C0-AKR-628

THE TEACHING OF
HOME ECONOMICS

THE TEACHING OF
HOME ECONOMICS
THIRD EDITION

HAZEL M. HATCHER
PROFESSOR EMERITUS, HOME ECONOMICS EDUCATION
THE PENNSYLVANIA STATE UNIVERSITY

LILLA C. HALCHIN
CHAIRMAN, HOME ECONOMICS DEPARTMENT
MANSFIELD STATE COLLEGE

HOUGHTON MIFFLIN COMPANY · BOSTON
ATLANTA   DALLAS   GENEVA, ILL.   HOPEWELL, N.J.   PALO ALTO

Copyright © 1973 by Houghton Mifflin Company.
Copyright © 1963 by Hazel M. Hatcher and
Mildred E. Andrews. Copyright 1945 by Hazel M.
Hatcher and Mildred E. Andrews. All rights reserved. No part of this work may be reproduced
or transmitted in any form or by any means, elec-
tronic or mechanical, including photocopying and
recording, or by any information storage or retrieval system, without permission in writing from
the publisher.

Printed in the U.S.A.

Library of Congress Catalog Card Number:
72–5119

ISBN: 0–395–14039–0

Dedicated to Mildred E. Andrews
in appreciation for her earlier contributions
to **The Teaching of Home Economics**

CONTENTS

PREFACE

Some teachers see only turmoil when they look at education today. In part, this is because life is changing more rapidly than it was ten years ago when the last edition of **The Teaching of Home Economics** was written. In general, teachers are like other people, in that they are afraid of change, and the more drastic the change, the more uneasy they become. Some react by discarding everything that is old in education; others cling to what has given them security in the past.

Fortunately, many teachers study past and present patterns and retain what seems good of the old as they look ahead to tomorrow. They evaluate new ideas and try to utilize those which will improve today's education. These teachers can be a challenge to the student teacher and the beginning teacher, as well as to experienced home economics teachers confused about change.

Today's changes lead to greater challenges to be faced than ever before. It is an exciting time to be a teacher. This new edition of **The Teaching of Home Economics** is intended to help home economics teachers meet the needs of today's society.

The most outstanding problems of teachers include: (1) developing relationships with others while growing as individuals, (2) being able to choose and use a variety of teaching techniques and resources, and (3) using, adapting, and developing home economics curriculum. Each of these problems has been developed as a complete book in a series of three books which comprise the third and present edition of **The Teaching of Home Economics.**

Home economics has expanded to offer a far greater variety of educational positions than was true ten years ago. People in home economics today represent all ages and both sexes. Although it is not possible to write extensively about all of them, the illustrations used throughout have been chosen to include as many kinds of situations and groups in home economics as possible.

New terms have come into use in the last ten years, such as the **humane teacher, life styles, self-actualization, empathy, accountability, people knowledge,** and **change agents.** New ideas have been added to our fund of knowledge about teaching. Such terms and ideas have found a place in the present edition in order to help not only student teachers but all teachers who feel a need to be up-to-date.

In line with today's emphasis on giving the learner more responsibility for his learning, the use of cooperative procedures has been developed in the present edition as in the two previous ones. New techniques and resources are described along with older tested ones. Teachers are urged to use a wide variety of techniques and resources while constantly evaluating these in terms of research which deals with the effectiveness of the newer ones.

In the past teachers have needed to be able to use curriculum materials developed by others, and this will still be true in the foreseeable future. However, with rapid and continuing change in home and community life, curriculum development will be an ever-present responsibility of nearly all teachers. Moreover, adapting to such frequent changes will become an increasing challenge. The present edition has developed the area of curriculum development to a greater extent than have previous books of this kind.

The authors wish to express appreciation especially to Pennsylvania teachers of home economics who have, through classes, visits, and observations, offered so many helpful suggestions. Miss Anne G. Eifler, formerly Senior Program Specialist in Home Economics Education for the Pennsylvania Department of Education, helped by contributing to some of the material as it was being developed, especially Book 3 and the Appendix. Other state supervisors generously cooperated in the use of needed materials. Miss Katherine Stooksburry, assistant professor of Child Development at The Pennsylvania State University, suggested ideas on curriculum materials for child development. Faculty members and students at both Mansfield State College and The Pennsylvania State University contributed illustrations, ideas, and encouragement.

Hazel M. Hatcher

Lilla C. Halchin

ONE

THE
HUMANE
TEACHER

INTRODUCTION

The teaching of home economics begins and ends with human relationships. Whether we are dealing with human development and the family, home management and family economics, foods and nutrition, textiles and clothing, or housing, our focal point is the individual and the family. People in the home economics profession are always concerned with improving some aspect of living, such as the nutritional level, the near-environment, physical appearance, decision-making, child rearing. Our central mission in home-economics education is the improvement of the quality of life, a goal sought by all kinds of people. Most individuals and families need and desire changes that will bring the reward of a better life. Home-economics education aims to help them achieve those changes.

However, essential to helping people change is an understanding of them as individuals and in group interaction. The professional home-economics teacher asks questions such as: What are people like? Why are they different from one another? How are they alike? Why is he like that? How much does he want to change? How can I help people learn to respect one another? To trust one another? How can I involve people in helping others?

Before the professional home-economics teacher is able to answer any of those questions, she must ask, "Do I understand myself?" Self-understanding is the keystone to all relationships including that of teacher and learner. Self-understanding includes recognition of one's own strengths and weaknesses, release of one's creativity, definition of one's values, formulation of a personal life style, identification of self-goals, and the continuous development of a philosophy of life.

After self-understanding, the goal of the home-economics teacher is to develop in herself, so far as possible, those attributes that facilitate positive relationships with others, particularly learners and fellow members of the educational team, both professional and volunteer. A positive relationship is characterized by trust, true concern, empathy, authenticity. The characteristics that contribute to one's humaneness as a teacher are developed continuously through interaction with others and a concerted effort to become more humane.

The beginning teacher and the experienced teacher alike may begin at any time in life to develop a humane self that will contribute to making learning an adventure, and to fostering in students a desire for improving one's life and situation.

PART ONE

INITIATING AND MAINTAINING GOOD INTERPERSONAL RELATIONSHIPS

The school bus was filled with chattering boys and girls on the way to the big game. There was singing, good-natured teasing, cheers, boasting, laughing, and much conversation. As usual, the talk turned to teachers. Professional ears would have burned.

"Mrs. Winters is tops in my book. There isn't a thing I wouldn't dare tell her if I needed to!" Debbie emphasized her statement with a toss of her head.

"Yeah," chimed in Linda. "And she's fair to everybody. It's not just the way she treats me, but the way she respects even the kids who don't do what they ought to—the goof-offs."

"I know what you mean," said Sally. "Take Mrs. Clarkson. She's great if you do things the way she tells you, but it's downright embarrassing the way she treats some of the kids. Mrs. Winters seems to know me better than I know myself, sometimes. Do you suppose she's a mind-reader?"

"No," declared Debbie, "but she has a way of putting herself in your place. Not that she acts like a teen-ager. She doesn't, but she seems to know what's important to me. It's kind of uncanny."

"Well, I only wish more teachers were like her," sighed Jean, who had been listening quietly. "If they had been, my brother might *have stayed in school. He said none of the teachers understood him and he wouldn't stick around to listen to all their insults. Oh, don't get me wrong. Ted's far from perfect, and he's the first to say so. But a Mrs. Winters might have made the difference."*

ONE

WHY HUMANENESS IN TEACHING?

ATTRIBUTES OF THE HUMANE TEACHER

In the years following the Second World War, burgeoning scientific developments and expanding technology, including increasing computerization, have deemphasized humanity in many segments of life, even education; man sometimes seems subordinate to the machine and to the system. In spite of our increasing ability to solve technological problems, many factors in the world are not conducive to healthful living and the happiness of people. We have achieved the almost impossible task of placing man on the moon, but we have not been so successful in coping with man's problems on earth. We continue to wonder why, and to seek ways of achieving a permanent peace and improved conditions of living, including better housing and nutrition, racial equality, happier lives, improved family life.

However, we are now beginning to observe in our society a shift from emphasis on material values to interest in the human values of humaneness, self-identity, authenticity, empathic relationships, sensitivity, self-actualization, commitment. These terms are not synonyms, but each expresses a value placed on the human personality and the interaction of people.

There is no better place to foster humaneness—the sincere concern of one person for another, or the helping relationship—than the educational setting with which all individuals are associated for varying periods of time. George Isaac Brown (1971) presents the challenge to education in this way: "The greatest potential for change and significant improvement in our individual predicaments and in our dilemma as a society lies in the school. It is the one institution in western civilization outside the family that most profoundly affects the human condition [p. 8]." This concept of the school places an enormous responsibility upon teachers. If schools are to focus on humaneness then teachers must be humane people. They must be thinking, feeling, responsive individuals, and not just dispensers of knowledge. It is the person inside the teacher that counts.

To be not just a teacher, but *the teacher who makes the difference,* is a worthwhile goal for any teacher, whether she is a beginner or nearing retirement. The teacher who makes a difference is different in many ways from the general run of teachers. Many people have attempted to identify the characteristics that contribute to effectiveness as a teacher. Almost any elementary school student has some basis for judging teacher effectiveness. By the time a person enters a teacher education program she will have developed criteria that can be translated into a list of "do's and don't's" for the teacher she wants to be. However, being the teacher who makes a difference is not quite so easily achieved as devising and following a list of "do's and don't's." The teacher who makes a difference is humane as a teacher and as an individual. She never ceases in her life to devote effort to developing humaneness, because every experience and every association throughout life contributes to what she is becoming. What the teacher *is* rather than what she *does* determines her effectiveness as a catalyst or facilitator in the teaching-learning environment, more simply defined as the classroom. The true measure of a teacher's success is the effect she has on the enrichment of the lives of her students. The person who teaches must herself have a rich and self-fulfilled life from which to enrich the lives of others.

HUMANE TEACHERS CARE

According to Thelen (Hamilton & Saylor, 1969), "Humaneness is a quality of experience of interacting. You cannot be humane all by yourself. . . . The fact that it takes a society to make humaneness possible, and the fact that society is changing continually, means that interactions have to change [p. 18]." Thelen describes one aspect of humaneness as caring, an unselfish wanting to do something for someone else because he is a human being needing help. Caring becomes the least common denominator of all human relationships. One cares for the other person simply because he is a human being and thus a person of worth, whether the relationship to him is professional or personal. Caring is not an attitude that is put

on and taken off at will, as in the hypocritical dealings of those who will "scratch your back if you'll scratch mine." The quality of caring is basic to the personality, permeating all relationships, and it is characterized by sincerity, honesty, straightforwardness, and altruism. Thelen summarizes, "Caring is not just a technique—it is a whole way of life."

Caring is not new to the discipline of home economics, and it continues to be a special contribution of this discipline to the educational scene. Although the body of knowledge encompassed in home economics is needed to help people improve the quality of life, knowledge alone will not achieve this goal. Concerned and committed transmitters of knowledge are needed. Home-economics teachers who have genuine care and concern for every student, regardless of race or national origin, status, and personal deficiencies or capabilities, will facilitate the integration of home economics learnings into personal and family living.

HUMANE TEACHERS ARE EMPATHIC

The humane and thereby effective teacher possesses a high degree of empathy that enables her to achieve teacher-student relationships characterized by mutual understanding and respect. It is necessary for a teacher to use excellent teaching methods and to possess firm command of subject matter, but she will be effective only if there is also a positive relationship or supportive interaction between teacher and students. Empathy is defined by Dymond (1950) as "the imaginative transposing of oneself into the thinking, feeling, and acting of another, without losing one's own separate identity or point of view [p. 343]." Empathy is expressed in the Cherokee prayer, "Oh Great

Spirit, grant that I may never find fault with my neighbor until I have walked the trail of life in his moccasins." Empathy makes students feel capable of having an understanding, warm, and approachable relationship with teachers. Conversely, teachers low in empathy are thought by their students to be lacking in understanding, cool, and unapproachable.

A review of the personality correlates for high and low empathy may help one to identify her position on the continuum of empathic development. Individuals who possess high empathic ability are more secure and better adjusted than those who have low empathic ability. They are more extroverted and more adaptive to others, and show fewer signs of anxiety and depression. They are sensitive to the feelings of others and have more social tact. High empathizers are warm and affectionate, and they have many friends. Their happiness requires good relations with others. They perceive of themselves as sensitive, idealistic, with a keen sense of awareness to social problems, and with sympathy for the underdog. They feel a need for others in order to achieve self-fulfillment. They are emotional, but their emotionality is well controlled and richly enjoyed.

Low empathizers are more rigid, rather immature, introverted, and motivated from within. They are relatively nonconforming, impatient with customs and authority, and disinclined to plan and accept schedules. They want to be in the limelight. They are not strongly motivated to seek contact with others. They are inclined to be self-centered, and prefer to avoid strong ties with others. They are afraid of emotions and are not capable of forming many good emotional contacts with the outside world. Their emotions are more explosive. They tend to mistrust others, and they seem to compensate for lack of emotional development by stressing the abstract and intellectual approach to life.

One can identify some teachers she has known as fitting the description of a highly empathic individual or the description of a low empathic individual. Probably the majority of teachers fall somewhere between the two extremes. However, if we are to achieve greater humaneness in teaching, more truly high-empathy teachers are needed. Diskin (1955) supports the thesis that the presence of harmonious interpersonal relations in the classroom climate may function as a basic factor in teaching effectiveness. He further maintains that the empathic ability of the teacher is fundamental to the initiation and maintenance of such relationships. The empathic teacher becomes involved in the lives of her students because she possesses an understanding attitude that enables her to perceive the situation from each student's viewpoint. She readily comprehends the values and motives of her students. At the opposite end of this continuum, teachers of low empathic ability often create a classroom climate of fear and insecurity, and this climate may even jeopardize the mental health of students.

While the empathic relationship is of great value in all teacher-student contacts regardless of grade level or subject, it is particularly important in the teaching of home economics. The content of home-economics subject matter—personal and family living—and the informality of the classroom climate typical of home-economics classes make an understanding relationship between teacher and student necessary. Conversely, lack of understanding between teacher and student in an area as personal as home economics can cause irreparable damage.

One of the writers, in conducting a study on teacher empathy, collected many comments from students describing teachers. Some of the typical descriptions of high-empathy and low-empathy teachers are included here because they provide considerable insight into teacher behavior as evaluated by students.

Student comments concerning a high-empathy teacher:

> She is always interested in everything you do, out of school and in. She helped me get settled in this school when I moved here.

> I feel she is truly interested in each one of her students as an individual.

> She is always willing to help you if you need help of any kind. She is generous, kind, and would help anyone.

> I feel that Mrs. S is a wonderful friend to have. She is kind and always ready to help anyone she can. She has a wonderful personality and can get along with everyone.

> I chose her because she has always been interested in my activities and has often been helpful and understanding.

> She has been the only teacher I ever talked about any of my problems with, and she seemed very sincerely interested in me.

Student comments concerning a low-empathy teacher:

> She is the type of person that criticizes everything and is never satisfied with what is done for her.

> When I had her as a teacher I was never able to learn anything because she wasn't the type of person. No matter what you did it was wrong. I was actually scared to ask her a question.

> She always has a mean look on her face, and is always criticizing. I feel very uneasy when I see her coming up the hall. Nothing ever satisfies her.

> This teacher has always bothered me for some reason. I have never had her for a class, but there is something about her that I do not like. I based my opinion on the feelings of the students who have her. She just seems cold and uninterested in students.

> She is changeable from day to day. I don't feel that I could talk with her very easily.

> I guess I really didn't try to get too acquainted with her and when I had her for class I just could not understand or get close to her.

These comments from high-school students are indicative of marked perception on their part as they evaluate teachers. It is evident, too, that students are, for the most part, fair in their evaluation of teachers and they do not employ vindictive tactics. In several of the comments, not included here, students pronounced a teacher unapproachable but thought this person to be a good teacher. Frequently, the students may not have been concerned for themselves but sensed the negative effect of certain teachers on their classmates. It should be noted, too, that a few students assumed some responsibility for a lack of rapport with teachers who had been identified as low-empathy teachers. Students appreciate having teachers who are friendly, understanding, considerate, helpful, fair, and who keep confidences. They do not identify the quality as empathy, but they do sense the difference between teachers who are understanding of students and those who are not.

People seem to vary in the amount of empathy they possess and evidence. While certain individuals may be born with a greater capacity for the development of empathy than others, there is support for the assumption that empathic ability can be developed. Rogers (1962) proposes that the development of empathy may be fostered by a study of great literature, by acting in dramatic productions, by psychology courses, and by the process of living.

In a study conducted by one of the writers, it was found that the high-empathy teachers shared certain common factors in childhood and family background which contributed to their high empathic development, and that the low-empathy teachers had similar factors in common which contributed to their low empathic development. The family climate within the childhood home of the teachers was a very important influence. The families of the high empathizers celebrated holidays together, and the high-empathy teachers felt greater satisfaction because their families had few family quarrels. They shared belongings with family members and felt that their families considered them thoughtful children. High-empathy teachers recalled that they shared creative efforts and discussed personal problems with their fathers, and they recalled with high satisfaction sharing creative efforts with their mothers. Reading aloud was a family pastime in the homes of the high-empathy group. Low empathizers recalled that father's work kept him away from home more than other fathers, and they felt great dissatisfaction because of this. Those in the low-empathy group quarreled with their siblings, and their parents quarreled with each other. They felt much dissatisfaction because of the quarreling. Low empathizers did not share creative efforts with their fathers, and their mothers seldom spent time helping them with things in which they were interested. Only occasionally did they select gifts for others. Seldom did their families celebrate holidays together.

The parents directly or indirectly influenced those in the high-empathy group and those in the low-empathy group. When a relationship with a friend or teacher was disturbing, the parents of the high empathizers tried to help them understand the other person's point of view. The parents of high empathizers showed consideration for people in ways other than giving money or material things. People of a different race were welcome in their homes. Those in the high-empathy group recalled with satisfaction that their fathers seldom or never criticized people because of their values. Low empathizers recalled that both mothers and fathers were critical of certain people because of their race, class, and religion. Mothers, in particular, were critical of others because of their values. Parents of the low empathizers seldom showed consideration for people in ways other than giving money or material things. They grew up in homes where people of a different race were not welcome.

Participation of the family members in groups and activities outside the home had some significance. The high-empathy group felt high satisfaction because their parents belonged to the same church and because their mothers and fathers participated in church activities throughout childhood. Families of the high-empathy group visited other families together. Parents of low empathizers did not both belong to the same church. The low empathizers as children had not actively participated in church activities; nor did their parents. Fathers of low empathizers participated to a lesser extent in social activities. Only occasionally did their families visit other families together.

Some interesting data on relationships with others outside the family were obtained. The high empathizers reported that their closest friends were not the same age as themselves. During adolescence they had close relationships with one or two friends older than themselves. During childhood they had particularly close relationships with adults outside the family. The high-empathy teachers recalled the high satisfaction they felt because all of their friends were welcome at home. Most of their sex information, they said, came from friends of about their own age during later childhood. Throughout childhood more of the homes of the high-empathy group had others besides immediate family residing there. While both high- and low-empathy teachers recalled to about the same extent being mealtime guests and over-night guests in the homes of friends, and visiting in others' homes, the high empathizers recalled doing these things with greater satisfaction. As children they said they resolved differences with playmates. Closest friends of the low empathizers were of the opposite sex, and usually all their friends were approximately the same age as themselves.

Enjoyment of certain activities was typical of the high-empathy group. Members of this group participated in creative play and dramatic play in later childhood, and in early childhood they participated in mimic play. The high empathizers read newspapers, "lived" the books they read. The high-empathy group reported that in early childhood they enjoyed reading fairy stories, nursery rhymes, and religious stories. In adolescence they enjoyed reading plays. Crying at sad episodes in movies was typical of the high empathizers. As children, high empathizers enjoyed going on picnics and shopping with their peer group, and with the family they enjoyed singing and attending carnivals. Low empathizers, as a group, did not indicate strong interest in any particular activity.

It is not feasible to conclude that specific home- and family-background factors are more important than others, but rather that a constellation of factors are conducive to fostering empathic development. Some high-empathy teachers have reported home and family situations hostile to empathic development. However, these same teachers have been exposed to empathy-nurturing experiences in their educational background. Certain factors in the home environment seem to be related to empathic development. If these factors are not present the result is decreased empathic development, unless other environmental factors are substituted. There is some evidence to show that when the factors that promote the development of empathy are minimal in the home and family environment, then the factors in a school situation can be so planned and executed as to further empathic development on the part of students.

An example of a high-empathy teacher coming from a family background that was not conducive to empathic development was a young industrial arts teacher known to one of the writers. He grew up in a home rent with parental quarreling and drinking. When he was fourteen, his parents were divorced and he was awarded by the court to his mother. Deciding that no judge was to tell him with whom to live, he spent his remaining high-school years living for one week with one parent and the next week with the other. In the meantime both parents had remarried. He related that by the time he was sixteen he was drunk almost every night, went home only for a change of clothing, and was failing in school. Then two teachers, a woman teaching English and a man teaching industrial arts, assumed the roles of his parents—the "father" outlining rules of conduct and showing a sincere and fatherly interest in him; the "mother" being sympathetic, understanding, and sincerely interested in him. In a short time he was on the honor roll and playing a "star" position on the high-school basketball team, and he had regained much-needed self-respect. After graduation from high school and subsequent army service, he was encouraged by the two teachers to complete his college education. His chief goal in teaching is to "help kids the way I was helped."

There is reason to believe that an individual can develop greater empathy in his relationships with others when he makes a conscious effort to do so. Such an effort involves training one's skills of perception to become aware of the way others perceive situations. The person who is developing greater empathy trains himself to be a listener, to withhold judgment, and to be open to the thoughts, ideas, beliefs, and understandings of others. To be empathic does not mean that one must believe as others do, but that one should be able to develop a relationship in which the other person feels free to be himself and does not feel threatened by what one may think of him.

HUMANE TEACHERS ARE PERSONALLY ADEQUATE AND SELF-ACTUALIZING

Teachers are human and experience all the joys and problems of human existence. However, when a teacher becomes too preoccupied with her personal life, she does not have sufficient time, energy, and interest to develop a helping relationship with others. Students sense this preoccupation on the part of some teachers with comments such as, "He's too busy," "She has her own problems," "He doesn't have time for me and my problems," "She doesn't even know what I say, let alone how I feel or what I think." There is a breakdown in the communications process which is necessary in teaching-learning relationships. The effective teacher has learned to use herself as an instrument in carrying out her own purposes and the purposes of the educational process.

Combs (ASCD, 1970) volunteers that there is good evidence to suggest that effective teachers are personally adequate people. He outlines four characteristics that are closely related to the personality correlates one of the writers

found to be essential for teacher effectiveness.

They tend to see themselves in essentially positive ways. That is to say, they see themselves as generally liked, wanted, successful, able persons of dignity, worth, and integrity. They perceive themselves and their world accurately and realistically. They do not kid themselves. They are able to confront the world with openness and acceptance, seeing both themselves and external events with a minimum of distortion or defensiveness. They have deep feelings of identification with other people. They feel "at one" with large numbers of persons of all kinds and varieties. This is not merely a surface manifestation of "liking people" or a question of possessing polished social graces, but a feeling of oneness in the human condition. They are well informed [p. 183].

In research reported by Combs (ASCD, 1970) he indicates that effective teachers can be distinguished from poor ones on a number of bases. The personally adequate teacher identifies with others, rather than emphasizing how she is different. In her relationships with students she builds on the ways in which they are like her and like each other. She possesses a strong sense of personal adequacy, and while she is well aware of the abilities she lacks as well as those she possesses, she accomplishes what she sets out to do because she believes in herself. Combs also found that good teachers see themselves as wanted and worthy individuals. They visualize the teaching role as one of freeing students to learn, to be creative, and to be themselves, rather than one of controlling students. Good teachers tend to be concerned with larger rather than smaller issues, and they can distinguish between the two. They are said to be self-revealing, rather than self-concealing. Thus, they dare to be themselves and to expend their energy on being who they honestly are rather than manipulating themselves and situations in order to present a preconceived and invalid image of themselves. Personal involvement is characteristic of the personally adequate teacher. She uses the team approach to learning; that is, teacher and learners together inquire, investigate, examine, and experience. Without this personal involvement of the teacher, the learner feels alienated, loses trust in the teacher, and questions the value of what she is supposed to be learning. Finally, good teachers, Combs found, are concerned with furthering processes rather than achieving goals. They emphasize means rather than ends. The good teacher is a personally adequate person who feels wanted, who is confident, who is trustworthy, and who inspires students to become personally adequate individuals of worth.

Maslow's self-actualized theory of personality development (1962) is similar to Combs' definition of the personally adequate teacher. In fact, Maslow (1971) began his studies of self-actualization because he had two teachers he "could not be content simply to adore, but sought to understand [p. xvi]." In seeking the answer to why some people seemed to be more self-fulfilled than others, he conducted a lifetime study of subjects whom he identified as "healthy people," or people who embraced "full humaneness." One important distinction between Maslow's personality theory and that of other investigators is that he studied psychologically healthy people, whereas many investigators, beginning with Freud, developed theories of personality development based on the study of troubled people. It was Maslow's conviction that study should be made of the very best human specimens in order to answer the question, "Of what are human beings capable? [1971, p. 7]."

Maslow has identified the distinguishing characteristics of self-actualizing people and has described them as follows (1962, pp. 56–58):

1.   They are realistically oriented.

2.   They accept themselves, other people, and the natural world for what they are.

3.   They have a great deal of spontaneity.

4.   They are problem-centered rather than self-centered.

5.   They have an air of detachment and a need for privacy.

6.   They are autonomous and independent.

7.   Their appreciation of people and things is fresh rather than stereotyped.

8.   Most of them have had profound mystical or spiritual experiences, although not necessarily religious in character.

9.   They identify with mankind.

10.   Their intimate relationships with a few specially loved people tend to be profound and deeply emotional rather than superficial.

11.   Their values and attitudes are democratic.

12.   They do not confuse means with end.

13.   Their sense of humor is philosophical rather than hostile.

14.   They have a great fund of creativeness.

15.   They resist conformity to the culture.

Perhaps most helpful for the beginning home-economics teacher is knowing how one may more nearly achieve her own self-actualized state of being. At the risk of over-simplifying a process that involves a lifetime, the behaviors leading to self-actualization, as discerned by Maslow (1971, pp. 45–50), are outlined below:

"Self-actualization means experiencing fully, vividly, selflessly, with full concentration and total absorption." Forget your "hang-ups," self-consciousness, hypocrisy, and wondering about what others will think and be totally yourself.

Life consists of making choices, one after the other. Do not be inhibited by fear of making the wrong choice and doing the wrong thing. Maslow distinguishes between a "progressive" or "growth choice," and a "regression choice." One moves toward self-actualization daily by making "growth choices," movement which is the opposite of aiming toward defense and safety for oneself and being fearful. Taking the latter course places one in a state of indecision, frustration, and unhappiness.

When in doubt, be honest rather than not. Maslow points out that frequently when in doubt, people are not honest. Looking within oneself for the answers means taking responsibility. There is an actualizing of the self each time one takes this kind of responsibility.

Make decisions with full self-awareness and at the risk of being different, unpopular, noncon-forming. Do not wait to see your best friend's hand go up before you vote. Be courageous rather than afraid. At times this may mean going up-stream when everyone else seems to be going down.

Since self-actualization is a process and not an end in itself, it means realizing one's potentialities throughout life. Maslow cautions that this does not mean "doing some far-out thing necessarily, but it may mean going through an arduous and demanding period of preparation in order to realize one's possibilities." It means working to do well the thing that one wants to do, to be as good as one can be.

"Peak experiences which cannot be bought, cannot be guaranteed, cannot even be sought" are ecstatic and "transient moments of self-actualization." However, the conditions for "peak experiences" can be devised through

elimination of illusions and false notions or through learning what one's potentialities are or are not. One grows in self-actualization as one learns to recognize "peak experiences." Such experiences are incidents or situations that produce overwhelming joy and a sense of achievement and self-fulfillment.

Self-actualization means giving up one's defenses after one has identified them. This is a painful process because defenses protect one from unpleasantness. (Defense mechanisms are discussed later in this book. See page 18.) Maslow suggests that we need to move from the defense mechanism of *desacralizing* to *resacralizing*. He defines *desacralizing* as generalizing about or categorizing people, objects, or behaviors, and then assuming that the generalization is true of all in a given category because it fits the experience with a sample. An example of desacralizing is the feeling of mistrust on the part of youth for anyone over thirty. "Resacralizing means being willing to see a person [p. 50] " in the realm of "the sacred, the eternal, the symbolic." Maslow gives an example: "It is to see woman with a capital 'W' and everything which that implies even when one looks at a particular woman. Another example: One goes to a medical school and dissects a brain. . . . Open to resacralization, one sees a brain as a sacred object also, sees its symbolic value, sees it as a figure of speech, sees it in its poetic aspects [p. 50]." Finally, self-actualization of any one individual is larger and more encompassing than himself. Through resacralization there is a reaching out to all humanity throughout eternity.

Self-actualization is not achieved at any given time in a person's life, but as he listens to his inner voice, takes responsibility, is honest, works hard, and becomes more self-aware, he grows in self-actualization. He dares to be himself, to answer questions and problems honestly, directly, and responsibly, to be open to others. He knows his mission in life. He is, speaking accurately, self-actualizing rather than self-actualized.

HUMANE TEACHERS ARE AUTHENTIC

Another quality of the humane teacher is authenticity as advanced by Moustakas (1971). "Authenticity and genuine self-development require the teacher's presence as a whole person, not simply a professional worker with so many degrees and a certain kind of training, but a real person with feelings, with dreams, with courage and daring, with an alive interest and commitment to creative experience for himself and for the child [p. 21]." Such an individual does not play a teacher-role but rather is a person in her own right, who dares to be herself. She is a *real* person with honest feelings, which she expresses openly rather than hiding or covering them up. She laughs, enjoys, is sad, disappointed, happy, calm, or excited according to the situation. Above all else she prizes each learner as a worthy individual. Such a teacher receives complete respect from her students because, through her honest respect for each student, she engenders in them a feeling of respect for every individual that permeates the classroom. Rogers (1969) uses the words *realness* and *genuineness* to mean authenticity. "When the facilitator is a real person, being what he is, entering into a relationship with the learner without presenting a front or a facade, he is much more likely to be effective. . . . It means that he comes into a direct personal encounter with the learner, meeting him on a person-to-person basis. It means that he is being himself, not denying himself [p. 106]."

The authentic teacher is aware of and values the feelings and ideas of others, accepts the tempo and pace of each student, and perceives the dynamic situation in the classroom through the eyes of the participants. The authentic teacher, the teacher who relates well to others, the teacher who makes the difference, possesses the self-understanding that leaves her free to perceive more accurately the behavior of others.

Moustakas (1971, pp. 23–24) identifies the following principles that will help one on the way to achieving authenticity. The first six principles may serve as guidelines for any individual to follow in developing authenticity. The remaining four principles will aid in the developing of authenticity on the part of students:

1. The individual knows himself better than anyone else; only he lives with himself twenty-four hours of every day.

2. The individual's perceptions and expressions of his own feelings, thoughts, and experiences are a more valid avenue of relatedness to him than any diagnosis or evaluation.

3. Only the person himself can develop his potentialities, no matter how fervently and exhaustively another person may wish to do this for him.

4. The individual, to keep on growing as a self, must continue to believe in himself, regardless of what anyone else may think about him. The belief in a reality is a primary factor in the fulfillment of that reality.

5. Objects have no meaning in themselves. Individuals ascribe meanings to them, meanings that reflect a unique background of experience.

6. Every person is logical in the context of his own personal experience and the values he has created out of these experiences. He may seem illogical to others when he is not understood in his own world of thought and feeling.

7. When the teacher accepts and values the

student as a whole person, the student will perceive this as an affirmation of him, and will use his energies in exploring and actualizing himself; when he is rejected and forced into a meaningless existence, he will use his resources in maintaining and defending himself, even if that self is alienated.

8. Growth of the self does not require calculated and planned external motivation from the teacher. These growth strivings are present at all times and constitute the one central tendency in each man.

9. Under externally induced threat, the basic striving for self-actualization is impaired; the self is passive, controlled, and inauthentic. Freedom from externally imposed threat, freedom to be (which may itself involve pain and frustration), enables the self to be open to life and to strive toward actualization.

10. The educational situation that most effectively promotes significant learning is one in which (a) the external threats to the self of the learner, such as rejection, criticism, evaluation, reward, and punishment, are at a minimum, while at the same time, the individuality and uniqueness of the person are valued, respected, and trusted; and (b) the person is free to explore the materials and resources that are available to him in the light of his own interest, potentialities, and readiness.

The four attributes described in this chapter, caring, empathy, self-actualizing, and authenticity, all contribute to the development of the humane teacher. The humane teacher respects each individual student as a person of worth and dignity. The humane teacher knows she must first understand the student as a unique individual before she can help the student to change her manner of behaving and coping so that her quality of life will be improved. Teachers characterized by humaneness are needed in order to help students develop humaneness. The development of humaneness is not limited to any one classroom or condition of life. However, there are conditions, as will be pointed out in the next chapter, that foster the development of humaneness.

TWO

HOW DOES ONE DEVELOP HUMANENESS?

UNDERSTANDING ONESELF

How does one become the kind of individual who relates to people in such a way and to the extent that one becomes a motivating force in helping each person to achieve his own potential for development? Stated more simply the question is, how does one become a humane teacher?

The development of humaneness is not achieved by means of a formula nor by the application of rules or guidelines. Rather it is achieved through the integration of interacting experiences and relationships. Certainly one must have more than a casual exposure to people who manifest humaneness. Combs reaffirms (ASCD, 1971, p. 182) "Humaneness is learned from the quality of an individual's interaction with significant others." (*Significant others* is a term used by psychologists to designate those who are important to others. People learn who they are and what they are from the way they are treated by the important people in their lives, such as parents, teachers, clergymen, and counselors. Only significant people have much effect on the development of the self.) Combs continues, "For the teacher in training, humaneness is as important to his success as a learner as the humaneness of his future students will be in their growth and devel-

opment [p. 182]." Producing an effective teacher is not so much a matter of teaching her how to teach as it is helping her to *become* a teacher. At the crux of this phenomenon is the teacher's self—the person inside the teacher.

Self-understanding or self-awareness is an elusive, will-o'-the-wisp state, which is not completely achieved by most people. Yet that is not to say that self-understanding should not be a lifetime goal of everyone and especially of professional people who are in the business of helping others. Jersild (Hamachek, 1971) emphasizes, "The teacher's understanding and acceptance of himself is the most important requirement in any effort he makes to help students to know themselves and to gain healthy attitudes of self-acceptance [p. 8]." Hamachek (1971, p. 1) says that each individual is faced with three questions that must be answered in order to achieve greater personal maturity: "Who am I?" "Where am I going?" "Why?" The answers to these questions are to be found in one's values, strengths and weaknesses, way of life or "life style," philosophy of life, and goals.

How one feels about himself begins with the recognition that one has a self that is unique and separate from others. It is that part of the individual of which he is consciously aware. Jersild (1955) clarifies what the self is in this statement, "A person's self is the sum total of all he can call his. The self includes among other things, a system of ideas, attitudes, values, and commitments. The self is a person's total subjective environment; it is the distinctive center of experience and significance. The self constitutes a person's inner world as distinguished from the outer world consisting of all other people and things [p. 8]."

The development of the self-concept, or attitudes about the self, begins very early and continues throughout life. Experiences with significant others including parents, siblings, and friends contribute to one's self-evaluation. When these experiences are positive and supportive, when others are acceptant, the individual sees himself as a worthy person. A snow-balling effect operates, whereby the self-accepting individual then accepts others, who in turn accept him, and with this reinforcement he accepts himself. Hamachek (1971) describes the source of self-acceptance. "Feelings of self-worth and self-esteem grow in part from our perceptions of where we see ourselves standing in relation to persons whose skills, abilities, talents, and aptitudes are similar to our own [p. 9]."

RECOGNIZING ONE'S STRENGTHS AND WEAKNESSES

Everyone possesses strengths, assets, special abilities, talents. On the other hand, no one escapes having weaknesses, liabilities, negative traits, inabilities. The goal in self-understanding is to assess strengths and weaknesses accurately and then to work toward developing each strength in order to achieve one's opti-

mum potential. It is a matter, simply stated, of maximizing the positive and minimizing the negative. However, identifying one's strengths and weaknesses, and then accepting them, particularly the weaknesses, becomes a problem for many people.

Each individual develops personal levels of aspirations which, if satisfied, bolster his feelings of self-esteem. However, if there is a consistent discrepancy between one's aspirations and one's achievement, the personal feeling of self-worth becomes threatened and downgraded. Such a person is described as not facing life realistically. The goal in self-understanding is to close the gap between the real self and the ideal self, to develop expectations for oneself which are in true perspective with one's abilities.

Hamachek (1971) points out that, "An important first step along the road of self-understanding is the ability to be able to discriminate between those expectations which come from inside the self and those which come from outside the self [p. 13]." Fulfilling the expectations of others can promote behavior that might not have occurred otherwise. He continues, "The individual who moves away from compulsively fulfilling others' expectations becomes free to listen to his own expectations, and to become the person he feels he wants to be [p. 13]."

The following case illustrates the effect of expectations upon the behavior of the individual. Upon receiving a C in a course in sociology, a prospective home-economics teacher was advised by her mother that the C was to be expected if sociology had anything to do with social behavior, because neither the student nor her mother had strong social inclinations. "We don't make friends easily" was the mother's reasoning. Considering herself a social failure, this student would have given up and withdrawn from college except for a perceptive professor who helped her to see that a grade of C in sociology was not indicative of one's social performance. Prior to her mother's evaluation, the student had been showing signs of developing an outgoing personality, and with the professor's reinforcement, continued to develop socially. This young woman learned an important lesson about self-evaluation and self-fulfillment.

While it is easy to accept feelings of love and joy as part of oneself, it is particularly difficult for all of us to accept the fact that we have feelings of guilt, fear, anger, resentment, hostility, and anxiety. Considerable psychic energy is used up in denying or rechanneling the presence and effect of these feelings. Yet all individuals use "defense" mechanisms to help protect and reduce psychological threats to the self. Defense mechanisms help preserve one's sense of personal worth in stress situations unless they are used to such an extreme that they interfere with the maintenance of self-esteem. Psychologists have described and labeled a number of defense mechanisms. Some of the most generally understood, with not too technical names, are denial of reality, fantasy, compensation, rationalization, repression, emotional insulation, and sublimation. When defense mechanisms are used occasionally, and when the individual realizes why he is behaving in a certain way, the effect may be beneficial. Habitual defense responses are unsatisfactory because they warp the personality and they may lead to more damaging situations, which the self is even less able to meet. Criteria for testing the effectiveness of an escape or defense mechanism include the following, according to Cole and Hall (1969).

It should lead to a better relationship with other people.

It should be conducive to mental health.

It should make future adjustments easier.

It should benefit society.

It should not divert one from one's goals in life.

Relationships with others, or social interaction, provide the testing ground through which the individual perceives himself. The self, as expressed through personality, makes contact with the selves of other people, also expressed through personality, and these contacts elicit negative or positive responses causing the self to react. The individual may enjoy the interaction experience, or he may feel threatened by it. Whatever the interaction experience is, the individual does something about it. His responses add up to a pattern of behavior. Among friends and acquaintances one has learned to identify behavior patterns as dependable, happy-go-lucky, serious and trustworthy, untrustworthy, and conscientious. Thus the pattern of behavior becomes a manifestation of personality which is unique to an individual. From social interaction, the individual evaluates his own behavioral pattern in terms of others as "worse than," "no worse than," "no better than," or "better than." Hamachek (1971) contributes an important concept in self-understanding. "Self-awareness develops as we compare and contrast our physical bodies, attitudes, and achievements to those of other people [p. 11]." This matter of comparison with others becomes a measure for self-esteem. (I wear clothes well; I am attractive; I am personable; therefore, I am adequate.)

Total self-acceptance and self-understanding is probably not possible. But it is possible to more nearly approach one's optimum development, to come closer to being an authentic person, that is, someone who honestly and with courage identifies his real hopes and aspirations, his strengths and weaknesses, and who realizes that when he falsifies his feelings, he does so at the expense of self-esteem.

A reference written by a college supervisor for a graduating senior in home-economics education reads as follows:

> Miss Rosemary Stratton will be graduated in June, 1973 with a major in home-economics education. She performed ably in the classroom during her semester of student teaching at Stony Point Junior-Senior High School. She was always well-prepared each day for teaching, with well-developed unit and lesson plans. She successfully used a variety of teaching-learning techniques and showed real understanding of the subject matter. Miss Stratton maintained excellent teacher-pupil relationships, showing understanding of the students and their homes and families. She also was supportive of and cooperative with the other teachers and the administration. Miss Stratton is an attractive, well-groomed, and poised young lady. She completed her student teaching with a very good rating.
>
> As her student-teaching experience progressed, Miss Stratton began to show signs of genuine creativity and manifested qualities of leadership. If Miss Stratton's development continues to progress along these lines, I would expect her to become a superior teacher of home economics.

This is a fine recommendation, and it is hoped that she continued the development of both creativity and leadership qualities, because these qualities will make the difference between a run-of-the-mill teacher and an effective teacher. From the first part of the reference one gathers the impression that Miss Stratton is not a bad teacher. She seems to comply with what is expected of her and conforms to the student-teaching situation. Most administrators would be interested in considering her application after reading this part of the reference. However, the last paragraph shows that something dynamic was beginning to happen. Miss Stratton was commencing to find herself, to feel at ease in the teaching situation, freer, self-actualizing. She began to identify her strengths and to develop new abilities. Perhaps in the ongoing evaluation of her performance it was suggested that she could develop more of certain qualities, and the student-teaching climate was such that she felt uninhibited and motivated to analyze her strengths and weaknesses and plan a strategy for developing her strengths.

Any individual at any time may assess her own strengths and weaknesses, keeping in mind that these are the things that make one unique, and that one does not need to, in fact should not, emulate others. The home-economics teacher will develop her own style, her own unique way of teaching; she will be herself, believe in herself, and enrich the lives of students.

RELEASING CREATIVITY

Although releasing creativity is closely related to recognizing and developing one's strengths and weaknesses, creativity is such an important quality that the writers will treat it separately here in some depth.

Creativity is a measure used frequently in describing an effective home-economics teacher, and for that matter all effective teachers. Creative teachers are creative people. The classroom of the creative home-economics teacher exemplifies creativeness, imagination, originality. Creativity is visible in the things one sees around the classroom, such as bulletin boards, mobiles, exhibits, objects. Students display this quality in the variety and originality of activities in which a single class may be involved. They show it in the way they go about their work, with freedom to invent, courage to be different, and the conviction that their product is worthy of existing, whether it is an idea, a pillow, a meal, a toy, a decorative object, Christmas cookies, or a new approach to an old problem. Creativity is not simply a matter of doing what one wants to do when one wants to do it. It is a channeling of the components of eagerness, curiosity, wonderment, spontaneity, sensitivity, and imagination, in the direction of problem solving.

It is generally agreed that creativity is an essential part of a fully adequate personality, and that every person is potentially creative. The question for the beginning home-economics teacher, and for experienced teachers, too, if they have not yet posed it, is how to release the capacity for creativity that seems to be innate in every individual. Maslow (1971) says,

> The concept of creativeness and the concept of the healthy, self-actualizing, fully human person seems to be coming closer and closer together, and may perhaps turn out to be the same thing. The creative approach can be employed in almost every experience and association involved in daily living. First of all, it is concerned with the perceptions one has of his world, the ability to see with meaning what one is looking at and to enjoy as much of what one sees as possible. Each scene one passes by and each situation one experiences or observes is composed of a myriad of components most of which are overlooked. With persistence one can increase his powers of observation and perception [p. 57].

Secondly, the individual wanting to release his potential for creativity will approach problems within the context of the present and, Toffler (1970) would add, the future. As Maslow (1971) says, "This ability to become 'lost in the present' seems to be a sine qua non for creativity of any kind." He advises us to "give up the past [p. 61]," and he draws a distinction between the "digested past," which becomes a part of the individual and thus contributes to his authenticity, and the "undigested past," which causes him to approach life's experience with past guidelines that are not compatible with the present.

Finally, creativity is released when the individual feels free from fear and inhibitions. Then he can become absorbed in the idea or the object he is originating. The inhibitions of shyness, self-consciousness, concern about what others will think, must be eliminated, for they check the courage to think and act creatively. Rank (Maslow, 1971), as long ago as 1920, pointed out lack of courage often keeps one from being truly creative. He showed that an individual learning to release his creativity needs to progress through three phases of development, beginning with adaptive behavior, followed by conflict, and finally creativity. Other psychologists, more recently, have corroborated Rank's belief that one of the most pronounced traits of the creative person is courage. This theory can be validated by what happens to many people. The young child in the family is uninhibited, and almost every parent visualizes a budding artist, orator, writer, musician, or future president in his offspring as he moves freely in his little world. But then, parents, teachers, and other significant people begin to place restraints on the child until we have a conforming individual who feels guilt when he senses that he may be "out of step."

Some few individuals, because of unusually

acceptant parents and other acceptant authoritative figures, achieve the autonomy and the opportunity to assert their own will. They win for themselves some measure of individuality. Then, according to Rank, in the next phase of the development of creativity, which he identified as inner conflict, the individual experiences conflict between his drives for individuality and the somewhat static standards of society. If he is unable to resolve this conflict, he is said to be unfulfilled and has feelings of guilt, inferiority, and self-criticism, and lacks self-understanding. If he can resolve the conflict, and feel sure of his goals, ideals, and ethical standards, he can achieve the final phase, the release of creativity.

Another concept important for the person who wants to become a creative teacher is that of the expressive approach to problems as contrasted to the coping approach. The expressive approach is closely related to creativity. Maslow (1971) noted in his studies of self-actualizing people that they display more expressive behavior than coping behavior. Their behavior is directed toward being who they are and what they are. They are involved. They operate with complete psychological freedom, and such behavior is the essence of creativity, claims Maslow. They and their problems become one and these people may even find joy in the confrontation of problems. Coping behavior is less effective, as it is directed at the problem and there is slight involvement of self, and little or no creativity and spontaneity. Closely akin to the expressive versus coping behavior just described is MacKinnon's (ASCD, 1969, p. 203) concept of the "open-minded" and "close-minded" individuals. The more creative individuals may be said to be open-minded. They are keenly perceptive, open, and characterized by flexibility, spontaneity, and intuitiveness. Close-minded individuals emphasize an attitude of judging. They function in an orderly and controlled manner, and often are considered prejudiced.

As with other potentialities, even the most prosaic individual may begin at any point in his life to release his capacity for becoming more creative, first by viewing his world more accurately and in greater detail, and then by taking the initiative in shaping that world.

DEFINING VALUES

"Teachers must stand for something if for no other reason than to give children something to push against. Values, beliefs, and convictions must be admitted to the classroom situation." This is a quotation from Combs (ASCD, 1969, p. 21) as he promulgates the need for teachers to be themselves and to be free to communicate their humanity.

"Do you mean that I, the teacher, should let the students know what my values are? If I let them know my values, I'll never know theirs. I thought there was danger in having my values impinge on theirs. Besides, I am not absolutely certain what my values are. My values have changed since I came to college—since last year, even. What difference does it make what my values are?" Perhaps these questions have been forming in the reader's mind.

Recognition of one's values is basic to self-understanding. The teacher who denies his values does not ring true and students are most perceptive when it comes to identifying a "phony." Consequently, the future teacher will want to understand the imperativeness of value identification to increased self-understanding and to effectiveness in teaching.

Values enter into every phase of experience and include attitudes toward success, failure, competition, and problem-solving as well as the time-honored virtues of honesty, obedience, cooperation, conscientiousness. Values are organizations of meanings that serve as anchors for judging, making decisions, and performing in certain ways. According to Raths (Raths, Harmin, & Simon, 1966) values are ideas, actions, things, or guidelines that seem right, worthy, and satisfying to an individual. They contribute to one's consistency and stability of behavior to the extent that it is possible to predict how one will behave in a given situation, yet they are dynamic and everchanging. It is the dynamic quality of values that facilitates meshing gears with a rapidly changing society.

The formation of values begins with the fundamental physiological needs of the organism: the desire for food and warmth, and later the desire for physical activity and stimulation of certain zones of the body. These primary values are expanded into numerous other values that are stimulated by interaction in the family, first with the mother or mother substitute and then with other significant people. The developing individual learns to value the things that win him recognition and approval from these people. As a person grows older and matures, the physiological values are likely to recede in importance. For example, if the need arises, a mother will go without food in order to provide sustenance for her child. A student will remain awake all night to complete an assignment due the next morning so that he will receive the reward of a high grade.

Steps in the process of valuing have been devised by Raths, Harmin, and Simon (1966). They outline seven criteria that must be met to establish the presence of a value:

Free choice, with the individual freely and independently evolving it himself so that it will be truly valued by him.

Choice from a number of alternatives so that the value is truly compatible with the individual and his situation in life.

Choice after weighing each alternative with the individual deliberating and reflecting on the value in relation to his self-image and self-style.

Evidence of prizing and cherishing whereby genuine and intrinsic meaning makes the value precious to the individual.

A willingness to affirm the value publicly, providing a testing for the individual and the rightness of the value for him.

Proof of action that reflects the value, thus reassuring the individual that his value is viable.

Adherence to the value to denote a stable rather than transitory allegiance by the individual which affirms commitment to the value.

There is no place in a free society for prepackaged and instant values. College students should be encouraged to develop their own values and their own way of practicing them, rather than the "right" values and the "right" methods. According to Combs (Avila, Combs, & Purkey, 1971), students need to be exposed to teachers who stand up for their own convictions while respecting the ideas and beliefs of students. Further, it is important that student teachers work with cooperating and supervising teachers who have strong convictions and who are not threatened by other people with differing values and convictions. The beginning teacher must clarify her values so that she, too, does not feel threatened by the values of others. The values of each individual depend upon influences that helped to shape them; some are family-oriented, others are culturally-oriented. People rarely have identical sets of values, although one person may find crossing-points with others and this becomes one basis for forming friendships and making marriages.

Therefore, as important as developing values for oneself is the awareness that different people have different values to be respected and cherished.

Teachers of home economics will find it to their advantage to develop values, strong beliefs, and convictions regarding family life and their profession. One home-economics student teacher, because she was an academically able student, had achieved grades of A's and B's in home-economics courses. Yet during the student-teaching experience her performance was mediocre because she did not have a sufficiently strong conviction about home economics and what it has to offer in improving the quality of life. She did not recognize the value of transmitting to others the basic concepts and skills related to human nutrition, the environment, child rearing, family relationships, decision-making, human potentiality. She lacked the conviction needed to be a creative, enthusiastic, perceptive, interested, and interesting teacher. To her home economics offers but one value and a weak one at that: making clothing for herself and others.

On the other hand, the writers have noted many instances of student teachers and experienced home-economics teachers who, because of a strong conviction regarding the worth of home-economics education, became superior teachers. Their enthusiasm enlivened their teaching so that students, too, were initiated and caught up in a discipline that gave deep meaning to their lives.

Since many of the readers are about to take up their first professional assignment, it might be well to point out some fallacious assumptions sometimes acted on even by teachers with many years of experience. These unrealistic assumptions and irrational ideas have been suggested by Ellis and related by Combs (1962).

1. The idea that it is dire necessity for an adult human being to be loved or approved by everyone for everything he does: "I never spent so much time on anything as I did on that lesson and now no one cares." The student-teaching situation is one of evaluation and self-evaluation. A student teacher desperately wanting approval may become unduly discouraged by suggestions and comments from the cooperating teachers and the college supervisor.

2. The idea that one must be regarded as thoroughly competent, adequate, and achieving in all possible aspects: "I can't think of a single other way of teaching that lesson. The kids just aren't interested—that's all!" The student teacher expends time and energy needed for constructive approaches in defending her position.

3. The idea that one is dependent on others and that one needs someone stronger on whom to rely: "After all, it isn't my home-economics department." The student teacher does not take the initiative to suggest possible contributions for the home-economics program to the cooperating teacher.

4. The idea that the past is all-important and that because something once strongly affected one's life, it should have the same effect indefinitely: "But this is the way they taught us in college."

5. The idea that it is exceptionally difficult to find the right solution to many human problems, and that if the precise and right solution is not found, the results will be catastrophic: "I don't know how you make kids like one another—when whole countries are at war. We'll just have to leave that pair out of the plans for luncheon. Maybe they can go to study hall—or just give up the idea of the luncheon altogether."

Values constitute an integral part of the individual and they cannot be removed by a surgical process, nor added as a veneer. The individual teacher needs to identify realistically those things or ideas about which she feels strongly. Then she needs to test in real-life situations those strong feelings that she has identified as uniquely hers. She is then ready to cull, prune, and shape those ideals that will enrich her life and the lives of those whom she is serving through the teaching-learning relationship.

FORMULATING A LIFE STYLE

Values are closely related to life style because the way a person lives, his choice of housing, dress, friends, and food, his manner of eating, and the way he spends his working time and his leisure time, are all based on the values he holds and by which he lives. According to Toffler (1970) life style has become the way in which the individual expresses his identification with this or that subcult and is no longer simply a manifestation of class position. Life style also expresses the person's self-identification, how and in what manner he values himself. With hundreds of diverse possibilities from which to choose, Toffler predicts that how people will choose a life style, and what it will mean to them, may loom as one of the central issues of psychology. Choosing a life style becomes an intricate operation because it involves making hundreds of choices, including a place to live, furnishings, ideas adopted, friends, even vocabulary and values. All this affects and is affected by the way one feels about himself and what he thinks about himself.

This idea of a life style is not a new concept. Hamachek (1971, p. 50) reports that the essential pillar of Adlerian psychology is Adler's conception of the "life plan" of the individual and the purpose, the goal, the "end in view" that determine behavior. Adler views every person as having the same goal, the goal of superiority, and believes that there are numerous different "life styles" for achieving the goal. One person may strive to become a professional athlete, another an intellectual, another a "back-to-nature" ecologist. Each manages his life, including making a living and choosing environment, companions, dress and other manifestations of what he considers to be his life style, so as to achieve the goal of being superior. This concept is in accord with the humanistic idea that man can be the master and not the victim of his destiny.

One cannot change one's life style, once formed, without bringing about some change in self-image, for life style involves not merely the external forms of behavior, but the personal values that are involved in that behavior. A life style is a vehicle through which we express ourselves. Choosing a life style is, to use Toffler's word, a "super decision." It is an efficient way of eliminating many alternatives. When an individual has selected the best life style for himself, then he minimizes choice-making that can be threatening or frustrating. He facilitates a self-integrated personality and he becomes free. Toffler (1970) warns that when a person's life style is suddenly challenged and he is forced to reconsider it, the person is compelled to make another "super decision" transforming himself and his self-image as well.

The concept of life style is a most important one for the home-economics teacher—it is her "stock in trade." Home-economics teachers are in the business of providing the resources, the learning experiences, the knowledge that contribute to choosing and effectuating a life style. While the home-economics teacher selects one life style for herself, it is important that she recognize the countless possibilities of life styles from which the students come and into which they will go. For the sake of personality congruence, the individual, as she selects her life style, needs to understand herself as fully and honestly as possible. Prospective and present teachers of home economics would do well to experience many different life styles, either in homes of family, friends, and other associates, or through reading, study of case histories, and films. Because life styles vary radically, it is important to be accepting of even the most bizarre differences. This is not to say that one is to accept for herself every other life style, but one accepts the life style of another because it is chosen by a human being of dignity and worth and to whom it has deep meaning.

IDENTIFYING SELF-GOALS

The thinking and productive person, as he progresses through life, establishes high watermarks that indicate how much he has matured physically, mentally, and emotionally, and what he has achieved. Many of these high watermarks are established for us, such as promotion from one grade level to the next in school and receiving a high-school diploma. These indicators of achievement provide courage and motivation to continue on to the next step. They furnish a symbol of success.

As a person matures he becomes more autonomous and freer to decide for himself what he desires to attain and to be able to do. The more mature he becomes, the greater independence he has in determining how he will spend the rest of his life. He becomes increasingly more able to make decisions and thereby exercises greater self-will. He becomes the "master of his own soul," and determiner of goals or objectives that will guide him as he continues planning for his own self-development. A person who moves ahead with clear and well-defined convictions and plans about what he hopes to achieve is said to be *goal-directed.*

Clarifying one's goals does not necessarily mean that all of them will be achieved, nor even that the individual will hold to all of them. In fact, in the process of living it may be to his benefit to relinquish some goals, to redefine others, and to add new ones. The reason for defining one's own goals, in the beginning, is that goals that have been truly selected by the individual provide a direction for successful and personally satisfying future performance.

Jerilyn entered college as a freshman student in home economics committed to a major in home-economics education. Jerilyn had little doubt about what it meant to be a home-economics teacher since her mother had been one and she had spent many hours under the guidance and encouragement of her high-school home-economics teacher. She was a joy to all of her professors in college as she personified a most successful future home-economics teacher. The cooperating teacher to whom Jerilyn had been assigned for student teaching spent a delightful first week with the new student teacher. On Friday afternoon Jerilyn asked the cooperating teacher to spend some time with her. For an instant the teacher could hardly believe what Jerilyn told her. "I don't want to be a teacher. I never wanted to. I thought I could make it, but now I see that I can't, because my heart isn't in it. Merchandising is my first love for a career, but I could never bring myself to tell this to my mother, and my home-economics teacher, and all the professors at college. I couldn't disappoint them. But now I've just got to face it realistically and do what is best for me." Much more was said but the point has been made that life goals must be determined by the individual.

There may be input from other significant people, such as encouragement and even assurance of money for financing various aspects of the goal, but the goal must be self-chosen. Goals do not spring from a vacuum, but rather are painstakingly and resolutely built from the solid bricks of self-understanding and values, held together with the mortar of a realistic approach to life. An individual's goals should be compatible with one another. Life histories are shot through with disappointment, failure, and unresolved frustrations because life goals were not clearly defined, or were not in agreement, or were even opposed to each other.

Ginger entered college with considerable zest for life, for college, for home economics, and for becoming a teacher. She was well liked by her peers and by her professors. As the year moved along some students and a few faculty noted that Ginger seemed depressed at times. The periods of depression became more frequent, culminating in a suicide attempt. She was referred to the college psychologist. After many sessions with the psychologist it became clear that Ginger was pursuing two goals that in her life and at that moment were incompatible. One goal was to marry and establish a home, and the other was to achieve her home-economics teaching certificate, which meant completing the program at a college several hundred miles away from her fiancé's home and work. In Ginger's case both goals seemed to be equally strong and so were not readily resolved. Faced with the reality that "she could not have her cake and eat it, too," Ginger finally decided to withdraw from college, get a position near her fiancé, marry him and establish a home. For peace of mind, Ginger had to decide which goal meant the most to her and then to pursue that goal.

Fortunately, in these two case histories, the prospective home-economics teachers resolved the problems resulting from poorly determined and conflicting goals, and pursued goals that took them away from teaching. However, this is not always the case and there are home-economics teachers who have continued to "straddle the fence" to teach without caring about teaching or while pursuing some goal that interferes with their teaching. Both the personal and professional lives of these teachers are something less than they could be. And the students in their classrooms are the losers because the teachers do not have complete dignity and integrity in themselves nor in their associations with the students. Students are perceptive to problems of this kind. Combs (ASCD, 1962) emphasizes the importance of dignity and integrity in relation to effective teaching.

> To produce an atmosphere in which dignity and integrity are encouraged, we need teachers who themselves are given opportunities to be people of such character. Children learn from their relationships with others, but you cannot have a relationship with "the little man who isn't there." Effective relationships exist only with people who are important to us; the rest we ignore or pass by. Teachers who are going to have real effects upon children, therefore, must themselves be somebody [p. 223].

It is not easy to be somebody unless you have well-defined and attainable goals that will govern both your personal and professional life.

The person who has not faced up to developing any long-time goals for her own development or for serving in society may be in as much trouble as the person with poorly determined or conflicting goals. This person is inclined to be a drifter, to take the line of least resistance, to avoid rocking the boat. She is just there. Occasionally, such a person drifts into college and into a teacher-education program even in home economics. Sometimes she becomes "fired up," depending of course upon what factors originally caused her to be lethargic about the direction of her life. If she is lucky, she may experience growth factors, such as stimulation, motivation, development of interests, and success for which she is mainly accountable, and she then becomes more goal-directed. But, if none of this happens we have a teacher who "goes through the motions," and who contributes very little of herself. Again, students sense that this teacher places little value on herself. She lacks a real sense of personal worth. It is at this point that one can visualize the close relationship between values, a philosophy of life, and goals.

DEVELOPING A PHILOSOPHY OF LIFE

It is almost a truism that life today is complicated. There are many puzzling aspects about the nature of the universe and man's behavior, innumerable problems calling for wise decisions and good judgment, and difficulties in the eternal quest to achieve a personally satisfying life in a constantly changing world. Nevertheless, a person who takes time to think critically can live a satisfying and intelligible life. It is not one's surroundings that count, but one's reactions to them. A purposive teacher can decide for herself what is important, what is worth striving for, and what she believes. Attitudes, values, and beliefs are the essence of a philosophy of life.

In developing a philosophy of life a teacher's thinking may encompass many aspects of the world or only a few. As previously indicated, much depends on her personality and what she desires from life. For example, if her major purpose is self-gratification in terms of securing money, good clothes, and many pleasures and personal comforts, the philosophy of life may involve only those aspects of the world that lead to these goals. The result could be a selfish, petty, narrow philosophy of life. On the other hand, self-gratification might be interpreted in terms of attaining success in teaching, maintaining good relationships, and achieving happiness through creativity, appreciation of beauty, and service to others. This concept of self-gratification would necessarily involve many phases of everyday living. A teacher whose critical thinking is so extensive cannot fail to grow intellectually and develop a more complete philosophy of life.

Although an extensive philosophy of life is desirable, any system of attitudes, values, and beliefs is subject to change. Since new facts are constantly being discovered and new experiences encountered, it is necessary to discard some views, to reformulate others, and to accept new ones. However, there needs to be a core of beliefs sufficiently stable to enable the teacher to guide her daily behavior.

It is quite possible that a teacher may feel the need of standards or guiding principles to help formulate her philosophy of life. Some people who think critically believe that the consideration of one's fellow man is of primary importance. A teacher following this principle could organize her beliefs regarding the world and mankind around the humanistic point of view. Such a view permits no justification for personal biases, prejudices, or selfish behavior. Other guiding principles are truth, beauty, integrity, right and wrong perspective, creativity, mental health, security, power, and human relations.

Although different persons are aided in different ways by their particular beliefs, a good philosophy of life usually provides these benefits:

It guides behavior. Organized personal beliefs motivate a person to act on a basis of rational thinking rather than on a spontaneous expression of "feeling," and thus make it easier to arrive at wise decisions. A philosophy of life points up one's basic values. And since values reinforce one another, they provide a strength of conviction whereby a person can make selections and rejections without having to weigh, at the moment, all the factors involved.

It gives relative serenity to life. By organizing beliefs, establishing values and goals, and knowing what one wants and expects from life, one can establish a pattern that provides serenity and stability to everyday living. Such a pattern enables a person to meet experiences with some degree of equanimity, to feel secure, and to withstand the vicissitudes of an ever-changing civilization.

The job of the home-economics teacher is not to fill a role, but rather to fulfill a professional commitment that involves helping others to develop their unique potentiality so that they, in turn, may better serve their fellow man. The teacher is able to do this when she has become an authentic, empathic, and self-actualizing individual, who has emerged as a person free to be herself in almost every situation. Through freedom to act and to be, she is not bound in by personality complications, inhibitions, fears, and lack of trust. Rather, she is free to operate within the setting of the moment and to engender a spirit of joy, trust, worthiness, honesty, and zeal that culminate in enthusiasm for learning. And the goal for such learning becomes the positive one of improving the quality of life for an individual and for a group of individuals through the utilization of that body of knowledge identified as home economics.

SUGGESTED TEACHER EXPERIENCES

1. Conduct a small survey on empathic development by asking each of ten people to tell you where they think those who know them best, their co-workers, classmates, friends, family, would place them on a continuum of empathic ability. You might indicate the five points on the scale as follows: high-empathic, medium high, middle point, medium low, and low-empathic. Then, ask these questions:

Why do you think most of your acquaintances would place you at the point designated?

What do you think contributed most significantly to your being this kind of a person?

The class members might then report back to the group the findings from their survey.

2. At the beginning of the course write a statement in which you describe your philosophy of life. Then, near the end of the course write a second statement of your philosophy at that time. Compare the two statements of philosophy to see in what ways they are the same, and in what ways your philosophy may have changed. What do you think might have contributed to the change?

3. List six personal values that are very important to you. Next review the list and indicate, from one to six, your strongest value, then your next strongest value, and continue until you have identified what you think is your least strong value. At the end of the course, without looking at the first value list, repeat the above directions. Now compare the two lists. The comparison should tell you something about the extent to which your values have changed. It will be interesting to analyze why they remained the same, if that is the case, or why your values have changed.

4. Show the next five people you meet upon leaving your room or the classroom that you really care for them either by word, gesture, or action. Take note of how each "caring" approach was received, and also note whether it was easy for you to show that you cared about each one. Was it difficult? Or was it more difficult for you to show this feeling for some people than for others?

5. Select one of the concepts from Part One that intrigues you the most and illustrate it in some creative way by writing a poem or story, by making a collage or mobile, or by some other creative effort. These may be presented as "show and tell" for the entire class.

6. Some defense mechanisms were mentioned on p. 18. Using one of the books suggested in the Bibliography or some other psychology book, clarify and become familiar with the meaning of each of the following: denial of reality, fantasy, compensation, introjection, projection, rationalization, repression, reaction formation, displacement, emotional insulation, regression, sublimation.

Keep a daily log of the defense mechanisms you employ. After several days review your behavior with the objective of becoming more forthright and less dependent upon defense mechanisms as you cope with situations in life.

PART TWO

IMPROVING THE QUALITY OF LIFE FOR STUDENTS AND THEIR FAMILIES

Understanding people is the focal point of the teaching-learning process. This concept is simple to state but implementing it is intricate, demanding, involved, and even frustrating at times. The home-economics teacher has a fund of information, understandings, and skills to impart to others for the purpose of helping them to improve their quality of life. However, unless there is an open relationship between teacher and learner to create a climate conducive to learning, the student will absorb little of even the best and most complete content or subject matter of learning. With the learner as the sine qua non *in the teaching-learning phenomenon, it behooves the home-economics teacher to develop a deep understanding of people. This understanding is not a superficial and sympathetic comprehension of what people are thought to be like. The teacher's responsibility is not simply to keep learners happy and contented, to avoid differences, to evade grumbling and discontent. To know the learner, the teacher must be able to identify what a person is truly like, and in what direction he might go in order to become more self-actualizing and more self-fulfilled. The teacher must know how to spark the innate* energy within the individual so that the change process will be initiated and how to help him perpetuate the change process so that the change, the learning, if you will, can become more enduring.

Carl Rogers (1969) is the initiator and one of the leading proponents of teaching as a facilitating process, and this quotation emphasizes the value of the teacher-learner relationship:

> We know that the initiation of learning rests not upon the teaching skills of the leader, not upon his scholarly knowledge of the field, not upon his curricular planning, not upon his use of audiovisual aids, not upon the programmed learning he utilizes, not upon his lecture and presentations, not upon an abundance of books, though each of these might at one time or another be utilized as an important resource. No, the facilitation of significant learning rests upon certain attitudinal qualities which exist in the personal relationship between the facilitator and the learner [p. 105].

THREE

WHAT CONTRIBUTES TO WORKING EFFECTIVELY WITH DIFFERENT KINDS OF PEOPLE?

PEOPLE HAVE SIMILARITIES AND DIFFERENCES

The teacher has many approaches for learning more about people. First of all, self-understanding is a step in the right direction. In fact, it is not possible to truly understand someone else unless one has a pretty good measure of understanding of oneself. It is doubtful if anyone really understands himself completely and for all time. Development of self-understanding is treated more in detail in Part One of this book. Further information on becoming a teacher and a person who is growing in self-understanding may be gotten from the publications listed in the references at the end of Book 1. The individual with a good measure of self-understanding has developed a comfortable awareness of self and the reasons for his behavior, so that he is free to interact with another without feeling threatened. He is free to expend all of his psychic energy, if necessary, in relating to the other person. To be empathic in the teacher-learner relationship is psychologically demanding as the individual consciously attempts to see the world through the eyes of another, and another, and another.

The next step in maintaining good interpersonal relationships is to attempt consciously to learn more about others, what they are like and why, what seems to be important to them, and their own self-assessment. Realistically, however, this understanding of others does not follow the development of self-understanding in an orderly arrangement. Rather, the person is attempting to achieve both self-understanding and understanding of others at the same time, and neither self-understanding nor the understanding of others is completely achieved at any given time. Both are developing states of being to which the individual devotes a lifetime. Some people seem to approach both goals more easily than others.

An approach for the teacher who wants to refine the ability to relate to others is to develop understanding of the people she knows —her family, friends, teachers, associates— every person with whom she interacts. And she must do more than simply maintain good relationships with them, although establishment of good relationships is a contributing factor to understanding. The home-economics teacher must invest much of herself in learning about all kinds of people because she is committed to all people—older men and women and the elderly, young people, both boys and girls, persons handicapped either physically or emotionally, people of all racial, cultural, ethnic, and socio-economic backgrounds, and the culturally disadvantaged. No person is beyond the realm in which the home-economics teacher functions. While many home-economics teachers teach in middle schools and junior and senior high schools, there is an increasing number who teach in adult education programs, correctional institutions, Appalachia programs, inner-city programs, elementary schools, and special schools or special classes for people with special needs. These avenues for helping people improve the quality of life through home economics are increasing and offer a real challenge to home-economics education as it looks to the future.

LEARNING MORE ABOUT PEOPLE

The term "people knowledge" has been used by Selley (ASCD, 1969, pp. 116–117) for that area of learning which involves knowing why people behave and interact as they do. Some people have values like ours and therefore they act like us, and there are others who are unlike us because their concept of what is important in life is not the same as ours. A teacher must have "people knowledge" about those who are unlike her as well as those who are like her. A study of others begins with some general observations that apply to all of mankind. Then, there are specific characteristics which cause each individual to be uniquely different from every other individual. To establish a relationship that will help individual learners approach the optimum development of their potential, the teacher will need to be able to identify the common humanity and the uniqueness of each individual student.

To begin with, each person projects a personality "style" which is his earmark. According to Hamachek (1971) "When we talk about personality style, we are referring to the sum total of all that one is and does, to his characteristic patterns of perceiving and responding [p. 72]." An individual has several options in manifesting his personality style. Finally, these become intertwined into a unified pattern which is designated as personality. Generally, each individual expresses a consistency in behavior which results in a personality style. A variety of personality styles is evident in any group of students or other individuals— shy Sharon, energetic Eugene, happy-go-lucky Harry, quiet Kathy, dissident David, pessimistic Pat. For example someone will say, "You can always count on Carolyn for a good time!" and you pretty much can. Because of the personality style of a person, other people have expectations about how that individual will behave. Frequently, in turn, the more significant the evaluator is to the individual, the more likely the individual is to measure up to expectations, whether or not it is to his advantage to do so. The idea of a person responding in terms of what he thinks another person expects of him is not a new one, and it is receiving increasing attention in psychology. Hamachek (1971) records the effect of expectations on behavior in an interview which he had with a seventeen-year-old delinquent boy who had just been returned to the reformatory. He questioned the boy as to why he had gotten into so much trouble while he was back home for three weeks. "Man, what did you expect. The whole neighborhood knew I was at this place for nine months. Man, I wanted to do good—I tried, but even my grandfather wouldn't hardly talk to me. Some of the parents in the neighborhood —some with kids in more trouble than me— wouldn't even let their kids talk to me. They would say something like there goes that kid from the vocational school, watch out for him. They had their minds made up before they even looked to see if I had changed. They want me to be bad—I'll be bad." Past behavior determines expectations in the first place, but expectations influence the behavior expressed.

As a professional person working with people it is to the teacher's advantage to recognize that every human being has basic needs which must be satisfied in order for him to approach living a fulfilled life. Maslow (1962, p. 30) identifies these five basic needs, which are arranged in a hierarchical order from the most potent to the least as follows:

1. The physiological needs, such as hunger, thirst, activity, and rest.

2. Safety needs, security, and release from anxiety.

3. Love needs, affection, acceptance, and belongingness.

4. Esteem needs, including self-esteem, adequacy, and capacities, esteem from social approval.

5. Need for self-actualization through creative self-expression; need to feel free to act, and self-realization.

It is Maslow's premise that the physical well-being is of prime consideration, followed closely by reciprocal satisfaction of belonging and loving, and finally, positive self-assessment. When the basic needs are satisfied one may strive for the goals which lead to self-fulfillment. Motivational needs higher in the hierarchy keep man continuously striving as lower needs are fulfilled. For example, a student from a minority group in a classroom peopled by individuals of the majority group may feel very much out of things, and therefore threatened by the situation. His belongingness needs must be satisfied by structuring conditions so that he feels safe and secure before he will try to fulfill himself. The foregoing discussion has pointed up what people have in common. Every individual develops a personality style based on expectations of himself and others. Motivational forces for being, or needs as described by Maslow, are universal in scope.

Another way of looking at people is to recognize the uniqueness of each individual. Maslow draws a distinction between the uniqueness of the individual and what he identifies as "specieshood," or a point of contact with all of humanity. Maslow proposes (1971, p. 187) that identifying one's specieshood merges with identifying one's self-hood, and in the process the individual begins to know himself, his uniqueness, his potentialities, his style, his values. At the same time, Maslow says, the individual is learning what it means to be a human animal like other human animals.

That each person is unique is the most significant and most important fact for the teacher to master and to be guided by in the teaching-learning relationship. This means that each person, because of the experiences he has had, has something or knows something which no one else on earth has or knows. Too often the fact that each individual is unlike any other individual is ignored. Schools are no exception among institutions where the uniqueness of the individual is denied. In some classrooms students are treated like quart bottles to be filled equally with the content of learning and then capped. To continue the analogy, individual students come in all sizes and shapes, not just physically but mentally, psychologically, and in every other way. Yet in past and even in present-day classrooms conformity is rewarded and uniqueness punished. The teacher who really believes that the most important person in the classroom is each individual learner will first accept the uniqueness of that individual. Then she will help him develop understanding of the kind of person he is and the kind of person he is capable of becoming. She will help him to develop his aptitudes and to build upon his strengths.

Learning more about people becomes a lifetime occupation. Each person is a distinctly new discovery unlike any other, and the person who devotes a lifetime to learning more about people continues herself to grow and develop, so that her frame of reference is ever-changing. The most effective way to learn about people is to take advantage of every opportunity to interact with them empathically. The task is to keep as open as possible to experiences and opportunities which will broaden and expand one's perception of self, and which will provide interaction with other people. Learning more about the students will contribute to the teacher's effectiveness in helping each student to cope more satisfactorily with his problems and to develop his potentialities.

TECHNIQUES FOR LEARNING MORE ABOUT STUDENTS

Valid information about students, including educational and personal experiences they have had, demographic information, sociometric information, self-evaluation, values, interests, goals, special problems, and individual successes, provides a background for increased understanding of students. The teacher has a variety of techniques on which to draw in order to accumulate appropriate information for developing a climate conducive to enriched teaching-learning experiences.

The teacher has a responsibility for the wise and discreet use of information about students. She will want to be careful not to draw conclusions on the basis of limited or possibly prejudiced data. The professional observer avoids participating in conversation about students with people in other professions who may be less objective, and she is especially zealous not to divulge information regarding one student

to another student or to lay people. Students become wary of teachers who betray their confidences, and rightfully so. Most schools keep a cumulative record of each student, but the extent of the data included will vary in different schools. Such a record may range from academic achievement to test results of intelligence, aptitudes, and interests, along with extraclass activities, work records, occupation of parents, and other personal data. The classroom teacher is generally permitted to review the records of the students in her classes.

However, the home-economics teacher will find it convenient and satisfactory to keep a personnel file of her own. Data from the school's cumulative records can be placed in such a file along with other information the teacher herself collects for acquiring a better understanding of her students. A loose-leaf binder or a file drawer that holds medium-sized cards can be used. The form on the opposite page or one similar is suggested.

COLLECTING PERTINENT DATA

In addition to the school's cumulative records the teacher may obtain information from the students themselves, from observations of her own, and from adults who have been in contact with the students. The extent of the data which the teacher will collect from these sources will depend upon the kind and amount of information she has on hand and what she feels is needed to understand her students more fully. If she has reason to believe that a student has a severe problem requiring special counseling, she may need to use several sources to justify her diagnosis. Familiarity with a wide range of sources and ability to use them efficiently will also tend to put her in good standing with a trained counselor.

Name: Age:

Residence:

Occupation of parents:

Special physical characteristics: (too tall or too short, over- or underweight, handicaps that interfere with normal activities, etc.)

School record: (taken from cumulative record and including IQ, special aptitudes, interests, etc.)

Homemaking achievement:

Comments:

Personnel Data Form

AUTOBIOGRAPHIES

A student's own life story can be of considerable value to both the teacher and the student. In addition to providing the teacher with factual information, the story will reveal events that appear significant to the student. Also the emphasis he places on these experiences may give clues to his set of values. Writing about himself helps a student to clarify his relationships to people and events. Moreover, in trying to present a picture of his life to someone else, he gains insight and a better understanding of himself.

In using this approach, some teachers make out a list of detailed directions for a student to follow. Others feel that more satisfactory results are obtained by allowing a student complete freedom to write a life story. In either case, the student must know what the teacher expects from him and what the teacher will do with the autobiography once it is written. The following explanation will indicate how a teacher can handle the matter:

I should like to know you better than I do so that we can work together more

effectively. You can help me by writing the story of your life. No one other than myself will see what you have written unless you give your permission.

Begin with your early childhood and make an outline of the important events in your life. Include both your happiest and unhappiest moments. Put the outline aside for a couple of days and then go over it again, adding other events that you may have forgotten.

Write your story around this outline. Do not be concerned about grammatical errors while you are writing. You can polish the material later if you want to. The important thing is to tell your story as accurately and clearly as possible. You may turn your story in to me any time, but I'd like to have all of it within the next ten days.

The teacher should recognize that an autobiography cannot always be taken at face value. A student may omit events that were too unhappy or embarrassing, or he may reconstruct the past to make it the way he would like to have had it happen.

AUTOBIOGRAPHIES OF THE FUTURE

This approach may be used as an extension of the autobiography. A student can describe what he would like to be, the sort of life he would like to live, and the things he would like to do. A student feels less inhibited in this type of writing than he would in setting down formal plans for the future. The autobiography can be written about the events centering around a day or a week in the student's life five or ten years from the present time. The material written will help the student and the teacher to become better acquainted with the hopes, aspirations, and ideals that the student has set for himself.

PICTURE STORIES

The teacher can provide a collection of interesting pictures relating to the different areas of the program. She can approach a student who seems to be having difficulties in a way similar to that recommended for writing an autobiography. The student can select a picture from several areas and over a period of time he can write a brief dramatic story about each picture. The story should include what he thinks is happening at the moment, what events led up to the present situation, and what the outcome will be. Through a series of such stories a skillful teacher can tell whether the feelings expressed are temporary or, by repetition, perhaps indicative of a deep emotional state.

SOCIOGRAPHS

Getting along with age-mates is an important aspect of a student's development. Failure to achieve social acceptance may result in severe emotional difficulties. By means of sociometry,

represented in the form of a sociograph, it is possible for the teacher to gain insight into the interpersonal relationships of a class. She will find this approach a reliable way to identify individuals who are well-liked and those who are rejected.

Some teachers feel that they can tell which students are accepted and which are rejected without using any special procedure. However, research indicates that teachers do not know their students as well as they think they do, since they are not fully aware of the bases from which students, particularly adolescents, make choices.

A sociograph may be used to identify popular and unpopular students in classes where there are all girls, all boys, or both. The following explanation may be given to a group of both boys and girls:

I should like to know you better than I do so that we can work together more effectively. You can help me by writing down your name and the names of two boys in the class whom you would like to have as good friends. List them in the order of first and second choice. Then write down the name of one boy whom you would least like as a friend. Repeat the same procedure for girls. No one other than myself will see what you have written.

There is a possibility that some students will try to compare notes on their choices. This could result in great unhappiness for a student if he learned that he was not wanted as a friend by anyone in the class. Such a situation can be avoided, at least in part, by having the selections made at the beginning of the class period, collecting the papers immediately, and then proceeding to other classwork that will absorb the attention of the group.

When recording the choices, a teacher who is inexperienced in using this approach may find it easier to make a sociograph by studying the illustration shown on page 40. The papers on which the choices are made should be destroyed as soon as the findings have been recorded, and the sociograph placed where students do not have access to it. In order to be sure that the information is adequately safeguarded, some teachers prefer to use code numbers or letters rather than actual names of students.

It should be pointed out that sociometric patterns in a class are constantly being altered as friendships develop or regroup. Sometimes the change is in a favorable direction, especially if the teacher has been able to help the ones who were identified as unaccepted. On the other hand, some popular students may lose their social position, perhaps because they have failed to adapt social skills to the shifting interests and ideals of the group. The teacher will therefore want to take periodic sociographs every few months to see what changes, if any, have occurred.

There are also variations in the kind of question that can be asked to reveal social interaction patterns. The teacher may want to find out whom the students would like to work with on various committees. However, there may not be a high relationship between the choices made for one committee and those for another. Students often evaluate their choices on the basis of utility and fitness for a particular activity or situation. For example, they may select the brightest and more experienced students to work with on a committee for a panel discussion or a class tea, and choose those with the most dramatic talent for a school assembly program. The popularity of a student may not be a determining factor in some choices.

From the information acquired, the teacher can determine who are the best liked students and who are the least liked for a variety of purposes and activities. To maintain the confidence of the class the teacher should be sure that each student has at least one of his choices fulfilled, for the chief object of the questioning is to give each class member the most satisfying committee placement from *his* point of view.

SOCIOGRAMS

Some experienced teachers prefer to carry out the sociometric approach through the use of a sociogram. This is a diagram in which circles, squares, or triangles represent the different students in a class. The type of symbols used and their arrangement and size may vary in accordance with the teacher's interpretation of the ease in reading the findings. Lines are drawn from one symbol to another to show relationships, the arrows indicating direction of choice. Like the sociograph the sociogram reveals direction of choice, mutual selections, accumulation of choice around individuals, and patterns of choice.

By using as a basis the sociograph on page 40, two sociograms are reproduced, the one on page 41 taken in September and that on page 42 taken in March. Various changes in choice can readily be noted between the first and second sociogram. The latter choices may be due to class members becoming better acquainted or to the teacher's influence on social relationships.

Trained counselors find the sociogram very helpful and use it especially to find out particular personality characteristics of different students. Since the sociogram is more difficult to construct, trained counselors frequently show teachers how to make and use one. Sometimes the teacher may be asked to cooperate with the counselor by submitting a set of questions to the class and then turning results over to the counselor.

CHOOSER	CHOSEN												
	Anne	Barbara	Catherine	David	Eleanor	Francis	Gordon	Helen	Isabel	John	Kenneth	Laura	Others in class
Anne													
Barbara													
Catherine													
David													
Eleanor													
Francis													
Gordon													
Helen													
Isabel													
John													
Kenneth													
Laura													
and others in class													
No. times chosen													
Total score													

Anne Smith

Boys I would like as friends:
    Gordon—1st
    David—2nd
    Kenneth—least

Girls I would like as friends:
    Laura—1st
    Eleanor—2nd
    Helen—least

Illustration of a Sociograph. (*Directions:* To enter the choices of a student, reverse the weight: a first choice gets 2; a second choice 1. When all the choices have been entered, adding them up gives a measure of relative popularity; the higher the score, the more often chosen with first and second choices. The least popular can be entered as R in red and added separately.)

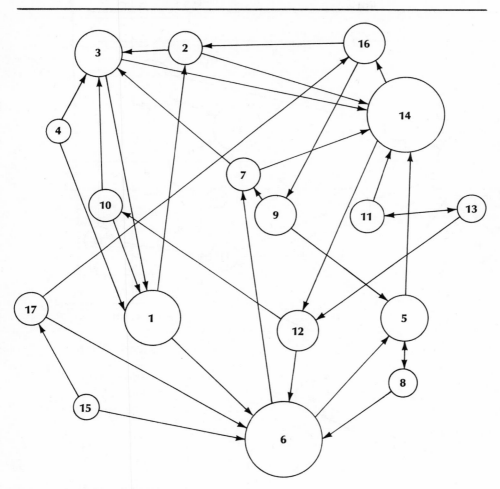

Illustration of a Sociogram Taken in September

DIARIES AND DAILY LOGS

Many students, especially adolescent girls, keep diaries in which they express their feelings about people with whom they are associated and about life in general. Although ado-

lescents consider their diaries private property, occasionally they will let a trusted counselor read the contents. A personal document of this type can be very valuable because it often reveals problems and attitudes that are not otherwise expressed.

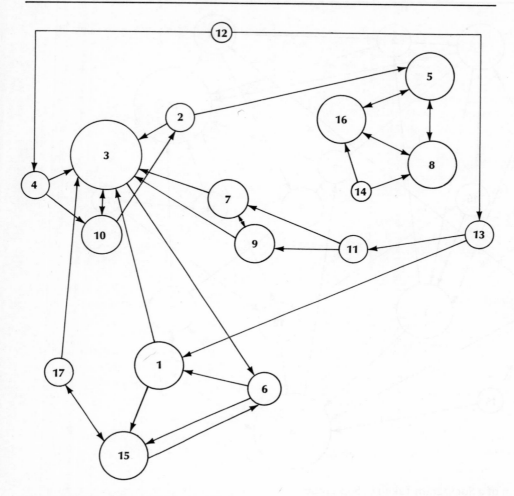

Illustration of a Sociogram Taken in March

A daily log of activities is less jealously guarded and also less revealing than a diary. However, a log has value because it indicates how a student spends his time and shows what he puts first in his daily living. A log can be used to help a student learn to use time more efficiently and to re-evaluate what he considers important in life.

PERSONALITY QUESTIONNAIRES

There are various standardized questionnaires which can be used to furnish a rough measure of qualities such as sociability, emotional stability, extroversion–introversion, tolerance, relative adjustment and maladjustment to home, school, and companions, and other traits. At one time it was thought that classroom teachers might use such questionnaires to identify problem cases. Now, however, it is deemed advisable for trained counselors to interpret the answers given.

OPEN-END SENTENCES

Students seem to enjoy responding to open-end sentences, phrases or words, and this technique provides some interesting and valuable information. Some responses are more valid than others but the teacher can readily discern by the tone of the responses those statements which are more accurate and those which are less accurate. The teacher can use other techniques for acquiring information about students to verify information recorded in response to open-end sentences. Responses are likely to be more valid if students are requested not to sign their names.

A variation of open-end sentences is open-end questions. A short paragraph is the expected response to open-end questions. Some suggested open-end sentences are listed on page 44 with sample responses.

GENERAL OBSERVATIONS

Any teacher can secure information for a personnel file by observing her students in their role of individual learners and as members of a group of age-mates. In regular classroom situations she can appraise scholastic abilities and limitation, special aptitudes and interests, and student relationships with the teacher and other members of the group.

IDENTIFYING STUDENTS WHO NEED SPECIAL COUNSELING

Something more than general observation is needed if a teacher expects to recognize students with special problems who do not respond to guidance integrated with the curriculum. Identifying these students is not always easy because they do not follow a standard pattern of behavior. However, there are warning signals which will indicate that a student may be having unusual difficulty meeting his problems. Since these manifestations will vary in extent and intensity with individual students, they will need to be corroborated by other sources before a final diagnosis can be made. Some of the warning signals which may be of help to the teacher are described as follows:

1. *Inability to respond normally to classroom procedure.*

   Works hard yet achieves poor results

   Is easily discouraged, gives up without trying to do the work

   Shows an indifferent attitude toward schoolwork

   Is timid and withdraws, prefers to work alone whenever possible

   Is uncooperative about carrying out suggestions agreed on by the class

   Finds it difficult to get along with classmates and is unpopular with them

OPEN-END SENTENCE	RESPONSE BY 15-YEAR-OLD BOY	RESPONSE BY 15-YEAR-OLD GIRL
The thing I like *best* about school	are the vacations	are the teachers
The thing I like *least* about school	are the teachers	are the tests
My mother	doesn't think much of me at times	is more like a friend
My father	is away from home a lot	works hard
I wish	I could quit school	I were grown up
I like most	playing football	being a candy-striper at the hospital
School is	not all that bad	O.K.
My brother is	Which one? Ted is in trouble most of the time	is a good kid
My sister	I wish I had one	is a nuisance now and then
My friends	are mostly like me	are great
I want to be	a truck driver	a nurse and then a wife
Drugs are	not for me	used by some of my friends
Girls are	what I'd like to know more about	are my best friends
Boys are	good sports	what I like a lot—certain ones

Suggested Open-end Sentences with Sample Responses

Is unable to concentrate on the task at hand and to make decisions

Is hypersensitive and feels discriminated against

Offers excuses such as headaches, digestive disturbances, and other illness when faced with responsibilities

Displays self-pity for a physical handicap, using it as a means of avoiding certain activities

2.   *Display of undesirable behavior, habitually or recurrently.*

Does an excessive amount of daydreaming

Is habitually lazy

Frequently becomes sullen and moody

Is constantly negativistic and quarrelsome

Becomes unduly excited and angry when things go wrong

Is tense and unable to relax

Constantly goes to extremes to attract attention by boasting, bragging, or being overly boisterous and noisy

Exhibits mannerisms, such as fingernail biting, eye twitching, fidgeting, and other nervous movements

ANECDOTAL RECORDS

As the name implies, an anecdotal record consists of a series of entries by the teacher describing incidents of a student's behavior as observed by one or more adults. This approach is a valuable way of acquiring a better understanding of a student. However, in most cases, the time element limits its use to students whom the teacher feels may need special counseling. The same format used for a personnel file is convenient for keeping such records. Since the series of entries will need to be kept over a period of time, each entry should be dated and filed accordingly. Certain other requirements are also considered essential. Each anecdote should have the following characteristics:

1.   Should be written while the details are still vivid. Notes taken at the time of observation will help to eliminate errors.

2.   Should tell briefly what the student said and did in a particular situation.

3.   Can include information about other people if they seem to be related to the situation.

4.   Should not be limited to classroom situations. Observations should be made in several places such as in the lunchroom, in the corridors, at school events, in the community, and in the home.

5.   Should not contain the teacher's reactions to the behavior recorded. It may, however, include her opinion as to whether a particular act is typical of a student's behavior or whether it represents something quite unusual. If cards are used for recordings, the teacher's interpretations can be made on the back of the cards.

If an anecdotal record is to be used as a source of substantiating a diagnosis of special difficulties, the teacher will need to provide some background information concerning the student. The example on pages 46–47 will indicate how this can be done as well as how the record itself may be kept:

Sylvia, a strikingly pretty girl fifteen years of age with above-average intelligence, comes from a family whose parents are separated. Sylvia and a younger sister live with their mother who works in a department store. They have a small house in a run-down neighborhood, but the furnishings are modern and well-chosen. Sylvia, who has had three semesters of home-economics, and her sister are responsible for keeping the house in order and for preparing the evening meal which has been planned by the mother. The living room was very untidy when a home visit was recently made.

CASE STUDIES

The case-study approach is an effective way to learn about and understand individual stu-

OBSERVER AND DATE	ANECDOTAL RECORD
Home-Economics Teacher Feb. 5	As class assembled, Sylvia in a loud voice said to Joan, "Aren't we going to cook today? No? Well, I don't want to sit around and talk, so I'm cutting class." Joan and several others told her to sit down. She finally sat down, but she took no part in the class discussion.
Feb. 11	Failed to do her share of a committee assignment by not giving her report. Said she had had a headache and did not feel like working.
Traffic Co-ordinator Feb. 25	Dropped a popcorn box from the second floor on a group of teachers. Was overheard saying, "Next time I'll drop something harder."
Home-Economics Teacher March 2	Asked Sylvia to stop in for a few moments after school was out, but she failed to appear.
March 7	Made same request. Waited for some time and was just ready to leave when she arrived. Talked with her about taking some responsibility for getting her work done on time and improving its quality. No comments from Sylvia. Finally said "Okay" and left.
Supervisor of Cafeteria March 16	Sylvia came in late but pushed her way to the head of the line saying, "I can't wait. I'm hungry. Didn't have any breakfast this morning."
Home-Economics Teacher March 28	At interschool debate Sylvia sat with a group of older boys. Wore tight-fitting dress, excessive make-up, and a considerable amount of costume jewelry.
March 29	Came to class in the same outfit as worn previous evening.
April 6	Especially noisy and boisterous. Laughed at the slightest provocation. Forgot to take notebook and several texts when

Sample of an Anecdotal Record

dents. The case study is a narrative account kept by a teacher or counselor of as many facts as possible concerning a student's life—past, present, and future. But because such a study requires considerable time and effort, its use is generally limited to students with severe problems. Through the information obtained, a per-

continued

OBSERVER AND DATE	ANECDOTAL RECORD
	leaving. Did not pick them up until next meeting of class.
April 11	Sylvia scored herself high on personality self-evaluation device. When students scored each other, her rating was very low. Became angry and remarked loudly, "What do I care what others think of me?"
Traffic Co-ordinator April 19	Created a commotion in the corridor when she saw a boy she did not like and rammed her head into his stomach knocking him down.
Office Clerk April 26	Inquired at office about baby-sitting jobs. When asked what experience she had, she replied "None, but that doesn't matter. Anyone can take care of kids."
Home-Economics Teacher May 2	Several students who walked down the street with me one day remarked that they did not like to be on committees with Sylvia, because she never did her share of the work. When she serves her turn as chairman, she makes no attempt to co-ordinate the work of the group.
May 6	During conference period talked with Sylvia about her work which has been getting progressively poorer. Was not successful in getting her to say much. She seemed tense and unable to relax, and her attention wandered. Leading remark, "As long as I pass, that's all that counts."
Art Teacher May 20	Sylvia had selected a free-style painting as an over-all project for the semester. When she turned in the painting, it was a mass of blobs. Asked what they represented, replied, "Oh, that is purely a personal matter."
Home-Economics Teacher June 2	During last meeting of semester she was heard to remark, "I've made a record in this class. It is the only one I haven't been sent out of the whole semester."
June 3	Recommended to principal that Sylvia be given special counseling.

son can learn much about the nature and cause of a student's difficulties and help him make a better adjustment to them.

In a school which does not provide specific instructions for making a case study, some such outline as that shown on the following page may assist the teacher to objectify the data that need to be included.

The Problem:

The reason for studying this particular student

Approximate length of time difficulty has been apparent

Concrete examples of the difficulties

The Student:

Name, address, birth date, sex

Educational status

Present grade

Mental ability, past and present achievement

Special aptitudes and interests

Extraclass activities

Vocational plans

Appearance and personality

General appearance: grooming, outstanding mannerisms

Personality traits: honesty, truthfulness, affection, and the like

Extent of emotional stability

Extent of social adjustment with age-mates and others

Physical status

Weight and height: normal or otherwise

General condition of health

Physical handicaps

The Environment:

The family

Socioeconomic status, cultural background, type of home

Number and age of persons living in the home

Parents' occupations

Parental attitudes: method of discipline, severe or lax; aspirations for children

Student's responsibilities at home

Pertinent facts regarding habits of student

Significant events in student's life: severe illness, frights, conflicts

The community

Type of neighborhood: urban, suburban, rural

Type of dwelling: single, apartment

Recreational facilities: clubs, parks, playgrounds, natural resources

Interpretation of the Data:

In relation to student's adjustment to the development tasks

Physical well-being

Emotional stability

Personal relationships with age-mates and others

Relative independence from parents

Vocational aspirations

Evaluation of himself, his values, and his attitudes toward everyday living

Avenues for Helping the Student Resolve His Difficulties:

School counselor or someone qualified to act in that capacity

Other teachers

School nurse and doctor

Parents and other family members

Social agencies

Religious groups

Youth organizations

Community clubs

TEACHING SPECIAL KINDS OF PEOPLE

The charge to home economics for the seventies and eighties is to help all people to improve their quality of life. *All people* is not to be loosely interpreted. Traditionally, since its inception, home economics has served principally girls in junior and senior high school, and some women in adult classes. The signs of the times as manifested in the identification of discriminatory practices involving sex, race, age, religion, and ethnic background, and the accompanying social action and federal legislation, have added impetus to making home economics more generally available to groups of people and individuals who have been neglected, not willfully, but because of limitations within the discipline itself. The old home economics, consisting principally of foods and clothing instruction with a little consideration given to family relationships, family health, child rearing, and management, was limited in its potentiality for serving all people of all ages in all walks of life. With increased emphasis on human development and relationships, nutrition, consumer education, decision-making, concern for adequate housing, and environmental control, it is generally recognized that the home-economics concepts are needed by everyone. Then too, a shift in sex roles has some additional implications for home economics. Women working outside the home (and an increasing number of them are) are carrying responsibility for the dual or even multiple roles of homemaker, wife, mother, and wage earner. By the same token men and boys are becoming more and more involved in the work of the home. Another influence is the goal to help handicapped people and the elderly to become more independent, and to be able to assume greater self-responsibility for personal care. It is now recognized that people who were formerly relegated to the wheel chairs can develop unique ways of serving their families and others, and possibly become employable. Home economics can contribute ways for these people to feel needed and wanted, and help them to live purposeful lives.

Exceptional students—those who have either less mental ability than most or considerably more than most—can be challenged through home economics, which contributes significantly to each person's way of life. People from subcultural groups may not always recognize the need nor even the desire for home-economics learnings, but they especially may be helped by home-economics concepts and skills to improve their quality of life.

Although they will not be discussed separately, there are other groups who gain from home-economics instruction, including girls and women with special needs, especially those in correctional institutions, unwed mothers, the mentally ill, and drug patients, to name a few.

Today's home-economics teacher, in serving humanity through her "people knowledge" and her specialized expertise in home economics, is limited only by her imagination and creativity.

BOYS IN HOME ECONOMICS

Increasing numbers of boys are being enrolled in home-economics classes. Sometimes they are included in classes with girls and sometimes there are separate boys' classes. Home-economics teachers report that boys revitalize the classes and contribute refreshing viewpoints. There is not an area of home economics which has not interested boys in one school and another. One of the writers, visiting a school where boys were in a separate class, saw a display case filled with ties and sports jackets which had been made by the boys. Signs identified each garment—"Tie constructed by John Taylor," "Jacket engineered by Garth Simmons," "Jacket built by Steve Parsons," "Tie fabricated by Terri Strong." Other units which had been included in the home-economics program for boys were: outdoor barbecuing, bachelor meals, preparation for marriage, making the old like new (furniture refinishing), stretching the food dollar, mother's day off (management).

In another school the eighth-grade boys and girls were in a class together. In a vegetable lesson the boys served the prepared vegetables to all members of the class over the protests of a few girls, some of whom said that they did not like the vegetables. It was noted by the observer at the end of the meal that each class member had eaten all the vegetables on the plate and had pronounced them very good.

Home-economics teachers who have had successful experiences teaching boys report some principles by which they have been guided:

1. Study boys' problems as boys view their problems. Such information can be learned from readings, consulting with school counselors, master teachers, and others who work well with boys. Discussions with boys who are the leaders in the school may provide some cues about what boys consider important.

2. Expect boys to be different from girls. They are inclined to be noisier, more direct, overtly curious. They may not be as neat as girls while working but they can usually be counted upon to clean up very well.

3. Do not be surprised to find that boys are different from one another. Within one grade level they show a great range of maturity. Boys undergo a period of rapid growth and many are perplexed by the mysterious changes taking place in their bodies.

4. Most boys in their up-bringing have not usually been exposed to taking responsibility for homemaking activities, and they may feel unsure of themselves, at first, but with experience they find such activities challenging and interesting.

5. Being a wife with a husband, or the mother of a son, does not necessarily guarantee that the home-economics teacher understands boys and men.

6. Boys need to be involved in the learning situation in a very real way; they like action and they like to complete a project with dispatch.

7. The scientific approach appeals to boys and they like to have the opportunity to evaluate and compare results objectively.

Different home-economics teachers have used a variety of ways to interest boys in home economics. Whatever approach is used, the teacher is wise to organize the class so that there is the greatest possible chance for success. Once an endeavor of this kind fails, it is difficult to initiate a successful boys' class for some time. Some teachers have used a screening procedure such as an interview, a questionnaire, academic achievement in other courses, or recommendations from other teachers in order to select boys for a class. Other teachers have offered a home-economics course for boys on a first-come basis. Sometimes a well-planned and effectively taught home-economics course has been responsible for holding boys in school. Mini-courses in "Outdoor Cookery," "Date-Raters," "Bachelor Meals," "Mr. Fix-it," "Dollar-Stretching," "Clothes Make the Man," "The Me Nobody Knows," or "A Man's Castle" have been popular introductory courses in home economics for boys. Home-economics teachers and agriculture teachers or industrial arts teachers have exchanged classes for a unit of work; or sometimes they have combined classes and used team teaching. In schools where it has not been possible to include boys in organized home-economics classes, home-economics teachers have taught aspects of consumer and homemaking education in cooperation with other courses, such as English or mathematics, for short periods of time. Other home-economics teachers have organized special clubs for boys. In some schools boys are active members of the Future Homemakers of America groups. This is in keeping with the changing role of men and boys. It is possible to offer FHA programs on selected topics of specialized interest: what to expect of girls, getting along with parents, drug use and abuse, minding-your-manners, chef's tricks, getting one's money's worth, use of credit, care and feeding of cars.

Having both boys and girls together in the same home-economics class or club group provides some advantages. It makes possible the opportunity for boys and girls to have a mutual sharing of viewpoints which can be quite different, and they develop understanding and respect for the roles of one another as well as for each other personally.

YOUTHS IN DEPRESSED AREAS

Awareness of the economically depressed segment of the population is in the forefront because of its size and the growing realization that society can be no better and thus life can be no better than the people who constitute that society. Almost every community is touched by the blight of poverty. Poverty-stricken people inhabit the ghettos and slum areas of our cities, row houses in industrial regions, Indian reservations which dot many of our states, and parts of rural America such as that part identified as Appalachia. They have several things in common, and one of them is that home economics holds one very important key to their release from a bondage which is self-perpetuating until enlightenment through educational resources is achieved. It must be a meaningful and relevant home economics

taught by teachers who are compassionate, perceptive, and knowledgeable about the people as well as the subject matter. The teacher must appreciate that there are decisions to be made and actions to be taken that are not within the context of the middle-class way of life. There is no choice to be made between buying or renting a home; rather one must learn how to mend a leaky roof and keep out the rodents. One does not choose between dining in the family room or on the patio, but rather clears a table and makes it clean so that all who are hungry may sit down together. The problem is not whether to make a packaged cake or a cake from scratch, but how to provide nourishment in meals at little cost and with a minimum of equipment.

What are young people from depressed areas like? What do they do, and what do they like to do? Do they have goals and aspirations? If so, what are they? It is impossible to generalize about all people in depressed areas because there are differences among them as with all groups. People who have had experience working with youths who are characterized as disadvantaged have described some common characteristics:

Usually they have experienced failure or defeat at an early age. Therefore their self-concept is weak and they cannot picture themselves as achieving and being successful, particularly in relation to academic pursuits. They mistrust the intent of people who are connected with institutions such as schools and social agencies. Their mistrust prevents them from responding in a positive manner to the classroom and all that it involves, including the teacher, teaching-learning techniques, and evaluation procedures.

The family and community environment of which these young people are a part lacks the stimuli for development of verbal, cognitive, and perceptual skills. The young people lack information and aids for health, sanitation, good grooming, and acceptable conduct patterns.

Self-motivation is at low ebb. The psychological impact of life in a depressed environment stultifies life goals and aspirations. Physical needs are not satisfied and lethargy and reduced efficiency result.

Because of premature exposure to life's adult realities, youths from depressed areas are forced into early adulthood roles for which they are ill-prepared. At ages when middle-class children are still playing with dolls and making believe, children in depressed areas are responsible for younger children, the infirm, and the elderly. As children they have first-hand experience with family problems and crises of desertion, divorce, poverty, unemployment, mental or physical handicaps, malnutrition, frequent and serious accidents, delinquency, legal entanglements. This experience causes them to seek immediate satisfaction of needs for affection, ownership, recognition, and status. They tend to solve one problem by taking on another.

Sound education for disadvantaged youths is far more than a "do-gooder" operation. Not every teacher possesses the understanding, the appreciation, and the ability to work effectively with students from depressed areas. However, some teachers are experiencing success in helping these students to improve their lives and their family situations. A first consideration is not to expect immediate success. The depressed-environment syndrome is often deeply rooted in a way of life that has been perpetuated through several generations. Changes of habits and patterns of behavior occur slowly, and may be besieged with setbacks beyond the control of the teacher and the learner. Since disadvantaged young people have learned well the lesson to trust no one, and especially not one who represents a way of life which is almost diametrically opposed to their own way of life, it becomes the teacher's guiding goal to develop and maintain trust above all else. Trust is engendered by having faith in the learner so that there is a positive force within the individual which can be discovered, released, and nurtured. The home-economics teacher, then, must use every resource available to her to identify those symbols that have a positive aura for the learner. In a foods and nutrition unit she must begin by using foods which are familiar to the students. Then, gradually, she may continue to expose the students to foods which are unknown to them. She is guided by the objective that some foods unknown to the student may be an inexpensive and rich source of a necessary nutritional element which is lacking in their regular diet. The purpose is not just to introduce new foods. The home-economics teacher also needs to help the families learn how to use the new foods. She must be sure that the food product is readily available, and within the means of the families. The introduction of any new learning must be able to satisfy the test of relevance. Does it satisfy a real need on the part of the learner? Will the value of the newly acquired skill or information be readily recognized by the learner? Will it receive acceptance by the learner and those who are closest to him?

A criterion for selecting any teaching-learning technique to be used with young people from depressed areas is that the technique must be based on student-input and the dynamic involvement of the learner. Factors necessary for implementation of the technique must be feasible without making impossible demands on the learner. Asking students from depressed areas to write a paper on the importance of specific foods in the diet is unrealistic because they do not possess the vocabulary nor the technique for writing, and are likely to have little appreciation for the written word. Yet they would appreciate feeding a good diet to one group of white mice, and a poor diet to another group of white mice, and then perceiving the effect of good and poor diets on mice. Many have a natural empathy for animals, and especially those who are being treated badly.

Evaluation or testing is a worrisome and threatening experience for students from depressed areas. The connotation of tests to them is failure, and failure is the beginning and the end of their frustration with schooling. The home-economics teacher needs to muster all her creativity to devise evaluation procedures which build up the individual and his self-image.

The teacher who has students from depressed areas in her classes has as much or more to learn than she will teach. She cannot teach these students effectively without learning first-hand about their life styles and how they view their world.

ETHNIC DIFFERENCES

Although students from different ethnic groups sometimes are from depressed areas, the word *ethnic* simply implies cultural or national origin. The home-economics teacher will recognize ethnic or cultural differences which seem to be typical of certain groups such as Mexican-Americans, Puerto Ricans, Indians, Ukrainians, blacks, Amish, Japanese, Chinese, and other identifiable groups. This recognition of ethnic groups will contribute to the effectiveness of her teaching and development of positive relationships with students and their families. Knowing the cultural characteristics of the

ethnic group, particularly as they influence family life, will facilitate the teacher's insight into family values and activities. This insight will help her in relating to students as individuals, and in planning curriculum offerings which will be meaningful to students and which will dignify ethnic influences. An awareness of some of the possible ethnic influences will alert the home-economics teacher as to what to look for in the larger community from which the students come.

Ethnic groups tend to be loyal to their culture, and they may be defensive about their beliefs and practices. Often they are suspicious of those outside the ethnic group and they may even actively resist change. Campbell (1971, p. 26) has identified in capsule form the cultural factors for the teacher to consider:

Family Life Style:

Composition and "closeness" of the family

Influence of the family on individual family members

Loyalty to the family or to authority figures in the family

Concept of the family group—nuclear or extended

Attitude toward unwed parenthood

Attitude toward decision making—democratic, autocratic or laissez-faire

Attitude toward aged members of the family unit

Overall focus of the family—child centered, paternal or maternal

Role expectations of each family member

Religion and Philosophy of Life:

Basic tenets of declared religion or personal philosophy

Rituals and traditions

Importance of religion to individuals and the ethnic group

Religious organizations and action within the community

Dietary restrictions and eating habits imposed by religious beliefs or personal philosophy

Ethnic Pride:

Degree of pride versus feelings of inferiority

Achievements and attributes which contribute to ethnic pride and a positive self-image

Outstanding individuals from ethnic groups —current and historic figures

Contributions of ethnic groups to the dominant culture in areas such as the humanities, medicine, research, law, education, entertainment, government

Strength of the relationship and ties with the country of an ethnic group's origin

Language Differences and Variations:

Extent of variation from the dominant group language and usage

Willingness to adapt

Weaknesses and strengths in oral and written communication

Language spoken at home—native tongue

Extent of communication problems among students, parents, teachers, administrators and the community in general

Colloquial and vernacular usages of language which result from regional, local, cultural and age factors

Education:

Attitude toward education as a means to an end or an end in itself

Differences in educational objectives for

boys versus girls in the family or subculture

Respect for—or suspicion of—teachers, administrators or other authority figures, and the school system

Educational level and aspirations of the family

Educational aspirations for youngsters

The presence of students from a different culture or ethnic group presents a challenge to the teacher. This challenge can be directed into a new and exciting thrust for home economics whereby the educational experiences of teacher and learners alike can be broadened. Rather than being a barrier between teacher and students, and between one group of students and another, ethnic differences can be drawn upon to enlighten all of the students and to provide a positive relationship among varying concepts of subject matter and among the individuals who make up the class. The teacher has a number of approaches she may employ to achieve a harmonious climate for teaching-learning and for the long-time goal of increased understanding of individuals and groups.

First, she needs to encourage active participation by the students in developing the curriculum in terms of cultural needs and interests. The students can indicate problems and concerns, and existing ways of coping with situations. Some of these may be effective and others can be refined or changed gradually and through the leadership of the students. Gaining insight into the life styles of students and their families becomes a major concern of the home-economics teacher. Developing communications with the home will be of utmost help. This communication must take the form of being helpful and friendly. Communication must be carried on in such a way that there is no chance it will be misconstrued as stemming from curiosity or being critical. Another approach to understanding life styles of ethnic families is to become familiar with the communities from which the students come. Familiarity with ethnic organizations, churches, recreational facilities, and mercantile establishments may be a rich source of background information for the home-economics teacher. The teacher should take advantage of the ethnic diversity and positive aspects of each cultural group. Sincere commendation of whatever is especially admirable in individuals and their cultural heritage builds rapport. The teacher must make an honest effort to know, to understand, and to appreciate the values which these students and groups hold. Language is frequently a barrier in understanding individuals and groups. The home-economics teacher will find it to her advantage to develop some understanding of the language, to recognize the meaning of certain phrases, and to be able to speak a few common phrases or words. By all means, she needs to be able to pronounce the students' names as they are accustomed to hearing their names spoken at home. She also needs to emphasize standard English usage to the extent required for the student to function competently in school and in situations outside of school.

The home-economics teacher who capitalizes on cultural differences in implementation of curriculum will promote a more viable home economics, and the self-concept of the individual will be strengthened so that he can become a contributing member of his family, his group, and society.

PHYSICALLY OR EMOTIONALLY HANDICAPPED STUDENTS

Present-day home-economics teachers have concern for a group of students identified as the physically or emotionally handicapped. This group is not limited to a given sex, age, or socioeconomic level. Perhaps more of those needing rehabilitation help are among the poor, and the problems of poverty compound the problems of physical or mental impairment. In public school classrooms there seems to be a larger number of physically or emotionally handicapped young people than ever before. At least two factors may be responsible for this: there may be more young people who are either physically or emotionally handicapped; more may be attending public school because of a changing view regarding the care of handicapped people. Formerly they were kept at home or institutionalized, and were often regarded as abnormal people, who would live out their lives being looked after by others. Present-day philosophy and facts tell us that handicapped people can learn to live normal lives and that they can be independent to the extent of looking after themselves and their basic needs, and can even support themselves financially, and contribute to the care of others.

Emotional problems seem to be on the increase. Because of the stresses and tensions accompanying contemporary life—pressure to achieve, to accumulate, to cope with unstable family life and resulting frustrations—an increasing number of people are displaying symptoms of emotional illness. People of all ages, including very young children and adolescents are not immune to adjustment problems.

Students with physical handicaps are not denied an education when formerly they have been. Their adjustment to life is more satisfactory when they are able to live and cope with problems along with unhandicapped people. Some physical handicaps are obvious such as lameness, blindness, and stuttering. Other physical handicaps, such as reduced hearing, reduced vision, epilepsy, and diabetes are less noticeable and the teacher may not be aware that a person has afflictions of this kind.

It is not enough for the teacher to include the handicapped along with the other students on the roll and in the classroom. She has a unique responsibility to help each handicapped person make the best adjustment of which he is capable. She can be instrumental in helping the student to gain self-acceptance, to develop adaptive behavior whenever possible and necessary, to develop skills that will help him to become more independent. She can also inspire other students to develop a positive attitude about handicaps so that they will learn how to be supportive of others less fortunate than themselves. In the event that they or family members may become handicapped these students will be aware of resources available to them.

In preparation for working with emotionally or physically handicapped persons in the classroom, the home-economics teacher will want to learn about each specific handicap, its limitations, the prognosis, symptoms of further regression, and suggestions for advisable classroom adaptation (such as seating students with limited hearing or sight near the center of activity). Depending upon the handicap she will want to be in consultation with the school nurse or doctor, the guidance counselor, school psychologist, school administrator, home-school visitor, rehabilitation counselor, responsible members of the family, or referral agencies.

All that is included here applies to all handicapped persons of both sexes and of all ages. Instruction in home-economics concepts and skills may provide for rehabilitation and therapeutic needs of handicapped people. Through home-economics learning they are able to become more self-reliant; they develop creative abilities; they learn to use their time more productively; they develop greater self-under-standing, and they are able to fulfill that right of every human being which is to realize one's full potential.

SUPERIOR STUDENTS

Superior students have been a neglected group in many schools as far as home economics is concerned. After an exposure to junior-high-school home-economics, the superior student's goal is usually college entrance with a prescribed high-school course of study which leaves little opportunity to elect home-economics courses. Therefore, a major concern of the home-economics teacher is to provide a curriculum which is sufficiently flexible so that the more superior students, both boys and girls, may elect home-economics courses.

Superior students differ among themselves as much as they differ from less able students. The longitudinal Terman study (Cole & Hall, 1969) has indicated that children who are superior in intellectual ability tend also to be superior physically, socially, and temperamentally. However, in spite of our knowledge about the general superiority of gifted children, teachers often are not able to identify them. It seems to be easier to identify the dull child, perhaps because gifted people display average ability while dull persons do not. When conditions are not challenging, some bright students may withdraw from participation in classroom activities. Others may rebel deliberately or unconsciously. An able student may be a passive participant, merely tolerating school, and then carry on more challenging activities outside of class from which he achieves his major satisfaction.

Another common error is to disregard the age of the student. An overage student doing excellent work with others chronologically younger is sometimes erroneously judged very bright by the teacher, as is the student who applies himself diligently and has fine character traits. The student whose general appearance and behavior is consistently annoying to the teacher is often judged to have less than average ability.

Since errors of judgment are possible without a careful systematic appraisal, the teacher needs to be guided by evidence that is considered reliable. In addition to tests and records, such evidence can be found in certain characteristics which able students are known to possess and which, when carefully noted, set these students apart from those with average ability. The following characteristics not only reflect the extent of mental ability, but indicate the influence of ability on emotional and social learning. It is important to recognize that this list does not give a complete description of the gifted student. Nor can any one individual be expected to exhibit all of these characteristics.

1.   Their span of attention is much beyond the average. They can concentrate for long periods and are not easily distracted.

2.   They can think logically and display superior organization in their work. Their judgments are generally sound.

3.   They can think abstractly and are able to generalize fairly easily. They are quick to recognize relationships. They speculate on moral and philosophical questions. They memorize rapidly and learn with little practice. They are able to transfer knowledge and experience to new situations.

4.   Their coordination is good, and they are relatively free from nervous troubles. Physical defects are uncommon.

5.   Their emotional control is better than average. They generally adjust to heavy restraints, sudden changes, or undue pressures without becoming unduly upset. They are not easily discouraged by failure or difficulty.

6.   They have many varied and mature interests, often carried on concurrently. They display eagerness to explore new fields and to tackle new problems.

7.   Their social consciousness is well above average. They participate in a wide range of activities and win recognition to a high degree. They are sensitive to needs of others, friendly and adaptable. They desire to excel. They readily accept personal and social responsibilities beyond their age expectancy.

8.   They are able to communicate easily. They write and speak fluently and use words accurately. They read quickly and with understanding. They like to express thoughts and ideas.

9.   They are critical of self. They are able to analyze abilities, limitations and problems. They are conscientious and trustworthy with a strong sense of responsibility.

10.   They are resourceful and imaginative. They can plan work with little direction. They show originality in problem solving and in writing. They are inventive and foresighted.

11.   Their personality is well integrated. They possess a high degree of common sense, breadth of vision.

If the teacher feels that she has some reliable evidence the student may be exceptional, she needs to begin immediately to study that student very carefully to ascertain his unique pattern of development and his special needs. The teacher should, however, avoid any indication before the class that such variations in ability may exist. Students, particularly adolescents, want to feel that they are like others in the group. Anything that tends to set them apart is apt to lead to a decrease in effective learning. Some bright students have been known to underachieve deliberately rather than be thought superior by their classmates. The teacher may modify her instructional approach for superior students, thus enriching the curriculum in breadth and depth. Able students do have problems with which teachers can help. A friendly, understanding teacher can have a great influence in the life of a superior student.

An efficient teacher modifies her instructional approach for superior students in the following ways:

1. Makes every effort to increase the range of their knowledge and skills. She can encourage extensive reading and study outside of school and see that the students are usefully occupied in school. Those who complete the classwork ahead of others can be encouraged to work on the same material more extensively, or be permitted to go to a new task. They can also be encouraged to engage in long-range experiences that call for a high degree of mental organization.

2. Motivates and develops critical thinking and analysis. Since high-ability students have superior reasoning ability, the teacher can arouse and maintain a questioning attitude that will stimulate reflective thinking. She can foster an unwillingness to stop with superficial answers and encourage a willingness to reach sound judgments. It is also important to encourage students to organize their ideas systematically and to integrate related ideas into basic generalizations.

3. Assists in developing an understanding of and ability to use problem-solving processes. Students can be helped to see how the techniques that are worked out in the classroom can be extended to meet all kinds of problem situations in everyday living. The teacher can also guide the students to learn to recognize problems that may be solved and those that can only be resolved.

4. Stimulates the desire for expanding creative abilities. Although every member of the class needs to be given opportunity to be creative, high-ability students can be encouraged to expand their abilities in many fields. It is especially desirable for them to formulate original ideas and to explore a new or different way of doing something other than the usual or common way.

5. Provides ample opportunity for working independently and for assuming responsibilities. High-ability students work better when supervision is at a minimum and when they are given definite responsibilities.

6. Develops leadership abilities. Opportunities to exercise leadership roles are important for all students, but especially so for those with high ability. Although there is no consistent pattern which characterizes all leaders, superior mental ability is generally regarded as basic to successful leadership. Of course, other qualifications such as learning to speak effectively and knowing how to deal with others in the group diplomatically are also necessary. Since there is a need for leadership in the world today, the teacher can encourage superior students to learn the skills of leadership, but at the same time these students need to recognize that there are occasions when it is just as important to be a good follower as a good leader.

MENTALLY RETARDED STUDENTS

In line with the current movement in home economics education to establish special programs for special people, there seems to be a need to develop and expand learning opportunities for the mentally retarded. Mentally retarded people can be taught to achieve useful and sometimes even independent places in society. Home economics has the potential to help each individual learn to live more independently as he clothes himself and looks after his physical well-being, as he feeds himself, as he adjusts the near environment to his needs, and as he makes decisions which influence day-by-day living. Home economics may be able to help the individual become more self-sufficient economically. Effort needs to be focused on establishing and evaluating curriculum, learning about resource materials, and helping home-economics teachers learn how to work with mentally retarded students.

The home-economics teacher needs an orientation as to what to expect mentally retarded students to be like. They may be young children, teen-agers or adults. Probably the most common of shared characteristics of many but by no means all of these students is economic and social deprivation. Achievement in subject matter, including reading and arithmetic skills, may reach between second- and fourth-grade levels by the age of sixteen years. Mentally retarded students will have the minds of children throughout life. They learn slowly and can forget quickly. Because there are many degrees of mental retardation it is not possible to generalize on the speed with which the mentally retarded learn. These students learn best through seeing, feeling, and participating.

Teachers of the mentally retarded have discovered some principles which generally lead to success in teaching students of low mental ability. They recommend that the material used in the classroom and the time schedule be kept flexible in order for the mentally retarded student to achieve a high degree of satisfaction and to develop security. More time is needed to provide for additional repetition and mentally retarded students are not frustrated by repetition. In contrast to more able students, mentally retarded students enjoy repetitive processes, such as those involved in knitting, cleaning, preparing vegetables, sorting items.

They also thrive on commendation and approval from the teacher because so much in life is frustrating to them, and they have experienced frequent and intense academic failure. The entire home-economics program must be supportive and should guarantee successes insofar as possible in the classroom. One failure leads to discouragement which can be almost impossible to overcome because it is difficult to reason with the mentally retarded student and to help him develop a philosophy regarding failure, as can be done with a student of normal intelligence.

To accomplish the goal of guaranteeing success requires very careful and complete planning in preparation for each activity and the teacher must provide constant surveillance. The successful teacher of the mentally retarded does not assume that a student possesses capabilities but, rather, she provides complete and simple instructions, and she observes his work carefully. Class periods must be orderly and well-planned, although flexible, because retarded students are more secure following a familiar routine. Sufficient time must be allowed for each step of the program so that concepts can be developed slowly, simply, and in sequential order over a period of time, and so that there can be meaningful repetition. Directions must be repeated often and in the same simple and concise terms. Instructions may be given verbally or in a combined form of simple words and pictures. Often many additional steps, which are taken for granted with normal students, need to be included. In planning for a simple breakfast students need to be shown the equipment they will be using. The names of the items and food need to be identified. It may be necessary to teach the students how to read the clock, how to make simple measurements, where to look for supplies and equipment. Much that is considered incidental information for normal students must become specific teaching concepts for the mentally retarded.

Teaching-learning techniques which involve the student directly are most appropriate for the retarded home-economics student. Preference should be given to providing real articles and real-life experiences. Simulation techniques and games which are not complex have proven successful. For more able students, home economics needs to present the challenge of many options. However, choices should be kept to a minimum for the retarded. For example, a few well-selected menus and recipes or one method of hemming or sewing in a zipper are most effective when teaching students of limited mental capacity. Measurements with fractions should be avoided except for the more able of the mentally retarded.

Teaching the mentally retarded has implications for the curriculum as well. The curriculum must provide for students who enter class at any point during the school year and for those who have been in the class for several years. It must also provide for students who are at the lower limits as well as those at the upper limits of educability. There will be non-readers in this group along with those who have some facility in reading. Care should be taken to prevent the less capable students from becoming dependent upon the more capable students. Like all students, the mentally retarded need to be encouraged to develop their potential to the fullest. Home economics has much to offer the retarded in the development of family and social skills. Most of these students will marry and become parents and so they need to learn in a simple way all that anyone else needs to know regarding nutrition, personal care, providing food, clothing, and shelter for the family, child rearing, consumer education, human development and relationships, and controlling the environment. Home-economics programs for the retarded which can be taught in a homelike setting will provide students with real-life experiences which will aid in developing self-reliance, cooperativeness, initiative, and some insight into harmonious family living.

OUT-OF-SCHOOL YOUTHS, ADULTS, AND THE ELDERLY

The swiftly changing conditions in the world today and their impact on personal, family, and community living make it necessary, as never before, for home economics to extend its program beyond the secondary level. The need and value of ongoing education for out-of-school youths, adults, and the elderly cannot be overemphasized. Socioeconomic and technological developments call for increased skill in using all our resources in ways that will bring satisfaction to one's self, one's family, and one's fellow man. The altered roles of men and women, and of parents, require a clearer understanding of human relationships and increased skill in living amicably and working constructively as a family group. Goals and values concerning family life need to be re-examined in the light of present-day situations to determine which should be retained, and which modified. Facts about the way men and women live and work in today's world indicate that the stereotype of the family with well-defined roles, with the husband as the wage-earner and the wife as the homemaker, is no longer accurate. The home-economics teacher can do herself and her profession a service by becoming more aware of how contemporary families function, with the role-exchange between the sexes becoming increasingly more evident.

The elderly constitute a group which is increasing in numbers, and in proportion to the total population. In many areas they are forming their own communities, because of common needs and interests, and they are discovering that in a loosely united grouping they are able to cooperate in coping with the unique problems of later life. The home-economics teacher will find an opportunity and a challenge here, too, because the special needs of the elderly for information about nutrition, clothing, health and safety, leisure time pursuits, housing, relationships, and consumer information and protection are important aspects of home economics. These and other factors indicate that home-economics teachers will need to assume responsibility for helping adults cope with and adjust to a rapidly changing society.

UNDERSTANDING CHARACTERISTICS
OF ADULTS

A successful program for adults depends markedly on a general understanding of what adults are like, for this knowledge will influence the procedures to be used. A teacher trained to think in terms of adolescent development will need to readjust her thinking when she works with adults, since the learning patterns of the two groups are somewhat different. Some of these differences are as follows:

1. Adults can learn but may take longer than adolescents. That adults can learn is well established. They may take longer than young people because of a general decline in physiological functioning and the fact that they are not in the practice of studying. But the quality of their learning can be much the same as that of young persons and may even be superior. The teacher will need to arouse adults to accept the ideas that learning can continue throughout life and that it will benefit and enrich their ev-

eryday living. As she works with adults, the teacher can take the time factor into account and not expect older persons to react as quickly as high-school students.

2. The range of interests of adults tends to be narrower and more stable than that of adolescents. With an increase in age there are few marked changes of interests but rather a narrowing of their range. Along with changes in duties and responsibilities, there is a shift of emphasis in existing interests. New interests are less likely to be established unless there are changes in environment and opportunities for development. As a rule, adult interests are centered on family needs with more long-term goals than those of adolescents. Most young adults tend to plan ahead for material things they would like to acquire and for their children's education. With advancing age and the concomitant slowing down of physiological functioning, interests are likely to be less active and more passive in nature. However, they will vary in accordance with the socioeconomic levels and cultural backgrounds of persons. In planning a program for adults, a variety of individual patterns of interest may need to be met.

3. Adults tend to resist change to a greater degree than adolescents. Most adults have acquired certain habits of thinking and acting and tend to question anything that involves change unless they can see some value in it. In general, adults like to believe that they have attained a good measure of growth and feel that admitting limitations, inadequacies, and inconsistencies is a weakness. They resist change partly to avoid self-disapproval and social condemnation. Adolescent thinking, on the other hand, is still fluid; answers to many questions are yet to be found. The teacher's responsibility is to arouse adults to an acceptance of new ideas, introducing these ideas slowly and showing how they are valuable and practical.

4. Adults are voluntarily interested in learning, and are not under pressure to learn like adolescents. Adults take courses because they are interested and eager to learn. Their selection is made on the basis of what they are interested in and want to learn. Consequently, the teacher usually has the task of sustaining interest in a course rather than motivating it, as in the case of some courses for adolescents. She will need to adjust the program to the adults and not try to adjust the adults to a program.

5. Adults, as a rule, are superior to adolescents in matters requiring reasoning, ability, judgment, and creative thinking. Through prolonged experience in encountering the many problems of everyday living, adults in general have acquired more skill in solving problems than adolescents have had time to develop. Adults have learned to see varied ways of doing things, to weigh alternatives, and to render judgments based on reasoning. The teacher will spend less time with adults than with adolescents in showing how to go about meeting problems. More time can thus be given to various aspects of a problem that adults might not have considered, or to the handling of more problems.

6. Adults can generally concentrate on a task for a longer period of time than adolescents. There are, of course, some adults who have not developed the self-discipline needed for prolonged concentration. Others may come to class so fatigued that they are physically and mentally unable to participate actively in anything requiring concentrated effort. But these people are in the minority. If interest is high and the subject challenging, instructional techniques and resources can involve a longer period of time than would be advisable for adolescents.

7. Emotional reactions of adults are somewhat different from those of adolescents. Adults tend to be less responsive emotionally than adolescents. They generally show less enthusiasm and often withdraw from taking part in a program because they feel self-conscious in a group situation or have feelings of inferiority. In early adulthood when there are usually innumerable adjustment problems, many persons are emotionally tense. A person working with adults will need to meet these emotional factors without becoming disturbed by them. This can be done by being patient and understanding, by showing a sense of humor, and by radiating happiness and enthusiasm for the good things of life.

HOW ADULT PROGRAMS ARE ORGANIZED

It is to be expected that the organization patterns of an adult program will vary from one community to another. The scope and size of the program, the availability of qualified teachers, and the necessary facilities for carrying out the work are some of the factors that govern the arrangements.

ADMINISTRATION

An adult program may be administered in various ways. In some cities a director of adult education is in charge of the school program with qualified teachers under his supervision. In other localities the supervisor of home economics is responsible for adult home-economics programs. In small towns or rural communities, the superintendent or school principal is likely to be the official administrator with one or more qualified persons planning the program, doing the promotional work, and teaching the classes.

FINANCING

Adult programs are financed from different sources and in various ways depending on the local situation.

1. Local funds. School boards may allocate funds in their annual budget for adult education. Sometimes community groups, organizations, and interested individuals make contributions to aid the program. In some localities where funds are difficult to secure, a small fee is collected from class members for the materials and supplies that are used.

2. State funds. In many states money can be obtained from the State Department of Education, which may have both nonvocational and vocational funds for adult education.

3. Federal funds. Communities which have a vocational education program and can meet certain specifications can be reimbursed with vocational funds allocated to the states by the federal government for the salaries of persons who teach adult home-economics classes.

FACILITIES

Providing facilities for carrying out an adult program involves various matters which need consideration so that the arrangements will be satisfying to the participants and at the same time help to bring about effective learning.

Many communities use the day schools for adult programs, provided that classes can be held at hours when space and equipment are not being used by the students. The home-economics department can usually be adapted satisfactorily for evening classes, but special storage should be arranged. If adult classes are held during the day and facilities are not avail-

able at the school, places such as churches, the public library, the YMCA, or the YWCA are sometimes used. Whatever place is selected needs to be convenient to public transportation and have available parking space. Suitable lighting, heating, and ventilation are also important, as well as comfortable seats, tables, chalk boards, and storage space for supplies.

TEACHERS

Various persons may be engaged to teach or to assist in teaching courses offered in an adult program. These may include:

High school teachers of home-economics, provided plans have been made to include this work as a cocurricular responsibility

Home-economics graduates who are in positions other than teaching and who have available time

Former teachers of home-economics, now homemakers

Homemakers without home-economics education but with special skill in some phase of homemaking

People in professions, industry, and trades who may take full responsibility for a course, or be brought in as resource persons to supplement the work of the regular instructors

In the last two groups there are likely to be some persons with little or no preparation for teaching who will need special help with instructional techniques before they begin. There may be others whose education for teaching home-economics dates back ten years or more. These people will need to be brought up to date on information regarding problems of relationships and child development; on recent findings in nutrition, textiles, housing; on new equipment; and even on new concepts of the philosophy of education and teaching procedures. Assistance can be given through individual consultations or group conferences with the administrator of the program or with someone equally qualified. Bulletins and other printed materials can also be distributed.

However, something more is needed than knowing how to present knowledge in a specialized field. Equally essential is the possession of certain personality qualifications which contribute to one's success as a teacher of adult classes. Some of the qualifications generally regarded as important are as follows:

A warm, friendly, outgoing nature with a genuine liking for people

Sincere respect for the dignity and worth of all individuals regardless of socio-economic and cultural background

An appreciation of the importance of the American family

A high degree of interest and enthusiasm in helping adults meet problems of personal, family, and community living

Ability to sustain interest and to stimulate creativity in the work undertaken

Ability to convey ideas and attitudes to others as well as to understand their viewpoints

A sense of humor, unlimited patience, and vitality

DEVELOPING A PROGRAM FOR ADULTS

Developing a program for adults requires advance planning and careful preparation. The person responsible for the program needs to know rather specifically what she is trying to do and what she hopes to accomplish, yet all plans need to be flexible, subject to modification if the situation warrants it. A program that becomes fixed or stereotyped is generally out of touch with the times. Although there is bound to be variation from one community to another, certain developmental procedures are applicable to most adult programs to assure some measure of success.

ASCERTAINING ADULT INTERESTS AND NEEDS

To be worthwhile any educational program should be related to the interests and needs of the people it will serve. The interests and needs of adults can be found in much the same way that the teacher would go about discovering those of her high-school students as she makes plans for their program.

The first step is to know the community in which the program is being offered. The social setting in which people live—their economic and cultural backgrounds—largely determine their interests and needs. Getting acquainted with people in all walks of life, visiting homes, and making contacts with civic, church, and business groups are sources for ascertaining the particular interests and needs of adults in the community. It is especially important to reach non-English-speaking people. In a community where such a group is present, it is often possible to get the help of a person who speaks their language and is familiar with their customs and problems.

Making a general survey is another possibility for finding out what subjects interest people. Such a survey can be made by sending out a simple questionnaire to representative groups in the community. Working in cooperation with the principal, the teacher could also give copies to the student body to take home and return. The plan for distribution and collection of the questionnaire should be one which will assure the greatest possible return.

During the process of ascertaining interests and needs it may be wise to set up a publicity program. It is only by knowing and understanding what home economics is that adults can identify their interests with the various aspects of personal, home, and community living which comprise the content of home-economics education.

COORDINATING INTERESTS AND NEEDS WITH POSSIBLE COURSE OFFERINGS

In setting up a program related to interests and needs, there are various factors to be considered. The interests expressed by adults, although important, represent only a part of the total picture. It is generally more acceptable to adults to express an interest in specific activities such as refinishing furniture or constructing slip covers and draperies than it is for them to admit that they want or need more knowledge about managing family financial situations or about developing better family relationships. In our society many adults are fearful that a study of these fundamental problems will reveal personal and family affairs which they consider private and highly personal matters. Furthermore, some of the expressed interests may also be "feeling," based on a condition or situation that is only temporary. For example, a parent, emotionally upset about a teen-age daughter who is "boy crazy," may be interested only in knowing how to handle this particular situation and not in studying family relationships in general.

It is therefore quite possible that the program leader's appraisal of what the adults need may be at variance with what some people think they want or need. For example, evidence may have been obtained that some fam-

ilies in the community are overextending their credit and that in several instances household furniture and equipment have been reclaimed because installment payments could not be met. Obviously, there is a need for a course in family financial planning although no interest in money management was expressed. Or evidence may show that in many homes the relationship between parents and their adolescent sons and daughters is far from satisfactory and a course in family relationships is needed, although no such interest was expressed.

The problem of the program leader is how to bring interests and needs together so that course offerings will be satisfying and beneficial. Some adult educators feel that it is wise to start with expressed interests, believing that expanded interests can grow out of or be developed from them. However, this may not happen unless the teacher plans to open up new learning possibilities as she helps the group work on their original interests. For example, the teacher of a group constructing slipcovers and draperies could use various techniques that would motivate interest in a course in home planning including aspects such as furniture arrangement, storage, or family needs for housing. Interest in buying furniture and other home furnishings might be created in a group refinishing furniture and then lead to the taking of a course in family financial planning. A group studying specific teen-age problems might well become interested in delving into family relationships. Thus the criterion determining whether an adult program is worthwhile is probably not its initial planning but the direction it takes.

LONG-RANGE PLANNING

In developing a program for adults it is generally desirable to plan for a longer period than one year. A program set up for such a relatively short time cannot, as a rule, begin to cover all the interests and needs associated with family living. The number of people to be served and the number of interests and needs to be dealt with would necessarily be limited. But a three- or five-year plan, taking into consideration present and anticipated interests and needs, could be worked out whereby a broader program could be made available to a wider range of participants. Organized courses providing systematic and consecutive learning experiences tend to sustain interest in on-going education and to yield valuable results.

There are various ways in which long-range programs are set up, each aiming to meet special interests that are known and urgent needs that are recognized. Some programs, centering on the various subject areas of home economics, emphasize different aspects of an area in successive years, with courses for adults of any age. Another type of program is designed for special age groups, and deals with interests and problems generally encountered at different stages of adult life. This procedure is frequently referred to as the life-cycle or family-cycle approach. Groups may include out-of-school youth who have become wage earners, young homemakers recently married, parents with children at different age levels, and elderly people. The cycle approach is considered especially valuable for young adults. It affords them an opportunity to learn to deal adequately with one stage of the cycle before going on to the next, thus laying a foundation of understanding for successive stages. In some communities it may not be possible to offer courses each year to all the groups represented in the adult cycle, but the program planners can begin with the stages in which there appear to be the highest interest and the greatest need. Regardless of the type of program planned, provision should be made for occasional re-evaluation, since changing conditions often lead to new interests and needs.

LENGTH OF COURSES

Short courses have proved to be more practical than those covering a long period of time. The courses may be independent or organized on a progressive plan, but a series of short courses has several advantages:

1. Wider variety of offerings and a consequent increase in individual enrollment. Since interests and needs vary, the more aspects of home economics there are to choose from, the greater the enrollments are likely to be. Some people hesitate to take a long course because they are only interested in certain parts of it, whereas a short course may cover just what they want.

2. More regular attendance. In a long course people tend to think that they can miss some of the meetings without losing much, but in a short course they feel that every meeting counts.

3. Opportunity to hold classes at convenient times for participants. A series of short courses that can be given at times when people are less occupied will have a greater appeal than long courses that may encroach on a busy period. The administrator of the program will need to be guided by local conditions in selecting the most appropriate time for the largest number of people to be served.

Some adults who may not be interested in a so-called course or class might be attracted by the idea of attending a "clinic" where their personal problems can be diagnosed. If this approach is used, resource persons who are specialists would probably be needed to assist the regular teacher.

The time of day for holding the classes will be determined by the hours most convenient for members of a class and for the teachers. The length of the class period will vary, depending somewhat on the type of work being done. However, two to three hours is considered an optimum period for both the teacher and group members.

PLANNING COURSE TITLES

The titles and subtitles given to the courses need careful thought and consideration. They should indicate the nature of the course in a way that attracts attention and arouses interest. The terms used need to be simple and the approach personal rather than general. A title such as "The Family and the Community" has little personal appeal, nor does it give much indication of what the course will cover. A more inclusive title might be "Your Family's Role in the Community." Again, "Is Your Home a Safe Place?" may be preferable to "Safety in the Home."

It is also desirable to use words which are familiar to the general public and avoid terminology that might be regarded as academic. Although this is a minor detail, it is an important one. Down-to-earth, familiar words are likely to stimulate more interest in a course than terminology that suggests something "over their heads."

HOW ADULT PROGRAMS ARE CARRIED OUT

As previously indicated, teaching adults is different from teaching high-school students. A teacher will find that the educational and personal backgrounds of an adult group will vary. Some adults will have a richer educational background than others. Some will have read a great deal and others very little. Some persons will be able to express themselves easily and readily whereas others will lack this skill. These and other differences will be strong factors in the selection of techniques and resources. Although each teacher will work out her own approach to these problems, some general information should prove helpful in all situations.

USING COOPERATIVE PROCEDURES IN ADULT CLASSES

The use of cooperative procedures in adult classes is a democratic approach that every teacher needs to consider. This approach tends to establish an informal atmosphere which helps to encourage freedom of expression and the give-and-take of ideas. In fact, the potential richness in a group cannot be released if individuals do not interact, and interaction is easiest in an informal setting. At first there may not be as much participation as in a high-school class, for helping to plan and carry out a program may be something entirely new to an adult group. Some people will have the preconceived idea that everything will be planned for them in advance and that all they need to do is to follow instructions. The teacher can modify this attitude by explaining to the group that, since the course is for their benefit, they may share in deciding what shall be learned, what experiences will best contribute toward these learnings, and how achievement will be evaluated. Once a group has had a hand in planning the work, they are likely to feel that the program is theirs and want to return for more learning.

SETTING GOALS OR OBJECTIVES

A course will generally get off to a good start

when members of the group know what the work is to include. Deciding on goals or objectives should not pose too much of a problem, since many adults are accustomed to daily, weekly, and even longer planning. A person who has planned class goals with high-school students can use some of the same procedures with adults. One feasible approach is to begin with a discussion, writing suggestions for goals on the board. If members of the group are hesitant about expressing themselves, the suggestions can be written. These may be tabulated by the teacher or a committee and submitted to the group for a final decision. Another approach is to show a film related to the course. It may stimulate a discussion of individual problems which can serve as a basis for group goals. Of course, it may not be possible to set goals in terms of all the interests and needs of the group, but the field can be narrowed to cover as many as possible that fit into the course as a whole. However, care should be taken not to have the goals too difficult for the group to attain. Success is an important factor in dealing with adults, and failure to achieve the stated objectives may cause them to lose interest in continuing their education.

Teaching-learning techniques for adults need be no different from those used for learners of other age groups. Techniques which involve adult learners directly and to which they contribute realistically, allowing them to visualize how the concepts and skills which they are learning can be applied to real-life situations, will catch the imagination of adults and will appeal to their sense of practicality as well. Then they will become devoted participants in adult-education programs and they will attract others to the programs.

FOUR

HOW IS FACILITATION OF CHANGE EFFECTED?

CREATING A CLIMATE CONDUCIVE TO CHANGE

Creating a climate conducive to change means providing an atmosphere in which positive learning for the benefit and enhancement of the learner will occur. It may involve tangible features such as the school building, the classroom facility with its equipment and furnishings, and light, heat, and air control, or the more intangible features characterized by freedom to investigate and explore, to adapt and adopt, to create and invent. This is in contrast to rigid structure and control, which is characterized by restraint and fear. The remainder of Part Two will be devoted to a discussion of the less tangible factors which are essential to creating a climate for learning that will, in turn, help the individual to become a person who possesses an adequate measusure of self-understanding and an increasing ability to relate well to others.

GUIDING STUDENTS IN
DEVELOPING SELF-UNDERSTANDING

Knowing oneself is one of the principal objectives of the developing individual, which stems from a self-awareness of being different from and yet being like others. Questions posed by young people, in their minds if not aloud, include: Who am I? How did I get this way? What am I like? Why am I like this? Whether or not these questions are voiced, one can be sure that they hover in the background and that they influence the behavior of the person, young or old.

In general young people who have a fairly true picture of themselves have a better adjustment than those whose self-concept is inaccurate in relation to the behavior they manifest (Cole & Hall, 1969). Those who experience considerable lack of self-understanding seem to reject themselves. They are said to have a poor self-image and are on the defensive, overly sensitive, discontented, and restless. Their responses to people and situations may be highly charged with emotion rather than displaying calmness and deliberateness. They are inclined to be unpredictable. They are identified as "square pegs in round holes," because they are unable to identify the kind of persons they are like and the kind of persons they are becoming. Such people attempt to assume roles for which they are not suited, hoping through a kind of subterfuge to achieve the goals they are seeking. This type of adjustment only helps to compound the already complex problem of self-realization.

Examples of a poor and an inaccurate self-concept are evident in almost every classroom. Sixteen-year-old Jane, who is inclined to be overly plump and not very attractive, yearns to be more popular, especially with boys. Her friends soon sense that Jane's glowing accounts of a boyfriend whom they never see, and of unusual gifts, which are never displayed, are figments of Jane's imagination. Seventeen-year-old Tom is nicknamed "Pouting Thomas" because he is rarely seen in anything but a sulking mood. Nothing is ever quite good enough to please him. These two individuals, in their own way, are saying that they are dissatisfied with themselves, that they do not know how to make constructive changes in themselves, and that they must therefore make some kind of adjustment in order to adapt to situations and feel less threatened. Unfortunately, this adjustment, good or bad, becomes a pattern of behavior which is strengthened through use to the extent that it is increasingly difficult to make a change even when desired. The behavioral pattern becomes a shield deeply rooted in the individual, and it is difficult to know where the real person begins and the make-believe person leaves off. The individual senses that he has to make some kind of adjustment when a strong need is being thwarted. He has to turn the situation from a threatening one into a more satisfying one for himself. Sometimes he chooses what seems to him to be the easy way and then he justifies the behavior as the most satisfactory and satisfying manner at his disposal in a given set of circumstances.

Experimentation with sex and drugs, petty thievery which may persist to become stealing, belligerent behavior, running away from responsibility or symbols of responsibility are all manifestations of immature and indirect ways of dealing with frustrations which develop because self-realization and self-understanding are at low ebb. Teachers see evidence in classroom behavior of the low self-esteem of some students. These students avoid positive interaction with others, they tend to promote disturbances, they are negative in thought and action. Through their behavior, they are crying out for attention and help, but they often deny that they are anything but self-sufficient. Because of their lack of self-understanding, these students require the utmost understanding on the part of teachers and the peer group. One of the major tragedies in lack of self-understanding is the resulting unhappiness, the keen disappointment in oneself, the dejection and self-rejection, the lack of self-worth, the futility which takes one up a dead-end street.

Self-understanding is a prerequisite for maintaining good relationships with others. The person who possesses self-understanding, who has a fairly accurate evaluation of himself, has a harmonious relationship to the situation in which he finds himself. He is said to be well-adjusted. He is able to function freely and without inhibitions and feelings of threat to his ego, to the extent that his self-understanding is translated into feelings of high regard for others. He develops and maintains positive relationships with others.

Because most human beings feel first and think next, it is important to recognize that how an individual feels about himself and others influences how he learns and the extent to which he learns. When feelings are denied in the teaching-learning situation, learning becomes an academic exercise and does not serve a real purpose. Learning lacks meaning and it is said to be irrelevant. It is not enough to learn for the sake of learning, or just to add to one's fund of information. There must be a reason for learning—a need, a desire, a want. The concepts of need, desire, or want are value concepts which appeal to the senses and which generate feelings. Learning and feelings go together. At the mention of any word or phrase one can conjure feelings of one kind or another. It would be a sterile learning, indeed, if it were devoid of feelings. Brown (1971, pp. 3–18) terms this "confluent education," which he defines as the integration or flowing together of the affective and cognitive elements in learning.

In order to learn one must feel free to learn. A classroom climate which is relaxed, warm, accepting, and unthreatening will foster the freedom to question, experience, and discover new learnings. Below are some guiding principles which may help in the development or promotion of positive self-images. However, the key to the facilitating classroom climate is the teacher. The teacher who possesses a positive self-concept serves as a model for the students. When she is a genuine person without a facade, the students realize that she can understand and appreciate them. The teacher . . .

shares her true feelings of joy, elation, excitement, and disappointment with the students.

shares special interests and achievements with the students.

expresses her honest enthusiasm for the discipline in which she has expertise and interest.

allows the students to challenge her ideas, opinions, and generalizations.

admits when there is something that she does not understand or know and then proceeds to secure the information, or she and the students together seek the needed information.

Students are involved in planning for the teaching-learning procedure and because they are, learnings and processes have real-life meaning for them. Students who have invested a personal stake in the learning continue to have intense and sustained interest in the learning procedure from beginning to end. The teacher . . .

provides an opportunity for each student to make comments and suggestions. Providing such an opportunity means more than just calling on a student.

accepts and values the contribution made by each student.

incorporates into each lesson a way for each student to participate and attempts to provide an opportunity for each student to serve in a leadership role.

provides recognition for each student when he makes a contribution to the class.

Students dare to learn when the teacher inspires their trust and confidence, and when she has demonstrated that she accepts each student for himself, including his imperfections along with his attributes. Mistakes are accepted, too, as a necessary part of learning. The teacher . . .

goes out of her way to gain the trust of each student.

offers sincere compliments to students whenever they are warranted.

places the burden of evaluation of student work on the individual student, always helping him to see the positive results first.

avoids use of learning techniques such as "read the chapter" or use of tests as disciplinary measures.

avoids being critical of a student's work in front of other students. A sense of humor on the part of the teacher when faced with stressful situations helps students to develop the ability to cope with unpleasant situations.

does not betray the confidences of students to anyone else.

avoids unfair and ruthless competition in the classroom.

provides support and encouragement for each student.

Students are treated as persons of dignity and worth. Then they develop a sense of being unique and important. The teacher helps each individual to accept and identify accurately his strengths and his weaknesses so that he has a realistic and positive self-concept. The teacher . . .

learns the students' names, and the correct pronunciation of each name.

treats each student courteously.

takes time for a quiet talk with each student.

avoids having pet students or favorite students.

makes favorable comments on things important to each student.

notices each student as an individual.

notices when a student is absent and welcomes him back to class.

helps the student to select tasks in which he is capable of having some measure of success.

Students function best within a classroom in which there is some semblance of organization and control. Basic to this is complete and good pre-planning and preparation for the teaching-learning process.

Students and teacher together determine guidelines for behavior in the classroom.

Both the teacher and students have a clear idea as to the kind of behavior that is acceptable and not acceptable.

Student tasks are determined in terms of student abilities and interests.

The teacher guides the students in determining evaluation procedures and standards.

GUIDING STUDENTS IN DEVELOPING RELATIONSHIP SKILLS

People, and particularly children and young people, have the option of choosing those other people with whom they wish to associate. Young children with parental guidance select their own playmates, and as people grow older they operate more or less autonomously in the selection of friends, marriage partners, and other associates. In the selection of others with whom he wishes to associate, a person tends to choose those who support his own self-image. The friend, the relative, the chosen associate may not be as supportive of the total self-image as the individual had hoped. Consternation and concern, which may develop into revolt, sometimes ends with an attempt to dissolve the relationship. Or at best the relationship is characterized by unhappiness and mistrust, and it may be emotionally charged. Examples of disintegrating relationships include the "hippie" in the youth culture, mistrust of anyone "over thirty," alienation between friends, alienation between parent and child, and alienation between groups of people as evident in today's society. These disintegrating relationships are the source of innumerable present-day problems.

In having good relationships with others, the primary need of the individual is to have self-understanding and a positive self-image, and to become self-actualizing to the extent that he is less dependent upon others for nurturing his own self-image (as was discussed in Part One of this book). He must develop relationship skills. These skills are many and not necessarily of equal value. They include having or making time for others, taking the initiative in relating in a positive manner to others, being considerate of others by performing acts of remembering or showing deference to others, anticipating the needs of others, expending effort directed toward helping others to achieve an expressed goal or satisfy a felt need, or both.

The focus of home economics on the family, service to others, and the welfare of others makes imperative the development of relationship skills on the part of the student of home economics. The majority of learnings embodied in home economics are in terms of others. These learnings include human development, family relationships, decision-making, planning for the satisfaction of food, clothing, and shelter needs of the family. Good interpersonal relationships, whether between teacher and learner, or between learners, cannot be learned from books or by listening to lectures and discussions. They can only be learned through a succession of successful interaction experiences with others. Guidelines, which home-economics teachers may find helpful as they guide students in the development of relationship skills, are included here:

1. In planning for teaching-learning activities the teacher attempts to provide, first of all, for real-life experiences, then simulated experiences, and finally those experiences which provide for vicarious learning, in that order. There shall be a minimum of the last.

2. "Teacher-talk" in the classroom is at a minimum. Conversely "student-talk" shall increase as "teacher-talk" is diminished.

3. The teacher exhibits honest respect and compassion for each individual student.

4. The teacher exhibits compassion in her relationships with students and their families, other teachers and staff personnel, and administrators. She knows that every individual has some worth, and helps students to identify that worth. She hates no one, and she does not pigeon-hole people. She helps students to understand and appreciate the behavior of others.

5. The teacher continues to experience and to learn about psychological, cultural, physiological, and socio-economic differences between people and between groups of people so that she leads and directs the classroom learning situation with "people knowledge" as her frame of reference.

6. The teacher recognizes that all students cannot be treated exactly alike at any given time, but all can be given equitable consideration.

7. Through selection and careful implementation of teaching-learning techniques, the teacher helps each student to experience joy in being a contributing member of a group and in sharing in the success of the group effort.

8. The teacher uses whatever professional means are available to her to identify students who are "loners" and to then encourage their participation in group effort, as well as to encourage the acceptance of the "loners" by others. Nor does she expect instant success in this effort to develop a cohesive group of several students including "loners."

9. The teacher recognizes that group experiences do not necessarily guarantee group participation. She must be prepared to serve as arbitrator, referee, resource person, and catalyst.

10. The teacher knows that the means—the working together—is of greater value than the results. She helps interpret to students the philosophy that the process which is involved in working together toward a common goal has greater value for individual students and the group than does the final outcome.

SUGGESTED TEACHER EXPERIENCES

1. Knowing more about students, regardless of their age or other circumstances, assists the home-economics teacher in providing more relevant teaching-learning experiences. Locate

a potential group of students in a public school setting or in a non-school setting, such as adults in a special housing area.

a. Select one or more of the techniques, as presented in Part Two, which would be appropriate for learning more about the students. Use the technique and then record the results.

b. Select an area of home economics which you propose to teach to this group of students, and determine the basic concepts you plan to include.

c. Show how the information gleaned from use of the technique in (a) above will influence the choice of content, teaching-learning experiences, and evaluation which you would like to use with this group of students.

d. What individual differences, as evidenced in the technique used in (a), would you need to take into account as you plan teaching-learning experiences for the students?

2. Divide the class into five groups with each group taking responsibility for one of the five areas of home economics as outlined in the conceptual structure (American Home Economics Association, 1968). Then, have each group indicate the difference in content in that particular area depending upon the backgrounds of the students. Suggested groups to be included are:

Middle-class suburban white girls in middle school

Ninth-grade boys of a low socio-economic level characterized by under-achievement

Young married men and women, mostly with one or two children

Elderly women living in an elderly housing area

Boy and girl senior-high-school blacks

Unmarried pregnant teen-agers

Mentally retarded teen-age girls

College-bound high-school senior girls and boys

Ninth- and tenth-grade Mexican-American girls and boys

Emotionally handicapped early teen-age girls

3. Arrange for observation of students in a public-school classroom. It need not be home economics. In preparation for the observation have the students in your class arrange in check-list format the criteria for developing a classroom climate conducive to change as given on pages 71–72. The students will observe the class using this check-list as a guide. Have the observers make additions of other criteria which may help produce a warm and accepting classroom climate.

4. Arrange for a panel of students from the class. Some students will report on real experiences they have had, or experiences other students whom they know have had, where the development of relationship skills was inhibited by the classroom situation. Other panel members will report on classroom experiences they or others have had which have promoted the development of relationship skills.

PART THREE

COOPERATING WITH SCHOOL AND COMMUNITY EFFORTS SIGNIFICANT FOR INDIVIDUAL AND FAMILY WELL-BEING

In considering the home, the school, and the community it is becoming more and more difficult to distinguish between where the responsibility of one begins and the responsibility of the other leaves off. Once upon a time each was a separate entity with its own specific concerns and responsibilities for meeting particular needs of individuals. The family was primarily concerned with the physiological, health, safety, love, and recognition needs of the family members; the school concentrated on training the mind; the community was called upon only in the event of a dire need which could not be satisfied by the family. Each unit was centralized and represented an autonomous authority of its own. Today there is a decentralization of each of the three units, the family, the school and the community. Some people speak of a breakdown of the family unit, but the phenomenon which is occurring seems to be a shifting of responsibilities.

The family looks to both the school and the community for support and provision for needs which can be more effectively and efficiently furnished by specially trained people, agencies, and institutions. An example of such a service is the school-lunch program in almost every school in the land, and a breakfast program in an increasing number of schools. Other evidence of a shifting responsibility is the fact that attention to all aspects of student health, sex education, mental-health service, family-life education, and occupational education are all provided by the school. Recreation is almost entirely centered in school and community programs. The community looks to the school to provide expertise and even facilities for many of its programs, and to provide trained people to perform the work of the community either as volunteers or employed workers. The school looks to the family for cooperation, information, and other even more tangible resources which will help the school to better serve the students. The school looks to the community for assistance in determining curriculum guidelines and for learning resources to be utilized in enriching the school's educational program. The school is continuing to play an increasingly more important role in the education of all individuals at all stages of life.

FIVE

WHY ARE INTERRELATIONS AMONG HOME, SCHOOL, AND COMMUNITY IMPORTANT?

HOME ECONOMICS IS AN INTEGRATING FORCE

Through the home-economics program the efforts of the community, the school, and the home are combined to enhance the welfare of families and individuals. While the aim of home-economics education is to improve the quality of life for all, the vehicles through which this goal is achieved are the home, the school, and the community. The home-economics body of knowledge and skills, which permeates the classroom, is of value only when translated into action in school, community, and homes of the community. Because of the interaction and interdependence among the three units the home-economics teacher needs to be aware of the uniqueness of each one, and the ways in which each one can supplement the work of the others.

LEARNING ABOUT HOMES AND FAMILIES

Knowledge about homes and families, particularly the homes and families of the students one has in home-economics classes, can be most enlightening and can be helpful in curriculum planning and selecting meaningful teaching-learning experiences. If home visiting by the home-economics teacher is acceptable in the community, it is one of the most valuable ways of learning about homes and families. However, with many mothers working outside of the home today it may be difficult or impossible to arrange for a time when the mother will be at home and not be occupied with home duties. In some communities the families will want to develop trust in the teacher before she will be welcome in the home. Particularly families living on welfare, families where a member of the family has been involved in legal action, or families of minority-group origin may be reticent about having someone from school visit the home. In such situations the teacher needs to first develop empathic relationships built on mutual trust, interest, and concern with the students before attempting to contact the homes.

By walking or driving around the community, the teacher may observe the prevailing types of housing and note their external care. These observations will give her a general idea of the prosperity of the people and the extent to which different socioeconomic levels are represented in the community. However, a more intimate knowledge of home and family conditions is necessary before the teacher can evaluate the needs and interests of community residents and plan a well-rounded program.

The home-economics teacher needs to be innovative in devising ways of learning about the home and family background of the students in her classes. A simple survey sheet to which the student may respond is often effective. Information provided by the student may be more valid if students are requested not to write their names on the papers. Some home-economics teachers have found an effective bridge to the home in the form of a newsletter which the teacher or the teacher and students together prepare for the families of the students. It may contain helpful hints, cartoons showing classroom incidents, recipes, an overview of classroom activities and concepts developed, news notes, and an open invitation to visit the classroom. Mothers have responded to such newsletters in kind and thus they have served to break down barriers which may have developed in some communities between school and home. Because homes and communities differ, the home-economics teacher may wish to attempt a variety of different approaches in order to find the most acceptable means of communication in the community in which she is teaching.

THE HOME VISIT

The home visit is one of the most effective means for providing insight and understanding of homes and families. However, home visits need to be carried out with complete understanding on the part of the teacher as to how to conduct them so that the results will be positive and will contribute to furthering the home-economics program at school.

Firsthand information on home and family conditions is invaluable. The knowledge gained by seeing the environment in which a student lives cannot be wholly duplicated from other sources. The general characteristics of the home—its location, size in relation to number of occupants, furnishings, and cultural background of the parents—all serve to give the teacher a better understanding of a student. Through observation of home conditions she can get background information which will be useful not only in the cooperative planning of class goals but in the selection of experiences that individual students may plan in carrying out the goals.

Meeting the mother in the home setting is also important, for she tends to feel more at ease and to talk more readily than she would if she visited the teacher at school. A teacher who is friendly and tactful can learn many things about individual students—what parents want and expect them to learn in home-economics, what responsibilities they are given at home, how much independence they have, what vocational plans are being made for them, and other helpful information. Some of this information can and often does come from the students themselves. But having the parents' point of view on such matters often brings to light hidden problems. The teacher thus gains a deeper understandng of the relationship existing between student and parent, and possibly between the student and other members of the family. These relationships may have an important influence on the student's classroom achievement and behavior. Becoming aware of them makes it possible for the teacher to give the student the kind of guidance needed.

CONSIDERATIONS IN MAKING HOME VISITS

It is difficult to make specific recommendations in reference to home visits that will be applicable to all teachers. Differences in local attitudes and customs and in the purpose of a visit affect the way in which visiting is carried out. There are, however, certain general considerations that every teacher needs to keep in mind.

THE COMMUNITY ATTITUDE
TOWARD VISITING STUDENTS' HOMES

However valuable home visits may be, each teacher will need to be guided by the community attitude, knowledge of which can be obtained from the principal or members of the teaching staff. There are some localities where people resent home visits and therefore none should be made unless an invitation is extended or special arrangements are made. Then again, there are communities where home visits are considered a part of the home-economics program and accepted as such by the parents. In many communities, however, visiting is possible if arrangements are made in advance. A disadvantage here is that the teacher may not see the home in its normal condition, since the parent may try to create a good impression by having the home unusually clean and neat. But most teachers can sense this situation and evaluate it accordingly.

General Visiting Procedures. The teacher needs to dress simply and in accordance with what the community considers appropriate. She will keep in mind that it is important to make the parent feel that the visit is for the purpose of getting acquainted with one another and with the work of the department. She will avoid giving the impression that she is making an inspection trip. Although it is essential for the teacher to observe carefully, she needs to do so unobtrusively. Taking notes or asking a barrage of questions concerning intimate family matters will not inspire confidence but will cause suspicion and resentment on the part of the parent.

After introducing herself, the teacher can "break the ice" by making favorable comments on something she sees around the home. The remarks, of course, should be sincere and can lead to a general question which will give the parent an opportunity to talk. From then on, the teacher can guide the conversation toward other subjects which will yield helpful information. If there are brothers and sisters older and younger than the son or daughter in the teacher's class, a few discreet questions can be asked, such as, "How do the brothers and sisters get along together?" "What chores do family members perform?" The latter query can bring out some of the things the parent expects or would like to have the student learn in home-economics.

The length of the visit will depend upon various factors:

The teacher's time

Pressing obligations which require the parent's attention

The attitude of the parent—whether she is interested in carrying on the conversation

How much helpful information the teacher has acquired

Upon leaving, the teacher can express her appreciation for the time the parent has taken to talk with her and extend an invitation to family members to visit the school and the home-economics department.

EXTENT OF VISITS

If home visiting is possible, a new teacher should plan to make some visits prior to the opening of school or soon after. With the assistance of the principal, the teacher can select a number of homes of the different socioeconomic levels represented by the students in her classes. This cross section should provide her with clues to some of the needs, interests, and problems common to her student group. The information thus obtained can serve as a basis for planning tentative class goals.

The number of homes to be visited throughout the school year will depend on various factors such as the area to be covered, transportation facilities, class size, and available time. In some communities it may be possible to visit the homes of every student. But more often than not, visits will have to be limited. Homes in which a student needs special guidance in carrying out a home experience, or in which a parent needs to be consulted about a serious problem with a son or daughter, are likely to be given priority.

PERSONALITY TRAITS
PARENTS LIKE IN A TEACHER

Parents become acquainted with a teacher directly or indirectly through various channels. These may include visits by the teacher to the home; visits by the parents to the school; meetings at civic, school, or church affairs; discussions about a teacher with other parents; or reactions of their sons and daughters to classroom situations. From these and other sources parents tend to formulate an idea of the personality traits they like in a teacher. Such ideas will vary with individual parents and are influenced by the community in which they live. However, a teacher can profit by studying the list of attributes which parents in general endorse. Then each teacher can decide which traits seem most essential to cultivate in the light of her particular situation. Parents like a teacher who has the following traits:

Is well-groomed

Is healthy and full of vigor

Has a warm, friendly disposition

Is open-minded without prejudices

Makes every student feel important

Can fire a student with enthusiasm to learn

Gives an honest evaluation of a student's work

Does not set herself up as an expert in personal problems but is able to handle most cases without sending the student to a specialist

Gets along with people of all ages

Keeps calm and does not lose her temper

Has imagination and a sense of humor

Does not consider teaching just a job

Keeps abreast of the times

Has ability to cope with individual differences

Can project herself into the minds and thinking of her students

Is a good disciplinarian—not too strict and not too lax

Can teach ideals

Is willing to cooperate with parents

Has social poise

LEARNING ABOUT THE COMMUNITY

Professional success is closely linked to the community in which a person is teaching. Planning and carrying out an effective home-economics program require a knowledge of the social setting in which students and their families live—their cultural, social, and economic backgrounds. In fact, the patterns of home and community life largely determine the people's needs and interests upon which an adequate program is based, not only for students but for adult members in the community. In developing an understanding of the community, the home-economics teacher will need to make a careful study of her surroundings and acquaint herself with various aspects of home and community living. It is important for her to meet many people and to learn what they value most in life. The teacher will also need to be alert for community resources that will aid classroom learning. All of these things need to be done with the intent of using the acquired knowledge to the best possible advantage.

GUIDES TO
UNDERSTANDING THE COMMUNITY

A teacher coming into a community for the first time cannot expect to acquire at once all the information and insight that will be needed to carry out a well-rounded program. Such an understanding comes slowly. It is acquired not only by making many personal contacts but by periodically becoming a part of the community through actual participation in its activities. There are, however, certain things a teacher can do—more or less systematically—which will help her to gain the needed understanding.

BECOMING ORIENTED AS SOON AS POSSIBLE

It is advisable for a teacher to get an overall picture of the community as soon as possible. Some schools prepare special booklets which are sent to teachers prior to their arrival. But such booklets are still so rare that they cannot be counted on. A teacher, however, can gain some preliminary knowledge about the community by subscribing to the local newspaper as soon as her contract is signed. She can note what news items are considered sufficiently important to make the front page. The editorials will help to reveal local attitudes on national, state, and community issues. The extent to which school news is mentioned will give some indication of the interest people are tak-

ing in education. The names of persons who make the society news frequently and those who appear to be active in local organizations can be jotted down for future reference.

If possible, a teacher coming into a new community should arrive in advance of the school opening. In some schools early arrival is expected of new teachers so that they can become familiar with the organization of the school and the nature of the work they will be doing. Some information about the community can be obtained from the principal and the teaching staff. Getting a general picture of the commercial, recreational, and health facilities and the prominent local organizations will help to orient a teacher. Such a picture can serve as a background against which she can evaluate additional information she may later acquire through other sources and through her own observations as she goes about the community.

GAINING INSIGHT INTO THE COMMUNITY

Getting an overall picture of a community by obtaining information from various sources and by making personal observations is helpful. But something more is needed. In order to understand a community, the teacher needs to get below the surface of things. Only in this way can she evaluate what she can do to fulfill her obligation as a teacher in home-economics education. She should learn about community attitudes, local prejudices, social practices, cultural backgrounds, and democratic values. This deeper insight involves knowing the attitudes that prevail toward national, state, and local policy issues and toward foreign relations. It includes knowing how the community feels about its leaders, what these leaders stand for, how stable such leadership is, and to what extent it represents major community groups.

The teacher also needs to become aware of sensitive conditions within the community such as the presence of minority groups, unemployment, slums, a large number of working mothers, delinquency, and crime. Knowing the prevailing attitude toward such conditions can help the teacher to weigh possibilities for taking steps to help improve a particular condition within the limits of her training and experience.

It will also be useful for the teacher to know what factional differences are prominent with respect to politics, economic interests, and religion. This knowledge will enable the teacher to handle situations diplomatically. She can avoid remarks and actions that will cause her to become identified with one faction and opposed to the other. This does not mean that the teacher should play up to local prejudices or avoid discussion on controversial issues. Instead she can decide what controversial matters are worth discussing and plan such discussion so that all sides are represented.

Sensing community feelings toward the school and particularly toward the home-economics department is also important. If such feelings seem to indicate interest and understanding toward education, then the possibilities for a well-rounded program are unlimited. On the other hand, the teacher may sense feelings of dissatisfaction or a lack of interest in, and understanding of, school policies. Awareness on her part can be a cue not only to finding out the nature and cause of such feelings but to taking steps to develop a more favorable impression and a better understanding.

GETTING ACQUAINTED WITH PEOPLE

Gaining an insight into a community can only be acquired by mixing and talking with people in various walks of life. In a small community this should not be difficult, since the school is often the center of social life and a new teacher is readily welcomed and soon known by everyone. In a large community getting acquainted is more difficult, because people generally have many personal interests and are less likely to be concerned about a newcomer. The teacher, therefore, may need to take the initiative.

She can begin by talking with tradespeople and others with whom she would naturally come in contact. Participation in religious activities will also enlarge the teacher's acquaintance. These casual, friendly contacts are bound to reveal attitudes that will give the teacher a broader understanding of the interests and needs of the community.

The teacher can also arrange to be introduced to civic leaders and to women who are active in various organizations such as the Parent-Teacher Association, the Woman's Club, and the American Association of University Women. She can ask them what is important for a newcomer to know about the community. Their answers are likely to reveal current community issues and problems. Becoming acquainted with key people and gaining their interest will also open up possibilities for publicity and promotional work in home-economics education.

In some cases it may be desirable for the teacher to become affiliated with one or more community organizations. Such membership would give her a more intimate knowledge of the attitudes and responsibilities these organizations are taking toward special community problems. However, the extent to which affiliation is possible will depend upon factors such as the time of day the organization meets and the amount of classwork the teacher is doing.

As the teacher tries to become acquainted with various people, she needs to make them feel that she considers herself a member of the community. If people feel that a teacher is genuinely interested in their problems, they are more likely not only to be motivated to do something about them but to cooperate with her in anything she may suggest. Sometimes, however, it may be difficult for a teacher to identify herself with the community. She may find local conditions quite different from what she expected or what she has been accustomed to. Social conventions may be so difficult to adjust to, or local prejudices so overwhelming, that she may feel she does not want to be considered a part of the community. In such a case the teacher will need to guard against being critical of local conditions or making unfavorable comparisons between the community she is in and another she regards more highly. And even when a teacher does not overtly display hostile feelings, many people can sense their presence. They will then hesitate to form friendships with a person who seems to be against the principles they represent. If a teacher expects to become widely acquainted in a community and really understand it, she must first accept the people as they are.

LOCATING AND UTILIZING
RESOURCES WITHIN THE COMMUNITY

Communities are rich with a great variety of resources which can be used in teaching home economics. These include agencies, organizations, programs and institutions whose sole commitment is serving individuals, homes, and families in one way or another. They provide a storehouse of information on people living in the community, their concerns, their problems, their hopes and their aspirations. Near the top of the list of things to do first when the new teacher arrives in the community is to investigate as many of the resources as possible. The

teacher may learn about available resources from the following sources: classified pages of the newspaper, yellow pages in the phone book, the public library, school administrators, the clergy. The following are some of the programs, agencies, associations, organizations, and institutions which may be located in many communities: Red Cross, Partners-in-Progress, meals-on-wheels, rehabilitation centers, groups for the elderly, day-care centers, youth centers, homes for unwed mothers, neighborhood houses with special programs for special people, homemaker aide programs, consumer programs, a wide variety of social agencies, nutrition aide programs, Y.M.C.A. and Y.W.C.A., Girl Scouts, Campfire Girls, nursing homes, hospitals, food-stamp programs. There are several ways in which the home-economics department and these agencies and programs may join hands. Frequently, the latter will supply speakers, information, and even equipment for class use. As an extension of the school home-economics program, the teacher may select one or more of these agencies or programs in which students may cooperate by conducting a service project. Students will learn firsthand about a particular community resource, its objectives and program, so that at a later time they may wish to serve it as volunteers or employed workers. Then too, the students will have an exposure to a resource which may serve them and their families now or later. Class visits to agencies, industrial and business establishments, and other places of interest enrich the home-economics program and contribute to its relevancy.

The new home-economics teacher will find that she has loyal supporters for the school home-economics program in other professional home economists. These are people she will want to contact early in her period of orientation to the community. They will have valid and useful information about the community which they will be glad to share with the home-economics teacher. They, too, are prepared to serve as resource people for the school home-economics program. Professional home economists may be employed in the following places: public utility companies, businesses and companies dealing with consumer products and consumer services, food-service departments of hospitals and other institutions, the Home Economics Extension Service located in the county seat, and social agencies. It is possible that there will be an organized group of professional home economists in the locality. Participation in a professional group of this kind will be useful in many ways.

Utilizing the resources of a community has many values:

The school and the community are brought closer together by sharing experiences to their mutual interest and satisfaction.

The community learns what home-economics teachers are trying to do.

Students develop a broader understanding of their community—its people and its problems.

Learning becomes more meaningful to students when the out-of-school environment is integrated with their classwork.

Students come to realize that people as well as books are desirable sources of information and inspiration.

Contacts with adults provide an opportunity for students to develop social skills, such as letter writing, making introductions, receiving guests, and carrying on a conversation.

Participation in local projects develops feelings of responsibility toward being a part of the community and toward making community life more wholesome.

LEARNING ABOUT SCHOOLS

The home-economics department is an integral part of the school. Therefore, the administration of the home-economics program, the financing, the curriculum, the scheduling of courses, enrollment of students, provision for facilities and equipment are circumscribed by the total school. The overall philosophy and goals of the school govern the direction of the home-economics program. The home-economics teacher needs to become familiar with the school's organization and policies. The school administrator will impart some of the information regarding philosophy, goals, policies, and organization, and may then delegate other school personnel to describe the many facets of the total school operation. These include regulations governing pupil conduct, the counseling service, the health service, the library, teaching resource center, visual aid center, school-lunch program, responsibilities involved in teaching, responsibilities outside the classroom, committee responsibilities, duplication of materials for teaching, janitorial service, budgeting and purchasing, faculty meetings, teacher institutes. Many schools publish a handbook for teachers which will include much of this information. In addition, the teacher will want to be alert to different kinds of educational programs with which she is not familiar. Many innovations are springing up in relation to education, some of which survive only a trial period, but others are adopted and become more lasting.

Some developments which are permeating public education today will be mentioned briefly. The reader may wish to investigate certain of these trends further. Computer technology is being introduced into schools and students are learning to use computers for information retrieval and data processing. An increasing number of schools are employing modular scheduling for the school day, making it possible for students to spend approximately one-third of the school week in independent study. Other outcomes of modular scheduling include eighty-minute or longer laboratory periods, seminar classes, open laboratories and self-taught units, student-initiated projects, and the continual ebb and flow of students from area to area throughout the day. A rather new innovation is performance contracting, in which a legal relationship is established between a public school and a private company, with the company providing instruction which is paid for on the basis of student performance. Differentiated staffing is a concept of organization that seeks to make better use of educational personnel. Different responsibilities are assigned to teachers and other educators based on new ways of analyzing essential teaching tasks and creative means of implementing new educational roles. A recent innovation is the "School Without Walls" or the "Parkway Program" in Philadelphia, with five hundred students organized into three basic units. Each unit is then divided into ten "tutorial groups" of fifteen students each. One full-time faculty member and one intern are assigned to each group with responsibilities for providing counseling, personal encouragement, support, and the acquisition of basic skills in language and mathematics. Each student is allowed to partic-

ipate in a management group whose function is to provide services necessary for the Parkway's successful day-to-day operation. Each student is also allowed to conduct a special problems course in an area of his own interest. Variations of this plan have been implemented in other schools in the country. The open classroom concept is possible in an architecturally designed building which eliminates walls between classrooms. Students are organized into small learning groups for more nearly individualized instruction. Several small groups are brought together when there is a common interest. The keynote for this concept is informality and individualization. The open classroom concept has also been implemented in the more traditional schools with walls. Mini-courses which are planned for a four- to six-week period make possible the scheduling of work in an elected area when there would not be time in a student's schedule for a semester- or a full-year course. This type of scheduling has implications for home economics because it enables students who under the more traditional pattern of scheduling are unable to schedule home-economics courses to schedule special interest courses of short duration.

New trends and innovations in education and school organization will continue to be introduced. The home economics teacher will want to keep abreast of each new development, so that the home-economics program will continue to be in harmony with current educational philosophy and practice.

SIX

HOW IS PARTICIPATION EFFECTED IN ACTION PROGRAMS WHICH AFFECT INDIVIDUAL AND FAMILY LIFE?

HOME ECONOMICS INITIATES PROGRAMS

The day of confining the home-economics program within the four walls of the classroom is past. The classroom setting may continue to be the base of operation for planning, evaluation, and some instruction, but it is agreed by many home-economics educators that home economics belongs in the mainstream of life in many communities across the land. Home economics with its many implications for improving the quality of life of all people everywhere needs to reach out to make contact with more people at the most auspicious times, in the most likely places, and with the most meaningful learnings. One natural vehicle for achieving these goals is the Future Homemakers of America. Then there are store-front operations, mobile units, and community home-economics centers, all striving to take to the people the home-economics information and skills which can improve the quality of life. Through efforts of this kind, the impact of home economics can be forceful, relevant, and lasting. A detailed description of the FHA organization follows. (Integration of the FHA program into the home-economics curriculum is described extensively in Book 3.) Some sample programs illustrative of special action programs directly affecting individual and family life are also described on the following pages.

An overall goal for the teaching of home economics is to help each student develop his potential for becoming the person he is capable of becoming. A vehicle for achieving this goal is the Future Homemakers of America, Inc., which is an integral part of the home-economics program at the secondary level. Both boys and girls are participating members of the Future Homemakers of America.

FUTURE HOMEMAKERS OF AMERICA

Future Homemakers of America, Inc., is the national organization of youth studying home economics in junior and senior high schools of the United States, Puerto Rico, and the Virgin Islands. The basic objective of the organization is to help individuals improve personal, family, and community living through programs organized as a part of the home-economics education curriculum in secondary schools. The Home Economics Education Unit of the Division of Vocational and Technical Education, United States Office of Education, and the American Home Economics Association sponsor the national organization because of the importance of its basic objective, both to its youthful membership and to the public. Cooperating groups are the Home Economics Education Association of the National Education Association, and the home-economics education division of the American Vocational Association.

Among the purposes of the Future Homemakers of America are the following:

To promote a growing appreciation of the joys and satisfactions of homemaking

To emphasize the importance of worthy home membership

To encourage democracy in home and community life

To work for good home and family life for all

To promote international good will

To foster the development of creative leadership in home and community life

To encourage wholesome individual and group recreation

To further interest in home economics, home-economics careers, and related occupations

With FHA activities which focus on individual growth, the family, education, development of occupational competencies, preparation for marriage and careers, and youth's role in society and the world, relevance to life is assured. Members gain in many ways through development of leadership qualities, cooperation with others, and opportunity for assuming responsibility and for service. They grow as persons and they form new friendships. With exposure to new views and new experiences provided through the FHA program, home-economics students become more adept at choosing goals and developing values. The local FHA chapter facilitates growth in human development and human relationships, for it is founded on the premise that every individual member counts and that he has a special contribution to make to the chapter. Provision is

made for the active participation of the individual in the many different activities. Through the cooperation of all members the chapter can achieve many goals that an individual cannot achieve alone. Provision is made for the youth members and the adult advisers to work together so that each gains from the other.

The role of the home-economics teacher, as adviser for the local FHA chapter, is to be responsible for helping coordinate class and chapter experiences in order that they complement and enrich each other. With the assistance of the adviser, members will improve their ability to evaluate themselves and their experiences in FHA, and become more proficient in setting and working together toward goals that affect their lives now and in the future.

The FHA National Program of Work in Action is devised for each new biennium. The major objectives and some suggested activities presently in effect (1970–73) will provide understanding of the FHA program as it relates to young people in today's world. (See pages 88, 89.)

Comments written by members of the Future Homemakers of America, former members, and advisers attest the viable and enduring part the organization plays in the lives of those who become inculcated with the goals of FHA and who become avid participators in the program:

FHA is a way of life and a way of thinking about life. It is an organization in which girls and boys become young adults and in which common interests in home economics are shared, values are realized, friends are made and family bonds are strengthened. It is a testing ground for the requisites of effective living; patience, determination, endurance, self-discipline, work, confidence, love, and faith. (Former FHA national officer.)

My years spent as an FHA member con-

Objective: To strengthen bonds within the family and between the family and community (FHA National Program of Work in Action, 1970–73)

CONCEPT	SUGGESTED ACTIVITY
Our Future As Homemakers To help prepare individuals for the responsibilities of homemaking.	Sponsor a program with a panel of boys to tell what homemaking qualities they would look for in a wife and what they view as the man's homemaking role.
Stable Home—Stable Life To stress the influence of the home on family members.	Become a big sister to a child who has an unstable home life.
Make Time Work for You To emphasize the importance of using your time wisely.	Arrange for your members to attend a meeting of adult groups such as the American Association of University Women to learn about their community activities. Ask them to share their experiences in saving time in order to be able to "give" time to community activities.
Decisions That Count To encourage youth to formulate and work toward educational goals contributing to future success.	Organize "empathy" interviews—women in careers interviewed by boys, and men in careers interviewed by girls. Find out their job satisfactions, how each sees his/her role, etc. Report findings at a chapter meeting.

tributed greatly in preparing me for the dual role of a working mother. FHA encouraged leadership training and fostered maturity and clear thinking. (Home economics teacher and mother of four.)

My membership in FHA strengthened my concept of the importance of a woman as an individual, a homemaker and a mother, and as a community person. I gained training and understanding of the problems involved in the fulfillment of my goals in each area. (A teacher.)

Family life has been strengthened and made easier and less tense through the activities and the lessons we do and learn at our FHA meetings. Here we have been shown the many responsibilities we actually do have in our family and just around our homes. FHA is the 'bonus' of the homemaking curriculum. Yes, more time is required, but it is through FHA that I am best able to challenge pupils to select

Objective: To help youth comprehend problems of society and contribute to their solution (FHA National Program of Work in Action, 1970–73)

CONCEPT	SUGGESTED ACTIVITY
To Dare Is To Care To work toward eliminating prejudices and inequalities involving differences in culture, race, and creed.	Volunteer FHA help to a foreign or new family in your community to help them begin to feel a part of the school or community.
Our World—A Growing Heritage To arouse youth interest and participation in solving of world problems.	Attend city council meetings to learn about the fundamentals of your local government. Offer to work with the council to see what youth could do to have their views reflected and how they might be involved in constructive civic action.
Preparedness—The Key to Opportunity To help youth develop initiative and resourcefulness in creating employment and preparing for work.	Invite a local high-school or college counselor to a chapter meeting to discuss creating jobs when none are available, or "selling your talents" to a potential employer.

worthy goals and develop and carry out plans for working toward the goals, evaluating growth as they proceed. (A chapter adviser.)

FHA is a very vital part of my life and to it can be attributed my success as a teacher, citizen and homemaker. (A chapter adviser.)

The privilege of working on chapter projects that interest us and serving on various committees has been profitable to me, as well as many of our other members. The FHA is the one school organization in which I have been able to express my creativeness and have had my imagination stimulated. It has offered me

many opportunities to express myself in both words and actions. (A chapter member.)

INTEGRATING HOME ECONOMICS, SCHOOL, AND COMMUNITY PROGRAMS

The home-economics program which reaches out into the school and the community is purposeful, alive, dynamic, exciting. Its first objective is serving others through the application of that body of knowledge identified as home economics, and it is characterized by understandings, information, and skills which help individuals and families to alter their behavior, or alter the near environment in such a way as to bring about a better way of life. The exciting aspect is that the application is direct, provided at the most auspicious moment, and it is made at the vulnerable point where the need exists. Such programs do not just happen. The home-economics teacher, as the architect and engineer for the program, uses her perception and expertise to detect the unique opportunity for extending the home-economics classroom into the school and the community. This extension should be within the realm of information and skills encompassed in home economics. If this extension of the school-home economics program is to be one involving home-economics students, then it must present certain evidences of feasibility, such as appropriateness of time for the students; availability of equipment, supplies, and a meeting place; and provision for sufficient quantity and quality of learning to be worthwhile for the students.

Some possible community involvement programs include providing child-care services or assisting in day-care centers or community play schools; demonstrating use of surplus foods or better-buys at a super market; being shopper assistants for shut-ins, the handicapped, and the elderly; reconditioning clothing for resale to migrant families, or for giving to people in need; providing services such as house cleaning, performing odd jobs, teaching crafts, or wrapping Christmas packages for people living in elderly housing facilities; providing "sounding boards" for young people on subjects such as, "parents don't understand me," "I wonder about drugs," "What's wrong with getting married, now?"; presenting specially prepared programs for radio and television.

Various types of home-economics programs featuring community involvement may be eligible for funding through the Vocational Amendments of 1968. This entails writing a proposal for application for funding, and submitting to the State Department of Education for approval. Guidelines for proposal writing are available from the local school administrator or from the State Department of Education.

Many excellent programs have been devised and implemented to serve students in the regular home-economics program. A few short synopses of such programs are included here. In one school a group of students in a class in consumer education were allotted a sum of five hundred dollars so that they might actually do comparison shopping for small electrical equipment. Upon the completion of the transactions the students took turns using the equipment in their own homes and they then reported their findings to the class regarding each piece of equipment purchased. They discovered that there is no test as valid as putting a purchase to actual use. Features which were most appealing in the store were of less importance in real life, they discovered, than some other features which had been taken for granted. They found, too, that price is not always commensurate with quality.

One group of students in another school purchased underclothing which their younger brothers and sisters wore for a controlled period of time. The students evaluated criteria such as wearability, durability, and care required, and then they drew conclusions about the selection of undergarments for young children.

In Philadelphia, through the efforts of the home-economics administrative personnel, a mobile van was outfitted as an instructional unit to be used principally in the area of consumer education. Included were facilities for care of young children while the mothers avail themselves of new information, a foods demonstration area, a clothing construction or alteration area, facilities for all kinds of projection equipment, facilities for experimentation with a variety of consumer items. The mobile unit is moved from one inner-city neighborhood to another for approximately one- to two-month intervals. A trained, indigent home-economics teacher aide mans the mobile unit and competently provides guidance, information, and skill development for the homemakers who drop in informally and those who come for special presentations. On occasion professional home-economics teachers present programs as well as prepare instructional resource materials.

A quite different kind of program, under the auspices of the school district and with federal funding through the Vocational Amendments of 1968, was provided in Chester, Pennsylvania for unwed girls of junior and senior high-school age who were about to become mothers. They became a special group of students meeting together with a home-economics teacher, who possessed empathic understanding for young girls when confronted with the problems of being unwed mothers. The curriculum included nutrition before, during, and after pregnancy; clothing concerns inherent in pregnancy and afterwards; decision-making regarding marriage, keeping the baby, further education and training; relationships in one's own family and with others; sex education including venereal disease; occupational preparation. Provision was made also for the students to continue study in other courses necessary for completing a high-school education. Specialized counseling relative to personal problems was a major contribution of the program. It is noteworthy that a large number of students who completed this program returned to the regular school and made plans to complete their education, when formerly the majority of students beset by the problems of motherhood dropped out of school.

In another city the home-economics teachers and student teachers from a nearby college devote Saturday mornings to students, both boys and girls, who live in a private school for mentally retarded children. The children learn how to prepare simple foods, how to set the table, how to conduct themselves while eating, and something that is important for everyone to learn, how to clean up after the meal. They enjoy the exposure to foods which are not usually the institutional fare. Children form close and lasting relationships with the teacher-friends under these circumstances and this experience contributes to the young students' development of positive feelings about themselves and self-acceptance.

These are a few examples showing the involvement and interaction of home-economics programs with a variety of community resources in order to more nearly satisfy the physical, emotional, social, and economic needs of individuals and families, and to provide a better way of life. There are many such innovative and imaginative home-economics programs which are being offered throughout the United States. All that is required is a spark of imagination, commitment to serve, and concentration of one's home-economics powers to provide one more program which will help a few more people cope with life in a better way—to express oneself through home-economics and to live a more self-fulfilled life.

SUGGESTED TEACHER EXPERIENCES

1. Form committees in your class to investigate particular aspects of the community in which the college or university is located, or a nearby community. Devise a plan for study of this community. Study each aspect of the community as thoroughly as possible by interviewing officials, business people, residents; visiting local government meetings; studying the local

newspaper; and consulting professional people such as a lawyer, a physician, a community planner, a member of the Chamber of Commerce, a social worker, and a policeman, who may have something unique to contribute. Report the findings to the class using slides, charts, maps. Upon completion of the cooperative study indicate the implications of your findings for a school home-economics program in that locality.

2.   Arrange to visit a home which is new to you. You may wish to select a home and family of a life style which is quite different from the one in which you grew up. Try to make this a learning experience for yourself and avoid judgment and evaluation. Suppose you had a person from this home as a home-economics student in one of the classes you teach, how might your plan for teaching be affected?

3.   Explore a community not too well known to you, by either walking or driving through the area. See how many evidences of home and family practices you can identify which might have implications for the school home-economics program in that particular community.

4.   Select the school situation you know best. Identify an extension of the existing home-economics program already being offered in the school, and show how your plan would enrich the lives of the students and the families concerned. Invite a home-economics educator or a home-economics supervisor to visit your class for the purpose of presenting guidelines on proposal writing for special funding. Then write a proposal for an extension of the home-

economics program in this particular school.

5.   Visit a school home-economics program for the purpose of learning more about the Future Homemakers of America. Discuss the program with the home-economics teacher and the student members of FHA, identifying the strengths and weaknesses of the FHA program in this particular school. You may wish to offer assistance with some particular aspect of the program.

6.   Tape record an interview with several FHA members for the purpose of playing back the tape to the rest of your class. As a basis for a discussion on FHA be prepared with discussion topics prior to the interview including:

Why did you join FHA?

What does FHA mean to you?

What opportunities have you experienced through FHA that you might not have had otherwise?

What is the most interesting thing you have done in FHA?

What is the most helpful thing you have done in FHA? for others? for yourself? for your family?

7.   Collect newsclippings describing activities of FHA groups. These may become part of a bulletin board exhibit describing the FHA program.

8.   Send a delegate from your class to an annual state FHA meeting or district meeting. Or invite a student teacher who may have attended such a meeting to report her observations to the class in person or in a taped interview.

REFERENCES

American Home Economics Association. *Concepts and generalizations: Their place in high school home economics curriculum development.* Washington, D. C.: Author, 1968.

American Home Economics Association. *Consumer and homemaking education: Opportunity and challenge.* Washington, D. C.: Author, 1971.

Baker, L. G. The enigma of men in home economics. *Journal Home Economics,* May 1969, **61,** 371–373.

Best, G. A. Home economics for the mentally retarded. *Journal Home Economics,* June 1969, **61,** 449–450.

Birnbaum, M. Sense about sensitivity training. *Saturday Review of Literature,* **52,** 82–83, 96.

Boots, H. B. The retarded teenager in the home economics program. *Journal Home Economics,* November 1968, **60,** 730–732.

Brown, G. I. *Human teaching for human learning: An introduction to confluent education.* New York: Viking, 1971.

Campbell, S. R. *Consumer education in an age of adaptation.* Chicago: Consumer Information Services, Sears, Roebuck, 1971.

Cavanagh, C., & Price, D. Teaching decision-making to the disadvantaged. *Journal Home Economics,* May 1968, **60,** 337–342.

Cole, L., & Hall, I. *Psychology of adolescence.* New York: Holt, Rinehart & Winston, 1969.

Combs, A. W., Avila, D., & Purkey, William. *Helping relationships: Basic concepts for the helping professions.* Boston: Allyn & Bacon, 1962.

Combs, A., Avila, D., & Purkey, W. W. *The helping relationship sourcebook.* Boston: Allyn & Bacon, 1971.

Cox, C. The citizen role of man in family education. *Illinois Teacher of Home Economics,* Fall 1966–67, **10** (1), 18–23.

Diskin, P. A study of predictive empathy and the ability of student teachers to maintain interpersonal relations in selected elementary classrooms. Unpublished doctoral dissertation, University of Michigan, 1955.

Dymond, R. F. Personality and empathy. *Journal Consulting Psychology,* October 1950, **14,** 343.

Fitzelle, G. A human relations laboratory. *Journal Home Economics,* November 1969, **61,** 277–682.

Flanegan, C. P., & Ridley, A. A profile of students enrolled in home economics courses for gainful employment and for homemaking. *Journal Home Economics,* May 1969, **61,** 363–365.

Future Homemakers of America. 1969–1973 *National Program of Work. Action Plan for the Future Homemakers of America.* Washington, D. C.: Author, 1970.

Greenberg, J. D., & Roush, R. E. A visit to the school without walls. *Phi Delta Kappan,* May 1970, **51,** 480–484.

Hackett, B. Dual-role double talk. *Illinois Teacher for Contemporary Roles,* May–June 1971, **14,** 209–216.

Hamachek, D. *Encounters with the self.* New York: Holt, Rinehart & Winston, 1971.

Hamilton, N. K., & Saylor, J. G. *Humanizing the secondary school.* Washington, D. C.: National Education Association, Association for Supervision and Curriculum Development, 1969.

Jersild, A. T. *When teachers face themselves.* New York: Bureau of Publications, Teachers College, Columbia University, 1955.

Lee, I., & Stith, M. Low-income negro mothers. *Journal Home Economics,* May 1969, **61,** 359–363.

MacLennan, E. W. Understanding human behavior. *Journal Home Economics,* May 1971, **63,** 320–324.

Martin, R., & Blashke, C. Contracting for educational reform. *Phi Delta Kappan,* March 1971, **52,** 403–405.

Maslow, A. H. *The farther reaches of human nature.* Esalen Publishing Program. New York: Viking, 1971.

Maslow, A. H. *Toward a psychology of being.* New York: Viking, 1962.

Merritt, R. Self-concept and achievement in home economics. *Journal Home Economics,* January 1971, **64,** 38–40.

Moore, M., & Beasley, C. Why the boys? *Journal Home Economics,* May 1970, **62,** 339–340.

Moustakas, C. *Personal growth: The struggle for identity and human values.* Cambridge, Mass.: Howard A. Doyle, 1971.

Murray, E. The teacher as a person. *Journal Home Economics,* October 1968, **60,** 645–647.

National Education Association, Association for Supervision and Curriculum Development. *Life skills in school and society.* Washington, D. C.: Author, 1969.

National Education Association, Association for Supervision and Curriculum Development. *Perceiving, behaving, becoming: A new focus for education.* Washington, D. C.: Author, 1962.

National Education Association, Association for Supervision and Curriculum Development. *To nurture humaneness.* Washington, D. C.: Author, 1970.

Oliver, J. L. The meaning and application of differentiated staffing in teaching. *Phi Delta Kappan,* September 1970, **52,** 36–40.

Raths, L. E., Harmin, M., & Simon, S. B. *Values and teaching.* Columbus, Ohio: Charles E. Merrill, 1966.

Rogers, C. R. *Freedom to learn.* Columbus, Ohio: Charles E. Merrill, 1969.

Rogers, C. R. The interpersonal relationships: The core of guidance. *Harvard Educational Review,* Fall 1962, **32,** 416–426.

Simpson, E. J. The American woman today. *Illinois teacher for contemporary roles.* May–June 1971, **14,** 217–222.

Smith, W. M. The family roles of modern man. *Illinois Teacher of Home Economics,* Fall 1966–67, **10,** 1–17.

Spitze, H. T., Stice, A., & Crowley, B. Consumer employment. *Illinois Teacher of Home Economics,* May–June 1970, **8,** 227–230.

Spitze, H. T., Stice, A., & Crowley, B. Consumer education for disadvantaged adults. *Illinois Teacher of Home Economics,* Fall 1967–68, **11.**

Spitze, H. T. Toward a definition of homemaker literacy. *Journal Home Economics,* May 1968, **60,** 333–336.

Thomson, S. D. Beyond modular scheduling. *Phi Delta Kappan*, April 1971, **52,** 484.

Toffler, A. *Future shock.* New York: Random House, 1970.

Torrance, E. P., & White, W. *Issues and advances in educational psychology.* Itasca, Ill.: F. E. Peacock, 1969.

Wax, C., & Tronc, J. Women's changing life styles: Some implications for home economics. *Illinois Teacher for Contemporary Roles*, May–June 1971, **14,** 223–226.

Whitten, E. B. Rehabilitation philosophy of today and the 1970's. *Journal Home Economics*, June 1969, **66,** 412–414.

Wolgamot, I. H. On aging. *Journal Home Economics*, December 1971, **63,** 656–659.

TWO

TEACHING-LEARNING STRATEGIES AND RESOURCES

INTRODUCTION

Today home-economics teachers are teaching all age groups from kindergarten through later adulthood. They are teaching in public and private schools, in general and vocational education, in rural and urban areas including inner-cities. Some are working with business, social, and religious groups. Some are teaching the handicapped, hospital patients, foreign visitors, and new citizens. Others are finding employment in housing developments and retirement homes. Some are working in other countries in government programs that include schools for dependents and in private programs of various kinds. Many are working in part for monetary rewards but some are contributing their services as volunteers. The list of employment or volunteer-service possibilities is almost limitless and will be even more extensive tomorrow.

What does this mean in terms of teaching-learning methods? The use of the word *learning* is important, for in any interaction with others a really fine teacher learns as much as he teaches. Thus, the teaching strategies developed in Part One of this book relate to the interaction of people in or out of school. The illustrations used have general as well as specific applicability. This means that a reader with other interests should constantly apply what he reads to his own field of interest.

Part Two deals with teaching-learning aids, which include techniques for effective learning, instructional resources, and types and forms of evaluation. So extensive are the teaching-learning aids, ranging from the newest to older, better-known ones, that one may find some aids useful for almost any interaction situation and others that will suggest ideas for the individual's own situation. Included in Part Two also is a Guide for those who wish to become more adept in the process of decision-making, as well as suggestions for managing the department.

PART ONE

UNDERSTANDING AND DEVELOPING FACILITY IN THE EDUCATIONAL PROCESS

"I've learned how much I didn't know about all the things I've been advocating. I'd like to find out the truth."

"Why am I doing this? What do I want? I'm the one who's responsible for what I'm learning—not anyone else."

"It's real queer. When the school used to pressure me I was unhappy. Now I pressure myself even more on school work and I love it. Maybe it's because what I am doing seems important now."

These statements were made by high-school students who were experiencing, for the first time, satisfaction with some of their classes. What was different about the classes they spoke of compared to other classes? How can home economics be taught so as to facilitate joy in learning and at the same time help individuals develop into mature persons capable of thinking for themselves and of continued self-education?

Many writers have expressed concern that our schools may be failing to produce individuals capable of taking part in a democratic process in a democratic way. One of these, Marvin Ack (1970), says further:

By modeling our schools after business

and military organizations rather than democratic communities, we have neglected to give students experiences in democratic living during their academic years to allow them to incorporate and integrate these concepts. Students grow up in an authoritative atmosphere that does nothing more than perpetuate and guarantee authoritarianism for future generations of adults. They are bright enough to perceive society's ills and inconsistencies, but for many experience has taught them that the only solution is to tear down the structure [pp. 647–51].

How can we make our teaching more relevant to today's society? Young people have more personal freedom, if not more academic freedom, than they have ever had and this trend is likely to continue. If we cannot develop individuals able to work democratically and to assume responsibility along with freedom, we can have no real expectation of students prepared for effective participation in our complex society.

Results obtained by autocratic teaching methods have not been regarded as successful by parents or students; total freedom for students has not been the answer either. It would seem that something between teacher dominance and student dominance offers more chance of success. Most of the ideas being advocated today are of this nature. They are not new but have been advanced (though too often not heeded) since the days of Socrates.

Socrates thought that subject matter could be assimilated if it were taught in such a way that it grew out of the actual experience of the individual, but that it could never be forced upon him. He believed that the pleasure derived from any form of activity tended to increase participation in that activity.

The history of education in western Europe and in the United States shows many attempts to stress individual development by increasing freedom of judgment, independence of thinking, and individual responsibility on the part of the student.

Dewey, the first great American educational philosopher of the twentieth century, advocated that, instead of having the teacher solve everyday problems of the classroom, the students themselves should learn the techniques of problem solving. He did not mean, as some have thought, that students should be placed absolutely on their own. Others have said essentially the same thing as Dewey, but in different words and with some modifications. Educational leaders have talked about child-centered teaching, goal-oriented behavior, discovery learning, developing mature individuals, and dozens of other closely related ideas.

Over the years there have been many studies of the effectiveness of different teaching methods. Most have been disappointing to those who think of education only as acquisition of knowledge. Such studies, in general, have not shown an appreciable difference in subject matter learned by students taught by different methods, but they have demonstrated differences in factors such as interest, attitude, carryover, initiative, flexibility, curiosity, independence, and judgment. In developing such qualities, authoritarian ways of working with students have not measured up to more flexible methods.

However, we shall no doubt continue to have teachers who believe their judgment is genuinely better at all times than that of students; others who want students to do only the things in which the students are interested at the moment; and finally, teachers who believe that the teacher and her students working together cooperatively can achieve more than either one working alone. It may be well, then, to point out something that applies to teachers in general, regardless of the method they use. Vocabulary changes frequently in education and many teachers are so busy trying to learn the new terminology that they never quite understand what they originally thought they knew, nor do they understand what they are currently trying to learn. Changes in terminology and modifications suggested in methods can be useful in improving teaching if individuals can relate the new to the old and do not discard the old for the new simply because it is new. It may be desirable to keep some of the old and add some of the new.

Education to be really meaningful needs to help students answer the following questions: What am I trying to achieve? In achieving, what will I learn? How will I learn? How will I know what I have achieved? Such questions can, of course, be answered for students by a teacher using any method, if she herself knows the answers. But all too often a teacher is satisfied with finding a program for action.

Part One is concerned with all four of the questions raised and it will stress the philosophy that the teacher and students working together will achieve more of what is needed in today's world than will be achieved by other ways of working. However, since all the questions raised are important in the educational process, teachers should find the discussion useful even if they choose to lean toward other ways of working.

ONE

WHAT AM I TRYING TO ACHIEVE?

UNDERSTANDING PURPOSES, GOALS, OBJECTIVES

Aristotle, a pupil of Plato who was in turn a pupil of Socrates, centuries ago stressed that all intelligent action is action for the sake of an end. Throughout the years up to the present, Aristotle's ideas have persisted, but the vocabulary used to express them has differed from time to time. Some of the many words that have been so used you will recognize—*purposes, aims, competence, competencies, goals, objectives, behavioral objectives, and outcomes*—and what they express is the subject of this chapter.

In studying the meaning of these various words, the reader may be able to make fine distinctions between some: for example, *goal* is defined as the end toward which effort is directed, and *outcome* is defined as the result or final consequence. Others will be recognized as synonyms: the words *competence* and *competencies* suggest the state of being competent; the synonyms for *objectives* include *goals, aims, purposes*. The reader should realize, however, that if she focuses attention on what the individual is trying to achieve or the significant behavior changes desired, rather than on the fine distinctions among words of a like vocabulary, her understanding will develop faster and be much deeper.

Aspects of setting goals or objectives discussed in this section will include: the sources of goals, types of goals, stating goals in a meaningful form, shared responsibility for goal setting, and evaluation of the goals chosen.

SOURCES OF GOALS

Most goals are based on studies of the learners themselves, studies of contemporary life outside the school, and suggestions obtained from specialists. Preferably the ideas gained are compared with some kind of a desirable norm.

Before the teacher is in a position to share responsibility for goal setting with students she will need to do preliminary thinking and planning. As a mature individual, she is likely to see alternatives, implications, and possibilities that students cannot, in the beginning, although they may learn to do so. Further, the teacher is likely to have more sources of help available than students can have. Even beyond these reasons, preliminary planning is important for the teacher because it increases her feelings of confidence and security. Such feelings will help her to appreciate better the ideas and suggestions offered by students. It is the insecure teacher who is likely to talk too much and to use autocratic procedures.

THE LEARNERS THEMSELVES

If education is to change people, to change not only their actions but their feelings and ways of thinking, it is important to study the needs, interests, and abilities of those to be taught. A comprehensive discussion of these is included in Book 1.

To determine some of the needs of students, the teacher of home economics should try to discover how various aspects of home economics relate to what students are already doing. What can home economics offer these students that will make a real difference for the better in their lives right now?

Interests are an individual matter at any age. They usually, though not always, become more stable and tend to be more narrow as age increases. Most people show satisfaction in activities that appeal to their interests. It is fairly easy to discover individual and group interests if one listens, observes, and shows concern for others. Many schools employ interest tests that are filed in the office of the guidance specialist and thus are available to teachers.

In most classes there is a considerable range in the mental ability and talents that determine, within limits, what students are able to accomplish academically. Knowing the abilities and talents of an individual without knowing how strongly she is interested in a particular goal or how hard she is willing to work toward that goal, may be misleading; such knowledge does, however, afford some guidance in considering possible goals.

The better a teacher understands some of the needs, interests, and abilities of her students, the more probable it is that she can work cooperatively with them in arriving at goals meaningful to all.

CONTEMPORARY LIFE OUTSIDE SCHOOL

There are many ways of studying the contemporary life of students outside the school but the following should be particularly useful:

Study the socioeconomic backgrounds of students—there may be several levels within a class group—and note in what respects students may want to improve their way of living.

Appraise the students' homes and consider how their patterns of living can be reflected in class goals.

Talk with parents and friends of students and take their suggestions into account.

When using any of these approaches, the teacher will want to keep in mind what home economics can offer that may be meaningful to students.

SUGGESTIONS OF SPECIALISTS

College teachers, supervisors, and other educational leaders may offer ideas about goals important to any or all ages and levels of students. They may present such ideas in discussions or they may refer those interested to courses of study published by states and some school systems. Such materials are not usually available without charge outside one's own state, but they may be available on loan from area or state leaders in the field. Further, such leaders may point out references that will be especially useful for study.

EVALUATION OF IDEAS GAINED

After the teacher has gained considerable understanding of her pupils and obtained the suggestions of specialists, she needs to evaluate the ideas about goals she has developed. How many of the following questions can she answer with a *yes?* Are the ideas consistent with her personal philosophy? Will goals based on these ideas be acceptable to the school and to society? Is each one important? Will it be possible to attain such goals in the existing society? Are ideas consistent so that students will not be torn by contradictions? Are the ideas in accord with what is known about the psychology of learning? For example, will they be feasible and realistic for the age level contemplated and for the home conditions each student returns to at the close of the day? Can several objectives be selected that can be developed together for greater effectiveness in teaching?

TYPES OF GOALS

There are individual and group goals, student and teacher goals, and immediate and long-term goals. Usually the teacher and the class are concerned directly with these and there may be further classifications of them. For example, a student goal may be an individual one, and either short-term or long-term. A goal for the class may be also a student goal, a teacher goal, or a student-teacher goal; it may be either a short- or long-term goal. Further discussion on the following pages should clarify these classifications for the reader.

In addition to the goals that students and teachers are most directly concerned with, there are other goals, such as those of teachers in the school, parent goals for themselves or their children, goals of the school or of groups such as social agencies. There are also goals of the profession of home economics and of vocational education, and these are the kinds of goals the teacher will want to keep in mind when formulating ideas for and then tentatively choosing other goals. For example, one of the professional beliefs of home economists is in the importance of good interpersonal relationships within the home and within the community. Individual and group goals may not all be concerned directly with this particular belief, but should not be opposed to it. If a social-science teacher whose class is studying a foreign country asks a home-economics class whether they would cooperate with her class on such matters as social customs, food, clothing, and housing of the country, it is important to see how the goals of the two classes are related. It may even be important to revise certain tentative goals for the home-economics class to enable them to participate in this new relationship within the school community.

At this stage in arriving at goals the important thing is to recognize that (1) nearly every individual and group has goals whether or not they are well-defined; (2) different individuals and groups may have the same or similar goals, or very different ones; and (3) recognition of the type of goal under consideration is essential when one thinks or speaks of goals.

STATING GOALS IN A MEANINGFUL FORM

Choosing important goals or objectives and stating them in a meaningful form is one of the most critical aspects of the entire educational process, because goals or objectives are the guide for all other activities. In the following pages the authors will consider: (1) variety in forms used, (2) the Taxonomies of Educational

Objectives, (3) adaptations needed for age and grade level, for individuals and groups, and for others. Additional characteristics of behavioral goals or objectives will be discussed also.

VARIETY IN FORMS USED

Objectives have been stated in many forms over the years. Most of the present day patterns for stating objectives have grown out of Ralph Tyler's concept of behavioral objectives first set forth in 1950 (Tyler, 1969). Various modifications have been and will be made by individuals. Any form for stating objectives is acceptable so long as it has certain characteristics: it must clearly indicate the kind of behavior expected of students and the area of life or the content to which the behavior applies; it should be understandable to all concerned. For example, the objective "To understand housing" indicates that education should bring about some change in students and, in general, the kind of change or behavior expected. But the wording is too general to have much meaning for most individuals. The wording, "to understand how housing is related to the environment," clarifies to some extent the area of life or the content to which the behavior applies. It may be necessary to define or delimit the word *environment* before all of the group understand the goal clearly.

Another objective might be "to appreciate reasons for different peoples' way of dress." This objective would have the necessary characteristics if everyone in the group understood the meaning of *appreciation* and agreed on the definition of "peoples' way of dress." Does the latter mean historic costumes, foreign costumes, clothing of special religious groups, clothing for everyday activities, or something else? Perhaps it means all of these or only part of them.

Sometimes individuals think they are stating objectives when in reality they are stating what someone is to do rather than the change desired in students' behavior. An example would be, "Have realtors and lawyers discuss the factors involved in selling, remodeling, and buying a place to live." Other persons think statements such as these are objectives: "A more satisfying life may result when one's heritage is reflected in housing" or simply, "one's heritage." These persons are listing topics, concepts, or generalizations. Their statements are not satisfactory indications of the kinds of changes to be brought about in students and thus are not objectives.

As said earlier, so long as an objective meets the criteria, any form of stating it is satisfactory. Some people like the form of questions. Others prefer gerunds ("understanding how . . .") to infinitives ("to understand how . . ."). What is especially important is to have objectives stated in the words of those who help choose them. Almost any form can be adapted to students' own words.

The Taxonomies of Educational Objectives (Bloom, 1959; Krathwohl, 1964; Simpson, 1966–67) have contributed so much to clarifying the stating of objectives that they should be discussed briefly at this point.

TAXONOMIES OF EDUCATIONAL OBJECTIVES

The Taxonomies of Educational Objectives categorize objectives under three major headings: cognitive domain, affective domain, and the psychomotor area. The cognitive domain is concerned with remembering, thinking, and problem solving. The affective domain is concerned with attempts to define behavioral characteristics in terms of thoughts, feelings, and actions. The psychomotor area relates to muscular action ensuing from conscious mental activity. In general, the Taxonomies are developmental, representing roads to travel rather than terminal points.

It should be pointed out that although teachers might like to have all students reach the point of being able to make value judgments, or to act in terms of what they believe, or to develop a high degree of skill in some psychomotor activity, in fact students will reach different points on the road; not all will reach the highest level even if they wish to do so.

The significance of the kind of classification considered here lies in its definition of abstract goals in terms of concrete behavior. It is true that at some points the different domains overlap, but nevertheless they are helpful in stating objectives more specifically than is often done.

It may be useful to look at the major classifications of one of the Taxonomies (realizing that it is further subdivided into a number of levels or steps). An illustration of an objective within each major classification is given to show the difference in levels. The sub-levels, not given, are set up so that each is equidistant from the other.

It is readily seen that such classifications

COGNITIVE DOMAIN

MAJOR CLASSIFICATIONS	EXAMPLES OF OBJECTIVES
Knowledge—Remember ideas, materials, or phenomena either by recognition or recall	Know that I have responsibility for improving my home
Comprehension—Grasp the meaning and intent of the material	Become aware of what my responsibility is for improving my home
Application—Can and will use knowledge in appropriate situations	Assume certain responsibilities for improving my home
Analysis—Emphasize the breakdown of the material into its constituent parts and detect the relationships of the parts and of the way they are organized	Analyze the responsibilities which should improve our home if assumed by all family members
Synthesis—Put together elements and parts to form a whole	Decide with the family which home responsibilities should be assumed by each member
Evaluation—Make judgments about the value, for some purpose, of ideas, works, solutions, methods, materials, etc.	Evaluate how effectively each home responsibility is being carried out

should help those working with objectives to be more specific in stating them.

ADAPTATIONS FOR OBJECTIVES

It follows that if goals or objectives are to be clear to the individuals concerned, they need to be adapted to the age level of those individuals. The goal "Know the processes of making decisions" might be stated variously as "Why do I have to make up my mind?" (young children), "Know how decisions are made," "Learn to make decisions and accept consequences," (youths) "Be able to distinguish day-to-day decisions and long-range decisions," "Understand the changing factors that may effect decision making" (adults of college age or older).

Individual and group goals may sometimes be the same; they frequently are in a homogeneous group of students. On the other hand they may be different. An objective of home economists (American Home Economics Association, 1959, p. 9) is to perform the tasks of maintaining a home in such a way that these will contribute effectively to furthering individual and family goals. Individuals other than home economists may have this goal or they may not.

The same idea applies to student goals and teacher goals. Often the teacher's goal for students may be the same as the students' own goal. An example might be "To be able to make clothes for children that suit their personality." The teacher may accept this goal for students but she may add to it the goal of incorporating into children's garments desirable construction features. A particular student may have a goal that goes beyond the class goal. She may think of the related goal of earning money by making clothes for children that suit their personality.

What matters is not that everyone within a group have precisely the same goal, but that the goals are closely enough related to suggest ways of achieving the needed learnings. As has been indicated, even if everyone in a group starts out with the same goal, they may achieve at different levels.

ADDITIONAL CHARACTERISTICS

Sometimes, when working with curriculum, teachers find that there are no clear distinctions among the learning experiences required to attain different behavioral objectives. It may be that the learning experience is comprehensive enough to cover several related objectives; this comprehensiveness may be very desirable. On the other hand it may be that the objectives are similar in meaning and only stated in different words. Such duplication of objectives leads to confusion throughout the rest of the educational process and should be avoided.

Goals need to be realistic if carry-over to students' lives is part of the teacher's aim. To choose goals impossible of attainment leads to disappointment in most instances. For example, it may be realistic for students in the inner-city to aspire to improved nutrition only when the teacher can guide them in achieving such nutrition through better use of *all* available resources. On the other hand, while goals need to be possible of attainment so individuals can experience feelings of achievement, goals that are too easy to attain provide little or no motivation and should be avoided also.

All too frequently individuals and groups setting up objectives formulate far too many. It requires time to attain educational objectives and sometimes so much is attempted that little is accomplished. It is far better to select only the number of important objectives that can be attained in the time available. Keep in mind also that students need to know and understand the objectives on which they are working whether or not they have helped choose them. As the list grows such knowledge and understanding may diminish.

The relationship of one objective to another should be clear. Usually objectives are closely related because they are concerned with one area, for example, a group related to meal planning. On the other hand it is possible to have a closely related group of objectives chosen from different areas. A low-income group with very little formal education might choose objectives related to better use of resources in the home. Such objectives could include wise use of resources in foods, in clothing, in housing, in care of children, and in any other related areas.

Related objectives should be consistent in form. The form in which they are presented to different groups may change, but in each case internal consistency should be maintained. Pages 296–298 show goals for a special group of children that are set up consistently in question form for this age level, whereas another form is used consistently for certain other groups of individuals.

Finally, a comprehensive list of objectives should be broad enough to encompass all types of outcomes for which the school is responsible, but the objectives must still have a relationship to one another. This aspect of objectives will be considered at great length in Book 3.

In conclusion, it may be said that while a number of criteria are important for setting goals and stating them, the most crucial one of all is that the goals finally arrived at have meaning to the student and indicate something she wants to achieve. The following section considers the responsibility of both the teacher and students in deciding upon individual and class goals.

SHARED RESPONSIBILITY FOR GOAL SETTING

Students need some of the freedom demanded today even though many teachers have failed to recognize that they do. But they need also some of the structure the school is able to provide. As one student expressed it so well, "We want to become involved in what we are learning, but we need someone in authority to guide us. We want to experience the democratic system in our daily lives at school." What can be more reasonable than this desire?

Perhaps the greatest difficulty in meeting students' demands is that too many teachers who have themselves experienced autocratic administration and teaching feel secure only when they treat students as they have been treated. The same is likely to be true of would-be-teachers who have not experienced democratic teaching. Such individuals need help in changing from this autocratic role and they need props or supports when they commence to share responsibility with students. Finally, teachers need to use all the creativity and sensitivity possible in guiding students.

THE TEACHER AS A HUMAN BEING

As was indicated earlier, the conventional form of student-teacher relationship is that of teacher dominance and student subordination. As long as a student believes it is necessary for her to learn her teacher's ideas and present them to her in the same or in different words, she may do just that or she may rebel. The role of the teacher needs to be changed if she is to work cooperatively with students. It may frighten the teacher to realize she needs to work in some different way with students because change is often frightening.

There are many ways for a teacher to explore. No one will be useful to every teacher or teacher-to-be. The following are worth considering:

1. Think back over an experience you had where you felt joy in learning because it was something in which you were very interested and in which you were able to use some of your own ideas. It may have been an experience in school or it may have occurred at home or elsewhere. Then think of several other such experiences. Attempt to analyze each of these in terms of whose idea it was. Did you do it entirely alone or have cooperation from others? How did you feel about the achievement? Was an adult concerned with it at any point? If so, what was his contribution?

2. Think about an experience you have observed of someone who gained joy from learning—not just a reward such as a gift, a grade, a trip. It may be a simple experience such as a very young child learning to put on his shoes. It may be the experience of an adolescent who has learned to create something he wanted but could not afford to buy. Analyze these experiences to see how they are different from many experiences in the classroom.

3. Ask yourself the following questions. Do you see children as individuals or only as a group? Do they see you as an individual or "just another teacher"? Do you believe that those you have been or will be teaching may have some ideas as useful for the class as yours? Do you think it possible to draw on these ideas without students taking over the class? If students are intent on what they are doing for the class and considerate of others, are you concerned when they move around? Do you feel less secure without rules you have made and can point to? It is questions such as these that a teacher needs to ask herself and answer honestly in order to decide whether or not she is the kind of person who can work cooperatively with students.

4. Have a friend ask several students what teacher they would go to if they had a problem and could not discuss it with parents or friends their own age. If several students name Miss X, try to analyze what there is about her that is different from most teachers. How do you need to change to become more like Miss X? Her strength may lie chiefly in student-teacher relationships, but such relations are one important part of successful teaching and of using cooperative procedures.

5. If you work autocratically with students you may exhibit some of the same characteristics in working with friends and others with whom you come in contact. It may be easier to try to change your way of working with friends before you attempt it with students.

In short, teachers need to be humane. They need to trust people, including students, and to be trusted in return. To enjoy democratic procedures, the teacher and her students work together as a team with give and take on both sides. It is sometimes difficult to know how much responsibility to take and what part the student should play. Whereas too much control may fail to develop self-direction and initiative, too much freedom can be equally unrewarding. The keynote is flexibility. It is important not only to remember its importance, but to accept the concept fully. In application, flexibility means the teacher may need to modify some of her ideas or even discard them on occasion if she is to demonstrate procedures that are truly democratic.

SUPPORTS IN SHARING RESPONSIBILITY

Remembering that generally students have done little, if any, thinking about class goals, a wise teacher is likely to use certain props or supports in helping students choose the goals most important to them. To do this she may focus attention on the general area under consideration by (1) using recent activities of students, (2) stimulating inherent interests, (3) using community needs, (4) affording choice among a number of goals planned by others.

Since events in and out of school interact, many student activities can provide background for possible goals. For example, advanced students in an affluent area may describe what their parents are trying to do for certain local people who have many needs and few resources. This description could lead to a class discussion resulting in a class goal on relationships with all individuals. Or there may de a student whose mother has recently died and the class learns that Kay is responsible for family meals but has a limited budget. In learning more about this from Kay, the class may want to consider goals to help Kay and at the same time learn more about management and financial planning. Sometimes students see such possibilities themselves, but, more often than not, it will be up to the teacher to encourage the use of such sources and, at the same time, make them general enough to avoid hurting the pride and sensitivity of an individual. As she attends school and community affairs in which students participate or are present, a teacher can often pick up clues that can be used to introduce goal ideas.

Adolescents have certain common interests that prevail to a greater or lesser extent throughout the teen-age years. Once the teacher is aware of these interests through study and observation, she can utilize them in setting goals. Sometimes the interest is so strong that teacher motivation is unnecessary as, for example, of boy-girl relations at a certain age. Other times interests need to be stimulated or brought to the attention of students in an appealing way. Any of the techniques and

instructional resources suggested in the preceding chapter, or others the teacher learns about or develops on her own, may be used. For example, films might point up some of the problems related to securing a job and thus suggest goals important to a class in employment preparation. A field trip to some of the homes in the community might suggest the need for classwork in home storage, furniture arrangement, or treatments for various types of windows. Sometimes "buzz sessions" help students think together and reports from these may form the basis for a general discussion directed toward possible goals. If the teacher has creative ideas and at the same time is sensitive to student needs, there is no end to the possible ways of bringing their own needs to the attention of students.

Sometimes a particular community situation is brought before the group by the teacher, a classmate, or someone in the community. The students may then consider possible goals that will not only meet their own needs but those of others in the community. For example, a city-wide safety campaign might lead to a goal in the area of home safety that ties in with the community project. Or a teacher and her students may be asked to demonstrate a variety of ways of preparing low-cost foods. This request might in turn suggest a goal related to arranging a temporary test kitchen and exhibit for interested persons.

After students have had some experience in helping to plan their class work, the teacher on occasion may find it useful to have students make choices among a number of goals planned by others. If the teacher is willing to let the group, usually an advanced group, omit, add, and change the ideas submitted, this support may be useful, particularly as a time saver. It may not, however, afford as much motivation as other techniques.

NEED FOR CREATIVITY AND SENSITIVITY

Creativity and sensitivity have been discussed at considerable length in Book 1. They are very important at every stage of the educational process. Only a teacher sensitive to others can differentiate between ideas to which students give lip service and those which are actually their own. Sometimes, as has been indicated earlier, ideas for goals should be dropped, but there are times when the teacher needs to help students accept goals of which they are presently unaware. If a teacher is to be able to do this, she needs to use creative ideas along with sensitivity. For example, a beginning class of rural students wanted to be able to prepare meals as good as their mothers served. This group urged the teacher to let them assist an employment-preparation group prepare lunch for a hundred guests by making biscuits. They appeared to be highly motivated. About half the class was certain that they knew how to bake biscuits because they had watched their mothers do it many times. The difficulty was that the mothers had been making biscuits so long that they used eye measurements rather than standard measurements. Most teachers would have said the class was not ready to assist at the luncheon, but this creative teacher suggested that they try an experiment before deciding about the luncheon.

The class was divided into those who were quite certain they knew how to make biscuits and those who were not. The first group divided into partners. One student made biscuits the way her mother did, while the partner translated the measurements to standard ones. The second group made biscuits by standard measurements. The two groups of biscuits were evaluated by the students with the help of the teacher. Among the first group there was only one plate of biscuits that rated satisfactory and the students who prepared them said their measurements proved to be what the other group had used. Among the second group there was only one plate of unsatisfactory biscuits and the two students who made these volunteered that they had not measured correctly. The teacher explained how some of their mothers measured by using their eyes, but that this would be very difficult for beginners. After the experiment, probably no class of beginners was ever more careful about measuring accurately. Such a sub-goal (accurate measurement) was necessary if the students were to reach their major goal in meal preparation. Later the teacher made an occasion to show students how it may be desirable to experiment with measurements after one has learned some of the science of food preparation.

There is no end to the creative ideas that could make education more enjoyable as well as meaningful. The difficulty is that many teachers are afraid to try new ideas: What if someone visited the class and saw those queer looking biscuits? What would they think of me as a teacher? It is to be hoped that more and more teachers will work toward greater creativity, remembering always that it is important to evaluate possible results of truly creative ideas before carrying them out.

In conclusion, many teachers find it difficult to know how effective they have been in working cooperatively with students on arriving at class goals. An experience of one of the authors pointed out how one may judge.

The author visited a high-school class to collect research data on teaching methods. She was met by three young students whose first question was, "What are your objectives for this study?" On a visit to another class during the same study, the investigator asked a small group of students what their objectives were for home-economics class during the last few weeks of school. The reply was, "I think the teacher might have it written down in a book." Which of the two classes has worked cooperatively with the teacher in arriving at plans for the home-economics program? Which is likely to achieve the most and at the same time enjoy what they do?

EVALUATION OF THE GOALS CHOSEN

Teachers who are attempting to gain greater facility in cooperatively choosing goals or objectives with students may want to analyze how successful they have been. The questions on page 113 offer a guide for self-analysis. The more questions to which you can answer "yes," the more successful you probably are in cooperatively choosing goals or objectives with students.

SUGGESTED TEACHER EXPERIENCES

1. Divide the class into groups representing different community backgrounds such as rural, suburban, urban, inner-city. Each group then considers how it might proceed in developing tentative ideas for possible goals meeting the needs, interests, and abilities of a group of specified students. How could the ideas obtained be evaluated? Illustrate several forms for stating ideas in the form of objectives that meet sound criteria. How could these tentative objectives be introduced to students who had not previously thought about them?

2. Choose a small group of persons of any age that you know and see if you can help them clarify ideas with reference to a purpose or purposes important to them. Analyze the purposes or goals decided upon to see if they

meet important criteria. Analyze how you felt in working cooperatively with these individuals. Whose goals were finally chosen—yours, theirs, or some of both?

3. Discuss some of the questions arising from goal setting with specified groups, such as the socially and economically handicapped, the very affluent, or any other group of special interest to the class.

4. In every classroom there may be some situations of unusual interest to students that might lead to the setting of a goal in which the class has little background. Try to think of such situations and consider what you would do if confronted with the selection of such a goal.

5. Class members may clarify their thinking by discussing such statements as the following:

> Greater permissiveness is associated with initiative and creativity of the individual. Conformity, anxiety, shyness and acquiescence, and lack of interest, are associated with excessive direction which may result in frustration and escape.

> It will take time for students to clarify their objectives.

> A teacher will benefit by knowing ways to secure the interest and cooperation of parents in determining possible class goals.

> Helping students to see goals of which they are presently unaware is an important responsibility of the teacher.

> Group consensus is an important force for encouraging learning.

> Certain capacities for behavior appear at specific stages of individual development.

> Individual differences become more important with increasing age; the teacher has the major responsibility for adapting instruction to fit the needs of the individual students.

6. Hold a class discussion of suitable ap-

QUESTIONS	YES	NO	NEEDS IMPROVE- MENT
Did I do preliminary planning to have possible objectives meeting the needs, interests, and abilities of my students?	_____	_____	_____
Did tentative ideas gained come from several sources such as a study of the learners, contemporary life outside the school, suggestions advanced by specialists?	_____	_____	_____
Were the tentative ideas evaluated in terms of the school, society, psychology of learning, philosophy of education and of home economics?	_____	_____	_____
Were the types of tentative goals chosen representative of individuals or groups for whom they were intended?	_____	_____	_____
Did I study a variety of forms for stating objectives before attempting any form of statement?	_____	_____	_____
Was I able to differentiate between forms that met sound criteria for such statements and those that did not?	_____	_____	_____
Do I understand the contribution of the Taxonomies of Educational Objectives for defining abstract goals in terms of concrete behavior?	_____	_____	_____
Was I pleased with my ability to set goals cooperatively with students?	_____	_____	_____
Was I able to use props or supports well in making goal-setting more satisfying and effective for students?	_____	_____	_____
Did I show sensitivity and creativity in guiding students in choosing goals?	_____	_____	_____
Were the goals finally decided upon			
adapted to the individual or group and to the age level for whom they were intended?	_____	_____	_____
mutually exclusive so that confusion would be avoided throughout the rest of the educational process?	_____	_____	_____
realistic?	_____	_____	_____
reasonable in number?	_____	_____	_____
stated to show a clear relationship to each other?	_____	_____	_____
consistent within a specific grouping?	_____	_____	_____
Most important of all, did the goals indicate something the students wanted to do and saw meaning in doing?	_____	_____	_____

A Teacher's Guide for Self-Analysis

proaches that might be used in setting some of the goals for a class in employment preparation. An area might be: Selected Factors in Our Job World. The following statements could be considered.

Many women say they would like to be gainfully employed outside the home and could be if employers were more flexible as to working conditions and hours of work.

There is need for workers and the employer to try to understand each other so better work will result.

The worker needs to have a good relationship with other workers and customers as well as his supervisor.

There is considerable discussion about what financial aspects are important considerations when seeking jobs.

7. A new term, called "performance objectives," or sometimes "'behavioral objectives," is being used (Mager, 1962; Mager & Beach, 1967), especially with reference to helping a learner progress through a pattern of learning experiences that are exclusively his. Such objectives "specify what he will need to do to complete a task, the nature of the task in specific terms, and the level of performance expected for completion [p. 20]." The class may wish to look into examples of so-called performance objectives and decide how useful they are (1) in programmed instruction and (2) in teaching the affective domain referred to on page 105.

TWO

IN ACHIEVING, WHAT WILL I LEARN?

DEVELOPING NEW LEARNINGS

Today, more than ever before, selective learning is important to individuals. What is known and what needs to be known so far transcends what any individual can learn that the greatest selectivity becomes a "must." No longer is it sufficient to learn a lot of facts that either will be forgotten shortly or, if remembered, will be superseded in part by other more recent facts. That is not to say that nothing learned today will be useful tomorrow; but rather that the way we learn may be more important than what we learn, because continuous learning will become even more important with the passage of time.

Just as *objectives* and *goals* are but two of a number of similar terms, different words for what is learned have been used over the years. *Content* was a popular word that included learnings of several kinds. In home economics, *learnings* or *supportive learnings* or something similar has replaced *content* in most instances, and tomorrow something may replace these. The term *important facts* is used today in about the same way it was used earlier. However, where individuals used to speak of principles, they are more likely to use the term *generalization* today. The words *attitudes, values,* and *skills* are still used, even though other words

may occasionally be substituted for them. In this chapter, the following will be considered: *important facts, generalizations, attitudes, values,* and *skills.* The word *concept,* which has been used in several different ways by home economists, will be considered first. It is important to remember that these various kinds of learning do not function independently, but that each kind of learning needs detailed consideration.

CONCEPTS

The dictionary says that a *concept* is an idea. It is a thought or a notion conceived in the mind. Concepts may represent an idea with related thoughts or ideas. A concept may be an abstract idea generalized from particular instances. In practice, the word *concept* has been used in at least three distinct ways by home economists; each is in accord with the definition. Rather than stressing one use over another it would seem more productive to employ whichever way or ways seem useful in situations and then, if necessary, indicate how the word is being used.

Everyone has ways of feeling and thinking about what he perceives or knows, and these are formed into impressions or images that are generally referred to as concepts. By the time a child reaches school age he is forming concepts, but more or less informally and haphazardly, and they are far from being fully developed. Some of his early concepts are related to the different areas of knowledge that the school is inculcating. One of the responsibilities of education is to help learners not only to expand, reorganize, and clarify these early concepts, but to teach new ones that can be developed to the best advantage within the school environment.

For years, teachers have been drawing upon concepts held by their students even though they may not have used the word *concept*. In setting objectives with students, effective teachers try to understand the ideas of their students and use them as a background from which to proceed. The creative teacher in the biscuit incident reported on page 111 learned what many of the beginning students regarded as measuring and built on this to expand their concepts and to teach new ones. A teacher whose class is commencing to study relationships among brothers and sisters will probably be far more realistic in teaching if she understands what her students' present thinking is about such relationships. In fact, without such knowledge, the entire educational process as it concerns the relationships among brothers and sisters may prove ineffective.

Some teachers have used the word *concept* to indicate the different parts of an idea. An example might be:

Job Orientation of the Student

a. employment opportunities

b. motivation

c. guides for job success

d. employment services

Listing thoughts related to, or subdivisions of, an idea as in the illustration above has been especially helpful to teachers attempting to organize their ideas about some aspect of home economics. Listing the different parts of an idea is even more useful to those engaged in curriculum planning and will be considered in more detail in Book 3.

Other teachers use the words *concept* and *generalization* interchangeably. This use is also correct, though it may confuse some who are more accustomed to the other meanings of *concept*.

It is well to point out that any concept becomes more meaningful when experiences with it can be related to everyday living. Concepts such as *responsibility* and *cooperation* cannot be adequately understood unless repeated experiences are provided in which their essential characteristics are found satisfactory and useful in day-to-day living.

In one sense, a concept is never completely learned, for added knowledge and increased experiences with the concept will develop new meanings and new associations. Furthermore, even though the teacher makes a systematic attempt to help the students develop adequate concepts, their points of view are likely to be colored to some extent by influences outside the classroom. This fact should not discourage the teacher, for any increase and enrichment of concepts is one of the valuable services a teacher can render.

FACTUAL INFORMATION

The learning of factual information requires distinguishing among facts, opinions, and generalizations. An illustration of each of these may be helpful:

Fact: In our society both governmentally required protective systems and systems of so called fringe benefits are built into our employment structure; the most important of these are unemployment insurance, Workmen's Compensation, Social Security, and fringe benefits.

Opinion: Suppression of the natural exuberance in a child is a serious matter.

Generalization: Critical and independent thinking emphasizes selectivity and discrimination as a basis for judgment.

Facts are proven truths that cannot be disputed. As a rule, students have little difficulty assembling many facts and gathering much information if they are able to locate reliable sources of information. However, there are so many facts associated with the various areas of a program that students cannot begin to learn all of them. Therefore, the teacher will need to guide them in recognizing which facts are most important and which have lesser value in relation to class goals. She can do so by giving the class frequent opportunities, during progress toward a goal, to identify and report on what is considered to be most important. Any type of summary may de used as long as it brings together the outstanding facts. The summary may be presented by the class as a whole, by committees, or occasionally by individual students or the teacher. Sometimes resource persons participating in a discussion related to some aspect of a goal will make a verbal summary of important facts. In this case students generally need to review what the resource persons said and to restate the information in their own words. Doing so will reinforce the learning and aid retention of the facts.

Opinions are personal beliefs that may or may not be based on actual facts. Sometimes opinions are important, but students need to be able to recognize them as opinions and not regard them as facts. The ability to make this distinction comes slowly and is developed by

learning to appraise carefully what one hears and reads. People often make general statements without indicating clearly whether they are really true or only personal opinions. Therefore, it is unwise to accept everything one hears as true without further corroboration, except, perhaps, in the case of statements made by persons who are talking about a subject in which they have had special training and experience.

Critical reading is as essential as critical listening. Many published materials are biased; that is, they do not express all points of view equally, since their aim is to influence readers to accept a particular way of thinking. Such aims may be perfectly legitimate, but the reader should be aware of them. Further, all too often writers are careless and make statements that on the surface appear to be facts, but that are actually only partially true or sometimes even untrue. Hence it is advisable for students to consult several reference sources on the same subject rather than to accept one source. When there appears to be agreement on the subject by various authors, it is more reasonable to assume that the material represents facts or accepted opinions.

Sometimes expressing one or more opinions in a classroom may be useful in helping students clarify what they think about a certain matter. Using an opinion as a fact or a fact as an opinion is what may lead to unpleasant situations.

A *generalization* is a complete thought that expresses an underlying truth, has an element of universality, and usually indicates relationships. In other words, the learning of generalizations involves the recognition of factual information that can be broadly applied; that is, related to many situations. An example might be: "Changes in our society have brought changes in the lives of women." Such a generalization might be one of the learnings an employment-preparation class derived from a panel discussion by middle-aged adults on how their lives differ from those of their mothers. Such a discussion should bring out any number of different situations in which lives of women have changed in even one generation. These illustrations may apply to one or more areas, such as foods and nutrition, textiles and clothing, housing and home furnishings, human relationships, and care of children. Thus the general statement above would be a generalization of facts drawn from these situations.

In a group studying clothing, several students at different times have had difficulty handling material that stretched too much. The teacher may have pointed out to them that certain materials are more difficult to work with and why, but a generalization can emerge quite naturally as the teacher and students actually work with the material. After experiencing or observing difficulties with certain materials students could more readily see that: Fabrics have varying degrees of stretch due to the weave and the handling of the lengthwise and crosswise grain.

As has been indicated, there are two ways in which a teacher can help students learn to see relationships. She can present generalizations herself and point out illustrations and applications. Or she can let generalizations emerge as the natural consequence of the classwork; this latter way is usually more satisfactory from the standpoint of learning and is more in keeping with cooperative procedures.

As students learn to identify important information related to class goals, they can be encouraged to look for information that can be extended and applied to different situations. At first, the teacher may need to point out some of these situations, because the ability to think critically and to generalize develops slowly even in able students who see and are able to state relationships readily. But even academically slow students may see certain relationships and express these in actions. For example, such a student may have seen someone substitute dry cake for bread and part of the sweetening and flavoring in bread pudding. She may apply the same idea using jelly doughnuts instead of dry cake. Who is to say she is not generalizing, even though she can not state the generalization, "Satisfactory substitutions may be used in some kinds of food preparation" in words, and may not realize that she is applying it?

Wherever possible it is important for the teacher to guide students in expressing related information in the form of generalizations. There is no standard form for such statements, but the terminology should be clear and simple and stated in the students' own words. Generally it is preferable to use as few words as possible in stating relationships. Verbal and written generalizations not only help to clarify meanings but aid in the retention of material. Sometimes many facts go into evolving a generalization, thus the generalization becomes more and more important as knowledge increases. But to insure the retention of this kind of learning, students need to realize that generalizations are valuable to the extent that they can be used in everyday living. It is the teacher's responsibility to apply the generalizations in a variety of situations beyond the classroom. Their frequent usage tends to motivate students to extend the generalizations in more ways in an ever-increasing number of new situations.

PSYCHOMOTOR SKILLS

Psychomotor skills relate to muscular action believed to ensue from mental activity, especially conscious mental activity. In such skills the pattern of action is not fixed or uniform, since by nature every person has a characteristic way of performing. However, there are desirable and undesirable forms of activity in exercising any skill, knowledge of which is important if effectiveness is to be attained. The teacher's responsibility is to direct the students' attention to the essential features of the skills to be acquired and to guide them in a course of action that will save time and effort in learning. She can do so through the use of procedures such as these:

1.   Helping the student to perceive the skill she wishes to develop, thus further clarifying her goal.

2.   Seeing that the student is prepared mentally and physically for the action and modifying the action to reflect actual conditions if it seems necessary.

3.   Giving guidance in the beginning stages.

4.   Encouraging practice to obtain proficiency in the skill.

5.   Guiding evaluation of performance and helping students to incorporate techniques and adjustments suited to her.

Each procedure will be discussed briefly as it applies to a goal in a class on employment preparation in clothing and home furnishings. The goal is "to develop skill in altering a variety of garments."

In helping the student perceive the skill she wishes to develop, it is especially important to present an overall picture of what is to be learned in a situation as nearly as possible like the one in which the skill is to function. Some experienced person can present a brief explanation, followed by a demonstration of making an alteration in clothing or some house-furnishing object. It is especially important to get an over-all picture of what is to be learned.

Since real understanding of some skills comes slowly, the initial stage needs to be as simple as possible. Too many details in an explanation or a demonstration will only confuse the students. If there are several processes to be learned, each can be demonstrated separately. However, opportunity should be given to summarize points of one process before another is demonstrated.

Sometimes it is necessary to see that students are prepared mentally and physically in relation to developing the skill. It could be that a student has some emotional blockage against developing skill in alteration. This blockage may be caused by some unhappy experience of failure in the past, or by a projected situation, such as a divorce, in which the individual might be required to earn a living using the skill. If progress is to be made, the student needs to be helped both physically and mentally at this point. Even though the demonstrator has tried to present the skill in a situation as nearly as possible like the one in which it will function, there may be further need for modifying the action to reflect what might be the working conditions of some of the students in their own homes or in industry.

The teacher can aid the learning of a skill by watching the beginning of a performance. In this way early faulty responses can be detected and eliminated as soon as possible. The amount of assistance or guidance will depend upon the individual.

Although practice does not guarantee expertness, proficiency in a skill is attained only through practice. The demonstration on alterations included simple alterations. As the student masters these successfully through practice she will want to attempt more and more difficult ones limited only by her goal and her ability.

Evaluation will be important throughout the entire process in order to show up any faulty responses being made and to indicate where improvement is needed. As the student becomes more proficient it may be possible to change or adapt some of the techniques so that they are more suited to the person using them. Chapter 8, which includes types of evaluation, should offer ideas on various ways of estimating progress.

Students themselves tend to think that they have reached a satisfactory level of proficiency when they can perform a skill independently. The teacher may need to point out that this ability does not necessarily mean that the skill has been perfected. Some skills require extended practice and use before they can be considered highly efficient. However, in general, a satisfactory level of proficiency is thought to be attained when a point is reached at which the normal use of the skill requires no further learning. Skills then tend to remain at a high level of competence when recurring situations call for their repeated use.

VALUES AND ATTITUDES

There is such a close relationship between values and attitudes that it is sometimes difficult to separate one from the other. Broadly speaking, values refer to the relative importance attached to different objects and activities, thus determining the selection of one line of thought or action rather than another. In general, attitudes may be regarded as a series of personal beliefs or ideas which cause an individual to feel and act in certain ways. This "feeling" aspect indicates an emotional content probably greater than that in other kinds of learning.

Every kind of learning develops values and attitudes which are often more significant than the knowledge and skills required. Such learn-ing contributes to development of a philosophy of life, of education, of home economics. It is especially important today where there is such widespread questioning of traditional values and goals in an American society that seems to be getting more complex and more technological every day. There is need for all Americans to redefine their values and take a harder look at their related attitudes. Many young people are troubled at the conflicts they observe or experience and need help in clarifying their beliefs that grow out of their values and attitudes. What is needed is a new perception of problems and issues that brings students, teachers, and parents together rather than pitting one group against another.

Each teacher and student already has a distinctive set of individual values stemming from a personal interpretation of cultural values. These values represent an individual's tastes; they serve as a basis for making choices and guiding behavior. The early patterning of attitudes reflects the value system of the family. With an increase in age and experience, values and attitudes tend to undergo change and modification. New codes that will replace old ones in response to the demands of changing conditions often begin on trial. If found to be compatible with personal needs and aims and with the results of previous experiences, they are likely to be accepted, at least temporarily. In time they may become more detailed, organized, and specific.

The teacher may help, but she cannot be expected to counteract some of the long-term influences in the limited time that students are under her guidance. She can assist students to clarify and test personal values. Desirable attitudes that will contribute toward satisfying personal and social adjustment can be emphasized and may be accepted.

Helping students to integrate their personal needs and interests with class goals and then to achieve these goals through pleasant experiences is perhaps the most effective method the teacher can use to influence values and attitudes. The following illustrate such goals, which will vary, of course, with the needs of different groups:

Appraise how cultural patterns affect the home life of individuals and of their social and economic groups.

Obtain personal satisfaction in carrying out sound health practices.

Realize that companionship is an essential element in the success of marriage.

Appreciate the role of social and economic factors in different life styles as, for example, the "earth people" tilling organic gardens in rural communities.

Develop self-expression in home arts and crafts as a means of personal enrichment.

Feel a sense of responsibility for conserving human and material resources.

Be ready to change behavior in the light of evidence indicating need for change.

Judge problems in terms of situations, purposes, and consequences rather than in terms of dogmatic ideas or wishful thinking.

The next chapter is mainly concerned with achieving such goals through pleasant experiences. There needs to be opportunity to identify and test personal values and attitudes in realistic situations. As experience and new information is obtained, such values and attitudes may be modified. Continuous reappraisal strengthens them and in the course of time contributes toward developing a satisfying philosophy of life. For example, Bill and Sue are hoping to be married soon and have saved $2500 for housing and furnishings. Bill's mother has to have an emergency operation and has no one on whom to depend financially or otherwise except Bill. What value judgments might Bill and Sue make? How satisfying their decisions are should help them not only to identify values more clearly but to test one kind of judgment against another.

In this chapter the authors have considered concepts, facts, opinions, generalizations, skills, values, and attitudes. In summary, these are the kinds of learning that students may expect to achieve in terms of different goals. Such goals are sometimes referred to as belonging to the cognitive, affective, or psychomotor domain. But as has already been indicated, there is considerable overlapping of kinds of learning for many goals. This overlapping need not disturb teachers; the important thing is that all the types of learning can and should be stressed in home economics.

SUGGESTED TEACHER EXPERIENCES

1. Class members may each present statements relating to home economics that appear to be facts, but that are really expressions of opinion or only half-truths. These statements can then be reworded so that they are true factual statements. The class may also want to discuss the question: Are there some facts that should be learned even though they cannot be applied immediately to the everyday life of a student?

2. The group may consider the following statement and then apply it to situations of their own choice: To help pupils build upon what is learned in one situation and to generalize to another situation, one presents the concept in various forms. One then encourages precise formulation of the general ideas and their application to situations that differ from those in which the concept was developed. In

so doing, one learns to draw generalizations.

3. Choose three goals, one of which is primarily cognitive, one primarily psychomotor, and one primarily of the affective domain. Determine the learnings that might be appropriate for each objective or goal. Note that the different behaviors involved in the different goals will require different types of learning experiences to achieve them.

4. Several class members who have developed skills of which they are proud may summarize how the skills were learned. Others in the class try to select points of agreement in the procedures described. Then choose the procedure that most simply and clearly summarizes the major points in psychomotor development. Are the suggestions in agreement with the literature in this field?

5. Class volunteers may describe personal experiences whereby they learned to make satisfying value judgments after having first made unwise choices or decisions. Members of the class try to summarize what appeared to cause the changes.

6. Several class members can volunteer to answer the following question: To what extent, if any, can factual knowledge and critical thinking counteract deep-seated emotional attitudes such as fear of criticism or fear of failure?

7. Each class member jots down the skill she would most like to learn. She also writes the value or attitude she would like to change. A sampling of these will indicate not only the wide variety of such possible learnings but their individuality. Next, each person in the group makes plans for learning the skill she has listed. She also outlines experiences that she believes might change the value or attitude she has written; then she attempts to provide the experiences which she has outlined.

THREE

HOW WILL I LEARN?

PLANNING AND CARRYING OUT LEARNING EXPERIENCES

As we have seen, various kinds of learnings are important in everyday living. In school these learnings are usually acquired through attainment of class goals. Such learnings are believed to be most effective when students participate in a variety of experiences related to their goals. The more students help to plan the experiences and the more they see the relation of the experiences to what they are attempting to achieve, the more meaningful will classwork be. And often these experiences will stimulate the desire for new learnings as well as make the present ones more meaningful.

Earlier in the history of home economics the term *activity* was used, and was generally thought to mean physical activity, even though mental and physical activity can rarely, if ever, be dissociated. As time went on, the term *experience* has been used more and more. Various modifications are also in use such as *learning experiences* and *evaluative experiences.* Whatever term is chosen refers to special activities carried out by individuals or groups to help attain goals. Although there is variety in form and content, experiences are intended to help students learn how to meet successfully

the problems of home, family, and community living. To do so, experiences may be planned as classroom, home, or community experiences, or they may be connected with the Future Homemakers of America. Whatever kinds are used depend on the individual or group for whom the experiences are intended and/or the place where they are to be carried out.

Learning situations for schools change. Open-space and no-walls classrooms are no longer unique. There are schools where teachers work in teams, where there are no bells, no rigid class-subject schedules, and no doors, but instead, great open classrooms, an auditorium, and a cafeteria area. In these schools, an atmosphere is created where the young adolescent can have continuous association with his peer groups in exploring social issues and problems that should help develop individual interests, values, and attitudes. However, most teachers will continue to teach in situations where there is less freedom to move and to work. In helping to plan interesting and meaningful learning experiences, these teachers may provide many of the same assets that some of the innovative schools provide.

USING TEACHING-LEARNING AIDS FOR
A WIDE VARIETY OF EXPERIENCES

Part Two of this book includes a discussion of the many teaching-learning aids available for use by the teacher and her students. There it is pointed out that teachers need to be as familiar with these aids and use them as skillfully as a doctor uses the tools of his profession. It is further pointed out that new teaching-learning aids are being developed all the time and that many of these originate with creative teachers.

The sampling of experiences that follow make use of some of the teaching-learning aids discussed at length in Part Two. The experiences may be individual, group, home, school, community or any combination of these. Some may be especially appropriate for meetings of the Future Homemakers of America. For the first experience, the objective and the generalization are given. For those that follow, the reader should decide the probable goal and major learning or learnings.

Objective: To discover how advances in technology have influenced today's housing.

Generalization: Developments in housing are related to advances in technology.

Experience: Building materials and the shape of the dwellings are directly influenced by advances in technology. This statement could be used as the focal point of a brainstorming session where all new ideas are recorded. Following the session, each student would research one topic, such as foam houses, modular homes, six-sided houses, cardboard houses tough enough to last twenty years in any kind of weather, plastics used in inflatable furniture. Reports would be brought back to class in the form of slides, collages, models, or whatever creative ideas students would develop. Plans could be made, wherever possible,

for individuals to visit the kind of house he or she was most interested in.

Other experiences follow:

1. A class that had worked on buying and storing food decided that each person in the group would plan with his or her family on how to use as much as possible of what had been learned. Examples of what a few individuals did follow. Joan did the weekly marketing for the family after shopping several Friday evenings with her mother. This provided time for other things her mother needed to do. Bill wanted to become an expert shopper for meats, poultry and fish. After he demonstrated what he had learned about these, his parents provided a budget for such foods with Bill in charge. Maureen helped her mother replan the storage of food in the kitchen and in the refrigerator. With your class, develop similar plans for using some learning to aid your family in its daily life.

2. Observe children in special education classes for (1) the educable retarded and (2) the trainable retarded. If possible, arrange a field trip to an institution caring for the totally dependent mentally retarded. Discuss the observations in class and formulate the characteristics of the educable, the trainable, and the dependent.

3. Compare size 14 basic patterns or sheets from the major pattern companies. Illustrate and discuss differences and similarities. Then compare dresses of similar design, some made from size 14 patterns and some size 14 ready-to-wear. State some similarities and differences. What implications do you see for an employer in the field of clothing and home furnishing services? For an employee?

4. Organize a friendship club in your class. Arrange to have some of the group send notes or cards on birthdays, in times of illness or sor-

row, and on other occasions. Others in the group can plan visits to the home when members are ill. They can also offer to perform some service that may be needed. All of these activities—and others that the class may think of—may be rotated among the group. Then everyone can have experience in each activity.

5. Have name tags labeled "mother," "father," "aunt," "brother," "sister," "grandmother," "cousin," "me," etc. Have children select a name tag and act out the different ways that such a person can help in the home, such as: dusting, vacuuming, making beds, dishwashing, picking up toys and clothes, feeding pets, mowing grass. Children tell how they can help in the house.

6. Three groups of students, one each from home economics, agriculture, and industrial arts, locate a disadvantaged family that is willing to cooperate with them. Working together and with the family, each group plans what its contribution can be to better living for this family. Carry out the plans when possible and desirable. Perhaps some community group without the know-how might supply materials needed.

7. Holding a "How would you handle the situation?" session may prove very interesting. You might start off with the following situations, and add others of the group's choosing.

Situation 1: One day four-year-old Nancy refused to eat her supper. She deliberately poured some of her milk on the floor. Then she began to play with the meat and vegetables on her plate.

Situation 2: Several children have built a garage with blocks. For some time they have been bringing in trucks and cars to be repaired, telling excitedly how they were wrecked. Suddenly one of the children accidentally hits the garage and the blocks begin to fall. Then bedlam takes the place of play.

8. Using her own personal situation, a person may be helped to decide what to use of her possessions and how to use them in a changing condition. This may be followed by a discussion of ways to share possessions with others who would really appreciate them.

Were you able to formulate goals and learnings that seemed appropriate for each experience? To do so you need to consider the group that might choose the experience. Did you see any that seemed especially appropriate for a class in employment preparation, for Future Homemakers of America, for kindergarten through elementary, middle, or junior high school, for post-secondary or adult education? If so, which one? What experience might be appropriate for several of these groups? Note that some experiences could be thought of as school-home-community experiences.

TEACHER'S ROLE IN CHOOSING EXPERIENCES

The teacher's role in choosing experiences requires the same general attitudes and techniques as were important in deciding upon class goals or objectives with students. Sources of experiences should be similar to sources of goals, and advanced planning, planning with students, and flexibility are as important here as in goal selection. In planning tentative goals, the teacher must arrive at some kind of reasonable organization of goals for the age and grade level intended without too much overlapping. This kind of organization is just as important in planning tentative experiences. There are other matters also on which the teacher needs to serve as guide. These include: (1) taking into account the cultural backgrounds of students, (2) considering other differences in students, (3) affording continuity in experiences, and (4) acting as intermediary in assessing suggested situations. Each of these will be considered in turn.

CULTURAL BACKGROUNDS OF STUDENTS

People around the world have many of the same goals, but their ways of reaching these goals differ greatly. The same thing is true of any group of students representing different cultural backgrounds or even a background different from the teacher's. Only as teachers understand the lives of those among whom they work will they be successful in reaching them. This understanding calls for some experience with and appreciation of the cultural backgrounds of the students and a relatively high degree of insight. For instance, black people have a culture of which they are proud, as do other groups such as Mexican Americans, Italian Americans, American Indians, and some religious groups.

Most of us are selective in learning, or should be, and before we accept new ideas we have to see how these ideas fit into our pattern of living. The same thing is true of students. This means, of course, that even though two groups have the same goal, the same experience may not be appropriate to both. A suggested experience may conflict with some value to which one group and their families ascribe priority. It may run counter to some well-established taste. There are other physical and psychological tests a new idea must pass before it may find a place in the lives of students.

As an example, home-economics teachers have sometimes used experiences for teaching meal service that are entirely appropriate for some individuals or groups, but which have almost no meaning for other students because they fail to see how such service can fit into their lives at home. It may be desirable to use the same experience but expand it to include at least one kind of very simple service that seems useful to everyone in the class.

Along this same line, it should be added that even though students do not see how a certain learning can be used in everyday living at home, it may seem important because they see other special uses for it. For example, a young girl told one of the writers that the kind of meal service she had learned at school was not practical in her family because the family was too large and the kind of service learned would take too much time. But she added, "I'm so glad to know it because I can use it on Saturday when I entertain two of my best friends for lunch." She was fitting the learning into her pattern of living.

OTHER DIFFERENCES IN STUDENTS

When considering differences in students, all too many persons think only of variation in mental ability. However, other differences may be as important, such as differences in social background, financial resources, special talents, manual dexterity, sensitivity, or creativity.

In a group where there is wide variation in mental ability, provision needs to be made for work commensurate with the levels of ability. Cooperative planning of experiences offers excellent opportunities for dealing with this situation without making it too obvious to the group that wide variation in ability exists. All students need not carry out the same experience even though all are working toward the same goal. Academically slow learners can be guided to select experiences in which they are interested and which will bring them some measure of success. Academically gifted students, who might be bored by such experiences, can choose others according to their interests and abilities. The teacher, however, will need to take special care not to minimize the experiences of the slow learners, no matter how simple or different. If intensely interested in a task, students with less mental ability will often do better work than more able students.

As an example, a class might choose the goal "Know how decisions are made," with this supportive learning: "Better decisions result when one follows the steps in decision making." An appropriate experience would be to print three simple steps in decision making on flash cards, one step to a card. Have the class choose a situation that is going to require a decision, such as choice of a winter coat. Use flash cards to go through each step in the decision-making process. As a substitute for the flash cards, several academically gifted students might write a skit involving each step and present it to their own class or to other classes. Students of differing abilities might take part in presenting the skit.

Often all students can work together on the same experience, contributing what is important to each one. Experiences 1, 4, and 6 on pages 124–125 illustrate experiences where such cooperative efforts would be easy to carry out. Moreover, a creative teacher who is sensitive to others can make suggestions for adapting almost any experience to students differing in mental ability.

Sometimes differences in social background or in financial resources can be taken care of easily by using case studies adapted to a particular group. Hypothetical or real problems in any area of home economics might be useful in challenging students to use whatever ingenuity or creativity they can muster. For example, three groups of students having the same goal, but allowed a very different amount of money, could each try to plan and prepare a nutritious meal, or a beautiful and satisfying room, or an attractive garment.

An inner-city group should find the following experience especially useful, though it would be important to almost any group: Tape a report on frauds in advertising, sales, and service by a representative of the Chamber of Commerce or Better Business Bureau. Play the tape for the class and provide opportunity to discuss and share experiences with fraud, including what was done about each example given.

Special talents may range all the way from outstanding musical ability to chalk drawing. A student with the latter ability may highlight with chalk drawings a summary the class is making or has made. There are any number of ways such a student could contribute to making the class more interesting. In addition, she might encourage other students to develop a similar ability. Almost any talent can be drawn on to contribute to class interest and at the same time help the student appreciate and improve her own special talent.

Individuals vary in manual dexterity as in other things. The home-economics teacher probably will notice such differences among young adolescent students more in finger dexterity than other kinds of dexterity. Handling a needle and thread with any ability at all may be difficult for a student at a particular time, whereas, six months or a year later it may be very easy. The same thing will apply to the use of certain other tools. Students develop finger coordination at different ages. If those who have not yet developed much are made to feel sensitive or unhappy about the situation, it may color their feelings toward later related situations.

CONTINUITY IN EXPERIENCES

There should be continuity in experiences that are chosen, so that new learnings that have been developed in the classroom are reiterated and strengthened through experiences both in and out of school. Such continuity makes it possible for students to see relationships among experiences and to make applications from one experience to another.

A class, for example, may have planned and carried out the details of a nursery-school experience that, in general, provided a favorable environment for satisfying the basic needs of pre-school children. But the environment did not enable a few children in the group to satisfy such needs. The class learns that these children are termed "disadvantaged" or "underprivileged." Such children may be found on all economic and cultural levels and may be disadvantaged in various ways. The class wants to assist in the establishment of an environment favorable for all the children in the group. Additional experiences are included:

1. Develop cooperatively a code of ethics for trainees to follow when discussing the intimate problems of nursery-school children and their families.

2. Invite someone who has been trained to work with disadvantaged children to speak to the class and answer questions that individuals have. Arrange for several representatives of the class to visit a nursery school where most of the children are disadvantaged. The representatives will report back to the class.

3. Plan nursery-school experiences that will be helpful to the disadvantaged children in the group. Keep a special record of their development.

In some instances, an overall experience may be comprehensive enough that through it a wide variety of related experiences are provided. A good example of this is number 6 of the experiences listed on pages 124–125.

ASSESSING SUGGESTED SITUATIONS

It is important to select situations, or the combination of circumstances, best suited to a particular experience. There may be many possibilities, but some will be better than others. Students may lack the sound judgment in making such selections that a teacher is expected to have. For example, a class may suggest a field trip that would take three times as long as another one just as appropriate. Someone in the class may suggest an outside speaker that the teacher knows would be excellent, but unavailable. Another person suggests an excellent experience but the timing is poor; it could be used to far better advantage later.

In short, there may be some experiences that are entirely inappropriate, some that need to be modified, and others that are ideal. The teacher should remember that planning experiences is in itself a new learning. Thus, she will encourage those who offer ideas, help where help is needed, and make use of all the suggestions that are possible. Especially will she be careful to use the ideas of students rather than her own whenever such ideas can be used successfully. But sometimes, especially in the beginning, students may not have ideas for experiences. If this happens, the teacher may propose several that she considers appropriate so that students will have the opportunity to assess such experiences and choose one or more among them.

TEACHER'S ROLE IN
CARRYING OUT EXPERIENCES

When students carry out experiences, it is again important for the teacher to assume certain responsibilities in order that the students may acquire maximum value from the experiences.

HELPING STUDENTS ORGANIZE

If small groups work together, as they frequently do whenever cooperative procedures are used, the question of the basis for group formation arises. The importance of flexibility in organizing such groups cannot be overemphasized. The needs and interests of students can best be met by providing opportunities for them to serve in a variety of groups. Sometimes groupings may be based on the interests of students in a particular aspect of the problem. Other times students want to select a group working on a subject or activity about which they know the least in order to increase their understanding. It may occasionally be wise for groups with different levels of proficiency to work together so those with a high level of proficiency can assist those desiring to increase their achievement. Again those with specific skills or individuals with talents and special abilities may contribute the most by working together as a group. Miscellaneous procedures are occasionally used. These include drawing numbers, matching cut-outs, counting off numbers and matching like ones, or simply considering students sitting next to each other as a group. The important question for the teacher and students to ask themselves is: What kind of group composition will best meet our needs for this situation?

Once groups are organized, it is important to remember that students work more effectively when they have a clear plan of work. The kind of plan needed depends on the person or persons carrying out the experience. Academically slow students may require a detailed step-by-step plan, whereas someone else can work best and more creatively from a general statement.

A plan to be carried out over a long period of time, or at home, or in the community, may need to contain more details than other plans.

Before proceeding very far with any plan, students should summarize what they already know in order to decide what further learning is needed. They may wish to check with the teacher to see that they have not included too many or too few new learnings, but just enough to be a challenge and yet assure some measure of success.

MAKING STUDENTS AWARE OF USEFUL RESOURCES

In almost any community there is a wide variety of possible resources to help with learning experiences. It may be useful for students to check what their community offers in terms of the many kinds of teaching-learning tools described in Part Two. Sometimes both teachers and students fail to recognize resources that will make an adequate contribution to an experience, or fail to use them wisely. The teacher will need to stress that the use in an experience of several resources rather than one usually results in more effective learning. Evaluating the effectiveness of the use of resources will help students become more adept at planning for their own learning.

ENCOURAGING INDEPENDENT WORK HABITS

After students know what they want to do and how to proceed, the teacher may find it encourages the use of more independent work habits if she provides guidance rather than actual participation in experiences.

Some students will work more independently than others because they have previously assumed responsibilities. Such students will generally require less assistance than those without this training. When individuals decide that help is necessary, the teacher can point out several courses of action. Those with similar problems can form small groups and try to find satisfactory solutions for themselves; this procedure tends to stimulate independent thinking on the part of students. Or an individual conference or a joint conference of several students with the teacher may be indicated. The teacher should announce early in the year that she will be available for conferences as needed and post a schedule for consultation with students. For situations that cannot be anticipated in advance, either a class period when classwork can proceed without the participation of the teacher, or, in some instances, time before or after school can be used.

In many instances, students can obtain information for themselves by consulting references and should be encouraged to do so. Using reference materials helps students to learn to analyze what they read and to develop the ability to think independently. The student who is able to draw his own conclusions after he has studied the evidence finds the experience stimulating and satisfying.

INTRODUCING STUDENTS TO EVALUATION

The term *evaluative experiences* was mentioned at the beginning of this chapter. The function of evaluation has been extended so greatly in recent years that it is especially important for students to be able to plan and carry out evaluative experiences along with other learning experiences. Illustrations of evaluation are given in Part Two of this book; evaluation as part of the total educational process will be considered in Book 3.

SUGGESTED TEACHER EXPERIENCES

1. Individuals or groups in the class may each choose at least two objectives differing in character and suited to a specified individual or group. After selecting major learnings for each objective, develop several appropriate learning experiences.

2. Choose at least one goal that would seem appropriate for each of the following:

An academically average employment-preparation group of out-of-school youth

An academically slow middle-school group

An adult group containing members with special designated talents

A group of Future Homemakers of America that cuts across all abilities and all economic levels

Plan appropriate learnings and one or more experiences for each objective, including illustrations of those that might be carried on at home, at school, and in the community.

3. It should be interesting for the class to analyze one or more of the following statements:

"Experience is the best teacher; in fact experience is the only teacher."

"The purpose of any experience guided by the teacher is student growth in desirable ways toward the objectives of education."

"In general, the procedure for choosing goals with students is suited also to choosing experiences."

"The chief criterion of whether an experience is a class, home, or community experience is where it can best be carried out."

"For big things they help, sometimes on little things I have to go ahead," is the way one teacher expressed cooperative working with students.

4.   Assume that you as a teacher overheard two students discussing what was taught in one of your classes. One student said, "It didn't mean a thing to me. We don't have any living room because we need every room for sleeping. Even if we did have the room there wouldn't be enough money to buy all those fine things." The other student replied, "I agree with you, only I would like to have things prettier and more convenient at our house. I don't suppose it's possible because we have only a little money that could be spent on fixing up things." List as many suggestions as you can for improving the teaching in this class.

5.   "If an individual is to change his way of living in any way, changes he adopts will have to fit his culture, be brought to his attention in an interesting way, be economically possible, and most of all, appear to fit his pattern of living." Consider the statement carefully. Select something you have added to your way of living and analyze it according to the statement. What implications does the statement have for teaching?

6.   A certain junior-high-school class is carrying out an experience concerning storybooks for kindergarten children. One group of students has obtained a standardized list of books for various ages. Another group has chosen an evaluation technique for evaluating books for young children. However, there seems to be a feeling that the experience is incomplete. How would you clarify the goal? What kind of continuity of experience might be provided? What suggestions could be made to the students at this point?

FOUR

HOW WILL I KNOW WHAT I HAVE ACHIEVED?

EVALUATING ACHIEVEMENT

John Gardner (1962) has written, "Happiness, despite popular notions to the contrary, is not best conceived as a state in which all one's wishes are satisfied and all one's hopes fulfilled. For most human beings, happiness is more surely found in striving toward meaningful goals. [p. 103]" The last chapter was concerned with how teachers can guide students to plan for and then strive toward goals meaningful to them. But at this point the matter of evaluation arises. Most people feel very strongly that students must be tested and graded by the teacher to know what is being learned, if anything.

DIFFERING VIEWPOINTS

What do home-economics teachers believe about evaluation? First, there is the "learn-and-then-test" kind of teacher, who thinks of evaluation as grades and grades only. To her, grades are a threat to hold over students, for without grades as a penalty students would not study. This teacher makes no direct recognition of such things as ability in food preparation, improved buying habits, becoming effective in decision-making or, in fact, of any of the things

that should rate high in importance. Her grades depend on how well students behave in class or how well they do on examinations, usually oral ones, or a poor essay test given at the end of the term. In the main, the tests sample unimportant subject matter.

Our learn-and-then-test teacher gives students no explanation of what grades are based on. Her grade book is kept locked up, and great secrecy prevails about grades. Many low ones are given, and students are coerced to make high grades regardless of individual ability. Superficial rewards such as honors and awards are employed. The teacher thinks that by using this kind of evaluation, she can make students study more and pay better attention in class. Actually in such classes some students develop all sorts of undesirable personality characteristics, such as cheating, lying, jealousy, and unwillingness to help others less able. They become nervous and more concerned about pleasing the teacher or parents with good grades than with real goals.

Then, second, we have the "evaluate-when-administration-requires-it" kind of teacher. Such an individual has no strong beliefs or security of her own but follows along, trying to do what the administration or her supervisor suggests should be done about evaluating and grading. This teacher is not conscious of goals, but plans from day to day with no long-term picture in mind. Students are not clear about what they are trying to do, and there is no interrelatedness in their work.

For this second teacher, evaluation is haphazard and is carried out generally at the end of the term or when the administration requires it. Various forms are used but with too little understanding. Such forms are derived almost wholly from others and passed on unchanged to students, who are interested in them, if at all, primarily as grade-getting devices. The gradebook is kept haphazardly so it has little meaning to anyone. The teacher is willing to answer questions about grades if asked. Parents' attitude toward grades are likely to have more effect than the teacher's.

Our evaluate-when-administration-requires-it kind of teacher expects very little except to satisfy the administration. The reaction of her students will vary. Some will be indifferent toward grades. In others mental and emotional confusion will result because they fail to perceive clearly what they are trying to do. Still others may develop feelings of persecution, frustration, or resignation.

And finally there is the "evaluate-as-you-learn" kind of teacher. She thinks of evaluation as a tool for helping students see their own growth along many lines. She sees it functioning in one's personal life and in the overall home-making and school program. To parents she stresses the desirability of a student's doing his or her best, regardless of what others in the group may achieve. She wishes grades were not necessary but recognizes that they are still required in many school systems; therefore she aspires toward something more satisfactory than the present-day grading system. This third teacher attempts to:

1. Check at intervals to be certain students are very clear about what they are trying to do.

Know that sometimes temporary confusion may arise even when students have helped plan class work and ways of achieving it.

2. Use students in planning evaluation so it has meaning to them. Realize it may be a new experience at first and therefore students may need help in knowing what to do and how to carry on.

3. Use evaluation related to the goal at all stages of learning, weaving it into what students are doing, so that sometimes it seems inseparable from the curriculum.

4. Use as many types as her imagination and that of her students can create, adapting these to situations, individuals, and/or groups.

5. See that whatever evaluation is used is in terms of specific goals accepted by and clear to students; it is as accurate as it can be made.

6. Face the fact that at first students will evaluate too high because their standards are different from those of the teacher. As students learn to evaluate, they are likely to be far more critical than the teacher.

This teacher works with students in determining what should count toward grades and how much each thing should count. She realizes that there may sometimes be errors in the evaluation, but knows that no known method is without errors. She understands that we need to know much more about evaluating the truly important learnings than we now know, and is eager to try out any idea that sounds promising. The teacher does not expect each student to attain the same level of achievement. But she does expect each one to exert a reasonable amount of effort to achieve what the teacher can help the student to regard as worthwhile. The result should be students who are relaxed, well-adjusted individuals who get along well with others. Many will achieve more than the teacher expects and in so doing will form habits of working independently and skillfully.

Such students understand what their grade is based on because they have helped plan it. They are satisfied with its basis even though ashamed in some instances of their own achievement. They blame themselves for the poor grade, if they blame anyone. They have real understanding of how and where improvement can be made.

To some readers, beginning with marks is not the appropriate place to commence a discussion of the process of evaluation. Any teacher or would-be-teacher, however, needs to include marks in visualizing the overall process, and deciding whether she wishes to be Teacher One, Two, or Three, or yet another kind of teacher. She may be able to visualize a fourth or fifth or sixth pattern. In so doing, she should remember that evaluation is an important part of the total learning process, and that the tools of evaluation will be useful whatever she decides. Consistency is important also; that is, whatever pattern of teaching is adopted should be consistent in all aspects. Even though she is able to develop an open-mind philosophy that allows for a broad view of evaluation and grading she needs at the same time to understand and accept other views. Only as she can demonstrate successfully what she believes, can she contribute to changing the view held by certain students, co-workers, administrators, and parents.

The remainder of this chapter will be concerned, in the main, with considering a broad view of evaluation consistent with other aspects of working cooperatively with students.

CHARACTERISTICS OF EFFECTIVE EVALUATION

John Holt, in *The Underachieving School* (1969, pp. 53–55), says he does not think testing is necessary, useful, or even excusable. He does speak of tests people give themselves to check their own progress. These he considers important, but states that students are not, as a rule, tested to prove they can perform satisfactorily activities they have chosen for themselves. Evaluation, according to Charles Silberman (1970), "is an important and indeed intrinsic part of education—essential if teachers are to judge the effectiveness of teaching, and if students are to judge what they know and what they are having trouble learning [p. 138]." Where schools attempt to do what Holt and Silberman speak of as desirable the following characteristics of evaluation should be evident:

1. Further clarification of the goal would be promoted.

2. Teaching students to evaluate would be approached in the same way as other learnings.

3. Continuous evaluation, interwoven to appear inseparable from the curriculum, would be provided.

4. Ingenious ideas adapted to different situations, individuals, and groups would be used.

5. Certain additional characteristics would be regarded as important ones to strive for: validity, reliability, discrimination, ease of administration and scoring, reasonable cost.

FURTHER CLARIFICATION

Evaluation, to be effective, should help clarify the goal toward which a person is working. All of us have said or heard someone say, "I wanted to do it, but I had no real idea what I was getting into"; or, "It's clear to me now, but what I had in mind was rather vague in the beginning"; Or perhaps, "I have so much more confidence in myself now that I know more clearly what I am trying to do." These statements of course relate to what a person wants to do, that is, to his goal.

In analyzing and clarifying what progress is being made and where improvement can be made, most individuals are able to visualize their goal more clearly. In doing so, some individuals become self-confident and proceed at a faster pace. Occasionally someone decides that what he thought he wanted was a mistake. But whatever grows out of such insight, improved learning should be the result.

STUDENT PARTICIPATION

Evaluation becomes highly significant when a student is given an opportunity to evaluate herself. Self-evaluation has become more important in recent years. With emphasis on greater freedom and individualized instruction, self-evaluation may become the most important kind of evaluation in our schools. As a student develops in independence, she usually likes to find out for herself where she stands in relation to what she expects of herself and what others expect of her. She wants firsthand experience in ascertaining the results of her efforts and knowing how she should change or develop. Self-evaluation tends to give her personal satisfaction with her progress and to motivate further achievement. Moreover, she knows that she will have to make judgments of herself after she leaves school. The earlier she learns to do so, the more efficient she will become; the classroom seems the logical place to begin.

Although evaluation really involves everyone concerned with the growth and development of a student, the teacher and the student are the ones most actively concerned. It is the teacher who is responsible for guiding the student to develop skill in self-evaluation.

The techniques already learned in working cooperatively with students up to this point are applicable here. The proficient teacher works with students in developing evaluation; she discovers that the ideas of some students may be better than her own. After the evaluation has been developed, the teacher helps students to use it effectively. There is a tendency in the beginning for some students to evaluate too high. If the teacher and such a student rate the student's progress separately and compare ratings, it is generally possible to discover the reasons for any differences in ratings. As the student learns to evaluate, she is likely to rate herself lower than does the teacher—if there is any difference. It is a matter of learning to develop and use evaluation in the same way as any other important learning. The teacher working with students in this way will discover special teaching techniques of her own that will prove effective.

CONTINUOUS EVALUATION AND CURRICULUM

As long as schools make it clear that the purpose of evaluation is to produce grades, evaluation will be something to be done chiefly when grades are to be given. But when evaluation is intended to help students learn and teachers to know how effectively they are teaching, it becomes an intrinsic part of education. Students evaluate as they learn, not when they have learned.

The following descriptions are illustrations of self-teaching and self-evaluation:

1. A class preparing for employment in clothing and home-furnishings services may use role-playing skits to illustrate conflicts in work situations. Students attempt to evaluate each skit in terms of how the participants should act if they are to get along well on the job.

2. Young students just learning to change a machine needle may find a Guide located close to the machine. It lists five steps for changing the needle and provides a place for the user to check off each step as it is accomplished.

3. In learning to accept responsibilities for making and carrying out plans in a management class, each student may set up a plan suited to his individual needs. He tries the plan with reference to some phase of his daily life and adapts it as needed.

4. To clarify their goal relating to home repair, a group might use a check list that includes repairs usually done by the homemaker and those done by the professional service man or repair man. The results would indicate what should be stressed in the classwork.

In each of the examples given, it may be seen that the evaluation is a part of the total learning process, not something placed at the end. It is designed to help students achieve what has been chosen as important. In other words it is providing students with experience in self-teaching and self-evaluation.

VARIETY IN EVALUATION

Almost everyone uses evaluation even though he may not always think of it as this. A second-grader comes home from school and tells his mother he is the third best reader in his class. A housewife experiments with several kinds of the same product to learn which is best from the standpoint of flavor, ease of preparation, cost. A group of preschool children wants to know how many days it is until Christmas, so their teacher uses an Advent Calendar, which has one tiny door to open each day up to this special holiday. Leaders in Future Homemakers of America want to gain greater participation in evaluating the program of a large meeting. Shortly after the opening of the General Session, a Western Union boy delivers a group of mock telegrams to the presiding officer, who distributes them. The telegram says, "Tell us three highlights of today's meeting. Request Day Letter answer." Then there is a group of

school administrators who find it necessary to defend the school to parents; they collect evidence to show what has been effective and what needs improvement. These five illustrations help to indicate the range from informal to more formal evaluation and application of evaluation to different situations, individuals, and groups.

Adapting ingenious ideas is particularly important to evaluation. Almost everyone likes variety and unusual ideas but these are especially important as Torkelson (1971) points out to "members of the 'new' generation who demand excitement and current information. They have been weaned on television, they observe distant conflict while they eat their dinner, they are assailed by the stimulation of music, psychedelic art, and avant garde films which test social mores. This is a generation living in the midst of rapid change and rapid dissemination of information. The critical question for education relates to the retention of the main threads of man's development while striving for relevancy and appeal [p. 67]."

Even people short on creative ideas for developing evaluation can learn to adapt ideas found in game books, on television programs, at parties, in some papers and magazines. Individuals and groups will enjoy using as many interesting kinds as can be created by the imagination of all concerned. At this point you may find it helpful to look at the illustrations of evaluation given on pages 201–229. And as a teacher you will want to remember that certain students in your groups will come up with surprisingly good ideas for evaluation if given the opportunity.

ADDITIONAL CHARACTERISTICS

Additional characteristics of effective evaluation include validity, reliability, objectivity, discrimination, ease of administration and scoring, and reasonable cost. Each of these is important. Discussion of them has been left to the last because, without the four characteristics discussed on preceding pages, forms of evaluation with all these additional characteristics will have little meaning to those using them. On the other hand, such evaluation forms may have all the first four characteristics and fail to give students a true and accurate picture of what they are trying to learn.

Validity is generally regarded as the most important characteristic. It usually involves reliability, objectivity, and, sometimes, discrimination. Validity is the extent to which a form of evaluation assesses what it is expected to assess. To be valid, the forms of appraisal need to be based on the new learnings contemplated in connection with class goals. These forms need also to be appropriate for the age level of the group that will use it. In other words, if the objective is primarily one of developing appreciation among individuals in a twelfth grade, the content of the evaluation will be primarily concerned with appreciation, and it will be appropriate for the age level of the group. Evidence on whether specific evaluation is reasonably valid may be obtained by getting the opinion of competent persons. Although this is subjective evidence, it is usually the only practical source of help available to a teacher.

Reliability implies that there is a high degree of accuracy and consistency in the evaluation being used. That is, the same results can be obtained with each repeated use by the same person or by different persons. Forms of evaluation that have a high reliability generally have a high degree of objectivity and a low degree of subjectivity. Personal judgment or opinion is largely eliminated, and there is little or no disagreement in appraising the results. However, most educators believe that reliability and objectivity should not be increased at the expense of validity. For example, it is important to try to assess some of the less tangible aspects of education, even though doing so means using evaluation that is less reliable and less objective than one would like. And there are times when the goal is related to obtaining personal judgment or opinion, in which case the evaluation will also include judgment and opinion.

Discrimination, which has been important in the past, is likely to be less important in our schools of the future. Where each student is interested in his own achievement with reference to a particular goal without regard to the attainment of others, discrimination is not pertinent. The trend is toward helping each person achieve at his own pace, rather than obtaining different scores for individuals of different abilities in order to have a wide range of marks.

Forms of evaluation need to be adapted to classroom situations. Some classrooms will provide teaching machines, learning packets, or other of the newer types of materials, many of which have built-in evaluation methods. But whatever forms are used should be relatively easy to administer and to score. Any special cost needs to be considered, also.

It is difficult to obtain all the desired characteristics of effective evaluation. Therefore the teacher should consider which ones are the most essential for a particular need, remembering that, of the additional characteristics, validity is the most important of all.

FITTING EVALUATION INTO THE MARKING PATTERN

Silberman (1970) says, "The question of grades and their impact on the teaching-learning process is receiving increasing attention, with a growing number of students and teachers proposing modification of the present system, or its elimination altogether [p. 346]." In general, as has been indicated earlier, the new goal is to give each child greater responsibility for his own learning. Such efforts are increasing not only in private schools but in nearly five hundred public schools across the United States (*Time*, 1971, April, pp. 81–82; June, pp. 54–55). Obviously, the kind of evaluation discussed here would fit into these schools. The question is whether it would fit the traditional pattern of education. Whether we like it or not, there will be a wide range in methods of education these next years, ranging from "schools without walls," such as the Parkway Program in Philadelphia, to the strictly traditional programs we have known for many years (Silberman, 1970, pp. 349–50).

SELF-EVALUATION IN MARKING

The teacher who has let students help in constructing forms of evaluation and later use these for self-evaluation can fit such evaluation into almost any grading system. She can satisfy the school requirements and at the same time meet the needs of the students, to some extent at least. In order to do so, she will want to give students a share in deciding which evaluations will contribute toward the mark and how much each should count. However, the problem of deciding what should contribute to the final mark is frequently difficult even for the teacher. Perhaps it can be made easier by thinking in terms of which factors affect goal achievement directly and which affect it indirectly. For example, the forms of evaluation that best appraise the various learnings of the goal under consideration would probably count directly. On the other hand, interest, effort, and cooperation, are factors that may indirectly affect goal achievement but that should probably not be counted toward the final mark. Some schools give marks represent-

ing the individual's own progress as well as his relative standing in the group. The two should not be confused.

The example that follows was taken from a class where the school required marks at regular intervals. The evaluation indicates what the teacher and the students decided should contribute to the marks for a group studying child development and how much the various forms of appraisal should count:

Several check lists and a rating scale based on work with children—one-fourth.

Several written short-form appraisals scored by a flexible key—one-fourth.

One written long-form appraisal scored by a flexible key—one-fourth.

Appraisals of observations of preschool children in a play school—one-fourth.

The teacher in this particular instance did not feel that marks were important but did believe, if marks were required, they should be as fair as possible for each student. She explained in detail the method she used because it was objective enough to explain to parents and pupils. She said she tried, whenever there was opportunity, to help parents begin to develop desirable attitudes about the many weaknesses of the marking being used at her school. Her superintendent did not object and said he only hoped she could convince some of the parents to agree with her.

USE OF THE TEACHER'S CLASS BOOK

This particular teacher gave the following suggestions: Record only evidence that is likely to serve as a basis for grades; check the appraisals that are to contribute to the final mark, indicating how much each appraisal will count;

on the basis of the appraisals checked, determine the final mark.

1. If letter symbols are used for the appraisals, the teacher may find it easier to obtain the score by converting the letters into numerical values. The following equivalents are frequently used on a five-point scale: A = 11, B = 8, C = 6, D = 4, F = 1. Once the letters have been converted, the same procedures are followed as when numerical symbols are used.

2. The appraisals are then weighted according to the amount they are to count toward the final mark. For example, several written short-form appraisals may count the same as one written long-form. If the short-forms contain half as many items as the long-form, multiplying the score by 2 will give the short-forms the same value as the long-form.

3. The total score is computed by adding together all the values.

4. The scores are then arranged in rank order from the highest to the lowest. The distribution will usually show definite breaks. The teacher will then need to decide what the groupings stand for in terms of the school symbols to be used. In some instances the highest group may receive the highest mark; then again it may not. The question is, "Did these students in the highest group achieve outstandingly on the forms of appraisal used or were they only somewhat above average?" After this decision is made, the teacher can assign the school symbol to the different groups.

The example that follows illustrates how breaks might occur in the rank order of the total scores made by twenty students out of a possible score of 260. The symbols, or evaluations, given are those that might be used by any school, but were assigned according to the decision of the teacher:

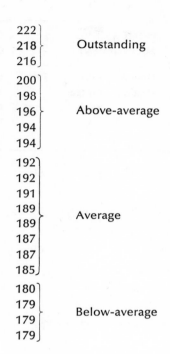

The table on page 140 is given as an example of the same teacher's record book, covering a nine-week period that was devoted mostly to child development, but also included some work in home management. The teacher and the students had decided that work in child development should count the most and that the tests would count less than half the grade.

AVAILABILITY TO STUDENTS

If evaluation is to be used effectively, students need to know: (1) how far they are from a goal at the beginning, (2) what progress they are making as they work and where and how improvements can be made, and (3) to what extent they have achieved the goal. When self-evaluation procedures are used, students ac-

STUDENT	HOME MANAGEMENT			CHILD DEVELOPMENT			FINAL GRADE
	Demon-stration	Com-mittee work ×3	Test	Play School Contri-bution ×12	Obser-vation reports ×6	Test	
Bennett, Mary	40	B	50	A	B	93	387 A
Brown, Susan	52	A	59	B	B	108	396 A
Daniels, Amy	47	A	60	B	B	110	394 A
Foster, Marie	24	C	48	C	C	94	292 C
Gordon, Jane	30	C	38	D	C	92	262 D
Jones, Edith	37	C	45	B	B	87	331 B
Kendrick, Ethel	38	D	50	C	D	88	284 C
Landers, Irma	42	C	62	C	B	90	332 B
Smith, Gladys	32	D	41	C	D	80	261 D
Thompson, June	49	A	58	C	C	100	348 B
White, Jean	35	C	39	C	B	79	291 C
Young, Helen	38	C	50	C	D	90	292 C

Example of Teacher's Record Book for Nine-Week Period
(Conversion scale: A = 11, B = 8, C = 6, D = 4, F = 1)

quire considerable knowledge about these three important aspects of the learning situation. As previously indicated, students can develop ability to rate themselves quite accurately with ratings similar to those of the teacher. If appraisals other than self-evaluation are used, the students need to know the results as soon as possible so that needed improvement can be made independently or guidance be provided if necessary.

PARENTS AND MARKS

Parents have long overemphasized the value of marks. This overemphasis is understandable, since in many high schools a periodic mark is the only indication parents have of how their sons and daughters are progressing. But all too often this mark is the only aspect of a student's development that interests parents. A high mark is the goal to be attained, and little or no attention is paid to the personal factors that influence this attainment. Many parents seldom try to find out anything about marks unless they are exceptionally low or do not coincide with what they expect or desire. Sometimes students are punished in one way or another in the hope that better marks will result. As a rule, this punishment deters rather than motivates the student, and an uncooperative attitude is often reflected in the student's daily classwork.

There are various actions the teacher can take to try to counteract an overemphasis on marks. She can begin by helping students develop desirable attitudes toward marks, and thus indirectly influence the attitudes of parents. This step would involve minimizing the importance of marks in connection with the classwork and helping students to acquire a better understanding of the meaning of progress. Emphasis can be placed on competing with one's own record rather than trying to outdistance the achievement of others and perhaps failing in the attempt. Students can be encouraged to show their parents, from one marking period to the next, where progress has been made or where deficiencies have been overcome. The parents may receive some measure of satisfaction even though there is not any great change in the marks of academic achievement. The value of progress can be further enhanced by the continued use of evaluation that shows the development of desired personality traits, attitudes and values, social relationships, and social skills. When there is evidence of improvement along these lines, students can be encouraged to exemplify these learnings by applying them to specific situations at home. It will, of course, take time for many parents to accept the fact that academic achievement is not the only goal to be attained. But if students themselves can learn to place a high value on the other aspects of development, then their parents may in time be influenced to modify their attitudes.

It is also possible for the teacher to help parents acquire a more comprehensive understanding of student progress. Visits to the home, interviews with parents at school, association with parents in various organizations, and other sources of contact provide opportunities for the teacher to explain about the marking problem and what it involves.

THE DILEMMA OF EVALUATION

Hawk (1971) points out that traditional grading and other authority-based evaluation systems have become outmoded in a system where each learner is functioning on his own. Rather, the learner must be accountable in a simple, logical, and easily managed manner for his day-to-day successes and failures.

Writers who deal with the question of evaluation in individualized instruction all make the same point: the authoritarian "passing down of judgment" upon learners is "out," and carefully documented profiles of achievement are "in." These writers point out that letter grading is dropped completely in individualized programs. In its place is a careful logging of progress based upon frequent and constant contact between learner and teacher [p. 76].

This method is appropriate whether each student is working independently with individualized instructional materials, or has been able to move out in an individualized program of his own, or is working as an individual within a group. The dilemma is that there is no universal understanding or acceptance of such procedures. Even individuals who say that evaluation must change as education changes are not always ready to change. They may give lip service to the fact that education now stresses the importance of producing individuals able to think for themselves and is no longer concerned chiefly with teaching knowledge for the sake of knowledge. But at this point a road block seems to appear in the case of far too many educators. The teacher of tomorrow must be concerned first and foremost with the development of each individual student. The school of tomorrow must redefine group goals. As Hawk says so well, "The unavoidable weight of social and technological change can not help but have a major impact upon the school of tomorrow [p. 80]."

SUGGESTED TEACHER EXPERIENCES

1. An opposing panel described on pages 155–156 should prove an interesting way to consider each characteristic of effective evaluation. Various viewpoints may be presented as class members grow in understanding of each characteristic. Whenever possible, actual examples should be used to illustrate points.

2. Two prominent educators gave their views on the grading system. One acknowledged that there were inadequacies in the system, but contended that grades are the only effective motivation to insure that students will put forth their best effort. Literally throwing up his hands in a gesture of futility, he asked, "What are we going to replace it with?" The other educator answered with two words, "Student interest." He said, "Student interest in the subject, rather than the antiquated grading system, will provide real incentives for education—not the artificiality of an arbitrary A, B, C, D, or F." What is your reaction to the statements of the two men?

3. Role playing or inviting appropriate persons to participate may be an interesting way to gain insight into such problems as:

What three community leaders who are regarded as progressive in their thinking believe about student participation in learning.

How a low-ability student who tries very hard feels about grades as compared with a gifted student who exerts himself very little.

How an inner-city parent feels about grades.

4. A first-year teacher who believed in student participation in determining grades asked a class of young adolescents what they believed should count toward the grade in a particular marking period. "Personality" was the answer given. How would you advise this teacher so that she can successfully work with students on the matter of student participation in grading?

5. Assuming that a senior-high-school class in employment preparation in food services had studied selected factors of the job and large-

quantity cooking during a particular marking period, suggest what might count toward the grade for this period. Using this information set up a hypothetical teacher's record book. If grades are not required, what kind of evaluation would you suggest?

PART TWO

USING TEACHING-LEARNING RESOURCES WITH SKILL AND SENSITIVITY

The teaching-learning resources available today to teachers of home economics are almost limitless and more are being developed each year. Some, but not all, of the new ones are primarily for individualized instruction. Paul Watson (1971), along with other writers, raises the question, "How individualized should instruction be to yield the greatest efficiencies in terms of learning, retention, cost and other parameters important in the educational system [p. 83]?" He concludes that we do not possess the basic knowledge to know the answer yet. He asks also, as does Patrick Suppes, "How much does society really want to commit itself to accentuating differences in cognitive styles, or to other individual differences [p. 84]?" Society is just beginning to face the practical problem of how much diversity is desirable.

Nevertheless, many educators would agree with Charles Reich (1971, p. 392) that students should be exposed and re-exposed to as wide a variety of experiences and contrasts as possible. To provide this variety, the effective teacher needs to learn about and use whatever available teaching-learning helps she and her students agree are most appropriate for a particular purpose. These would include long-established techniques and resources as well as innovations that appear in the literature and on the market.

Any classification of teaching-learning resources is arbitrary and there may appear to be some overlapping. Nevertheless, the classification chosen should make it easier for the teacher to acquaint herself with many of the helps available. A variety of long-established techniques and resources will be discussed first followed by some recent innovations and examples of evaluations.

FIVE

HOW CAN I USE BETTER-KNOWN TEACHING-LEARNING TECHNIQUES EFFECTIVELY?

ESTABLISHED TECHNIQUES

There are many uses for effective techniques. Some are used to develop specific information that is not generally found in reference books and that helps to enrich the home-economics program. Others are used to illustrate certain processes and skills, or to stimulate interest along new lines of thought. There are techniques that encourage the development of creative ability or provide experience not easily secured in any other way. Practically all techniques can be used to evaluate new learnings associated with the class goals.

Many of the techniques selected have long been in use in classrooms where cooperative procedures are considered important. Some of them have also been successfully used by teachers who have not yet adopted cooperative procedures. In either case, a review of familiar material may evoke a new and different viewpoint on the part of the teacher, resulting perhaps in a more profitable application of the techniques. Any technique new to a teacher may serve as a challenge to make learning situations even more interesting and meaningful.

It should also be pointed out that descriptions of some of the techniques are more extensive than others. The purpose is to help teachers understand these particular techniques more fully, and not to imply that any one is preferred. All the techniques have innumerable possibilities in a home-economics program and their potential value is limited only by the skill, ingenuity, and imagination of the teacher and the students.

DISCUSSION

One of the most effective techniques for stimulating the learning process is discussion. A good discussion involves group interaction in which individuals express themselves, listen to the opinions of others, and then pool the best ideas and judgments. Thinking aloud together is a valuable experience. Ideas tend to become more meaningful when they can be talked over, and misunderstandings are often corrected.

NEED FOR GOOD LEADERSHIP

Good leadership is needed for successful discussion. The responsibility of the leader is fourfold.

1. *To get the discussion started.* The details of getting a discussion started will vary in accordance with the way the discussion technique is being used. These details will be given later.

2. *To keep the discussion moving.* A good leader may toss out questions from time to time to keep the discussion moving, but he seldom answers one. If a question is directed toward him, he can refer it to the group. For example, he might say, "I would like to hear what some of the rest of you think first before I make any comments." Or "Would anyone like to answer this question?" Often the leader can keep from being the target of questions by partially withdrawing from the position of discussion leader. One way of doing so is to write on the board important points that are brought up. This has the added effect of giving members of the group the feeling that their contributions are acceptable.

3. *To see that participation is distributed.* Although aggressive individuals often take the lead in a general discussion, others in the group should also be given an opportunity to participate. One way of increasing group participation is to encourage circular discussion. When discussion passes freely from one person to another without having to be screened by the leader, more people are usually willing to make a contribution. It is not necessary for the leader to feel compelled to comment on every remark made. Occasionally, however, some person who is reticent about offering an idea may need an encouraging comment. The leader may also find it helpful to direct uncolored questions to different people, such as "Do you want to add anything to what has been suggested?" Or "Would you express it differently?" Or "Are there other reasons?" Such questions challenge thinking and give group members a chance to make judgments of their own. But every member of the group needs to feel that his ideas will be listened to

with respect and that an honest attempt will be made to understand them.

Of course, individuals often make statements that are incorrect or contrary to what the leader believes is desirable. A wise leader will not take issue with these statements at the time they are made. Instead he will wait until the end of the discussion period when a summary of ideas and suggestions is to be made. By then these statements will have become a part of the discussion and less a contribution of some particular individual. But even then, the leader will need to handle the situation carefully and sympathetically.

It is also important for the leader to work toward the point where he can make a direct suggestion to the group and have it examined on its merits just as though it had come from any other member. Because the leader is generally held in high esteem by the group, it is expected that his contribution will carry considerable weight. To overcome this advantage, the leader can wait until the members of the group have had a chance to express their ideas and then give his suggestions carefully without stressing them. However, any idea that the leader may offer should be evaluated along with those of the group.

4. *To guide the discussion toward a useful conclusion.* At some point in the discussion, the group should begin to select outstanding ideas and suggestions. The leader will need to guide the selections and to see that they are listed in full view of the group. The final conclusions, however, need not be identified with the persons who offered them.

PERSONAL QUALIFICATIONS OF
A GOOD LEADER

Persons who are considered good discussion leaders generally have the following qualifications: (1) a personal and lively interest in the subject under discussion; (2) the ability to suppress the expression of personal opinions most of the time; (3) an open mind about the final decisions or choices made by the group; (4) a sense of humor with a sense of the serious.

CLASS DISCUSSION

There are various ways in which discussion can be used in large or small groups. Each way is a technique in itself, since the methods of operation are somewhat different for each one. However, the general values of discussion and the basic considerations for good leadership are essentially the same, regardless of the procedure.

Learning to use the discussion technique as a classroom procedure is not easy. It involves much more than giving the students an opportunity to verbalize their thoughts and ideas. In addition to understanding the role of leadership, the teacher needs to know when and how to initiate a discussion, what subjects will yield the most fruitful results, and how to get the discussion under way.

INITIATING A DISCUSSION

One of the principal responsibilities of the leader is to know when various aspects of the current classwork can best be attacked by thinking aloud on those occasions, of course, when discussion is not an integral part of the general procedure. One such occasion may arise when a new area is being taken up and the students need to consider possible goals. Or if the classwork has reached a point where there is some doubt about a future course of action, a discussion may clarify the situation. Sometimes there are common problems connected with social situations or with family relationships that students want to talk over in a group setting. A discussion may help individual students later in making decisions that will be personally satisfying. Whatever is to be discussed, however, should have sufficient breadth and depth to provide critical thinking on various aspects of the subject. A subject that is too simple is soon exhausted, and ceases to be challenging to the group.

In addition to sensing the appropriateness of occasions for a discussion, the teacher will also need to take the time element into consideration. It is not advisable to initiate a discussion unless there is sufficient time to carry it through to a satisfactory conclusion. A worthwhile discussion needs the active participation of at least a majority of the class and sufficient time for pooling the ideas that can be used most profitably. The amount of time taken will usually depend on the experience the class has had with the discussion technique. More time should be allowed for an inexperienced group, who may be expected to flounder around until they have learned to express themselves aloud in the presence of others. Experienced students think more clearly as a group and know how to go about expediting the subject under discussion. It is possible, of course, to carry over a discussion to the next meeting of the class. But much of the initial interest and enthusiasm are lost and never regained. Even some of the best ideas and suggestions may lose their significance in the time that has elapsed since they were presented.

GETTING THE DISCUSSION UNDER WAY

There are various ways of getting a discussion started. The most elementary approach is one in which the teacher directs questions to the students and then discusses their replies. Or the students ask the teacher the questions. In either case the teacher does a considerable amount of talking.

A more effective procedure is to involve the group in an interchange of ideas with each other rather than with the teacher. She can start with a provocative question and then encourage answers from several students. Sometimes, however, this procedure may not be sufficient to motivate a discussion. The students may be shy and afraid that they might say something wrong. Often a new subject seems so puzzling that students hesitate to become drawn into a discussion. Such situations can be remedied through the use of small group discussions. After the outstanding points made by the groups have been summarized, the subject can be turned over to the class for general discussion. Once the discussion is under way, the teacher's responsibility has already been indicated in the other three aspects of good leadership.

BUZZING

Buzzing is an effective technique for increasing individual discussion. The class is divided into small groups and given a short time in which to discuss a specific topic. At the end of that period the class reconvenes and the various groups present their ideas. This technique has considerable value in a variety of situations:

1.   When there is difficulty getting classwork under way. As previously indicated, sometimes class members are unable or unwilling to express themselves in a large group. Small groups, on the other hand, stimulate individual thinking. This increases the flow of ideas in a setting where these ideas can be discussed freely without embarrassment.

2.   When it is important to save time. A buzz session is a rapid procedure for pooling ideas. If there are several questions that need to be discussed, small groups can each take a question and work out possible answers. Or if the class wants the opinion of each member in relation to a proposed activity, time can be saved by initiating a buzz session where every student can express himself.

3.   Midway through a long discussion period. When an extensive subject, such as planning a yearly program or setting goals in an area, is being carried out, a change in procedure from a general discussion to buzzing will help to sustain interest and relieve monotony.

4.   Following a movie or a filmstrip. Many films are so provocative that they act as a natural springboard for a buzz-group discussion. Everyone is eager to talk about what he has seen. A class discussion would generally not provide this opportunity, whereas a buzz session would.

ORGANIZING GROUPS

A buzz group will usually consist of five persons, although any number from four to six is effective. A group that is too small has few resources on which to call, whereas one that is too large tends to inhibit free discussion. Although the group can be selected in various ways, the procedure used should be simple and expedient.

Groupings can be based on the prevalent seating arrangement by having five or six persons sitting near together form a group, or if the seats are in rows, groups can be formed horizontally across the room or vertically from front to back. A counting-off procedure may be used, or numbered cards can be shuffled and passed out at random. After the groups have been organized, the cards can be collected and used another time. Needless to say, the same groupings should not occur each time a buzz session is held. Variation encourages a greater exchange of ideas and helps students to get better acquainted.

The time allowed for buzzing is generally from five to twenty minutes, depending somewhat on the topic to be discussed. It should be long enough for each group to put down several ideas but not long enough to exhaust the topic. However, too little time is better than too much. If the period given proves to be too short, the time can be extended three or four minutes. A skillful teacher knows from experience how long her students can talk about something productively.

If the group is fairly small and the topic brief, a chairman may be all that is necessary. But if the topic is more extensive and calls for a number of ideas, a recorder may also be needed. In classes unfamiliar with group work, it is advisable for the teacher to see that the groups are structured before discussion begins so that the work can get under way quickly. Some method, such as having the person whose name is nearest the top of the alphabet serve as chairman and the one nearest the bottom as recorder, can be used. As the students become more experienced in group participation, each group can decide on the roles.

GIVING REPORTS

In reporting on the decisions, it is advisable for each group to hear its own findings presented to the class. Students feel personal pride and satisfaction in being identified with a group's accomplishments. Usually the recorder will give the report. Occasionally she may write, or have someone write, the summary on the chalkboard. One way to avoid repetition and still have group recognition is to take a vote to determine the number of groups who have the

same findings. Sometimes it may be advisable to collect the reports from the various groups and have a committee consolidate them. A class discussion following the reports tends to reinforce the ideas presented.

BRAINSTORMING

Brainstorming is primarily a creative technique that allows the imagination to run riot. It works best when there is a specific problem that lends itself to many possible answers, since its chief aim is to accumulate a quantity of alternative ideas. Its value lies in limbering up the minds of the group; in getting directly at people's spontaneous ideas, which often lead to remarkable suggestions. A brainstorming session is never dull.

HOW THE TECHNIQUE OPERATES

At the beginning of a brainstorm session a recorder, or possibly two, if the class is large, is appointed to take down very carefully all the suggested ideas. The students understand in advance that they can offer any ideas on the problem under consideration that come into their minds—the wilder the better. Weighing an idea before it is presented is ruled out. Often impractical suggestions may "trigger" in other students practical ideas that might not otherwise occur to them. Criticism of the ideas offered is not permitted during the session, the main object being quantity and not quality. The greater the number of ideas, the greater the possibility that some really excellent ones will result. The screening and appraisal of the suggestions are best reserved for another meeting of the class. The intervening time gives the students a chance to mull over the ideas that have been offered and an opportunity to combine some and improve or eliminate others.

USEFULNESS OF BRAINSTORMING

It should be pointed out that brainstorming is not a substitute for analytical thinking, for it approaches a problem through imagination rather than through reasoning. However, there are occasions when the only way to get useful ideas is to exercise the imagination freely and without any restraint. Such occasions might include getting ideas for a school party or for entertaining the whole family at a picnic supper in the back yard.

CIRCULAR RESPONSE

As the name implies, members of a group sit around in a circle for a discussion. This technique is most effective with small groups of not more than fifteen and is suitable for mixed age groups. Circular arrangement encourages everyone in turn to participate and prevents a few people from monopolizing the discussion. In a mixed group of adults and young people, the latter feel closely associated with the group and less segregated because of their age; they tend to feel more at ease with the adults, and are encouraged to talk freely.

When the group is seated, the person selected as leader announces the topic to be discussed. The discussion begins with the individual on the leader's right. Then the person at his right has an opportunity to talk and this continues until the discussion has gone around the circle. No member of the group can speak a second time until his turn comes again. When the topic has been adequately covered, the leader summarizes the main points.

THE PANEL

A small group of people called "a panel" discuss a popular subject among themselves in the presence of a larger group. The chief aim of the technique is to stimulate cooperative thinking among the panel members and hence in the audience by offering various viewpoints for consideration. If the subject is well explored by panel members, many questions in the minds of the audience can be answered.

GENERAL PROCEDURES

The panel, consisting of five to nine people including the leader, is generally seated around a table in view of the audience. The leader introduces the topic and the panel members, explaining briefly the points of view each represents. Thus the audience is given an opportunity to orient their thinking to the topic. The panel members, exclusive of the leader, then carry on a discussion among themselves although the leader may enter into the discussion briefly from time to time. After the subject has been thoroughly explored so that its significance becomes clear, the audience is given an opportunity to direct questions to individual members of the panel. Before the meeting is terminated, the leader, or someone designated in advance, summarizes the pertinent remarks made by panel members and the audience.

SELECTION OF PANEL MEMBERS

The key to the successful use of panel discussion is the selection of panel members. They need to think quickly, to speak easily, to be fair-minded, and to be well informed on the subject to be discussed. On the basis of these general qualifications, there are several possible choices. The panel may consist of: (1) a group of experts; (2) persons known to represent different points of view in relation to the topic (they may be experts, but they do not need to be); (3) persons of different ages or occupations not necessarily representing any particular point of view; (4) members of the class who are well informed on various aspects of the topic.

PANEL LEADER

The importance of having a good leader should not be underestimated. In addition to having the same general qualifications as the other panel members, he needs to be resourceful, to be tactful but firm, and, if possible, to have a sense of humor. As the leader, he has the following responsibilities:

In addition to introducing the topic and the panel, he needs to know the name of each member so that he can address him by name.

He must keep the panel members talking on the topic under discussion and prevent them from rambling.

He should see that all members of the panel are actively participating in the discussion.

He needs to listen carefully to each member's point of view. Although he does not make any speeches, he helps to integrate the contributions made by panel members. At the same time, he avoids saying anything someone else might say.

He must see that the interest of the audience is sustained after panel members have brought out the main points of the topic. He can do so by asking the panel fast-moving questions that stimulate interest.

He must be prepared to lead the audience into a discussion or a question period following the panel discussion.

He needs to see that a summary of the pertinent remarks by panel members and the audience is given. This may be done by (1) making the summary himself, (2) leading the panel into giving the summary, (3) appointing in advance a recorder to make the summary, or (4) arranging for a group from the audience to make the summary. (The latter procedure is probably advisable when the leader is a student, since several persons will remember more points than the leader or an appointed recorder.)

PRELIMINARY PLANNING

In addition to the selection of a qualified panel, other advance planning is needed. The leader must know what he is expected to do. Other panel members need to have advance information on the topic and the line of thought each is expected to take. However, it is not recommended that they write down and later read what they are to say. A free and easy presentation, with brief notes if needed, is advisable, since informality tends to put the audience into a receptive mood. It is also desirable for the leader to formulate key questions that he may ask during the discussion. These questions should be agreed upon by the panel ahead of time so that they can think through the answers carefully. They will then be able to reply quickly and easily.

It is also advisable to plan the seating arrangements for the panel and to see that a supply of pencils and small writing pads is available. Any seating arrangement is satisfactory if everyone in the room can see and hear the panel. In a small room where the audience is limited to twenty-five or thirty people, the panel can be seated in front of the audience around three sides of a table with the leader in the center position. In a large room microphones would be needed if this arrangement were used. However, if there is ample room and microphones are not available, the panel may be seated in a V shape with the leader at the point of the V. In this position the panel can see each other and the audience can easily see and hear the panel. Individual tables or two longer tables on each side of the V with a small table for the leader should be supplied for their convenience. If the panel members do not know each other or are not known to the audience, a card with the person's name printed in large letters can be placed on the edge of the tables in front of each person.

THE FORUM

The forum discussion is also a speaker-audience technique. Two or more speakers offer differing points of view on a vital issue. Considerable time is allowed for the audience to ask questions or to express opinions. Listening to well-informed people present several sides of a controversial topic is a stimulating and challenging experience. In addition the opportunity for the listeners to express their views and to feel that personal ideas and opinions also have recognized importance makes the technique even more valuable.

Forums and panel discussions are much the same in that the speakers and the leader are carefully selected and know in advance what they are going to say and do. The chief difference lies in the way the meetings are carried out. The atmosphere of the forum is more formal than that of the panel discussion. Each speaker sits and stands in front of the audience, presenting his side of the topic for their consideration. There is no debating or questioning among the speakers themselves as in a panel discussion. Instead the time is given over to the audience to direct questions to the different speakers and to express personal opinions about the issue. This feature is an important part of the forum technique.

THE SYMPOSIUM

Like the panel and the forum, the symposium discussion is a speaker-audience technique.

However, the symposium has more of the nature of a conference. A topic of current interest is discussed by experts, each presenting his specialized field as it contributes to the main topic under consideration. The chief value of this technique is that it can be used to provide a background of general understanding on a subject that can best be discussed by well-informed experts.

The symposium is conducted in much the same way as are panel and forum discussions. Three to five speakers, selected on the basis of their specialized knowledge of the topic to be discussed, sit at a table facing the audience. Each speaker stands when making his speech and is given a specified period of time to present his point of view without interruption. The leader sees that each speaker keeps within the time allotment. After all the speakers have made their contributions, they discuss among themselves various aspects of the topic. There follows a question period for the audience, but it is not regarded as an important part of the meeting.

THE COLLOQUY

The colloquy discussion is another speaker-audience technique similar in nature to the panel. However, instead of one panel group there are two: one consisting of resource persons, the other selected from the audience. This procedure permits direct audience representation on an equal footing with the experts, thus giving the general audience an intimate feeling of association with the resource group. It also motivates the experts to consider more closely the needs of the audience and in turn stimulates the latter to listen more carefully and to participate more freely.

The basic set-up of the colloquy is similar to that of panel and forum discussions with a moderator performing the same functions. Each panel group consists of three to four members who remain seated in front of the class during the meeting. Resource persons are selected for their particular knowledge and interest in the subject to be discussed. Audience members are chosen on the basis of their interest in the problem and their ability to ask appropriate questions and to make intelligent comments. Advance preparation on their part is necessary to assure efficiency in performance and the judicious use of time. The audience representatives present the problem and ask questions of the resource members. These experts serve as consultants who contribute their opinions on various aspects of the subject, but refrain from speech making. Under the guidance of the moderator the general audience is encouraged to participate whenever they desire.

QUESTIONS AND ANSWERS

The question-and-answer technique involves asking and answering questions in a discussion setting. It can be carried out by the class itself or in conjunction with resource persons. This technique has several values: (1) questions encourage individual thinking and stimulate eagerness to know the answers; (2) questions and answers are particularly useful in situations needing clarification; (3) formulating questions helps students develop ability to pinpoint important information that is needed, and answers provide this information in concise form that can be easily assimilated.

HOW THE TECHNIQUE OPERATES

There are four ways in which the technique is generally carried out:

1.   The class sets up a list of questions to be answered by individual students or by groups of students.

2.   The class sets up a list of questions to be answered by a resource person—someone who has special information or experience with the material being considered.

3.   A leader—the teacher, an experienced student, or a resource person—introduces questions prepared in advance and calls upon the class for answers. Or the leader draws questions from the group and then turns the questions back to the class for answers.

4.   A leader introduces questions which he answers himself or calls upon some resource person to answer.

THE OPPOSING PANEL

Use of "the opposing panel" technique may be illustrated as follows: One-half of a group is known as "question raisers" and the other half as "question answerers." An important topic is selected, usually one that has already been discussed but about which there are still questions or misconceptions. The general aim is to avoid discussing well-known information but instead to discuss new ideas. This stimulates a deeper interest in the topic and develops clear thinking about it.

After a leader has been selected and the group divided into two sections, each half is divided into small groups of four to six persons. The groups who are "question raisers" think up an agreed number of good questions. At the same time the "question answerers" try to anticipate what questions might come up and how they can be answered. Fifteen to twenty minutes are allowed for preparation. One subgroup of "question raisers" then asks their questions. If they are not satisfied with the responses of the "question answerers," they can offer their own solutions. If this occurs, increased interest in the answers results and the solutions become more nearly complete. When one subgroup has given their questions, another group repeats the procedure, which continues as long as time permits. In concluding, the leader makes a summary of the high points of the discussion.

DEMONSTRATION

In home-economics education the demonstration technique generally involves the presentation of procedures or processes to be learned. Educators have long realized the value of this technique. Showing how something is done often leads to more effective learning than using written or verbal instructions that are sometimes vague and often subject to misinterpretation. In addition to providing concise information, demonstration is a means of exemplifying high standards for the process being presented. It also has value to persons who do the demonstrating. They not only develop poise and the ability to talk and act at the same time, but also learn the importance of organization and timing, which are essential aspects of the technique.

INITIATING A DEMONSTRATION

There is considerable variation in demonstrations. They may be given by the teacher, by students, or by resource persons. Or there may be combinations—students assisting the teacher, the teacher or the students assisting the resource person. Some demonstrations are fairly short, requiring a minimum of equipment or materials, and are often given to small groups. Others are longer, involving various kinds of equipment or materials, and are presented to large groups.

Regardless of the type of demonstration, only one process should be shown at a time.

Even when variations of a process are possible, it is not advisable to introduce them until after the fundamental procedure is thoroughly understood and practiced. For example, in demonstrating bedmaking, students need first of all to know how to make an ordinary bed and to practice this procedure before they learn about making a bed with a patient in it. To see these two procedures demonstrated at the same time would lead to confusion in the minds of the students when they try to remember the correct details that accompany each procedure.

PRELIMINARY PREPARATION

Whether a demonstration is given to a small or large group, preliminary preparation is important. The equipment or materials should be assembled and conveniently arranged in full view of the audience before the demonstration begins. Whatever is needed should be similar in kind and size to what the students will be using after they learn the process. For example, in demonstrating bedmaking, a normal-sized bed should be used and not a miniature copy. Or if cooking utensils are required, they need to be the same size and kind as those used in the foods laboratory.

Since a small-group demonstration generally involves a process that needs to be closely observed, the position of the demonstrator is important. She should plan to stand so that her right and left movements will be in the same relative position as those of the group. This makes it easier for students to learn the correct movements they will normally use in carrying out the process. Chairs for a small group can be arranged informally around the demonstrator.

Lighting for both small- and large-group demonstrations needs to be carefully planned. Strong or glaring lights should be avoided, *teach them how to look*

since they tire the eyes and cause the attention to wander. Adequate lighting is soft, yet of sufficient strength for everyone in the group to see what is going on.

Advance preparation of copies of directions for the process being demonstrated is highly desirable, especially when step-by-step procedures are involved. Each student should have one of these instruction sheets to serve as a source of reference during the demonstration. It can also be used later to check individual performance.

CONDUCTING A DEMONSTRATION

Students who will be needed to assist in the demonstration should be seated near the place of presentation to save time and avoid unnecessary moving around. If a resource person is giving the demonstration and calls for volunteers, students sitting near the front of the room should respond.

In a long step-by-step demonstration, it is generally understood beforehand that questions and discussion are to be reserved until after the presentation. Interruptions are usually disturbing to both the demonstrator and those watching. However, if the demonstration is given informally to a small group of students, the demonstrator may not object to a few questions, provided the interruption does not confuse the students or distract their attention.

During the demonstration, the undivided attention of the audience is necessary and important if the technique is to be effective. The demonstrator can get this attention at the beginning by giving an overall idea of what is to be done—perhaps in the form of a brief, stimulating explanation or a colorful picture or model of the finished product. From then on, if

the demonstration is well conducted, interest and attention will be maintained.

After the demonstration, an opportunity should be given for questions or discussion to clarify any points that may not be clear. However, learning is strengthened if students can practice the process as soon as possible under supervision. In general, the longer the practice is delayed, the more it will be needed. (See pages 118–120 on psychomotor skills.)

OBSERVATION

Directed observation, when carefully planned and carried out, can be beneficial as a learning technique. Through observation, students develop the ability to see things as they really are, not as they often seem to be. They learn to notice important details that might otherwise be overlooked. In short, observation helps students not only to see but to perceive.

Directed observation is generally carried out in two ways: (1) by large groups and (2) by individuals or small groups. Large-group observation helps students to develop an objective approach and makes it easier for them to participate more efficiently in individual or small-group observations. Large groups can make careful observations during demonstrations, on field trips, and while watching movies, filmstrips, or pictures. (Information on these resources is described on pages 165–167 and 186–188.)

Individual observation as a learning technique offers a broader experience than large-group observation. But more skill, greater independence, and considerable responsibility are required on the part of the students.

Small-group or individual observation may be directed either toward specific situations and conditions, with the aim to acquire a more comprehensive knowledge about them, or toward behavior, in an effort to develop a better understanding of different behavior patterns.

LEARNING GENERAL
OBSERVATIONAL PROCEDURES

The success of the observational technique when used with individuals or small groups depends markedly upon following certain procedures. These procedures need to be learned and understood before observation of an activity begins.

1. Observation needs to be systematic. Casual observation has little value. Students should have some preliminary knowledge, through classwork and references, of the situation they are going to observe. Specific activities within this situation can then be selected for observation. A prepared check sheet listing these activities, with space for writing pertinent information, will facilitate the recording and evaluation of the observations. (Information concerning check lists can be found on pages 176 and 201–207.)

2. Repeated observation should be made of the same activities by several students. Practically nothing of value is learned from a single experience of one student, and very little from scattered observation. A few students should observe the same activities several times to see how much agreement there is on the results of their observations. Unless there is some consensus, the observations are not being adequately carried out.

3. The observations need to be recorded immediately and accurately. An observation becomes increasingly vague as time elapses and thus decreases in value. The use of a check or observation sheet is therefore important, since recordings can easily and quickly be made during or soon after the observation.

POINTERS FOR STUDENT OBSERVATION OF
YOUNG CHILDREN AT SCHOOL

In many home-economics programs, individual or small-group observation is often directed toward the behavior of young children in a school setting. To minimize the inconvenience of the students' presence, it is particularly important for them to understand and carry out the following suggestions:

1. Be as unobtrusive as possible. If children realize that they are the center of attention, they tend to behave somewhat differently than they would otherwise. Moving around unnecessarily or grouping together with other observers should be avoided. However, an observer should feel free to walk around occasionally to follow a child's activity that cannot be watched from a distance.

2. Avoid talking. Observers' conversation with one another will disturb the children. However, if a child asks a question, the observer can answer it pleasantly and briefly.

3. Do not question the teacher or her assistants. No one engaged in supervising young children likes to be interrupted. An important question can be jotted down and asked after the school session is over or at another convenient time.

4. Maintain a casual, detached attitude. Any display of emotion showing amusement or concern over anything a child may do or say should be strictly avoided. Children are not in school for the amusement of adults, nor are they helped by a display of emotion from an adult when something unexpected happens.

5. Do not use doorways as observation

points. Standing in a doorway prevents the children from moving freely from one room to another.

6.   Wear comfortable shoes. Since observation requires a minimum of walking around, students will often have to remain standing in one spot for a considerable length of time. Uncomfortable shoes cause fatigue and distract a student's attention from his task.

ROLE PLAYING AND RELATED TECHNIQUES

An interesting and valuable learning technique that is being increasingly used in the classroom is role playing, or sociodrama, as it is sometimes called. This technique is the spontaneous enactment or dramatization of a situation in which students impersonate people of various ages and occupations. The action comes from the student's creative use of his own feelings and imagination.

VALUES OF ROLE PLAYING

By trying to speak, feel, and act like others, students develop a better understanding of how people act in real-life situations. Role playing also offers an excellent means of bringing out into the open emotional problems. Being free to impersonate someone else affords a student an opportunity to express and release his thoughts and emotions without feeling self-conscious and without making the problem appear to be his. Eventually these impersonations may help students to find more adequate patterns of behavior. Where it is unwise for the teacher to give specific answers to common family problems or to express opinions about them, the role playing technique may be advantageously applied. Through role playing

these problems can be acted out as they might be in real life, showing ways in which they can be satisfactorily met. In addition to this, undesirable and desirable social behavior can be dramatized without making the situations appear too instructive.

STEPS IN ROLE PLAYING

Since it is an informal procedure, role playing differs from the usual type of drama in that no script, no memorizing of lines, and no rehearsals are needed. In fact, its chief characteristic is spontaneity of presentation.

However, the technique involves more than the simple acting out of the roles. It is made up of a series of steps of which acting is only one. Once these steps are understood, they usually flow into one another quite naturally and easily.

Step 1: Selecting the situation.   The situation chosen for role playing needs to be a simple one directly related to the current classwork. Until students have had experience in using the technique, it is advisable to select a situation requiring two or three characters. Too many participants at first are apt to cause confusion and to retard the important spontaneity in action. A brief description of the roles to be played should be given so that the class will have the parts clearly in mind and will understand the significance of the interaction to occur.

Step 2: Choosing participants. Participants may be suggested by the teacher and the students or the students themselves may volunteer for particular roles. At first, however, the teacher will need to guide the selection rather carefully to avoid having a student take a role that will make him feel self-conscious or uncomfortable. Students with dramatic training are not necessarily the best participants when spontaneous acting is required. Role playing draws upon the individual's inner resources of imagination and feelings. Students who have imagination and self-assurance will be the most successful in showing others how to put the technique across. However, every student in the class should have an opportunity to build up experience in role playing.

Step 3: Setting the stage. After the participants have been chosen, they should be given a few minutes in some quiet place. They will want to discuss among themselves the roles they are to play in order to get the feel of the situation and the personalities. They may also decide staging details, such as how the scene should look, what furniture to use, and when entrances and exits are to be made. Sometimes a committee may be quickly selected to arrange these details. The observers should be encouraged by the teacher not to be merely passive spectators, but to watch the action as though they too were acting.

Step 4: Acting out the situation. The participants should be permitted to follow their own course of action, since a feeling of freedom contributes markedly toward creating a realistic atmosphere. However, if a student appears to be misinterpreting his role, the teacher can remind him of what he is supposed to do. And if the action continues beyond a point where the participants seem to be only marking time, then the presentation can be terminated. The teacher will need to sense such possibilities and act accordingly. However, as students acquire experience in role playing, such instances will seldom occur.

Step 5: Evaluating the presentation. As soon as the presentation is finished, students should be given an opportunity to discuss what has taken place. The observers will probably be eager to offer their comments on how fully the situation was covered, what could be added to

make it more meaningful, or how realistically the roles were played. The teacher should be on guard to forestall too much adverse criticism unless constructive suggestions are offered at the same time. The observers will need to realize that a perfect performance cannot be expected in a role-playing situation. The performers, too, should be given a chance to express their reactions to the way they felt in acting out their roles. They also may be aware of improvements that might lead to a more comprehensive enactment of their roles. In fact, so many constructive ideas may be presented that the class will decide to re-enact the situation with the same participants or with new ones. If it seems desirable to use a new group, the teacher should make it clear that the change does not reflect a poor performance on the part of the former participants. She can bring out the point that it is important for all students to get as much practice as possible in role playing. The class, of course, may decide that before re-enacting a situation more knowledge is required of the situation itself or of the personalities involved. A willingness to repeat and improve a performance should be very gratifying to the teacher, for it would seem to be an important indication of the effectiveness of the technique.

PANTOMIME

The pantomime technique is a variation of role playing, but differing from it in that the characters do not talk. Gestures, facial expressions, and vivid action replace words in the portrayal of situations and character roles. Although these conditions do not minimize its value as a technique, they do limit the extent to which it can be used. However, learning to express one's feelings and actions without words can be a challenging experience in classroom learning.

The considerations for operating this technique are much the same as those previously described for role playing. There are, however, two possible types of performance that may be given. The first type involves the selection of situations, such as those appropriate for demonstrating "do's" and "don'ts." This kind of performance needs to be rather brief, to have only two or three characters, and to be dynamic in action. Without these qualifications the situations being portrayed may not be clearly understood and may even become boring to the observers. The second type of performance can be longer and can have more characters, but it calls for an unobserved announcer who briefly describes the action of the performers as it is being carried out. This type can include many of the same kinds of situations previously described in the values of role playing.

SKIT-SCRIPT TECHNIQUE

Another variation of role playing is the skit-script technique that involves the presentation of a skit or short play in which the action is guided by a prepared script. This technique can have considerable value in stimulating learning when certain conditions prevail. The scripts need to be written by the students or carefully selected by the students and the teacher from commercial sources. In either case, they should be related to the current classwork. Also, the roles must represent the inner feelings of the students portraying them.

NATURE OF SCRIPTS

Writing a script requires only a minimum of technical skill. With a little experience any interested student who uses imagination and ingenuity can develop it. Although in most cases the actual writing of a script is an individual experience, deciding on its general content and the way it will be used are matters for the class to determine.

Several types of scripts are popular in home-economics programs. One kind may be designed for a mock-radio or mock-television broadcast. Sometimes roles for resource people may be included in the script. If the content of a script has a universal appeal to other students, the broadcast can be used at a school-assembly program, or in connection with a Future Homemakers of America meeting. Some scripts may be of interest to the Parent-Teachers Association. In fact, some scripts may prove to be so interesting and stimulating that they will warrant tape recording. In such cases a local radio station may be willing to use some of the best ones.

Another type of script is the double script, often referred to as "before-and-after" or "do-and-don't" scripts. As the name implies, two situations are set up with the wording of each carefully prepared to portray contrasting situations.

Both types of scripts will need to be checked by the teacher for accuracy of facts and soundness of home-economics policies.

PROCEDURES FOR SKITS

The same procedures that were described for role playing are used in presenting a skit. The chief difference is that the students will need time to become familiar with the script. Brief rehearsals may even be advisable. Unlike role playing, the content of a script has been carefully prepared to convey definite ideas and impressions. Memorizing the lines or having only brief notes usually results in a smoother, more realistic performance. But if lines are not memorized, the performers will need to become so familiar with them that they can read easily and naturally. At the same time the action of the performers should be coordinated with the lines. However, regardless of whether the lines are memorized or read, each performer should interpret his role in the light of his inner feelings. Otherwise, the performance may seem stilted and unnatural.

EXHIBITION

Techniques of exhibition, such as setting up exhibits, arranging bulletin boards, and making posters, have long been a part of many home-economics programs. All these ways have considerable value. Active participation in the operation of the exhibition technique develops creative and artistic ability, encourages responsibility, and improves the use of management procedures. The results bring great personal satisfaction to the students carrying out the technique, and this helps to sustain their interest in the classwork. Thus, the technique may also be a means of stimulating constructive action.

BASIC CONSIDERATIONS

To develop effective learning, the considerations for setting up exhibits, arranging bulletin boards, or making posters are much the same:

1. The content needs to be directly related to the home-economics program. This consideration, of course, is essential when any of the three activities is being used for class purposes. But it also applies to exhibits and posters to be viewed by other students in school or by people in the community. These are ways to arouse interest in and acquaint people with the work of the department.

2. One outstanding idea or impression should predominate. The influence of an exhibit, a bulletin-board arrangement, or a poster is lessened if more than one idea is emphasized.

For example, if an exhibit centers on play equipment for young children, it is advisable to arrange the content into several small exhibits, each one set apart from the others and emphasizing a particular type of equipment. One exhibit could show the types of toys that can be made at home, another the kinds that are safe, and still another the types especially suited to different age levels. The viewer would thus have an opportunity to concentrate on a particular type of toy that is of special interest to him. If all the play equipment were assembled together in one exhibit, the viewer would get only a general impression of toys. That would soon fade.

Similarly, a bulletin-board arrangement or a poster whose content is not focused on a single idea has a cluttered and diffused appearance. There is nothing to catch the eye and hold the attention. The viewer takes a passing glance and that is all. It does not seem worth the effort to find out what the content represents.

3. Special knowledge is needed to plan the content effectively. It is important to know how to make discriminating selections between the materials or objects that are important and those that can be eliminated; how much space and lighting will be required to display advantageously the material or objects selected; what colors and combinations go well together; how proportion, balance, emphasis, and rhythm are involved in making an attractive and pleasing arrangement.

4. The content needs to be neatly labeled and to show clearly what is being presented. As viewers study the content, they like to know what the various materials or objects represent

so that the message is complete and interesting.

STUDENT PARTICIPATION

The number of students actively participating in setting up an exhibit, arranging a bulletin board, or making a poster will necessarily vary. However, the more students involved, the greater the value of the exhibition technique. Active participation in carrying out the procedures is superior to merely viewing the presentation after it is completed.

SETTING UP AN EXHIBIT

Setting up a large exhibit, which generally includes a number of small exhibits, offers considerable opportunity for student participation. In fact, it is usually possible for the whole class, with the guidance of the teacher, to assume responsibility for the entire exhibit. As a group the class can decide on the general content of the exhibit, when and where it will be held, for whom it will be presented, and how the responsibilities will be distributed. Small groups can then carry out the details. These may include assembling the materials or objects to be used and later returning them to their proper places, taking care of any needed promotional work, issuing any special invitations that may be desirable, and acting as hosts and hostesses if they are needed.

On the other hand, small single exhibits, which are generally held more frequently than large ones, do not require the active participation of all the students at one time. The class as a group may decide on the content and then delegate the responsibilities to a few students. Or some students working as a committee may decide on the content and carry out all the procedures themselves. If small exhibits are held frequently enough for everyone in the class to have experience in planning and carrying them out, then the small exhibit can be as beneficial as the large one.

ARRANGING A BULLETIN BOARD OR MAKING A POSTER

Arranging a bulletin board or making a poster seldom involves the active participation of the entire class at one time. These activities are similar to making small exhibits; hence, their content may or may not be decided on by the class and the procedures delegated to a few students. More frequently, students working as a committee for arranging a bulletin board will decide on the content and carry out the procedures. Although a committee may decide on the content of a poster or a series of posters, the actual work is usually done by one or two students. The involvement of fewer students does not necessarily decrease the value of learning to arrange a bulletin board or to make a poster, provided every student in the class is given an opportunity at one time or another to plan and carry out the different procedures involved.

INTERVIEWING

Interviewing is a technique frequently used in home-economics programs as a way for students to obtain helpful information related to the current classwork. When interviews are with people of widely differing ages and occupations, interviewing can also help students to develop poise and self-assurance in meeting people.

OBTAINING INFORMATION

Interviews are generally used to find out how people think and feel regarding a particular situation, or how and why they follow certain procedures. For example, students may hold interviews with mothers of young children to find out what they expect of a baby sitter. Or they may interview older students to get their opinions on dating etiquette. Interviews may be held with various homemakers to learn about their weekly, monthly, and seasonal cleaning procedures. Or grandparents living with their sons or daughters can be interviewed to find out how they get along with younger members of the family. The information received can be referred to the class for discussion and then used in the classwork wherever it is needed.

CONSIDERATIONS FOR
HOLDING AN INTERVIEW

Students need to understand that certain considerations are important if interviewing is to produce good results. These considerations are essential for interviews outside the students' homes, but they should not be ignored within the family circle. Consideration is just as important for the members of one's own family as for those of other families. The following points need to be taken into account whenever the interview technique is used:

1. Interviews are best conducted singly, in pairs, or by three students at the most. Too many people are apt to confuse the person being interviewed.

2. Advance arrangements contribute to the success of an interview. The interview is less hurried when time is set aside for it. A brief explanation of the nature of the interview gives the person an opportunity to think about the subject to be discussed.

3. Interviews run more smoothly and efficiently when students prepare their line of questioning ahead of time. Having in mind two or three informal questions will tend to keep the interview focused on the subject under discussion. Or the student may take along a series of questions requiring short answers to be recorded by the student during the interview.

4. A neat appearance is important. Careless dress and a sloppy appearance create a bad impression and thus the interview may start off unfavorably.

5. A pleasant, friendly greeting helps to establish rapport. If the student is not well known to the person being interviewed (even though advance arrangements have been made), he should give his name and state briefly the reason for his visit to start the interview amiably before the questioning period begins.

6. Attention and interest in what is being said are a mark of courtesy. The student should never argue, interrupt, or take exception to any remarks made.

7. An interview needs to be kept within a moderate time limit. Even though the student has not secured all the information he wants, the visit should end if the person being interviewed becomes inattentive or seems reluctant to carry on the conversation.

8. An expression of thanks and appreciation for the interview is a must. This is a courtesy that cannot be omitted.

9. An important part of an interview is the resultant summary. A summary should be made by the student as soon as possible after the interview. Impressions tend to fade and important points are often forgotten if too much time is allowed to elapse. The essential points listed can then be reported to the class for general use.

VISITING

The technique of visiting, as used in home-economics programs, involves trips to various places in the community to obtain information directly by seeing things as they really are. Such visits, generally referred to as field trips, serve many useful purposes. Students are challenged by the new ideas and impressions they receive and are influenced by them long after they return to the classroom. Critical thinking is developed and horizons are broadened by seeing how people work in different activities. Classwork thus becomes more meaningful as it is related to real-life situations. Through these trips students also develop the personal traits of responsibility, cooperation, dependability, and courtesy.

SOURCES FOR FIELD TRIPS

Sometimes long trips that require extensive preparation are taken by the class as a whole. Sometimes short trips are made by smaller groups. The sources available for either long or short trips are much the same in any community. These often include the following:

Factories manufacturing household items, such as equipment, furniture, textiles, china, glassware, or foods

Markets handling fresh fruit and vegetables, meat, poultry or fish

Stores of all types including the department store with its various departments related to homemaking; and specialty shops carrying clothing and accessories, furniture, or native and foreign foods

Utility companies which demonstrate correct lighting, efficient kitchen planning, and home management in general

Radio and television studios when programs are being broadcast

Museums holding special exhibits, such as colonial furniture, unusual textiles, jewelry, or period costumes

Community agencies such as the Departments of Welfare and Health

Homes exemplifying some aspects of current classwork

PROCEDURES FOR LONG FIELD TRIPS

A long field trip in which the entire class participates generally involves the use of school time in addition to a single home-economics period. Because of the interference with other classwork, the approval of the school administration and the cooperation of other teachers are essential before any plans for a trip can be made. The teacher will also need to make satisfactory arrangements for her other classes. These conditions may impose a limit on the number of trips that can be taken during the year; hence, the trips need to be carefully planned and efficiently carried out if they are to have optimum value.

PRELIMINARY PLANNING

If field trips have the approval of the school administration, they can be tentatively planned when the teacher and the students are setting up the yearly program. Or they may be decided on when the class goals or the experiences leading to the goals are being considered. In any case, sufficient time should be allowed to make all the necessary arrangements well in advance. Three details need to be taken care of:

1. Contacting the place to be visited. Con-

tacts may be made by telephone, letter, or a preliminary visit by the teacher and a small committee of students. It is important to find out the time of arrival, the length of the visit, the number of students who can be accommodated, what is to be seen, and what information is to be given.

2. Making the trip more meaningful. There are several ways in which students may prepare themselves for a field trip. A special list of readings can be posted on the bulletin board. The use of resource materials such as a film, a series of slides, or pictures can stimulate interest in the subject and at the same time provide valuable information. A committee of students can interview people connected with the trip and report their findings to the class. A few key questions to be asked during the visit can be agreed upon by the class.

3. Arranging incidentals. If the trip is to run smoothly and efficiently, the following details need to be worked out by the teacher and the students, and the information made available in printed form to everyone taking the trip:

The expense involved and what it includes— transportation, meals, and other incidentals

The trip's schedule—time and place of departure and approximate time of return

Appropriate attire to be worn—with stress on comfortable shoes

Persons who need to be informed about the trip—school officials, parents, or others concerned with the trip

Acceptable conduct during the visit—when questioning is in order, when notes can be taken, and other matters relating to courtesy to the host or hostess

AFTER THE TRIP

A class discussion should be held shortly after the trip. The high points can be brought out and summarized with indications of how the trip has contributed toward the current classwork. An evaluation of the way the trip was carried out and constructive suggestions for improving subsequent trips will also be profitable. The teacher and the students should arrange to express thanks and appreciation to the person or persons who made the trip possible.

CONSIDERATIONS FOR SHORT TRIPS

Short trips are usually made by small groups of students during or after the regular home-economics period and are planned with one of several purposes in mind. Students may want to get ideas and firsthand knowledge of a particular phase of current classwork. Or they may desire to see how some of the new learning they have acquired in class is applied to real-life situations.

Examples of students wanting additional information might include a group especially interested in learning more about modern furniture. Visits could be made to stores featuring such furniture or to homes where this kind of furniture is used. Or a committee may want information and suggestions for general class use on planning a young child's bedroom or playroom. Seeing homes where plans for these rooms have been successfully carried out may give the group new and interesting ideas.

Examples of students wanting to see how learnings can be applied might include groups from a class that has learned about arranging utensils, chinaware, and supplies in the school kitchen. Now they want to see how kitchens in some of the community homes are arranged. A class has learned ways of meeting living-area problems, such as making a room appear larger or smaller than it is, or making a dark room seem sunny. Students who each have a particular problem of this nature in their own homes want to see how other homes with the same problem have met the situation.

Although arrangements for these visits are not as extensive as those for a long trip, advance plans and certain considerations need to be taken into account:

1. Contacting the place to be visited. A contact is usually more effective when a preliminary visit is made by one or two students. An explanation regarding the purpose of the visit, what the group would like to see, the size of the group, and the approximate length of time available to the group should be given. The date and time of day can then be agreed upon.

2. Preparing for the trip. Actually not much preparation is needed for short visits. However, students in a particular group making the trip for a specific purpose may want to agree on key questions ahead of time. Otherwise, the main points to keep in mind are the date, the place or places to be visited including the expected time of arrival, and when and where the group will meet before the visiting begins.

3. Social courtesies. Students who visit in small groups need to be especially courteous and thoughtful to the host or hostess. Little courtesies, like being careful not to track dirt into a home, pick up and examine objects without first asking permission, or converse loudly with other members of the group, should be observed. Although a few key questions may be asked, a constant barrage of questioning is distracting to both the host or hostess and those in the group. Each student, of course, needs to express thanks and appreciation upon leaving.

4. After the visit. Each visiting group should get together as soon as possible after the visit to discuss what has been seen. A summary of the important points can be prepared and reported to the class. If the group has a chairman, as most groups do, he should be responsible for writing a note of thanks to the persons who made the visits possible.

RECORDING ANECDOTES

Recording anecdotes is a technique often used in home-economics programs. Students keep a written account, similar to a diary, of incidents that have occurred in connection with a specific aspect of the classwork. When efficiently used, this technique has considerable value. By keeping records, students learn to express themselves objectively and accurately, and in so doing acquire insight into their own behavior.

CHARACTERISTICS OF GOOD RECORDING

Good recording has a few simple but important characteristics:

It needs to be done individually—not in groups.

It should deal with a single situation over a specified period of time.

It must relate briefly and clearly to what happened and to what the student did concerning the situation.

It should not include at the time of recording any personal appraisal or interpretation by the student of the incidents described.

It needs to be written while the events are still vivid in the student's mind.

PROCEDURES

The class as a group or individual students can decide on the particular situation that is to serve as the basis for the anecdotes. At the same time, it is advisable to set up a general guide to follow in order to make it easier for students to record and later analyze the material.

Analyzing the records may be difficult until students have had experience in using the technique. The teacher will therefore need to take several examples and show the students how to appraise each record. She can point out records that show adequate or inadequate knowledge of the prescribed situation and whether attempts were made to increase this knowledge. She can indicate records that reveal desirable or undesirable behavior on the part of the recorder, and can point to instances that show evidence or no evidence of learning. If learning seems inadequate or behavior needs modification, the teacher can offer suggestions for improvement. In some cases it may be desirable for students to continue, especially if they can be encouraged to feel that further records and another analysis will be helpful.

After the class understands how to make an analysis, small groups can work together appraising each other's records. Eventually students may learn to make their own appraisals. However, there are occasions when the teacher and a student may need to work together on the analysis. Such cases are generally those that involve personal problems.

The example described is an arbitrary one set up for a specific situation. Because of space requirements, many of the details that would ordinarily be recorded by students are omitted. For this same reason the appraisals selected represent a random sampling and do not follow any particular sequence. It is hoped, however, that the material will indicate how the technique can operate effectively.

Situation: Buying wearing apparel

Period: Three weeks

Directions: Record the name and date of each purchase, and comment briefly when each purchase is made on the four questions listed below. Then make comments on the results of the purchases.

1. What do I know about the article I plan to buy?

2. What is the maximum amount I should spend? Did I go over or under that amount?

3. What information, if any, did I try to obtain from the salesclerk?

4. Was I satisfied with what was available? If not, what did I do?

ANALYSIS	COMMENTS BY PURCHASER
Considerable	Question 1: Pantyhose is sized according to height and weight; comes in a variety of stretch yarns and in jersey or mesh knits; long-wearing hosiery is reinforced at places where there is strain (heel, toe, panty), but for reasons of appearance reinforcements may not be wanted (as with sandals).
Moderate amount	Shoes need to be about half an inch longer than the end of the big toe; good-quality leather feels firm but not stiff.
Not much	A sports jacket should fit comfortably.

Satisfactory behavior	*Question 2:* I spent a few cents over what I had planned.
Unsatisfactory	Went way over the amount. Had to borrow some money from Jack to pay the difference. Will ask my father for an advance on my allowance.
Fairly satisfactory	I had to pay two dollars more to get the color I wanted.
May be satisfactory	I spent less than I planned but I think I got good value.
Considerable	*Question 3:* I asked the clerk what denier meant. We also discussed the merits of the various yarns and of mesh and jersey knits.
A little	The clerk told me the inside of the heel should fit snug so that the heel does not slip as you walk.
Did not ask for any	I can tell by looking at it whether I like it or not.
Satisfactory behavior	*Question 4:* Yes, I found just what I wanted at the first store.
	No, I tried several stores before I got what I wanted.
Unsatisfactory	No, I could not find what I wanted at the first store and did not want to bother to look around. Will ask mother to buy it for me next time she goes shopping.
Fairly satisfactory	No, I spent several hours looking around but could not find anything that was exactly what I wanted.
Evidence of learning	*Results of Purchase:* The pantyhose fits fine but is too sheer for everyday wear. But if I handle it carefully and keep it for special occasions, it may last me quite a while.
	I got more for my money, but the quality was not as good.
	The shoes are too narrow. I should have gotten a size wider. Maybe I can have them stretched a little.
Evidence of no learning	I think it was a good buy because it was cheap and the salesman told me it was a great bargain.
	The dress looks good on me but I do not know

	how it will wear. I forgot to ask whether it should be washed or dry cleaned.
	The jacket is a "knock-out." Everyone raves about it.
Learning doubtful	I have had a lot of compliments about the color of my coat, but I am not sure how well it will fit into my wardrobe.
	My woolen skirt looks and fits fine. I hope it does not shrink when it is cleaned.
	My wash-and-wear shirt is marvelous. All my friends are getting them.

COMMITTEES

Using committees within a class group is a technique that has been found to have many values. Students learn how to work cooperatively and to think for themselves more easily in a small group than in a large one. Although freedom of expression is encouraged throughout a cooperative program, there is a greater possibility for its development in a small group, possibly because the feeling of belonging and intimacy motivates students to put forth their best efforts. Committees also provide a greater opportunity for developing leadership and responsibility, because such jobs as chairman or recorder can be passed around more frequently than in a class group. Committees also make it possible to explore a particular problem more extensively and to solve it more quickly. Different committees can work on various aspects and pool their findings and ideas for general class use.

ORGANIZING COMMITTEES

The importance of flexibility in organizing committees cannot be overemphasized. The needs and interests of students can best be met by providing opportunities for them to serve in a variety of groups whose membership is based on various considerations. Some of these are:

1. Special interests. When the class is working on a general problem, committees may be based on the interests of individual students in a particular aspect of the problem, provided that no one group becomes too large to benefit from small-group participation. Sometimes, however, the teacher cannot be quite sure whether some students have a genuine interest in a specific aspect of the problem or an interest in certain committee members. The matter may not be too serious unless the students continue to maneuver membership in every group where these others are.

Sometimes several students who go around together outside of school want to form committees. Students who have the same social interests often adjust more quickly to small-group procedures and work more efficiently than mixed social groups. However, this basis for committee organization needs to be carefully considered, since students not identified with any social group may feel discriminated against.

2. Social needs. Another basis for organizing committees may be individual needs. Students

may want to select a group working on a subject or activity which they know the least about in order to increase their knowledge for some special reason.

3.   Level of proficiency. Sometimes it is desirable to form committees with a level of proficiency as the basis for membership. Students who already have considerable knowledge of a subject may want to group together to increase their knowledge or to work on a related subject. Other groups can be organized on the basis of extent of achievement in relation to expected achievement. This arrangement is also satisfactory when the development of a particular skill is involved. A committee of students who have attained a high level of proficiency and do not need further practice can supervise the practice of individual students or groups of students.

4.   Specific skills. There are also occasions when the class will want to form small groups to learn and practice specific skills which may be needed in working out individual problems common to a group.

5.   Talents and special abilities. A combination of talents and special abilities may draw a committee together; for example, when a class is planning a social affair in which dramatic or musical talents and leadership and management abilities are needed.

6.   Miscellaneous procedures. Drawing numbers, counting off by odd and even numbers, or matching cut-outs are also used as a basis for committee organization. Occasionally when time is limited and the activity is a simple one, students sitting near one another may be considered a group.

OPERATION OF A COMMITTEE

Before committee work begins, each group should know definitely what it is expected to do and in general what the other groups are going to do, in order to prevent overlapping and save time and effort. Each group also needs to know the length of time it has for completing its work, and when a final report is to be made to the class. When committee work is to be carried on in the classroom, the teacher and the students can decide where the different groups will sit. Adequate source materials should also be made available.

Each committee needs a chairman and usually a recorder. These people may be selected by the group, but no two persons should serve in these capacities from one committee to another. Everyone in the class should get as much experience as possible in these jobs.

ROLE OF THE CHAIRMAN

The duties of a chairman should be defined by the teacher and the students when committees are first considered as a part of the regular classwork. Otherwise, there may be conflict among groups about a chairman's responsibilities.

In cooperative procedures the role of the chairman is that of a leader who guides the group in determining individual tasks and in making policy decisions. If the work of the committee is to be done outside the classroom, such decisions may include when and where committee meetings will be held and in what form the final report will be given. The chairman will then be responsible for seeing that these meetings are held and conducted efficiently. Although members can work independently, the chairman will need to see that all the work is coordinated. If advice is needed, he should be willing to give it to the best of his ability. In case of disagreements among members, he should avoid taking sides but let the group work out the solution.

ROLE OF THE RECORDER

Like the chairmanship, the role of the recorder also needs to be defined in advance by the teacher and the students. In general, his duties may include keeping track of the decisions made by the committee, summarizing all its findings, and presenting the final report to the class, unless some other arrangements have been made for the presentation.

USEFUL OCCUPATIONS FOR GROUPS WHO HAVE GIVEN A FINAL REPORT

The problem of finding useful occupations for groups who have already given a final report may be met in various ways. They may continue to do further work on the experience itself. Or one group, or possibly two, can work together to make a summary of important facts which the other groups are presenting. Or one or more groups could observe and evaluate the work of the other groups with the idea of improving group techniques. However, the best approach to the problem might be to let the students work out their own solution.

CHARACTERISTICS OF A GOOD COMMITTEE MEMBER

A good group member recognizes the value of working with others cooperatively and effectively. He is willing to take responsibility for himself and others and tries to see where the group is going and how it is progressing. He listens attentively to others and uses their ideas, or, if he disagrees, does so in a constructive manner. In turn, he feels that his contributions will be welcomed and received in the spirit intended. A good member also realizes that it is just as important to be a good follower as it is to be a group leader. If he is more capable than

some of the others in the group, he takes on only his share of the work, letting others do tasks which they can perform. At the same time, he notes and appreciates what others can do. By sharing experiences in this manner, he learns to understand his own capacity.

JINGLE WRITING

Although it may seem unusual, writing jingles is an effective learning technique as well as a kind of creative experience. The jingles bring out important points that students will long remember after the facts on which the jingles were based are forgotten.

No special organization, type of structure, or particular talent is needed for jingle writing. Everyone possesses some creative ability. The difference in people depends largely on the extent to which creative self-expression has had a chance to develop. All too often students are unaware of this ability, possibly because there has been no specific time or place in which it could function. But once they have been given an opportunity to express themselves creatively, the ability develops. Skill in writing jingles is also aided by the development of the sense of rhythm and the ability to manipulate words and, of course, by practice. Students generally derive much personal satisfaction from the results they achieve.

GAME PLAYING

Nearly everyone, young and old, likes to play games. Some home-economics teachers may not realize that this type of enjoyment can be used in the class-room to facilitate learning, but games are valuable in many ways. Among other things, they provide an opportunity for students to see familiar material in a new light. In every program there are certain aspects of the classwork, such as learning new terminology or modifying undesirable work habits, which as such are not particularly interesting. However, when games are adapted to these situations, not only is interest motivated and sustained but retention is perceptibly increased. Games can also be set up to reveal students' attitudes and to indicate how well certain material has been learned.

The teacher and the students can work out any number of helpful games. Ideas may come from books on games or other sources. Imagination and ingenuity are needed to adapt these ideas to the current classwork. Care should be taken, however, to avoid competitive situations in which able students outshine other members of the class. Games in which one wrong answer eliminates the participant and prevents this person from further participation tend to defeat their usefulness. In such cases the able students, who usually remain in the game the longest, are generally the ones who need less practice than those who are eliminated earlier.

Generally speaking, this technique adapts itself to two types of games—those that are played with cards and stress individual accomplishment and those that involve teams or small groups.

CARD GAMES

There are numerous ways in which games with cards can influence classroom learning. A few examples are given to show how such games might operate as a learning technique:

Example 1:   A game called "What Would You Do?" could reveal students' attitudes toward certain subjects such as health habits, family relationships, and social behavior. It could also indicate knowledge of a subject before and after studying it. The game is played as follows: A set of cards—one for each class member—is prepared, describing a particular situation. The cards are shuffled and distributed. Each student reads aloud the situation on his card and tells what he would do. The class members discuss the answer before going on to the next situation.

Example 2:   A variation of "What Would You Do?" is called "Conversational Cutups" and is played as follows: Various situations are written on a set of cards—the number of cards corresponding to one-half the number of students in the class. The cards are then cut into two sections, each card being cut in a different way. After the sections are shuffled, the students each draw one section and then match it for a partner. The partners then dramatize in conversation the situation written on their card. A few minutes may be given each pair for preparation, with time at the end of the conversations for discussing what has been said.

Example 3:   Another type of card game may be used to review material that has been taken up in class. A catchy title related to the subject will stimulate interest in the proceedings. Directions for the game are as follows: The class decides on a number of questions and answers pertaining to certain material. These are put on separate cards until there are at least five pairs for every player. A question and its answer equals one pair; one pair is called a book. An extra card containing the title of the game can be used for either a question or an answer. The cards are shuffled and five cards are dealt to each player, the remaining cards constituting a "kitty." In the first round of play, each player lays down on the table one answer card from his hand. If he does not have an answer card, he draws from the kitty until he gets one. Beginning with the second round of play, each player either continues to lay down an answer card or to match a question card from his hand with any of the answers on the table to make a book. If he runs out of answer cards, he again draws from the kitty until he gets one. The person who plays all his cards first ends the hand. Several hands are necessary to make a game. The game ends when a player reaches the score of 200. Scoring of each hand is done in the following manner: subtract 15 points for each question in possession, subtract 5 points for the "extra" card in possession, add 10 points for each book.

This same type of game can be set up to review new terminology and to reinforce the understanding of familiar terms that are infrequently used. The word can be put on one card and the definition on another.

TEAM OR SMALL-GROUP GAMES

Games in which the class is divided into two sections or in small groups of four to eight students can also be used to facilitate learning. Several examples are given:

Example 1:   Games called "Baseball" or "Football" can be played to see how much knowledge has been acquired in a particular area or in a goal within an area. The game is played as follows: The class is divided into two teams, A and B. Each team appoints a pitcher. The four corners of the room are named to represent home plate, first, second, and third bases. Pitcher A hurls a question on a subject, previously agreed on by the class, to members of Team B who are lined up at bat. If the first member answers the question correctly, he goes to first base. If teammates answer the following questions correctly, they move to first, second, and third bases, and finally to home plate to score a run. If a member answers a question incorrectly, he strikes out. After three outs, Pitcher B takes over and questions Team A until three outs are made. In the second

round for Team B all contestants again line up at bat including those who have previously struck out. The game proceeds through nine rounds. Score is kept as in regular baseball and may be posted on the board. Questions for the pitchers can be prepared by the class and printed on small cards with answers on the reverse side.

Example 2:   Another game called "Furniture Cut-outs" may be used to illustrate what the class has learned in relation to furniture arrangements for different rooms. Directions for arrangements in a bedroom are as follows: Each student is given a sheet of paper and an envelope containing an assortment of furniture cut-outs. A drawing on each paper represents rooms of various shapes and sizes. The idea is to arrange and paste the cut-outs in a bedroom to be used for a variety of purposes. The class is then divided into small groups. One group can arrange the room primarily for sleeping and dressing. Another group can set up a study area in addition to a sleeping and dressing area. A third group can plan the arrangement in which a leisure-time area is stressed. Other groups can plan the room to be shared by one or two more persons. After a certain length of time, the papers without names are collected, shuffled, and then redistributed. Each group studies the papers they have been given to determine whether the arrangements are satisfactory on the basis of what they have previously learned in class. Comments and suggestions for improvement are then made in a class discussion.

Example 3:   Night letter-telegram games are always interesting and are adaptable to all areas of a home-economics program. The game is played as follows: The class divides into groups of six to eight persons. Half of the members of each group write a telegram to the other half, asking advice on a certain problem. The reply is given in the form of a night letter of no more than fifty words. After a given time the questions and answers are read to the whole class. A discussion follows on the appropriateness of the questions and answers.

Example 4: After a class has learned about correct walking posture, a game can be played to see how well students are able to follow what they have learned and note where improvement is needed. Directions for the game are as follows: The class appoints two referees, preferably students who have already developed good posture. The teacher can also serve as a referee. The class then divides into two groups who line up single file on each side of the room. At the signal "go" the first player of each group places a book on top of his head. Without using hands to balance the book, the players walk to a given point and back again. The book is then given to the second player in both groups and the same procedure is followed. Each player returns to the end of the line when finished. If the book is dropped, the player has to stop, replace the book, and continue. The referees stop anyone who keeps the book on his head by assuming poor posture. That person is required to start all over again. Each group is timed to see how many minutes it takes for all its members to reach the specified point and back again.

SPECIAL TECHNIQUES FOR SECURING INFORMATION

Throughout every home-economics program there are occasions when students want to get specific information in concise form. They may do so in several ways—through questionnaires, check lists, and inventories. All three of these techniques are similar in some respects. But they all have significant value in that students learn how to organize material in such a way

that the information sought can be readily and efficiently obtained, and easily evaluated.

QUESTIONNAIRES

As the name implies, a questionnaire consists of a series of questions so constructed that the answers can be given by marking down an appropriate symbol, writing a word, or writing out a detailed reply. Questionnaires are generally developed to secure information from older students, parents, and other people in the community. In some cases the questions are asked verbally with replies jotted down by the questioner. Or a questionnaire may be submitted to people for them to read and fill out. Sometimes it is used in connection with an interview. In any of these situations, considerable thought and planning are required for developing a good questionnaire. The following suggestions may therefore prove helpful to teachers who are unaccustomed to this technique:

1. A questionnaire should be developed cooperatively by the teacher and the students. When students share in formulating the questions, they are better able to interpret the answers and to make a sounder application of the information received. However, adaptations can be made from other questionnaires. Many times using a good questionnaire as a model to develop one's own in terms of the students' needs is preferable to taking time to make one up.

2. During its development, the purpose of the questionnaire should be clearly understood and kept in mind. This is important because every question needs to be directly related to the purpose for which the questionnaire is being used. Writing down a statement of the purpose will be helpful. It will not only keep the attention of the class focused on the prob-

lem, but suggested questions can be checked against the statement to see whether they are really needed. Sometimes a question may be followed by a choice of possible answers. This method tends to clarify the question and to facilitate answering it.

3. The questionnaire should be fairly short and the questions brief. No one likes to answer a long, involved list of questions which may require several readings before the content is understood.

4. The form of the questionnaire should lend itself to easy tabulation. If directions are needed for filling out the questionnaire, they need to be brief and easily understood. Aligning the questions on the page with the answers to be given on one side only and numbering each item facilitate the answering and make it easy to summarize the results.

5. In most cases a person's name should not be identified with the answers given. People are generally more willing to give information or opinions when they know that their names will not be used.

When submitting a questionnaire to parents or other people in the community, students should follow procedures similar to those for holding an interview. (See pp. 163–164.) If people in the community are asked to fill out a questionnaire at their convenience, an advance appointment may not be necessary. But if answers are to be given on the spot, a scheduled appointment is desirable. A busy person may resent an unexpected request to answer a list of questions. He may either refuse to consider them at all or answer them so hurriedly that the information given does not represent the real situation. Parents also need consideration. A mother should not be expected to answer questions thoughtfully when she is in the midst of meal preparation or some other household activity. Nor can a father be expected to show

interest in school affairs if he is fatigued after a busy day. The time for a questionnaire is when parents are relaxed and can give unhurried thought to the questions.

CHECK LISTS

Check lists generally consist of a series of statements or questions to be checked with an appropriate symbol of with short word-answers such as "almost always," "sometimes," "almost never." As a rule, in home-economics education check lists are used with students to obtain information concerning knowledge acquired, current progress, achievement, social behavior, attitudes, and habits. The considerations for developing questionnaires are also applicable to check lists. The key to their success lies in an objective approach, ease of tabulation, and the facility with which the results can be evaluated. There are many kinds of check lists that can be developed and used throughout a home-economics program. Some of them will be described in Part Two of this book.

INVENTORIES

There are various occasions when students can benefit by knowing how to take an inventory. This technique is a systematic procedure of finding out and recording what is on hand in a particular situation.

One begins an inventory by first getting a picture of "the whole"—what is to be inventoried—then breaking it down into parts or categories and recording or checking items in each category. Sometimes students assist the teacher in taking an inventory of the equipment and supplies in the home-economics department. For such a purpose the principal may have a printed form, or he may suggest the kind of form to be used. Or the teacher and the students may decide to take an inventory of the living area at school for their own purposes. Any form that will give a true picture of what is on hand is acceptable. A particularly useful inventory that students need to take periodically at home is of clothing and should involve more than merely checking the number of different garments on hand. It could include separating these garments into four groups: (1) those that can be worn just as they are, (2) those that may need some repairs or alterations, (3) those that have been outgrown but are still wearable by others, and (4) those that are no longer usable. Once this is done, group (1) can be hung up and group (2) can be set aside for future consideration. Parents should be consulted about groups (3) and (4), since they probably have definite plans about what should be done with these garments.

SUGGESTED TEACHER EXPERIENCES

1. Members of the class who want to experiment with an unfamiliar technique can discuss it with several persons who have used it. Comparisons of the different ways it was used and the extent of success may justify trial attempts.

2. Several members of the class can tell about good class discussions they have observed. They can bring out such points as (a) leadership by the teacher or a student, (b) how the discussion got under way, (c) to what extent participation was distributed, and (d) how the discussion terminated.

3. With the class, make a list of several subjects that might be suitable for the following types of discussion: (a) panel, (b) forum, (c) colloquy. Give reasons why the subjects suggested are more applicable to one type of discussion than another.

4. Divide the class into small groups, each group taking an area of the home-economics program and giving examples of demonstrations that might be used effectively.

5. Get information from several experienced teachers about some directed observations that were not particularly successful and learn what might have been done to insure more effective results.

6. With the class, list several situations in each area of the home-economics program that would lend themselves to role playing or a related technique. Each member can select a situation and briefly describe the characters and the setting and perhaps the desired outcome.

7. Several members of the class might like to set up some role-playing situations relating to problems they have recently faced or expect to face in future teaching. Several different groups can dramatize these situations, giving their version of a particular problem and how it could be met. Individual summaries can be made of any new insight into personal problems.

8. Hold a class discussion of the relative merits of an exhibit displayed by a commercial concern and one set up by a class.

9. Make up a list of topics for bulletin-board arrangements and posters designed to create interest and to motivate a class in attacking certain problems. The list can be kept on hand for future use.

10. Several members of the class might be willing to tell about personal interviews not too successfully held in connection with previous classwork. The incidents can be evaluated in terms of the considerations for holding an interview described in this chapter.

11. Use the following account of a field trip as the basis for an interesting discussion on (a) how the situation might have been prevented,

(b) what should be done to relieve the present situation, and (c) how the recurrence of a similar situation might be prevented on future field trips.

A class carefully planned and carried out arrangements for a field trip to the furniture section of a local department store where an exhibit of living-room arrangements was being held. Everything went according to plan until the class started to leave the exhibit area. Several members of the group became noisy and boisterous, playfully pushing each other around and occasionally knocking against pieces of furniture and even some customers. The manager of the department, with whom previous arrangements had been made, reported the inci-

dent to the school principal, who in turn called in the home-economics teacher conducting the field trip to discuss the situation.

12.   Obtain a series of unanalyzed student anecdotes from teachers who have used the technique of recording anecdotes. Several members of the class can analyze the same series individually on the basis of the example described in this chapter. Then comparisons can be made of the different appraisals of the same series to see how much agreement there is on various points.

13.   Discuss how different committees might be organized in connection with various problems encountered in each area of the homemaking program.

SIX

WHAT INSTRUCTIONAL RESOURCES SHOULD FACILITATE LEARNING?

SELECTION AND USE OF RESOURCES

Various resources are available to increase the interest in the techniques described in the previous chapter and to offer variety and efficiency in their operation. In this chapter, the resources are classified thus: resource persons, material resources, and miscellaneous resources.

Since students' interests and abilities vary, the teacher will need to see that a wide variety of resources is made available. For some students printed material such as books, periodicals, and the like are highly significant in the learning process. For others who do not read easily, learning may come more readily by looking at objects, observing processes, and watching people at work. For still others, sounds and feelings, such as those engendered by television, movies, and talks by resource persons, may make learning easier. Although certain resources may be more effective with some students than with others, their general use is not precluded. Skillful teaching can make it possible for each student to benefit from a variety of resources.

As the teacher acquaints her students with various resources, she will need to guide the students in their use. She can help the class to make selections on the basis of whether or not the use of a particular resource will contribute to the current classwork. For example, using a film just because it happens to be available is a false economy, unless the content of the film is related to classwork being planned or carried out. Likewise, listening to a well-known resource person who happens to be available would have little intrinsic value unless his talk contributed to some phase of the prevailing classwork. However, with careful guidance, students can develop ability to use many resources wisely and advantageously.

PEOPLE AS RESOURCES

In both the school and the community there are various persons who can make worthwhile contributions to the current classwork—people skilled in a particular field, parents, seniors and recent graduates, and young children.

SKILLED PERSONNEL

Home-economics departments have long been accustomed to having people who are skillful in special occupations talk to their classes. Students enjoy seeing new faces and usually listen attentively to what is said. They are often challenged and inspired by these adults. Some resource persons also give demonstrations, hold exhibits, or participate in various discussion techniques.

More often than not in small communities, a person invited to the classroom is a highly respected citizen whose general qualifications are known to the teacher and the students. In large cities, however, little may be known about a person other than his occupation. Since being skilled in a particular line of work is only one qualification for a classroom speaker, the following questions might be considered before inviting anyone to speak:

1.   Is this person genuinely interested in the welfare of young people? If a person takes a critical, negative attitude toward the general behavior of students, whatever message he may bring to the class will be completely overshadowed by this attitude. To have influence value, the speaker needs to be sympathetic and understanding toward student problems.

2.   Does he avoid expressing strong prejudices? The classroom is not the place for a person to express personal dislikes. Animosity directed toward any group represented in the class or toward conditions over which students have no control creates an unpleasant atmosphere.

3.   Can he speak in terms that students can readily understand? A person who uses highly technical language cannot expect to hold the attention and interest of the class. Although students do not like to feel that a person is "talking down" to them, they want to be able to understand what is being said.

4.   Is he able to cope with students' questions? If a speaker becomes irritated and shows annoyance at questions that seem stupid to him,

he creates an unfavorable impression with the students. Patience, poise, and understanding are necessary to establish good rapport.

Finding answers to these particular questions is important. Certain characteristics such as a poor speaking voice, odd mannerisms, and an unawareness of good public speaking can be overlooked; but the qualifications just mentioned cannot be ignored if a classroom visit from a resource person is to be valuable.

PARENTS

Although some parents may be included as skilled personnel, the majority of parents who come to the classroom serve in other capacities. For instance, they participate in carrying out a particular learning technique. Parents may be members of a panel, a forum, or a symposium. Or they may come for a question-and-answer session. Sometimes they assist in or give demonstrations, or they may serve as consultants on special problems. Occasionally they appear in mock television or radio broadcasts. Parents also attend special class functions, which may include a class tea for parents to get acquainted with one another or to meet a well-known person associated with home-economics education. The occasion may also be an exhibit the class has set up, a fashion show, or a skit.

RECENT GRADUATES AND SENIOR STUDENTS

Persons who are slightly older than the class group can often exert more influence on this group than adults. A panel discussion or a mock television or radio broadcast with recent graduates or senior students is an excellent way of helping the younger group develop desirable social behavior. However, those selected for participation need to be held in high regard by the class.

YOUNG CHILDREN

Young children are considered resource persons when they help students acquire knowledge and experience in child care and development. These children may already be present as part of the school curriculum, usually in a kindergarten or nursery school. In such cases small groups of students may take turns observing and recording the behavior of these children and can note procedures that are being used with the children.

Children may also come to the home-economics department for a short period of time in connection with a play-school planned and carried out by the students themselves. Sometimes an organization, such as the Parent-Teachers Association, may sponsor a play-school and arrange with the administration to use some of the school facilities. In such a case the department may cooperate with the organization in operating the play-school for a period of time. Daily contacts afford an excellent opportunity for students to learn a great deal about these children. This knowledge is often increased by occasionally planning, preparing, and serving a meal to the children.

Occasionally arrangements can be made for the school nurse or the public-health nurse to give demonstrations on bathing a baby. Frequently mothers bring small children to the classroom to demonstrate practical types of clothing.

MAKING CLASSROOM VISITS
PLEASANT AND PROFITABLE

When resource persons are invited to the classrooms, making such occasions pleasant and profitable for all concerned involves the following considerations:

1. Advance arrangements need to be made with the visitors. Most people have a busy schedule and need to plan ahead for a visit to the classroom. They also like to be briefed on what they are expected to say or do and how long the visit will be. Preliminary arrangements also include finding out what equipment, if any, guests may need and planning for these needs. It also involves ascertaining whether transportation is desired, and, if so, making plans accordingly. When parents are bringing small children to the classroom for a special occasion, a few toys can be provided to make the children feel more at ease. All these arrangements can be made by committees.

2. Visitors should be welcomed when they arrive. As a rule, the teacher and the students acting as hosts and hostesses can greet guests when they arrive at the classroom. However, if a person is visiting a large school for the first time, a student can be delegated to meet the guest at the school entrance and conduct him to the classroom.

3. If the guest is to give a talk, the teacher can ask permission to interrupt if a point does not seem clear. This can provide a break if the talk becomes rambling, or if the students appear to be losing interest.

4. A student chairman for the occasion should introduce the guest or guests. This introduction should be brief. In most cases it can include a few remarks about the background of the guest and how he is going to participate in the meeting. When parents or other persons are invited as a group, explaining the occasion for the meeting is all that is necessary.

5. At the close of the meeting the chairman and the teacher should express thanks to the guest or guests for coming. If a visitor was met

at the school entrance, he should be escorted back to the entrance.

6.   A letter of appreciation should be sent to individual persons who have contributed their services. The letter can be written by a committee and, if desired, a note from the teacher can be included.

7.   Each occasion needs to be evaluated on the basis of the contribution it has made to the current classwork. For obvious reasons it is best to avoid an appraisal of any of the participants. Some unfavorable reactions may be justified, whereas others may be based on unimportant details which in no way reflect on the worth or integrity of the person. Although a guest may prove a disappointment, there is generally something worthwhile to be gained by his visit.

MATERIAL RESOURCES

There are many material resources that have long been a tangible part of home-economics programs. In recent years scientific research has made many more available, so that, at the present time there is a wealth of materials that have great potential value in bringing about effective learning. Some of these materials can be obtained through the home-economics department budget or can be secured upon request. Others can be made by students or borrowed from various departments in the school. Still others are purchased by the school for general use. Many of these resources are considered so necessary that there is no problem in obtaining them. Others, although regarded as important, are not provided because of the expense involved. Many more are not used because their potential value is unrecognized. Since it is the teacher's responsibility to make learning as effective as possible, she needs to become acquainted with and use a wide vari-

ety of material resources that will enrich the home-economics program. In so doing, she may need the cooperation of the school administration in securing some of the resources that involve the expenditure of money not provided in the department budget. Doing so will probably not prove an insurmountable difficulty if the teacher herself is convinced of the value of these resources.

PUBLISHED MATERIALS

The home-economics teacher has access to a limitless supply of published materials. The problem is to select only the publications that the teacher and the students have time to evaluate on the basis of actual needs and available finances. Quality rather than quantity of publications is important.

In order to be most effective, published materials need to be suitable to the level of ability of the students using them. Highly technical materials are usually too difficult for students to understand because of their limited experience. College publications are also not particularly helpful to the majority of high-school students, although there are various levels of reading ability even in a high-school group. An alert teacher, knowing what materials her individual students enjoy and can assimilate, will have as wide a variety as possible. In order to encourage reading, one corner of the classroom can be attractively arranged for that purpose.

BOOKS

Selecting suitable books is not an easy matter, since it is not always possible for the teacher and the students to evaluate a book by reading it in advance. However, publishers issue brochures giving detailed descriptions of their books. By studying this information carefully, the teacher and the students can try to make a wise selection. It is also possible for the teacher to get helpful ideas by talking with other home-economics teachers and looking over the books they are using. Regardless of the procedure, books should meet several requirements to be selected for the department:

1. Up-to-dateness is essential. What constitutes up-to-dateness depends largely upon the extent of current research in a particular field. For example, a book published five or six years ago containing information on the use of color in the selection of clothing and home furnishing may still be useful. On the other hand, knowledge of nutrition is increasing so rapidly that it is difficult to have the most recent material on hand. When a book is no longer useful, it should be clipped for worthwhile illustrations or information and then discarded.

2. A book should adequately cover all the areas it claims to cover. Some books may cover only a single area, whereas others may include all the areas generally regarded as essential for a well-rounded program in home economics. If a book claims to be useful in all areas, the material in each needs to be equally strong.

3. The content needs to have depth. Superficial material has little or no value. Home economics is a field with many learnings, and related books need to clarify and explain some of them well.

4. The material should be well organized and of appropriate reading level. The clearer the organization, the easier it will be for students to understand and retain what they read. But the vocabulary, and the sentence and paragraph structure also need to be at the appropriate reading level for those who will use the book. All these factors help to motivate reading.

5. The book needs to be stimulating. Suggestions for using the book, for planning student experiences, for evaluating progress and achievement, and for making practical applications of new learnings help to make a book interesting and challenging to its readers.

6. The illustrations should be related to the main ideas expressed in the book. Since most books must necessarily be limited in length, too many illustrative materials will restrict the subject content. It is therefore desirable that pictures, charts, tables, graphs, and other illustrations be directly related to the main ideas brought out in the book.

7. The Table of Contents and the Index should be comprehensive. The outstanding features of each chapter need to be presented in the Table of Contents. The Index should be given in such detail that no difficulty will be encountered in locating various subjects.

8. The format should be pleasing. Good features include paper that is not too glossy, print that is easy to read, and binding that is durable yet attractive. The book should be a size that is convenient to handle—not too large and not too small.

MAGAZINES

At the present time there are many periodicals that can be very useful in a home-economics program. First choice is the *Journal of Home Economics* to which every home-economics teacher should subscribe as a part of her own professional equipment. Having this periodical also available for classroom use helps students to get a more comprehensive picture of home economics. Other magazines that describe activities of home-economics classes throughout the country are popular with students and provide them with a basis for comparison.

There are periodicals that specialize in a particular area of home economics, such as foods, clothing, or family relationships. The so-called women's magazines also contain interesting articles on various aspects of home and family living. Students can be encouraged to clip and bring to class pertinent items from publications available at home.

After magazines are no longer current, they should be stored away if space is available. Then students can use them from time to time as references in future classwork. When space is not available, committee groups can take turns clipping worthwhile material. These clippings along with others brought to class can be placed in a resource file. One way to prevent damage from handling is to mount the clippings on large cards, each card to contain several articles related to the same topic.

BULLETINS AND PAMPHLETS

There is a great deal of printed matter in the form of bulletins and pamphlets available at the present time, but it is often difficult to know exactly where to obtain what is needed. There are, however, several sources that may be used. Government departments and agencies are constantly issuing up-to-date material on many aspects of home and community living. These may be secured from the Superintendent of Documents, Washington, D.C., or directly from different branches of the government, such as the U.S. Department of Agriculture, the Children's Bureau in the Department of Labor, and the U.S. Office of Education. Some of the bulletins and pamphlets are free upon request, and others may be obtained for a nominal fee. Then there are various state sources that publish a great deal of printed material for public use. Agricultural experimental stations connected with land-grant colleges

and universities and extension departments in many schools for higher education provide material based on the latest research in many areas pertaining to home and community living. Another rich source are the publications of professional and commercial groups, such as those connected with the medical and dental professions, consumer-buying agencies, and dairy groups. Large retail stores in various sections of the country also issue valuable information on different aspects of home living.

Before ordering a supply of bulletins or pamphlets it is wise to get a sample copy first for evaluation. Indiscriminate ordering is wasteful and costly and should not be encouraged even for materials that involve no expense to the home-economics department. Requests for materials should be written on school or department stationery, or sent in the teacher's name.

In evaluating bulletins and pamphlets from commercial sources, it is advisable for the teacher and the students to learn to recognize desirable and undesirable characteristics.

A useful pamphlet would have the following characteristics:

Contains information on using and caring for the product.

Describes the operation of the equipment as well as its use, care, and storage.

Shows distinguishing differences in products or in equipment of similar types.

Shows ways in which the product or equipment can save time, energy, and money.

Gives information on cost.

Keeps advertising to a minimum.

One should avoid using pamphlets with these characteristics:

Shows the historical development of the product or piece of equipment, or explains steps in manufacturing or processing an item—all of which are relatively unimportant as a rule in a home-economics program.

Overdramatizes the content, thus detracting attention from important facts.

Promotes contests that generally overemphasize the importance of one person excelling over another and encourages students to work only for prizes.

Expresses the content in such a way as to produce anxiety, or uses fear as a basis for creating interest.

Includes advertising that overshadows descriptive information.

GRAPHIC AND PICTORIAL MATERIALS

In general, graphic and pictorial materials include cartoons, charts, motion pictures, still pictures, posters, and television. Although some of these resources do not provide as much descriptive information as the resources previously mentioned, they exert considerable influence on the learning process in other ways.

CARTOONS

Most cartoons used in connection with classwork are clipped from current newspapers or periodicals and brought to class by students. Selecting appropriate cartoons indicates that these students are able to see relationships; that is, they recognize that the content of the cartoons is related to the current classwork. Some students do not see this relationship unless it is pointed out to them. A discussion of the cartoons may therefore be needed to help everyone in the class understand their symbol-

ism and to interpret their meanings. Occasionally cartoons are drawn by class members, but since a special talent is required, active participation is limited to a few students. However, a class is likely to show more interest in something depicted by someone they know personally. In such cases the cartoons may be more effective than those clipped from periodicals. Like all clippings, cartoons need to be filed away for future use.

CHARTS

Generally speaking, two types of charts are used in home-economics programs: commercial and student-made.

Commercial charts give information in two ways—pictorially or by tabulation. Students enjoy picture charts, especially those in color. Although the information given is minimal, it is pinpointed so that it is readily assimilated and remembered. For example, a chart showing cuts of meat that are labeled helps students to learn to identify the different cuts before they become actual buyers. Color charts picturing foods needed for a balanced diet, or those featuring desirable personal appearance, tend to create favorable attitudes toward these subjects.

Charts that give information by tabulation are less interesting to students but offer considerable information. Because of their impersonal nature and the fact that it takes time and effort to digest the information, they lack the natural appeal of pictorial charts. Reading and using a chart of this type efficiently are abilities that must be developed. Students are not expected to assimilate all the information contained in the tabulation at one time. It is best first to obtain an overall view of the chart, noting the main points of reference. Then the details under these points can be studied as the information is needed in the classwork. Charts containing a wealth of tabulated information for all areas of a home-economics program are readily available from many of the sources previously mentioned. Like clippings, the charts can be kept on file in the classroom for future use.

Student-made charts generally contain information in tabulated form. Many teachers encourage students to make charts, believing that chart-making develops ability to identify and to present important information in concise form. The charts will need to be simple and easy to read, and should be checked by the teacher for accuracy. The making of charts lends itself to small-group participation in assembling possible information, then to class participation in the final selection of material to be used and in the manner of tabulating it. Committees can then do the tabulation, the number of groups to be used depending on the extent of the information to be tabulated and the manner of tabulation.

MOTION PICTURES

Motion pictures have long been recognized as one of the most valuable resources for effective learning. Some films provide important facts and information or demonstrate processes and skills. Others are shown to arouse interest and to stimulate imagination in a particular subject. Some are designed to reinforce desirable attitudes and social behavior.

Using motion pictures requires a projector, an operator, a screen, and a semidarkened room. Every teacher can benefit from understanding how to operate a projector and how to take proper care of the machine and the films. If it seems advisable, and ordinances permit, a student with mechanical ability can operate the machine, thus freeing the teacher to attend to other details. Many schools have one

or more projectors, usually for 16-millimeter films, for general class use.

Advanced preparation is particularly important when films are to be used. In fact, the teacher and the students can make tentative plans for possible films when the yearly program is being set up. There are many sources from which films for all areas can be obtained. The Educators' Progress Service, Randolph, Wisconsin, issues a catalog, revised annually, called *Educators' Guide to Free Films*. Brief descriptions of the films are included. In each state the United States Department of Agriculture has a depository of films at the land-grant college or university. Other colleges and universities maintain film libraries. Various commercial sources also provide films related to home and family living. In many cases they can be borrowed or rented at a slight cost plus transportation charges. Catalogs generally designate how long in advance a film should be ordered. However, for those that are especially popular even more time should be allowed so that the presentation can be synchronized with the presentation of a particular area in the home-economics program.

It should be kept in mind, however, that the showing of a film alone does not produce the best results. The class needs to be prepared for the film, to help select it, and to discuss its content after it has been shown. It is also desirable for the teacher and a committee to preview a film before it is shown to the class. Then any new or unfamiliar terms can be explained in advance. Because most films are projected at a constant speed, interruptions during a showing are not practical. Therefore, explanations and comments must be made before and after the showing. Although some films end with a summary of the contents, a follow-up discussion immediately after the showing is important to give the students an opportunity to verbalize what they have just learned. Doing so aids their retention of the material. Note-taking during a film showing should not be encouraged since important details may be missed when students are not looking at the screen. It is better to take notes in the form of a summary after the film has been shown.

When motion pictures were first used in the classroom, it was believed that a film should be fairly short, about ten minutes. This theory was based on the assumption that this amount of content was all a class could absorb. Research has shown, however, that this is not true in most cases. Although the rate of absorption decreases somewhat after ten minutes, students continue to learn from a film even for as long as an hour. However, for most classes the length of the film might be gauged by the length of the class period, allowing sufficient time for introduction and a follow-up discussion.

Criteria for the selection of a film are difficult to establish, since most films must be selected from brief descriptions given in catalogs. However, teachers may get information from one another about a successful film. Or a teacher who has used films which have proven satisfactory for her classes in the past may be guided by these results when other classes are considering selections. Such experience might well provide the teacher with the following criteria:

The film serves the purpose for which it is being shown.

The content is up-to-date and accurate, suited to the age and grade level for which it is used.

The presentation is of suitable length to hold the interest of the class.

There is not excessive commentary about action not seen on the screen.

The film is not so overpacked with material that the students have difficulty assimilating what they have seen.

The film, if a commercial one, is free from objectionable or excessive advertising.

STILL PICTURES

Still pictures in connection with current classwork are also considered an effective source for making learning more meaningful. But in order for presentations to be successful, students need to learn to "read" pictures. Although a picture is supposed to be an accurate record, it does not tell the whole story, nor does it always portray the situation as it really is. The person taking the picture shows what he wants to by selecting the point of view of the camera, by controlling the lighting, and by arranging, in some cases, the composition of the picture. Using these controls, he can make objects appear larger or smaller, longer or narrower, and even more beautiful or attractive than they really are. All these factors need to be taken into account in studying a picture. Furthermore, since pictures contain a great deal of irrelevant detail, the students will need to learn to select the elements that are most important in relation to the classwork under consideration.

It is interesting to note that students with different levels of ability "read" pictures in different ways. Slow and average students tend to see only some of the items in the picture. Bright students identify more details and relate these details to the total meaning of the picture. They may even add imaginative touches and associate the picture with their own experiences. These differences indicate that when pictures are used, the selection needs to be broad and varied enough to interest those of all levels of ability. In general, there are four types of still pictures: (1) flat pictures, (2) filmstrips, (3) photographic slides, and (4) transparencies. The last three must be projected to be seen and therefore involve the use of a projector and screen, an operator, and a partially darkened room.

1.   Flat pictures may be photographs, illustra-

tions in books, magazines and other publications, and paintings and drawings. When the latter are made by artists who have selected important elements and eliminated others, they may be more helpful than photographs or illustrations. Flat pictures can be used in various ways. They can be held up, passed around for individual inspection, or displayed on a bulletin board or a poster for further study. Some may be used in an opaque projector.

2.   Filmstrips are also known as slide films or film rolls. They are still pictures printed on short strips of standardized width, nonflammable motion-picture film. They can be projected serially or singly, and forward or backward as desired. A picture can be held on the screen for any length of time and the strip can be turned back to pictures previously shown. A disadvantage is that the pictures have to be shown in a fixed sequence. However, filmstrips possess great flexibility in that the teacher can stress certain pictures as they are held on the screen. Both silent and sound types are available. The sound type can be run without sound if the teacher wishes to supply explanation or if the class wants to discuss certain pictures as they are being shown.

3.   Photographic slides are made of glass or plastic and have several advantages over filmstrips. They can be shown in any order and are more durable and less likely to be damaged by heat. Taking photographs to be made into slides requires some knowledge of the use of a camera, but many students and most teachers already have this knowledge and can make slides for class use. Colored slides can show the role that the effective use of color plays in making a home attractive and enjoyable in relation to furniture, draperies, wall and floor coverings, and decorative arrangements. Certain foods in a balanced diet become more appetizing when shown in color. Slides showing services for buffet meals or informal suppers on the porch or in the back yard may also influence some students to introduce at home something new and different in the family meal pattern. Color is especially interesting and helpful to students learning to select a wardrobe and accessories to accompany it. These ideas, however, are not meant to minimize the value of slides made from black and white film. Many pictures, such as those of different styles of furniture, various kinds of textiles, and most home appliances, need not necessarily be shown in color to create interest and to give information.

4.   Transparencies are materials that can be shown in an overhead or opaque projector, the operation of which is simple enough for most students to handle themselves. Materials used generally include photographs, illustrations from books, reading material or drawings put down with a wax pencil on a transparent plastic sheet, or small objects. Many slide projectors have an adjustment feature that makes it possible to show either slides or opaque materials.

POSTERS

Two types of posters are generally used as resources for creating interest in learning situations: student-made and commercial. Making posters in connection with the current classwork has already been described as a technique, since it involves certain procedures that need to be followed to insure successful results. Obviously the student-made poster has considerably more value than the commercial type, because it offers students an opportunity for creative expression and is often pertinent to the local situation.

Commercial posters, however, when stylized in attractive and colorful presentations with a minimum of advertising, often have considerable impact upon students. Such posters need to be placed advantageously and need to be visible across the room. They should also be changed frequently to provide variety in color and content.

TELEVISION

An interesting resource with great potential value is television. Research has already shown that television instruction can be as effective as an educational film or regular classroom teaching. In fact, a television presentation is similar to the average classroom lesson. The person giving the broadcast usually looks directly at the camera and therefore appears to be looking at everyone in the room. Apparently, the psychological effect causes the students to give close attention to what is happening on the screen.

Television instruction is carried out under the supervision of school authorities by a closed-circuit system, which operates within a limited area in contrast to the open-circuit type, which operates within unlimited radius. A closed-circuit system, for example, can link together all the home-economics departments in a large city or throughout a county, thus making it possible to channel instructional material to a large number of students at one time. The television instructor works closely with the classroom teacher and students, preparing material to be used in their joint handling of the classwork.

A successful television lesson operates in the following way. At the beginning of the class period there is a warming-up session which may consist of a review discussion and an introduction to the current television lesson. A guide sheet to be followed while watching the lesson and to be used for taking notes has proved to be very helpful. It can also be used for reference in a follow-up discussion after the broadcast, which is an important part of the total procedure. The length of a presentation may vary, but will generally be from fifteen to thirty minutes. Since the interest span of the average high-school student is thirty minutes, most of the value of television instruction beyond this point is lost. Material that is complex or highly emotional will necessarily be presented in planned intervals to permit the students to ponder on what they have seen, heard, and felt. A chairman and an engineer are needed for efficient class management. The chairman distributes and collects materials and conducts the meeting, the engineer adjusts the television set before, during, and at the end of the presentation. Both positions can be rotated among class members.

The level of television instruction is necessarily aimed at the average student. However, the classroom teacher who knows the different abilities of her group can see that the television material is supplemented in various ways. Bright and average students can be encouraged to explore the subject at greater length. The slow learners may need further instructions or special activities to foster retention of the television lesson.

It is not expected that television teachers will replace classroom teachers. Both can play an important part in the learning process. Television teachers can be responsible for the functions that seem to be best suited to the medium of television. At the present time these appear to include the following:

Motivating and stimulating interest

Giving information

Holding demonstrations

Showing applications

Enriching backgrounds

Raising questions

Suggesting activities

Challenging students to assume more responsibility for their own learning

On the other hand, there are certain functions that seem to be handled more efficiently by direct contact with students. Some of these include:

Holding class discussions

Helping students to meet personal problems

Providing guidance and assistance when needed

Helping students to establish desirable attitudes and satisfying values

Caring for individual differences in students

Providing opportunities for students to exercise critical judgments

Helping students to establish relationships between what is learned and everyday living

Guiding students to evaluate their achievements

MISCELLANEOUS RESOURCES

There are certain resources that do not lend themselves to any special classification, but which are nonetheless considered effective aids in the learning process. These include anecdotes, decorative objects, the flannel board, models, samples, short stories, tape recordings, and newer resources discussed on pages 195–199.

ANECDOTES

Anecdotes told by students in relation to some aspect of the current classwork are often used in various areas of a home-economics program to bring out points needing emphasis. Students not only enjoy listening to incidents that have happened to others, but they like to relate experiences of their own. These experiences generally bring to light personal habits and behavior that can be improved and often lead to classwork that will benefit everyone in the group.

The telling of anecdotes may be planned in advance by the class or may be extemporaneous. When planned, students who feel they have something to contribute toward the classwork under consideration can volunteer to relate their experiences. The teacher may need to point out that these anecdotes should be fairly short. A long, drawn-out account is generally less effective than a brief one. Too many descriptive details tend to draw attention away from the main points to be emphasized. Occasionally in the course of the classwork the teacher or some of the students may remember an interesting experience of a certain member of the class and suggest that she tell them about it.

A class accustomed to listening to anecdotes soon learns to recognize students with narrative ability. They will listen attentively to someone who speaks clearly, easily, and pointedly without rambling. And they particularly enjoy a person who has a sense of humor and the ability to dramatize a situation.

DECORATIVE OBJECTS OR ARTIFACTS

Decorative objects or artifacts of various kinds are considered necessary resources for every home-economics department. They add to the attractiveness of the classroom and help the students to develop an appreciation and knowledge of color and design. They also provide an opportunity for students to learn pleasing arrangements and placements for similar objects in their own homes.

It is important for the class to share in the selection of the objects to be used. Although every department starts out with a number of items, each year something new can be added. This is not to imply that a department should accumulate a large supply. The quality of the items is more important than their quantity. Having a sufficient number from which a selection can be made for different arrangements from time to time is all that is necessary. Those not in immediate use can be stored away. If space is not available for keeping a supply of objects on hand, items can often be borrowed from the art department.

FLANNEL BOARD AND CHALKBOARD

The flannel board, often used in various areas of a home-economics program, might be regarded as a portable bulletin board. It lends itself to many uses and affords an opportunity for creative expression.

Flannel boards may be purchased or student-made. The commercial type offers the advantages of a wire folding easel to hold the board in either a horizontal or vertical position and a carrying case in which the larger boards can be folded in half. Commercial boards are available in several sizes.

There are no standard procedures for making a flannel board, which in some cases may even be a series of boards hinged together. Plywood or wall board is generally used for the board itself. Any size that is easily seen by the group and large enough for the purpose is satisfactory. Outing flannel—any color desired—is stretched over the board and tacked or secured with tape on the back. Whatever illustrations or printed matter are to be used are mounted individually on light cardboard. Then flannel or size 00 sandpaper is cut to size and glued with rubber cement to each section of cardboard. These will adhere to the board when pressed against the flannel, but they can be taken off and put on as desired.

The flannel board can be used for small exhibits, such as pictures showing certain aspects of room arrangements. It is also suited for highlighting important points in a talk or discussion when these points can be prepared for board use in advance.

The chalkboard may be movable or portable, and offers many of the advantages of the flannel board. Some teachers find it easier to use and consider it a satisfactory substitute for the flannel board. In addition the chalkboard serves other uses as well. In fact the use of both resources is limited only by the imagination and ingenuity of the teacher.

MODELS

Models have long been recognized as a valuable resource for classroom learning. A model represents something completed and as such gives the students a concrete picture of what can be accomplished. It not only creates interest in getting started toward a definite objective, but it serves as a guide as the work develops. For example, if a class plans to make children's toys, models of various toys will tend to stimulate interest in toys and give them ideas for constructing similar ones. Sometimes several models of one kind are brought together to compare their relative merits. For example, students learning about different kinds of kitchen knives may assemble various types not only to learn the most effective use of each, but to find out general criteria for selecting knives. However, whatever models are used in connection with the classwork should be similar in size and kind to what the students will be making or using at school and at home.

DIORAMAS

In a diorama, models and objects are arranged against a background painting to create a three-dimensional effect, giving the illusion of a natural setting. Dioramas are especially well adapted to such areas as food, home furnishings, home care of the sick, and clothing.

SAMPLES

A resource that is particularly helpful in many learning situations is the use of samples, which, generally, are small quantities or portions of items being used in the current classwork. They are shown as evidence of the quality and character of the "whole." For instance, students can assemble a representative sampling of labels used on various kinds of products. By studying and comparing different samples, they can learn whether the information given on a label is adequate for consumer satisfaction. Or by looking at samples of different fabrics, students can learn their names, what fibers they are made of, how they can best be used, what service they may be expected to give, what care is needed, and other essential information, all of which is important to know before a purchase.

Sometimes students can secure the samples needed, but the teacher will probably have on hand samples of different kinds of materials for clothing and for household furnishings, such as draperies, chair and floor coverings, and wall paper. It is generally difficult for students to obtain samples large enough in size for their real

content and quality to be studied and in sufficient quantity so that time will not be lost in examining them. An efficient teacher will have selected samples on the basis of what the students and their families can afford to buy and their availability in several stores. She will also see that the samples are adequately labeled according to width or size and cost, that certain patterns or designs are available in different colors, and that the materials can be purchased. Periodically she will bring her supply of samples up to date.

SHORT STORIES

The use of short stories in connection with classroom learning is receiving considerable recognition. Adolescents enjoy hearing or reading a story, especially if it concerns young people their own age and deals with matters in which they are genuinely interested. Sometimes the students themselves bring in stories which emphasize certain aspects of the classwork and which they feel will be of interest to other members of the group. But more often than not, the teacher herself will use a story for one purpose or another.

For example, reading a story to the class is an excellent way of opening the first meeting of the school year with a beginning group who may be feeling ill at ease with their new teacher. The story needs to have action and humor. By the time it is completed, the students will be relaxed, and they will begin to feel at home in their new surroundings. If the story is a provocative one, a class discussion will probably result.

The teacher can also use an appropriate story to point out undesirable behavior, bad habits, or unpleasant personality traits that may be present among class members without making the need for improvement seem too personal.

The story draws their attention and stimulates interest in these unrecognized needs and generally leads to concerted action on the part of the students.

There are other occasions when a story can be effectively used, and a wise teacher will have several stories on hand that will be appropriate for a number of situations. It hardly seems necessary to point out that the story used should be suited to the age level of the class.

TAPE RECORDINGS

The use of tape recordings in connection with learning situations is becoming increasingly popular because they can be employed advantageously throughout a home-economics program. Two types of recordings are generally used: those obtained from sources outside the school and those made by the teacher and the students.

Recordings from outside the school can be obtained from various sources. The United States Department of Health, Education, and Welfare has publication lists of recordings which may be borrowed as well as bought. The Association for Educational Communications and Technology, an affiliate of the National Education Association, issues such information also. Other resources include commercial recording companies.

Many schools have recording equipment which is available for general class use. (The use of cassette tapes is discussed on page 197.) The cost of operation is low, since the spools can be used many times without loss of fidelity. The machine is portable and easy to operate. A recording or parts of it can be repeated as often as desired, thus providing students with an opportunity to evaluate the strengths and weaknesses of a performance. Recordings may

be made of various discussion techniques, demonstrations, role-playing situations, children's conversation during play, stories as they are told to children and many other situations. Some recordings may be filed away for future use. Others no longer desired can be automatically erased from the spool and a new recording made.

SUGGESTED TEACHER EXPERIENCES

1. The class might carefully consider the resources discussed in this chapter to see if it would like to include other resources. Then each member of the group could choose one or several resources to present to the class. The presentation might use any of the techniques or other resources mentioned. The important point to keep in mind is that each member of the group needs to understand how best to use each resource under consideration.

2. Assemble various commercial listings of available bulletins and pamphlets, graphic and pictorial materials, charts, motion pictures, filmstrips, slides, posters. Divide into teams to evaluate such lists and exchange findings with each other. It should be helpful to find out which of the resources are available in your state. At the same time it will be important to learn under what conditions these resources may be secured.

3. Choose two or more techniques and resources that might be used together and describe how you might use them. For example, you could use role playing to demonstrate desirable and undesirable features of certain household equipment along with a display of charts illustrating certain points that need to be stressed. The term *multi-media teaching aids* sometimes refers to using several aids at the

same time or to using several aids in relation to a problem but not necessarily together. Describe several situations where you would like to use at least four or more such teaching-learning aids. One or two of the resources discussed in this chapter should be included.

SEVEN

WHAT IS KNOWN ABOUT NEWER TEACHING-LEARNING RESOURCES?

INNOVATIVE TECHNIQUES AND RESOURCES

It is not expected that any one teacher will use all of the more recently developed teaching-learning helps any more than she has heretofore used all the long-established techniques and resources. But she needs to learn about new ones and try them out whenever appropriate and possible. In time the literature will carry an evaluation of each new resource and any up-to-date teacher needs to acquaint herself with such reports. Kopstein (Watson, 1971) points out that "the reward system in education is often conducive to the introduction of one fad after another and is counter to any consistent and integrated evaluation of effective educational processes [p. 85]." Nevertheless, it is reasonable to assume that some of the innovations will prove useful and will endure. Some of the others will be improved in time and proven to be worthwhile; these also will survive.

THE COMPUTER

"Of all the technological innovations which support individualization, no single tool has had more impact," according to Hawk (1971).

"The computer is useful in a number of ways, but generally in one of two categories: (1) either as a tool for direct instruction, or (2) as a management tool wherein record keeping, testing, and scoring are done on an automated basis [p. 76]."

Hawk believes that although many examples of individualized instruction are available around the country there is no universal understanding nor acceptance of such proposals. Because this aspect of the educational enterprise is innovative, change will come slowly. Acceptance may come as everyone gains familiarity with the principles and techniques, and as the problems encountered along the way are solved. Among the problems that are the most clearly identified at the present time are: (1) shortage of material, (2) need for re-organization within school, (3) arranging staffing levels and assignment, (4) dehumanization of students and teachers, (5) social isolation or lack of interaction with people.

In spite of present problems, the computer is likely to play a dominant role in the future of American education. Leaders in educational technology generally agree (Hawk, 1971, pp. 78–79) that at present they need to familiarize in-service teachers with more machine systems, encouraging them to use some of those currently available on the market. The initial purpose would be to overcome the fears teachers have of such machines and to demonstrate possible uses. Later, interested teachers could be helped to develop materials according to their interests. They could also be made aware of other commercially available materials designed to assist the educational process.

LEARNING PACKAGES AND CAPSULES

Designed by Shear and Ray to play a supplementary role in home-economics curricula, Learning Packages were developed at the Pennsylvania State University and made available through Penn State and later through the American Home Economics Association.

Shear and Ray (1969) write, "A Learning Package is a self-instructional unit developed for learning one basic concept or idea in which the idea to be learned is broken into its several components. The teacher constructs the three- to five-lesson package in such a way that the individual learner may proceed at his own pace and learn in his own style by selecting from among alternative resource materials and activities. Built into the package is a pretest designed to diagnose the learner's status in relation to the concept and to assist the student in selecting materials and experiences for the areas of greatest need with reference to the objectives sought [p. 768]."

Five hundred capsules or independent learning guides have been developed by Mrs. Eleanor Cochrane, instructor in home economics, Brookings High School, Brookings, South Dakota. These are in use with both girls and boys at the Brookings High School and are for sale along with seventy tape scripts, all part of a set.

Other individuals and commercial concerns have also developed programmed instruction available to teachers of home economics.

Programmed instruction appears to hold promise for individualizing instruction in learning certain concepts, especially those concerned primarily with information. Teachers need to become acquainted with these materials and experiment with ways of developing and using them most effectively. Many adaptations are possible, such as substituting pictures for some of the words in programmed-learning materials developed for slow learners in junior high school.

SELF-INSTRUCTION LABORATORY

One or several teachers sometimes set up a self-instruction laboratory to meet individual differences of students in their background of training and experience. The extent to which instruction is individualized, or programmed, varies from situation to situation, but a multimedia approach is included. The plan is generally flexible and changes can be made when new media become available or old media prove ineffective. The success of such laboratories is likely to depend to a considerable extent on good judgment in planning the program including evaluation.

SINGLE-CONCEPT FILM AND
TAPE RECORDING

The single-concept film or film loop (Gausman & Vonnes, 1969) is a short motion-picture film wound in a continuous loop for use in a relatively inexpensive, small, ultra-simplified projector. The tape recording provides verbal instruction either simultaneous with the picture or separate from it. Film loops on a variety of subjects are available from commercial sources; local film production may be desirable also.

Such films and tape recordings provide students with an aural-visual experience on an individual basis that would otherwise be provided by a demonstration and lecture. The success of this approach is likely to depend on the availability of adequate film and tape resources. It appears to be a new tool with which teachers need to experiment in terms of student goals.

CASSETTE TAPES

Cassette tapes are a technical improvement in tape recording. The ease with which they can be used has led to the making of recordings by authoritative speakers on a variety of subjects. These cassette tapes offer a unique and convenient means of keeping in touch with the latest developments. The availability of subjects suitable to home economics is limited at the present time, but some tapes appropriate for individual and group use should offer an opportunity for home-economics teachers to experiment with the method, even developing tapes of their own. It should be interesting to follow the evaluation of this tool as more and more cassette tapes become available.

In some situations listening-learning centers have been provided. Here students have dial-access by means of the telephone to whatever tape they wish to hear. Such arrangements make it possible for more than one student to hear the tape at the same time.

TELE-LECTURE

When a group wishes to have an outside speaker not able to appear in person, they may arrange a tele-lecture. The equipment for a tele-lecture, which is rented, enables an entire group to hear and respond to what is said over a telephone.

Plans for the tele-lecture must be made beforehand by someone representing the group and by the distant speaker. Then, at the appointed time, a station-to-station telephone call is made to the speaker, who then proceeds to carry out his part of whatever plan has been made. He may speak, answer questions, or even carry on a discussion with the group meeting together at an arranged place. Sometimes students speak directly or they may have arranged to pass their comments or questions to one or two persons who relay them to the speaker.

In the room where the group is meeting, a picture of the speaker may be shown or films or slides of other materials illustrating the speech may be shown at the appropriate time. This of course requires a careful plan and coordination of effort by the leader of the group or whomever he designates and the speaker. Although extensive evaluation has not been made of the technique it would seem to serve a unique purpose.

SIMULATION TECHNIQUES

The simulation technique (Bogniard & Dalrymple, 1970) has been used to allow individuals to act through a certain situation in order to see the consequences of different choices before the situation has to be actually faced.

Sometimes games developed for a specific purpose are used. These games may have been purchased from producers in the same way as other school materials. Or the teacher and a student or group of students may devise such games.

In preparing prospective teachers, real-life teaching situations may be created by would-be teachers who then enact and analyze their own teaching behavior in a simulated classroom situation.

Early evidence indicates that the use of simulation techniques may be popular with students and at the same time improve their ability to understand and critically look at specific problems. They are somewhat related to role-playing, discussed on pages 159–160. At this point there is need for more well-developed games and situations. Experimentation in more effective ways of using such materials may be expected to add to their usefulness.

ENCOUNTER GROUPS

Encounter groups vary widely, but in general they attempt to increase a person's inner awareness and modify his behavior through confrontations and frank self-disclosures in the group. Sessions may be short or could run for several days.

The encounter group technique began expanding in 1968, especially at the college level, but other groups have participated also. The behavior of the leader is probably the key to how successful the technique will prove to be in any particular instance. The first study indicated that encounter groups may be harmful to some participants. Further experimentation by well-trained leaders and research on effectiveness of the technique may result in a different picture.

INTERACTION ANALYSIS

Interaction analysis (Amidon & Flanders, 1967; Baird, 1970) is a system of categorizing and analyzing the verbal behavior of teachers and students in a classroom. A trained observer may observe such behavior and record it at 3-second intervals for 20 minutes. There are ten different categories for recording. Analysis shows the proportion of teacher and student talk, the proportion of direct and indirect influence used by the teacher, and the proportion of class time spent on each category of behavior. The teacher may tape-record her own class and then analyze results in the same way if she so desires.

Research related to interaction patterns of home-economics teachers has been limited. Jorgenson (1968) categorized the teacher-influence patterns of first- and second-year teachers in this field. Other home-economics educators have tried out interaction analysis without doing it as a research project. More study with different groups is needed on the technique before definite conclusions can be drawn as to its usefulness.

VIDEO TAPES OF MICRO-TEACHING

Video tape used with micro-teaching and in other ways (Crews et al., 1969) appears to be a useful technological aid. It has been used in at least three different ways and doubtless others will be developed as individuals carry on further experimentation. The three ways include:

1. Using micro-teaching situations in which the prospective teacher is video taped while he teaches a short—usually five- to ten-minute—lesson to a few students. The replay encour-

ages the participant to evaluate his teaching performance for both strengths and weaknesses. Peers as well as the instructor and coordinating teacher may participate in the evaluation if desired. Further teaching should demonstrate the desired changes in presentation.

2. Having the camera operator include classroom views of young students where such views may serve as a motivation for improvement or show desirable behavior in carrying on some activity, perhaps a certain skill.

3. Building a library of edited tapes of different performances to be used in teacher-education classes, seminars, or otherwise.

WORK EXPERIENCE

Home-economics programs of wage earning are not new in some sections of the country, but received new challenges under the Vocational Education Amendments of 1968. Such programs are usually set up to include work experience related to home economics. A number of individuals and groups have worked on providing such experiences. The most helpful conclusion at this point is that as many ideas as might prove practical for providing such experiences should be tried out, evaluated, and then reported with recommendations for other interested persons. Reference is made to wage-earning programs at a number of places throughout this book.

TEACHER AIDES

As enrollments have increased, some schools have tried to meet part of the new problems by using teacher aides to increase efficiency in operation. The work of these aides varies in different situations, but in general their work is to assist the classroom teacher in whatever way proves most helpful. Such aides are paid by the school but at a lower rate than teachers. Generally the success of such programs have depended on the cooperation of the teacher as well as the personality, training, and background of the aides.

TEAM TEACHING

In team teaching, two or more teachers operate as a team under the direction of a team leader. The teachers may divide the work in any number of ways—by subject matter, by method, or something else. The students are divided into groups as the teachers think best. Such teaching brings teachers together to discuss educational problems of concern to all. It can have real possibilities as a means of improving instruction. Sometimes, however, it means only a new kind of division of labor, and is considered a useful but limited device. The potential is great enough that more study and experimentation could provide a brighter picture than is clearly evident at this time.

SUGGESTED TEACHER EXPERIENCES

1. Some member of the group may know a great deal about one of the recently developed teaching-learning aids and be willing to teach the group what she knows. The report could be a visit to see the aid, a demonstration, or whatever form of presentation is preferred. The aid itself could be one discussed briefly in this chapter or another about which someone in

the group knows. Outside sources could be drawn upon for teaching more about aids with which the group is unfamiliar.

2.   Decide with the class for what purpose each of the aids mentioned would probably be most useful. For example, the matter of recognizing different alternatives might be shown best by simulation techniques or perhaps a learning package. It should be interesting to examine both and draw whatever conclusions seem justified.

3.   Secure information from as many persons as possible who have used each aid discussed.

This information could be in the form of an interview, anecdotes, or something else.

4.   Do any of the teaching-learning aids discussed in this chapter appear to be modifications of those discussed in Chapters 5 and 6? If so, what possible similarities or relationships do you see?

5.   Make a search of recent publications for other innovations in learning aids. The American Vocational Association, the *Journal of Home Economics*, and other journals in the field of education would probably give such information.

EIGHT

WHAT KINDS OF EVALUATION CAN BE USED ADVANTAGEOUSLY?

TYPES AND FORMS OF EVALUATION

Since successful teaching calls for the competent use of evaluation, it is important for a teacher to understand the types and various forms which can be used advantageously. There are three general types: (1) check lists, (2) questions, and (3) combinations and variations of check lists and questions. Any of these can be used in conjunction with the various techniques and instructional resources discussed in the preceding pages. In fact, the techniques themselves serve as a basis for evaluating new learnings.

The three general types, and various forms of them, will be described, accompanied by illustrations showing how some of them have frequently been constructed and used. Additional material and examples will indicate how some of the forms can be modified to increase their effectiveness. However, it is first advisable to refer back to pages 134–137, where the desirable qualities for all types and forms of evaluation were considered.

THE CHECK-LIST TYPE OF EVALUATION

The term *check list* usually refers to a series of words or statements to which an individual in-

dicates his reaction with a symbol, a word, or a brief phrase. The term *score card* is usually used interchangeably with *check list*. This type of evaluation generally includes four forms known as (1) check-off, (2) two-response, (3) multi-response, and (4) rating scales. These four forms are not distinct from one another, but need to be considered as levels requiring discernment on the part of the user.

CHECK-OFF

This form generally consists of a series of items or statements which are to be checked as they are accomplished. Shopping lists and important steps in developing a new skill or process are examples of the use of this form.

Situation: An employment-preparation class in clothing and house-furnishing services is learning how to care for a sewing machine. A list of essential procedures is set up by the group. Copies are available so that each person may check the procedures whenever his machine needs cleaning and oiling.

Directions: In the space to the left, check (✓)

as you carry out each procedure. When you feel confident that you can use and care for the machine satisfactorily, ask another student to check your performance. You will want to use the check list until you can carry out all procedures without referring to it.

PROCEDURES

_____ 1. Have on hand equipment consisting of small and large screw drivers, absorbent cloth, brush, and oil.

_____ 2. Carefully clean all parts of head above table.

_____ 3. Clean bobbin case.

_____ 4. Lift the head and clean all lower parts.

_____ 5. Apply one drop of machine oil at each place as shown in the manual.

_____ 6. Saturate the red felt near bobbin with oil.

_____ 7. Run the machine for a few minutes and remove all surplus oil with cheesecloth.

_____ 8. Return parts of machine which were removed to proper location.

Note: This check list should be adapted to the type of machine which is being used. The illustration is incomplete but gives enough of the contents to indicate how the form is constructed and used.

TWO-RESPONSE

The two-response form involves a series of statements to which an individual replies in one of two ways, in terms of the presence or absence of certain attitudes, performance, or qualities of a product. Or he may simply give a positive or negative answer to each question. The response terms commonly used are *yes* and *no*, but such terms as *I have* and *I have not* or *I agree* and *I do not agree* may be more appropriate as answers to some questions.

Situation: A group of early adolescents in a family finance class are planning to study allowances. Before deciding on goals the group chose to prepare and use a check list to discover group attitudes toward allowances. Part of the check list follows.

Directions: Check (✓) under the appropriate column to indicate your attitude.

YES	NO	ATTITUDES
_____	_____	1. Teenagers who work should not have an allowance from parents.

_____	_____	2. The money that a teenager earns should be spent for whatever he wants.
_____	_____	3. A teenager should save some of his allowance every week.
_____	_____	4. A teenager's allowance should be cut in times of a family's financial emergency.

MULTI-RESPONSE

Another check-list form frequently used offers several alternative answers—usually three, but sometimes more. To some extent this is a rating scale, since the descriptive terms represent ideas which are approximately equi-distant in value. Choosing an answer calls for discrimination on the part of the user. The sets of descriptive words may vary, but an example is "seldom," "sometimes," and "generally." Words such as "always" and "never" are usually avoided, because most people hesitate to be absolutely positive or negative.

The following illustration shows how the multi-response may be used.

Situation: A class studying for gainful employment as a caterer's helper or a home caterer agreed in the beginning on certain needed attitudes, skills, and knowledge. Now each member plans to evaluate the extent to which he or she complies with these aspects of catering.

Directions: Check (✓) in the space under the word which applies to your situation.

ASPECTS	SELDOM	SOME-TIMES	GENER-ALLY
1. Works well with others	_____	_____	_____
2. Shows initiative	_____	_____	_____
3. Uses time effectively	_____	_____	_____
4. Presents a clean and neat appearance	_____	_____	_____
5. Keeps work area in good order	_____	_____	_____
6. Uses food materials wisely	_____	_____	_____
7. Is safety conscious of self and others (List incomplete)	_____	_____	_____

RATING SCALES

The fourth form of the check list is known as a rating scale. It is generally used to indicate varying degrees of quality or adequacy. The rating scale requires the user to exercise more judgment and make finer discriminations than other check-list forms. It also differs from the others in that the responses are assigned numerical value. Three degrees of discrimination are commonly used: values of 1, 2, and 3. Descriptive words, such as "below average," "average," and "above average" are sometimes used to indicate these values. Zero is seldom used to indicate complete failure since no individual likes to admit its existence. Sometimes a rating scale is constructed with as many as ten values. Obviously this requires very fine discrimination.

The following example shows how a three-value rating scale can be constructed and used.

Situation: The students are evaluating a com-

mercial film recently used in connection with a class goal. They have previously summarized important factors contributing to a film's appropriateness for class use. The evaluation is to be made on the basis of these factors.

Directions: Rate the film 1, 2, or 3 in terms of each item listed, and place your response in the right-hand column. The number 1 will indicate the undesirable quality in the first column; 3, the desirable quality in the second column; and 2, a mixed reaction or a degree between.

FACTOR	1	2	3	
Purpose	Not oriented to class goal		Related to class goal	1. _____
	Not suited to age and grade level		Suited to age and grade level	2. _____
Content accuracy	Information unreliable		Information reliable; based on research and recognized authority	3. _____
	Limited; gives only partial information		Gives adequate information	4. _____
Timeliness	Information out of date		Information-up-to-date	5. _____
Prejudice	Subject matter biased: limited in theory or ideas		Free from bias; broad interpretation of subject	6. _____
Form of presentation	Dull; uninteresting		Stimulating; interesting	7. _____
	Organization not clear; subject matter confusing		Material well-arranged; subject matter clearly presented	8. _____
Propaganda	Advertising excessive and objectionable		Free from excessive and objectionable advertising	9. _____
Photography	Picture blurred at		Picture clear and	

| | times; image not always clear | distinct at all times | 10. _____ |
| Sound | Sound not always clear; words sometimes indistinct | Sound clear; words distinct at all times | 11. _____ |

VALUES OF THE CHECK-LIST TYPE

Every type of evaluation has its strengths and weaknesses. Some of the values of the check-list type are as follows:

1. It is easy and not too time-consuming to construct. With the guidance of the teacher, students can develop ability to help make appropriate lists, although rating scales are generally more difficult to construct.

2. It is exceedingly versatile. It is adaptable to all ages, to different levels of ability, and to individual or group participation. It can be used in a wide variety of situations in all subject areas. The same form can function any number of times to evaluate the same situation.

3. It is usually easy to interpret. Responses can be made within a short period of time, and the results quickly tabulated and evaluated.

4. It contributes to self-teaching and encourages self-evaluation. Setting up a check list is a good way of summarizing what has been learned in a particular situation. It is also an effective way of getting an overall picture of what needs to be learned in developing a specific skill. Students are thus encouraged to make their own appraisal of the extent of their achievement and to find out where and how improvement can be made. Frequent self-checking of the same situation is a way of showing each student whether progress is being made and minimizes any delay in making needed improvements or in providing for necessary guidance.

WEAKNESSES OF THE CHECK-LIST TYPE

Check lists have one major weakness: they may be lacking in reliability. The extent to which the evaluation is accurate may depend largely on how tangible the content is. In general, the more concrete the items, the more accurate will be the appraisal. The evaluation of relationships, attitudes, or values is likely to be less accurate than an appraisal of a film, food products, or an exhibit, because it is unusual to find complete agreement on these aspects of growth. Their very nature indicates that some personal judgment is likely to be present in the evaluation.

Even when the content is concrete, agreement is sometimes difficult, especially when too many different aspects or unrelated qualities are included in an item. Unless provision is made for scoring each aspect or quality, disagreement on the appraisal usually results. To provide a place to score each characteristic would often make the form too long and cumbersome for practical use. The content usually needs to be telescoped, as shown in the illustration on pages 204–205; that is, two or more closely related characteristics are included in a description and one rating is made for the group as a whole. Accuracy is increased when the evaluation asks for observation and immediate response rather than recollection.

When students first begin appraising themselves, their evaluation will probably be too high and at variance with the teacher's. However, with experience, students can develop ability to rate themselves quite accurately and obtain results similar to those of the teacher.

In spite of some weaknesses, the check-list type of evaluation gives a fair approximation of what the teacher and the students want to know.

MODIFICATIONS OF THE CHECK-LIST TYPE

At the present time check lists are undergoing various modifications. People familiar with check lists believe that one way of making them more interesting is to vary their construction and content. Another way is to let students use their own terminology in construction and evaluate their own progress. The illustrations that follow will show variations in check-list construction. Except for the first example, only enough of each check list is given to show form.

EXAMPLE 1

Situation: A class of early-adolescent girls learning to improve grooming habits helped to construct the check list on page 207, "Keeping Clothing Clean and Neat from Top to Toe."

Directions: Check each of the listed statements, indicating whether you are Glamorous Gladys, Average Anne, or Sloppy Sal, by placing a dot in the center of the block and drawing a connecting line from one block to the next. The profile will show where you need improvement in your grooming habits. Although you are likely to be a mixture of all three types, you need to strive toward becoming as nearly like Glamorous Gladys as possible.

EXAMPLE 2

Situation: Individuals who believed that they wanted to prepare for employment in child care services wondered if they possessed qualities important for such work. Each person rated herself and then had a conference with the teacher to discuss why she had rated herself as she did on each quality.

Directions: The positive and negative qualities listed on each side of the scale can have important effects on children. Draw a circle around the number that best describes you. Place that number under "Your score" and add the numbers to get your rating.

QUALITY						YOUR SCORE
Gloomy	1	2	3	4	Cheerful	_____
Unsure	1	2	3	4	Confident	_____
Blunt	1	2	3	4	Tactful	_____
Uncooperative	1	2	3	4	Helpful	_____
Undependable	1	2	3	4	Reliable	_____
Totals	5	10	15	20	Total	_____

(Note: Add other points as desired.)

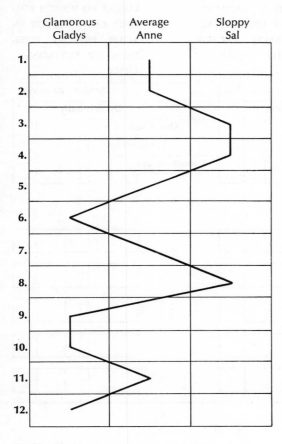

	Glamorous Gladys	Average Anne	Sloppy Sal
1.			
2.			
3.			
4.			
5.			
6.			
7.			
8.			
9.			
10.			
11.			
12.			

Profile Chart

STATEMENTS

1. I change and wash clothing worn next to the body daily if at all possible, and other garments frequently.

2. I wash sweaters and other simple garments whenever they are soiled.

3. I remove common stains from washable clothing as soon as they appear and consult an experienced person about spots on other fabrics.

4. I keep my clothes neatly pressed.

5. I air all clothes that are to be worn a second time before putting them in the closet.

6. I sew on missing buttons.

7. I keep my socks darned and my stockings free from runs.

8. I repair broken seams and loose hems.

9. I keep my shoes in good condition.

10. I see that my socks and stockings are well supported and seams straight.

11. I keep suits, coats, heavy skirts, and dresses free from lint and dust.

12. I wear appropriate clothes for work or play.

Keeping Clothing Clean and Neat from Top to Toe—Checklist

EXAMPLE 3

Situation: An adult class of men and women were interested in making greater contributions to their community. Two persons in the group had seen the check-list form of questionnaire shown on page 208 and offered to secure copies for the group. They thought this check list would help individuals understand themselves better. Such understanding should provide some basis for decision making with reference to the community.

Directions: This check list is concerned with relationships with people, intra-personal feelings, working conditions, and community and environmental conditions. Place a check (✓) in each set of boxes indicating your feelings. There are no right or wrong answers.

FACTORS WHICH MAY YIELD SATISFACTION OR DISSATISFACTION	AMOUNT OF SATISFAC-TION OR DISSATISFAC-TION EACH FACTOR YIELDS TO YOU IN LIFE	EXTENT TO WHICH YOU FIND EACH FACTOR IN YOUR PRESENT POSI-TION OR ENVIRON-MENT
	High dissatisfaction / Some dissatisfaction / Indifferent / Some satisfaction / High satisfaction	Seldom or never / Occasionally / About half of time / Frequently / Almost always

Intra-Personal Feelings:

22. Having sufficient energy for work and other interests

23. Finding new ways of thinking and doing things

24. Being unable to feel a sense of personal growth

25. Opportunity for doing things with one's hands

26. Opportunity to develop one's own thinking

THE QUESTION TYPE OF EVALUATION

Questions can be answered in a variety of ways depending on the form and construction of the question type of evaluation that is used. The forms identified with this type of evaluation are as follows:

1. Recall

   A. Oral

   B. Essay

   C. Free-response

   D. Completion

   E. Identification or association

2. Recognition

   A. Modified true-false

   (1) Cluster true-false

   (2) Circling word or words which make a statement false and substituting the cor-rect response

   (3) Two-choice

   B. Multiple choice

   C. Matching

   D. Ranking (sometimes regarded as a modi-fication of matching)

In order to give a clear picture of the na-ture of these forms, the following material shows several examples of different forms, indicating their strengths and weaknesses, and offering general guides for their construction and use. In a later section other examples will be presented to show how some of the forms can be modified to make them more comprehensive and effective.

RECALL FORM—ORAL

Situation: The previous day a panel of mothers discussed mealtime problems of preschool children. The class is reviewing important information brought out by the panel.

Sample Questions:

1. What emotions may affect a child's appetite?

2. What is the advantage of small servings over large ones?

3. Is it desirable to let a child be the judge of the amount to be eaten? Give reasons for your answer.

4. How can a child's appetite be stimulated so that he will enjoy eating foods which are needed?

5. What foods are not considered good for small children?

Strengths:

Is generally a challenging and stimulating activity for both teacher and students

Affords an economical way for the teacher to determine whether students possess certain information

Errors made in answers can be discovered and corrected immediately

The total number of questions answered by a class may be greater than those that students can write in the same period of time

There is less paper work for the teacher

Can be used with students individually—not in connection with class participation—to ascertain background knowledge or the extent and quality of particular learnings attained.

Weaknesses:

May not give an accurate indication of what a student knows, since he is generally allowed to answer only one or two questions

Usually tests ability to recall factual information only, if questions are the short-answer type

Penalizes students who are limited or handicapped in oral expression

Does not permit an evaluation of the difficulty of questions; some may be more difficult than others

Evaluation of replies may be biased by the teacher's personal opinion of what she expects answers to include

Guides for Construction and Use:

It is advisable to prepare questions in advance so that attention can be centered on the answers given.

Questions need to be concise and specific so that they can be answered in a limited time.

It is generally considered desirable to direct each question to the entire class before an individual student is called upon to respond. This makes it possible for each student to frame an answer and thus participate indirectly in the learning experience.

Repeating a student's answer is questionable except when there is need for specific emphasis. Otherwise the class may tend to wait for the teacher's repetition rather than to concentrate on what the student has to say.

RECALL FORM—ESSAY

Situation: The class is learning some of the things they need to know when visiting away from home. Reference materials were consulted and discussed along with personal experiences related by some of the students. Demonstrations were given on packing.

Directions: Answer the three questions below about visiting. Total time allowed—45 minutes, approximately 15 minutes to a question. Each question will have equal value.

Questions:

1. What are some of the important things that need to be considered before making a visit? Comment on at least three.

2. How can the guest make the visit a pleasant one for the hostess? Indicate at least four things. Discuss each.

3. What are the customary procedures for a guest to follow after a visit? Comment at length on one.

Strengths:

Generally requires minimum preparation to construct

Useful in evaluating ability to organize, interpret, and apply what is being learned

Helpful in estimating ability to see relationships and to form generalizations

Permits originality of expression instead of response to a set pattern

Gives the teacher a fair basis for comparison of results, since all students answer the same list of questions

Weaknesses:

The time allowed for answering provides too limited a sampling of what is being learned

Penalizes students who are handicapped by limited vocabularies and by inability to express themselves in writing

Students are apt to become involved in the mechanism of writing and wander from the subject

Answers are difficult to evaluate correctly because of the teacher's judgment of what she expects the answers to include. Other factors may also affect the evaluation, such as the halo effect of other students' replies, or the teacher's attitude toward or opinion of individual students.

Evaluating the results is time-consuming

Guides for Construction and Use:

Increasing the number of questions and restricting the length of response will tend to make evaluation of the results easier and more accurate.

Extreme care should be taken in the selection and preparation of questions. Emphasis needs to be placed on those involving reasoning, judgment, application, and organization.

Questions need to be stated so that the meaning is clear. They should not contain words that are ambiguous or beyond the students' range of experience.

Students need to understand the purpose of the examination and what considerations will be given to sentence structure, spelling, and punctuation as well as subject matter.

The approximate time to be given to each question can be specified, but sufficient time should be allowed so that students can make revisions if they desire.

It is highly advisable to assign in advance specific value to each question with a possible answer key. Students may be told what value each question has.

Evaluating one question at a time for all papers and ignoring the identity of the student whose question is being appraised are advocated.

If time permits, papers can be divided into groups by scores and some reread to see whether the quality of appraisal is consistent.

RECALL FORM—FREE-RESPONSE

Situation: The students are learning to use cup measurements for foods. A few items are given to show how the form is sometimes constructed.

Directions: What are the correct cup measurements for each item listed below?

CUP MEASUREMENT	ITEMS
(1)	1. Two sticks of butter
($\frac{1}{2}$)	2. One quarter pound of butter
(2)	3. One pint of cream
(2)	4. One pound granulated sugar

Strengths:

Easy to construct and to use

Economical in space

Well-adapted for use when numerical answers are required

Weaknesses:

May cause memorization of facts with little regard for their significance

Situations in which it can be used are limited

Guides for Construction and Use:

The construction of the form needs to be

such that the question can be answered by a word, phrase, or number.

It is advisable to use the form only when important information needs to be recalled and remembered.

RECALL FORM—COMPLETION

Situation: The class had recently used a resource person to learn more about illness. A partial list of questions will indicate how the completion form was constructed and used to find out what was learned.

Directions: What did Dr. Barton's talk bring out regarding the following statements? Use the blank spaces for the appropriate information.

1.   Fever is nature's way of providing an environment (*unfavorable*) to the germ.

2.   Respiration is the inhaling of (*oxygen*) and the (*exhaling*) of carbon dioxide, one breath taken in and one breathed out.

3.   A normal mouth temperature may vary from (*97.6° F.*) degrees to (*99.0° F.*) degrees.

Strengths:

Relatively easy to construct and economical in space required

Especially useful for recalling important information to know and to be remembered

Possible to construct a key on which there is reasonable agreement

Weaknesses:

In some instances may tend to encourage students to memorize isolated bits of information

If the questions are not well constructed, the meaning may be obscure

Guides for Construction and Use:

Care needs to be taken not to lift statements

verbatim from textbooks or reference materials being used by the class.

It is advisable to avoid using too many blank spaces in a statement.

Directions need to be made clear so that the response words or phrases will be clearly understood.

Questions need to be as direct as possible and call for brief responses.

It is advisable to have the response lines of the same and of adequate length.

The evaluation of results can be facilitated by setting up a key with correct alternatives if one correct answer is not possible.

RECALL FORM—
IDENTIFICATION OR ASSOCIATION

Situation: Mary's committee has set up an exhibit of indoor toys important to the development of preschool children. In her report Mary brought out different toys that would aid development in various ways. Sample aspects of development will show how the identification or completion form can be used. Note there are several alternatives in the selections of a toy.

Directions: After carefully studying the exhibit, indicate a toy associated with each aspect of development in the following list.

DEVELOPMENT	TOY
1. Motor skills	(wagon or tricycle or ride-on toy)
2. Mental activity	(picture books or puzzles)
3. Creativity and imagination	(clay or crayons or paints)

Strengths:

Same as for Completion

Weaknesses:

Same as for Completion

Guides for Construction and Use:

The last four items under completion apply to Identification or Association.

RECOGNITION FORM—
MODIFIED TRUE-FALSE
CLUSTER TRUE-FALSE

Situation: The class is studying ways to finish walls. A sampling of statements will show how the form can be constructed and used.

	STATEMENTS
×	1. Smoothly plastered walls are easier to clean than roughly textured ones.
0	2. Plastered walls painted with an oil-base paint in a flat, dull finish are less expensive than water-base paints.
0	3. Wallpaper made with a fast-color ink is easier to wash than a plastic-coated type.
×	4. Plastic-coated wallpaper is more expensive than ordinary wallpaper.
×	5. Water-base paints on plastered walls will not wear as long as oil-base paints.
0	6. It is desirable to use regular wall paper in a room that is subject to heavy soil.

Directions: Check X before each statement which is correct information. Mark O for each incorrect statement.

Strengths:

Relatively easy to construct

A wide sampling is possible because many items can be answered within a given time

A well-constructed form usually shows discrimination, indicating the range of abilities within a class group

Possible to set up a key on which there is reasonable agreement

Weaknesses:

Fosters guessing when students do not know the content covered

Statements which are not wholly true or not wholly false are apt to be included

Guides for Construction and Use:

It is advisable to use a series of brief statements based upon a specific situation which is described in more or less detail and which needs to be considered in making each decision. Long, complex sentences are apt to be confusing.

Care needs to be taken to make the statements unequivocally right or wrong.

Approximately the same number of items for each kind of response are desirable, but this need not necessarily be the case at all times.

Directions need to indicate that students should reply to every item instead of only to those which they consider correct. Otherwise the scorer will not know whether the student disagreed with the statement or whether he failed to make a decision.

RECOGNITION FORM—
MODIFIED TRUE-FALSE
CORRECTING WORD(S)

Situation: The students have been finding out ways in which a living room can be made attractive. Sample statements, shown below, will show the construction and use of the form.

Directions: In the shorter space to the left of each statement listed in the table, mark X if the information is true and O if false. If the statement is false, circle the word or words which make it false and substitute the correct ones in the longer space.

	STATEMENTS
O size	1. Keeping the (shape) of objects in pleasing scale with one another and with the room as a whole adds to the room's attractiveness.
O more	2. A room is (less) attractive when pattern is used sparingly.
×	3. To make a room wholly attractive there needs to be some spot on which attention is immediately focused.

Strengths:

Decreases the possibility of guessing

Results show whether students really understand the subject matter on which the statements are based

Can be very discriminating in identifying the range of abilities within the class group

Weaknesses:

Difficult and time-consuming to construct

Only a limited number of statements can be answered within a given time because of the careful thinking required

Useful in only a limited number of situations

Guides for Construction and Use:

The phrasing of the statements requires careful thought so that students will interpret them correctly.

The statements containing the false words should not be too long and should center around one idea rather than several.

Care needs to be taken in deciding on the key words.

TWO-CHOICE

Directions: In each situation listed below, two introductions, (1) and (2), will be made, one correct and one incorrect. After each set of introductions, indicate A for the correct one and B for the incorrect, in the space at the right.

SITUATIONS	**DEMONSTRATIONS**	
	(1)	(2)
1. Girl introducing a friend to her mother	_____	_____
2. Boy introducing a pal to another boy	_____	_____

3. Teacher introducing a new boy to a girl _____ _____

Strengths:

Fairly easy to construct

Economical in space

Not time-consuming to answer

Evaluation of results can be made with reasonable agreement

Weakness:

Useful in only a limited number of situations

Guides for Construction and Use:

The statements need to be short and to the point.

The form is best used where the correct answer cannot be questioned.

RECOGNITION FORM—
MULTIPLE CHOICE

Situation: The class is holding a play school to get firsthand experience in learning about young children.

___C___ 1. Three-year-old Anne sucks her thumb. What is considered the most advisable way of helping her to stop? Write the letter to the correct response in the space to the left.

A. Remove the thumb from her mouth whenever you see her sucking it.

B. Tell her big little girls do not suck their thumbs.

C. Ignore the thumb sucking.

D. Put adhesive tape or bitter medicine on the thumb.

E. Punish her every time she does it.

Strengths:

It can be used in almost any area of content

A wide sampling of knowledge is possible

Well-constructed questions are likely to be discriminating

Guessing can be practically eliminated

Weaknesses:

Time-consuming to construct; difficult to find relevant and plausible responses with only one correct answer or one better than the others

A great deal of space is frequently required

Guides for Construction and Use:

Construction usually consists of two parts: (1) a statement or a direct question or an incomplete sentence and (2) a series of alternative responses, only one of which is to be chosen on the basis of being correct or better than the others. Occasionally the incorrect or less good response is the one to be selected.

Putting a statement or an incomplete sentence into question form sometimes makes the content clearer. Preceding the question by a description of the situation also tends to increase clarity.

It is advisable to provide four or five responses of equal length and to make each incorrect response sound plausible. No clues should be given to indicate the key response.

Listing the responses in column form is preferable to putting them in a paragraph. The latter practice may save space at the sacrifice of clarity. Possible exception may be when the responses are single words.

Care should be taken to avoid a pattern, as in having the third response consistently the correct or best one.

Graphic presentations such as drawings, diagrams, or pictures are frequently used in setting up either the response or the situation.

RECOGNITION FORM—MATCHING

Situation: The students are learning how to prepare an evening meal so that it can be served on time.

Directions: Select from the list of time periods given in the following table an appropriate one for carrying out each of the tasks listed. Place the letter of your responses in the blank spaces provided. All your answers need not necessarily be the same as those of other classmates.

MENU

Pot Roast	Hot Rolls, Butter
Mashed Potatoes	Frozen Marlow
Fresh Green Beans	Vanilla Sugar Cookies
Tomato and Lettuce Salad	Tea

	TASKS	PERIODS OF TIME FOR 6 O'CLOCK DINNER
A or B	1. Prepare lettuce and refrigerate	A. In the morning
D	2. Arrange salad on plates	B. In the afternoon before 5 o'clock
D	3. Place butter on table	
B	4. Shape rolls	C. Between 5 and 5:45 o'clock
D	5. Put rolls in oven	
D	6. Fill water glasses	D. Last 15 minutes before meal is served
B or C	7. Set table	
C	8. Peel potatoes and start water boiling	
D	9. Make tea	
A or B	10. Mix dough for rolls	
A or B	11. Prepare frozen Marlow	
C or D	12. Mash potatoes	
C	13. Start beans to cook	
A or B	14. Prepare Pot Roast	
A or B	15. Make vanilla cookies	

Strengths:

Can be adapted to almost any content area

If well-constructed, may be discriminating

Especially useful for evaluating students' ability to recognize relationships

Likely to be economical of space

Weaknesses:

Sometimes necessitates the use of single words or brief phrases, thus possibly reducing clarity

There is probability that clues may be given

Students may build up false associations if the material is not carefully constructed

Guides for Construction and Use:

Construction usually consists of two parts: (1) the stimulus list which includes definitions, descriptions, or other statements and (2) the response list, consisting of single words or short phrases. Each should be given a descriptive label. Directions need to explain clearly how the matching response is to be answered.

The two lists can be of equal length, or the stimulus list can be longer with some items in the response list being used more than once. But no stimulus item should have more than three answers. When more than one answer is considered correct, the directions should clearly explain this.

It is generally advisable to use four to eight response alternatives. If the responses are in groups, all the items in a group need to be related or similar. The arrangement of the responses needs to be kept in alphabetical or some other logical order. Using capital letters helps to make students' answers clear.

The response list should be clearly visible during the selection and recording of the answers. There are three such possibilities:

1. It may be located at the right of the stimulus list if both lists consist of single words or short phrases.

2. It may be placed above the stimulus list.

3. It may be on a separate sheet to which students can refer. This is often the case when the response list involves long descriptions, diagrams, or pictures for which there is not sufficient room on the page containing the stimulus list.

The form is sometimes used, as in the illustration, to show the order of preparation for a menu to be served at a given time. Other situations for which it might be used could include showing the comparative cost of menus prepared by a specific number of people, or the cost of operating different kinds of equipment.

RECOGNITION FORM—RANKING

Situation: The class is studying meal preparation. Several members are having difficulty preparing hot foods to be ready at the same time.

Directions: Mary is preparing dinner for four people and is using an electric range with three burners and one oven. Indicate the order in which Mary needs to commence the actual cooking of the foods listed below. Rank as 1 the food which should be started first.

RANK	FOODS	
1	A.	Hot steamed pudding
4	B.	Broiled steak—medium rare (not frozen)
3	C.	Fresh green beans, buttered
2	D.	Baked potatoes

Strengths:

  Reduces guessing

  Can be discriminating if well-constructed

Weaknesses:

  Time-consuming to construct

  Has limited use; difficult to find practical situations and to obtain a key that can be agreed on

Guides for Construction and Use:

  Care needs to be taken to select situations in which the form has practical use. In addition to the illustration given, these could include the comparative cost of menus prepared for a specific number of people or the cost of operating different kinds of equipment.

MODIFICATION OF THE QUESTION TYPE OF EVALUATION

Since more teachers have acquired knowledge and experience in using the question type of evaluation, they have been able to modify many of the forms illustrated on pages 208–217. They have experimented and discovered ways of constructing these forms to make them more meaningful and interesting. Several examples of modifications will be presented. As a general rule, these forms can be adapted to most areas of a home-economics program and to all adolescent levels.

EXAMPLE 1

Situation: A film was presented to bring out a particular aspect of the class goal under consideration. The students used the rating scale shown on pages 204–205 for appraising the film. It was then decided to obtain further evaluation of the students' reaction to the film. A copy of the questions in the list on page 218 was given to each student to answer outside of class and to hand in at the next meeting.

QUESTIONS

1. What are the main points you learned from the film?

2. Is there anything in the film you did not understand? If answer is yes, comment.   Yes _____   No _____

3. Do you have any questions concerning the film? If you have, state question(s).   Yes _____   No _____

4. Did the film show any relationship to your present-day life? If it did, give example(s).   Yes _____   No _____

5. Can you suggest any way(s) in which the film could be improved? If the answer is yes, indicate suggestion(s).   Yes _____   No _____

6. Do you think the film helped in carrying out class goal?   Yes _____   No _____

7. Would you like to see the film again?   Yes _____   No _____

                                        Name _____

EXAMPLE 2

Situation: A class of early adolescents is learning about the care of young children. Since most members are interested in babysitting, emphasis is upon what they need to know in this situation. Evaluation was made in two interesting ways: (1) Several students planned to relate their personal experiences while babysitting and to indicate how they had or had not applied the information a competent sitter needs to know. Comments from the class would also be given. (2) Other students kept diaries each time they went babysitting. Extracts from one of the diaries (Hatcher & Andrews, 1959, pp. 477–78) is presented below to show how the evaluation was made.

The diary contained two columns for (1) "What happened" and (2) "Comments." The student wrote down as soon as possible in the "What happened" column incidents that occurred while on a particular babysitting job. Then in the "Comments" column she indicated what a competent babysitter would do in each incident. She also had a classmate offer other suggestions which are shown in the form of questions following the student's remarks.

WHAT HAPPENED	COMMENTS
Oct. 20th. Had a phone call at 4:00 p.m. to be at Mrs. Dean's house on Front Street by 5:30. Regular sitter had suddenly become ill and had	

just telephoned she could not come to take care of Tommy while his mother and father went to a church supper.

Mom was out shopping, so left a note about where I was going. Was supposed to make a dessert for supper, but did not have time. Had to phone Jessie and Anna. We talked so long that I missed the bus. Did not get to Mrs. Dean's until 6 o'clock.	A sitter should always let her family know where she is going and when she expects to be home. Might have made a quick dessert instead of talking with Jessie and Anna. A sitter needs to arrive at the time she is expected. Promptness is important.
Supper was on the stove, ready to heat. Called Tommy several times, but he didn't pay attention to me. Went back into the living room and found him playing with toys. Told him supper was ready. He said "no." I said "yes." This went on several times. Finally I said "no" just for the fun of it, and Tommy said "yes." Then we both laughed. I let him take a small toy with him while he ate.	If it is mealtime, let him help you in the kitchen. Get a child's attention before making a request. Give a child warning before mealtime. Do not argue with a child. (How about washing his face and hands before eating?)

EXAMPLE 3

Statement: June always reads the labels on the new garments she buys.

___b___ 1. Indicate best comment on the above statement.

　　　　a. Many of the new materials today do not need to be dry cleaned to prevent shrinkage and to retain original appearance.

　　　　b. It is not always easy to identify the materials in a garment; therefore, statement of the fiber content and suggestions for care are often given on the label.

　　　　c. If a garment shrinks during laundering, one can look on the label to find what the fiber content was.

EXAMPLE 4

Study carefully the situation described before answering the questions in the table on page 220.

Situation: Jane, who had just completed her first year in college, was at her home in the city for the summer vacation. Her parents were very concerned over her behavior. They blamed themselves to a considerable extent, because from the time she was a small child they had given her everything she wanted in so far as they could. They had been proud to learn that Jane was always popular at college dances and had lots of dates. However, after Jane had been at home for a few weeks her parents faced the fact that Jane's "lights were turned on only in company." They admitted to themselves that she was nonchalant and cynical, as if nothing really mattered to her. She appeared to think her bored manner was superior and sophisticated. She pursued a make-believe existence that left her dissatisfied and unhappy when she came back at intervals to the realities of life. Her parents decided that what Jane most needed was a new point of view and a new sense of values. They thought the situation would be helped if they could guide Jane in wise use of time during the summer vacation.

Directions: For items 1–6, write in the space to the left of each item the letter corresponding to your evaluation of the suggestion.

EVALUATION

a.   If the suggestion was followed by Jane it would probably lead toward *greater* happiness.

b.   If the suggestion was followed by Jane it would probably lead toward *less* happiness.

c.   The suggestion involves so many unexplained factors it is not possible to judge whether it would contribute to Jane's happiness.

a	1.	Search through newspapers for new things to attend—things which Jane never dreamed were available in city life.
c	2.	Spend part of the vacation with grandparents who are lonely and want someone young around the house.
b	3.	Utilize a considerable part of the summer for lying around and reading popular novels for which there is not time during the school year.
a	4.	Make a practice of learning something new all the time, even during vacation.
b	5.	Avoid planning any routine for living during the summer vacation; leave that for next year in college.
c	6.	Spend as much time as possible with a college acquaintance who lives a few blocks from Jane.

EXAMPLE 5

Situation: A class of middle adolescents has been working on the goal "getting along with my family." Each student, selecting a personal problem, planned and carried out a solution. Some of the classwork involved formulating generalizations associated with the various problems. The following illustration is based on the generalization that consideration of others is the basis of good family relationships, and was part of a written long-form appraisal.

The problem: Lucy, age 13, the youngest member of the family, has become very much concerned about her personal appearance. She spends considerable time in front of the bathroom mirror which is the only well-lighted one in the house. The other members of the family have complained to Lucy's mother that they have difficulty getting ready for work and school on time because Lucy monopolizes the bathroom each morning. What would you do if you were Lucy's mother?

PROCEDURES

Mark × the wise procedure(s) and 0 for any that are unwise.

0	1.	Tell the others Lucy will get over being concerned about her appearance.
0	2.	Tell Lucy to stop spending so much time looking in the mirror.
×	3.	Make arrangements for a well-lighted mirror for Lucy's room.
×	4.	Have a private talk with Lucy about sharing the bathroom with other members of the family.
0	5.	Ignore the complaints.

Mark × the best reason(s) for your answer and 0 for those you did not use.

×	6.	Lucy should be encouraged to be well-groomed.
0	7.	Lucy's concern over her appearance is only temporary.
0	8.	Spending too much time in front of the mirror may cause Lucy to become vain.
0	9.	Lucy needs special attention even though it inconveniences the rest of the family.
×	10.	It is important for Lucy to understand that what she does affects other members of the family.

EXAMPLE 6

Situation: A class of late adolescents is learning how to make a living room attractive. Part of the evaluation was made through the use of pictures. Each student was given four pictures illustrating some of the things they had learned and a copy of several room descriptions.

Directions: In the column at the left, write the letter of the picture which best matches each room description.

	ROOM DESCRIPTIONS	PICTURES
_____	1. Objects are especially well related in form and shape to create a feeling of harmony.	A
		B
_____	2. The wise use of lines produces the effect of height.	C
		D
_____	3. Pattern is used particularly well.	
_____	4. The furniture tends to make the room appear larger than it is.	
_____	5. The general effect contributes to making the room appear small and cozy.	

EXAMPLE 7

Situation: A class of middle adolescents studying child care is learning how to give directions and suggestions to preschool children. A sampling of one evaluation form follows.

Directions: Read carefully the directions given to the child related to each situation listed in the table. Then in the space provided at the right, try to improve the directions. If you think improvement is not necessary, leave the space blank.

DIRECTION	IMPROVEMENT
Situation 1—Judy holding the door open	
Don't hold the door open, Judy. You're letting in all the flies.	(Judy, please shut the door as quickly as you can so the flies won't come in.)
Situation 2—George putting his feet on an upholstered chair	
Don't put your feet on that chair. You'll ruin it.	(George, our shoes aren't clean on the bottom, so we have to keep them out of chairs where people sit.)
Situation 3—Susan taking several magazines from the living room table	
Leave those magazines alone, Susan. You'll tear off the covers and you know how your father hates to read torn magazines.	(Let's look at one magazine together, Susan. We'll hold it like this so it won't get torn.)
Situation 4—It's lunchtime for Amy	
Wash your hands, Amy, or you can't come to the table.	(Amy, it's time to wash your hands for lunch.)

EXAMPLE 8

Situation: A class of middle adolescents is working on the goal "learning what makes a living room attractive." A sampling of one form of evaluation used follows.

Directions: The colored pictures A, B, and C represent three living rooms. Study the pictures carefully, noting the details and general appearance of each one. In the list below are several statements pertaining only to the areas that can be seen in the pictures. These statements may apply to one, two, or three of the pictures or to none of them. Circle the letter which corresponds to each picture for which you think the statement is true. If you believe that the statement does not apply to any of the pictures, leave the letters unmarked.

ROOM	STATEMENTS
A B C	1. The coloring of the walls makes the room seem small and cozy.
A B C	2. The furnishings are in scale with the room.
A B C	3. The furniture is in keeping with the character of the room.
A B C	4. Lamps are placed where they are convenient to use.
A B C	5. The room has a chief center of interest.

Listed below are suggestions for altering the rooms. Circle yes the suggestions that you believe would be desirable and no those that you think would not be an improvement.

Room A would be improved if:

Yes No	1. The furniture were regrouped to form a center of interest around the sofa.
Yes No	2. The walls were painted a light bright yellow.

Room B would be improved if:

Yes No	1. The large rug were replaced by several smaller ones.
Yes No	2. A conversation grouping were made.

Room C would be improved if:

Yes No	1. More pattern were used throughout the room.
Yes No	2. Less furniture were used.

EXAMPLE 9

Situation: Two teachers were interested in learning to develop programmed instruction to support main points or for make-up work with absentees. Two examples of questions taken from different frames of one of these teachers are shown on page 224.

Directions for use as a teaching tool: Read each frame and try to complete the statement without referring to the answer column. If you cannot fill in the missing word or words, unfold the answer column for the correct answer.

Directions for use as an evaluation device: Keeping the answer column folded under, complete the frames, writing the missing words on a blank sheet of paper placed to the right of the frames.

STATEMENT	ANSWER
1. Of all the home factors in early years of life which influence the child's social behavior and attitudes, perhaps the most important is the type of _____ methods used by parents.	child-rearing
2. Close associations with persons whose emotions are uncontrolled frequently lead to undeveloped emotional _____ in the child as he imitates the behavior of others.	control

Two examples taken from a frame of another teacher follow.

Directions: The answers can be written in the spaces provided for each question or on a separate sheet of paper. When you have completed your questions unfold the pages and check your answers.

---

1. Which one of the following diagrams shows the best proportion? _____

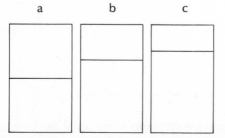

    a   b   c

2. Harmony demands that sizes, shapes, textures, colors and ideas be _____.

COMBINATIONS AND VARIATIONS OF CHECK-LIST AND QUESTION TYPES

In addition to modifying the check-list and question types of evaluation, teachers have experimented in using combinations and variations of the two, resulting in a more varied and broader scope of evaluation procedures. A few examples will be presented to show how this has been accomplished.

EXAMPLE 1

Situation: A class of early adolescents working on the goal "to develop good posture while sewing" helped to construct the form of evaluation on page 225. This type of appraisal is carried out by dividing the class into two groups, the chairmanship rotating at each class meeting. After a certain period of time the final scores made at each meeting are combined. The group having the higher total score wins and can then ask a special favor from the losing group.

Date									
BEGINNING SCORE									
Deductions									
Additions									
FINAL SCORE									

Scoring:

100 points to be given at the beginning

10 points to be deducted if the chairman does not maintain good posture; decision to be based on the majority of the group

5 points to be deducted for each group member who has poor posture; decision to be made by group chairman

If one group has no deductions, the deductions of the other group are to be added to the total score of this group.

EXAMPLE 2

Situation: A class of middle adolescents is learning to use time spent outside of school more effectively. Each student kept a record of activities for one week, using the form on pages 226–227.

At the end of the week the records were brought to school where a committee summarized the time spent on the various activities. The results were put on the board and discussed by the class. The students summarized the important points in the discussion and on this basis set up a list of questions to use in evaluating their records. A sampling of the questions follows.

QUESTIONS	YES	NO
1. Do I waste a lot of time?	_____	_____
2. Do I have a variety of interests?	_____	_____
3. Are there things I would like to do but don't seem to have time for?	_____	_____
4. Can I organize my day more effectively?	_____	_____
5. Do I try to do too much and as a result not do some things well?	_____	_____

A second week's record was kept and evaluated by the students who felt that considerable improvement was needed in their schedule. All the records were eventually given to the teacher who used them to evaluate students' interests.

ACTIVITIES	DATE	TIME SPENT	COMMENT
A. Studying			
B. Entertainment Radio listening TV viewing Movies Concerts, lectures Other _____			
C. Games Playing games Watching games Supervised sports Unsupervised sports Other _____			
D. Social pursuits Parties School affairs Club meetings Loafing with friends Other _____			
E. Solitary pursuits Reading Hobbies Loafing alone Other _____			
F. Special instruction Music Other _____			
G. Religious affairs Church attendance Church work Church societies Other _____			
H. Home work Duties connected with meals			

Housework Outdoor yardwork Other _____			
I. Outside work _____			

EXAMPLE 3

Situation: A class of early adolescent girls completing their first project in clothing construction helped to construct a check list, of which only a part is shown below: "How Does Your Skirt Rate?"

Directions: Check the space in the column which applies to you and your skirt.

	It's almost perfect	It's only fair	I need more practice
	1	2	3

GENERAL APPEARANCE

15. The skirt is clean and well pressed

16. The hem hangs even

17. The length is becoming to me

18. The seam hangs straight

How many 1's did you check? —— How many 2's? —— How many 3's? ——

If you have more checks in column 1 than the other two columns, you can be proud of your skirt.

If most of your checks are in column 2, you have learned a lot but still need to improve.

If you have more checks in column 3 than the other two columns, you have learned enough to make your skirt, but need more help on the difficult parts.

What did I enjoy doing most about my skirt?

How satisfied am I with my skirt?

The new processes that I learned were:

My family thinks my skirt is:

My teacher thinks my skirt is:

EXAMPLE 4

Situation: A class of middle adolescents helped to construct a self-teaching, self-evaluation form (shown on page 229) to appraise their achievement toward the goal "to practice good methods of cooking vegetables." Copies of the form were posted in each kitchen and checked by the students whenever they cooked vegetables. In the left-hand column of the form, important clues were listed and represented by drawings. In the right-hand column there was a list of questions regarding the clues, along with reasons for using the appropriate methods to cook the vegetables.

GUIDES FOR CONSTRUCTION

It is important for every teacher to become familiar with the types and forms of evaluation previously described and illustrated. This takes time and requires careful and systematic work. But as teachers, and even students, gain experience in using various types of evaluation, the process of construction generally tends to become less difficult. The following suggestions should prove useful:

1. Determine the emphasis to be placed on different learnings. A balanced evaluation emphasizes the relative importance of the various kinds of learnings related to each goal. It does not place undue emphasis on some learnings while others are neglected. This is true whether the evaluation is to be used for determining grades or as a part of programmed instruction. Sometimes, however, balanced evaluation is not possible when the goal is such that valid, reliable evaluation cannot be developed for lack of know-how. This may be true for certain goals in relationships or other areas also.

2. Select forms of evaluation. Knowledge and experience in constructing and using various forms will help the teacher to decide which are best suited to a particular situation.

3. Prepare and organize the items. The guides listed, if followed, should result in more satisfactory items.

Prepare items dealing with the evaluation of a particular goal at one time.

Decide how many items will be needed and then allow a few extra as some will probably have to be discarded.

Construct appropriate items well in advance of the time they are to be used. Formulate concise, complete, and clear directions.

Organize the items to facilitate the use of different forms. Sometimes the most difficult items are placed in the middle with the easier ones toward the beginning and the end. Items are generally numbered consecutively.

Decide on key responses and include these when asking experienced persons to look over the evaluation. Reactions of such individuals will help to obtain a key on which there is likely to be general agreement.

Secure a higher reliability by having clear, accurate reproduction of the evaluation used.

ADMINISTERING EVALUATION

Whether evaluation is used for self-teaching, which may or may not be programmed instruction, or for determining grades, certain factors need to be taken into account:

1. Have all necessary materials available as needed.

2. Be certain that students understand clearly what they will be doing and how much time is available. There is usually a time limit for evaluation if the results are to be used as a partial basis for grades.

	CLUES	ARE YOU DOING THIS?
	You may have trouble on your hands. Don't pass it on.	Washing hands before working with vegetables. (This helps prevent the spread of disease.)
	Please leave me in my jacket.	Cooking in skins whenever possible. (Foods retain more vitamins and minerals when cooked this way.)
	Why make an old soak out of me?	Washing vegetables but not keeping them standing in water. (This preserves vitamins and minerals.)
	Don't drown me!	Using only the smallest amount of boiling salted water that will cook the vegetables without burning. (This helps to retain vitamins and minerals.)
	I'm green and I like it.	Preserving the color of most green vegetables by bringing them to a boil rapidly without a cover; then reducing heat and covering. (This preserves their bright color and fresh flavor.)
	Please don't keep me waiting.	Serving the vegetables as soon as they are prepared. (This makes them look and taste better.)

3.   Provide as much quiet as possible while students are working, because certain students are seriously disturbed by noise or confusion. However, some evaluations may require moving around quietly, such as those based on objects or pictures, or being conducted during a field trip.

ANALYZING AND INTERPRETING RESULTS

In the future more and more evaluation will probably be used to help all students achieve while functioning on their own. Carefully documented profiles of achievement will have more meaning to those concerned than today's traditional grading. Nonetheless, both teachers and students will want to know how good the evaluation is that they have developed. Most forms lend themselves to continued improvement. Sometimes questions or ideas of students as they work will suggest needed change. Sometimes the teacher will gain new ideas through conferences, meetings, or study which will suggest improved evaluation for students.

The question then arises as to whether item analysis as presently in use is needed in individualized instruction. It is expected in such programs that able students will not be held back by synchronizing their learning with other students less able. At the same time, students who learn more slowly will have an opportunity to achieve the same as abler students though less quickly. The answer to the question about item analysis probably lies in the kind of evaluation used in particular programmed instruction. Any evaluation question which is formulated so as to be more confusing to those with superior ability than to low-ability students will not achieve at least one of the purposes of individualized instruction. In such circumstances, the able student may not learn more quickly than other students. Further, for

some time to come, many schools will continue to use traditional grading and other authority-based evaluation systems. For this reason, making an appraisal of items will be considered here.

APPRAISING THE ITEMS

An informal appraisal can be made when a small group of students have used the series of items. In making this appraisal, the teacher will need to watch out for three situations which would indicate that improvement is necessary: (1) a high percentage of the class may fail to answer correctly a large number of the items; (2) most of the items may be answered correctly by a high percentage of the class; and (3) some items may be answered correctly by more low-ability students than those with superior ability.

A more exact appraisal, generally known as item-counting, will also show whether or not the same conditions have resulted. But certain procedures are used to obtain this information. The series of items will need to be given to a large number of students. At least sixty papers are generally considered necessary for an adequate appraisal. From these papers the teacher selects the highest fourth and the lowest fourth, disregarding the middle half. On a separate sheet he records the errors made on each paper, first of the superior group, then of the lowest fourth. It is easier to complete one paper before starting the next. The recording would be similar to the illustration shown on page 231.

In appraising the results, the teacher will need to decide which items are too difficult or too easy, which are reversals, that is items answered correctly by more low-ability students, and whether the percentage of difference between the high fourth and the low fourth is significant. An arbitrary standard of a 15 per cent

Items	High-ability Group No. = 15	Low-ability Group No. = 15

Item-Counting Method of Appraising Student Performance

difference is regarded as satisfactory. Thus a sampling of the items shown above can be appraised as follows:

Item 1 is too easy, since a high percentage of both groups answered it correctly. It is therefore not discriminating.

Item 2 is discriminating because more high-ability than low-ability students answered the item correctly. The difference was much greater than 15 per cent.

Item 4 is a reversal.

Item 5 is too difficult, since a high percentage of both groups failed to answer it correctly. The item is therefore not discriminating.

INTERPRETING THE FINDINGS

Having appraised the series of items, the teacher will want to interpret her findings. Interpretation requires careful thinking, good personal judgment, and an insight into various factors that might have adversely influenced the results.

If she discovered that a high percentage of the class failed to answer correctly a large number of items, she may consider several possible reasons why this happened.

1. Could it be due to her instruction? Maybe the students did not understand the material on which the items were based. Or perhaps

they were not sufficiently interested in it to make an earnest effort to give the correct answers.

2.   Were there factors associated with the administration of the evaluation? Perhaps there was undue noise or disturbance which prevented the students from concentrating on their work. Quite possibly the group was under pressure to answer the items in too short a time.

3.   Were there upsetting circumstances outside the classroom which affected the group? The students may have been emotionally disturbed because the school had just lost the state championship in football. Or an approaching class trip may have been so absorbing that they failed to work to the best of their ability.

4.   Could the items be at fault? Perhaps the phrasing was ambiguous or too many unfamiliar words obscured the meaning. On the other hand, if most of the items were answered correctly by a high percentage of the class, what could be the reason? It might be that the teacher had not made sufficient differentiation among different levels of ability. Thus the material covered in the series of items was so easy that all the students knew it. Or a great deal of emphasis may have been put on the material so that everyone in the group learned it. Or after the material was taken up in class, the students may have continued to learn more about it elsewhere. Still another possibility might be that the phrasing of the items suggested the correct response.

Why should some items be answered correctly by more low-ability than high-ability students? In such instances, the superior students may have had a more comprehensive knowledge of the material and may have given the items a meaning which was not intended.

Once the teacher has clues indicating why

some of these conditions may have occurred, steps can be taken to remedy the situation. Any of the following suggestions may prove useful:

Re-evaluate instruction and try to make it more effective.

Be more careful in administering evaluation and see that extraneous factors are minimized or eliminated.

Try to improve the series of items so they are clearer and less ambiguous.

Change the content of items to meet different levels of ability.

Discard poor items and construct new ones in their place.

SIGNIFICANCE OF A SCORE

Most written forms of evaluation calling for student responses can usually be summarized by a score. Such a score has little significance in individualized instruction other than to indicate to students what is yet to be learned or accomplished. But where grades are required, the score needs to be translated so that it will indicate a student's relative position in a particular performance. For example, the scores made by all members of a class on a particular form of evaluation may be arranged from the highest to the lowest. Or they may be grouped into upper quarter, middle half, and lower quarter. Both arrangements show a student's position in relation to that of other students in the class. This position may not necessarily remain the same throughout a series of evaluations. A student who is in the middle half of a group in one performance may, through exerted effort or acquired knowledge, score high enough in another performance to be in the upper fourth of the group.

Once a student's position is determined in a particular performance, some kind of symbol is often needed to indicate different levels of achievement. This symbol is known as a grade or mark. Fitting several grades or marks together for a term grade was discussed on pages 137–141. It may be noted that in determining the final grade a symbol may or may not be needed up to that time.

GENERAL REMARKS ON GRADES AND EVALUATION

To give grades or not is one of the many difficult problems facing educators today. A few schools have used substitutes for grades such as conferences with parents or a written description and analysis of accomplishment. In some instances, these substitutes have worked reasonably well, particularly at the lower grade levels and where the teacher-student ratio is relatively low. In secondary schools where one teacher may work with several hundred students a day, the problem seems insurmountable even though many teachers enjoy grading less than any other part of teaching.

Evaluation itself adds to the plight of the teacher. As schools begin to place increasing emphasis on developing creativeness, sensitivity, and other less tangible abilities, additional ways of evaluating accomplishment may be needed. However, the first thing for any teacher to do is to recognize that now and in the future there will be many changes in education bringing surprising innovations. The teacher who has an open mind and a willingness to experiment and evaluate new ideas will be the successful teacher of today and tomorrow.

SUGGESTED TEACHER EXPERIENCES

1.   Working with a group, assemble examples of evaluation from a particular source such as books, magazines, pamphlets, courses of study. Evaluate the various examples found in terms of suggestions on evaluation in this chapter.

2.   In learning to construct appropriate evaluation,

a. the group may set a goal in any area of a home-economics program, indicating the age level desired and the major learnings to be taught;

b. working individually or in small groups, each person selects a different technique or instructional resource that would be useful in working toward the goal;

c. each person then constructs as many forms of evaluation as possible that could be used to appraise achievement of the goal, using the selected technique or resource as a basis for the evaluation;

d. the various forms of evaluation are then compiled and studied by the group as a whole. A general discussion can bring out points such as whether the forms are suitable and what check lists or question type of forms were not constructed and why;

e. several of the most appropriate forms can then be selected and arrangements made to try them out in high-school classes.

3.   Help the class to collect materials or sources of materials which provide ideas for adapting to ingenious evaluation. Each class member can then try to make at least one such adaptation. If possible, try out the evaluation developed with the age group intended. These individuals will probably be able to contribute useful suggestions.

4.   The group may want to have a brain-storming session to consider what it would like to substitute for grades in our schools.

EPILOGUE:

Some teachers who have used earlier editions of this book have written the authors about the teaching-learning methods they have been experimenting with. They have stressed how much they enjoyed trying out many of the suggested instructional techniques, resources, and illustrations of evaluation. Many spoke of two other matters with which they had problems:

1. Choosing which techniques and materials to use for a certain specific purpose.

2. Knowing what to do about the things generally referred to as "business of the department." Many teachers have come to realize that these things are really necessary supporting resources which need to be managed if teachers are to be effective both in and out of the classroom.

What they are really saying in bringing up both problems is how important decision-making is. Teachers have studied management in one or more of their university classes in which decision-making certainly was stressed. They have been told that decisions and responsibilities that were not a part of teaching in a less complex society are being forced on individuals today. An example follows: "At the university I became acquainted with all kinds of new teaching equipment which I know is now available for use in relatively few schools. Some administrators do not even believe in much of what I would like to work with. There is a school I would like to teach in, and I have the opportunity to do so, but I would need to adapt to having very little of the newest teaching equipment. I am not certain I could do the kind of teaching I want to do." A teacher's decision on this and other problems may not resemble that of anyone else. The problems, the setting, the resources all differ among individuals; thus the decisions may be expected to differ also.

We are including a Guide for Development of Decision-Making Ability, which we trust will be a helpful summary. The teacher may want to modify it to make it more useful for her as an individual. Certainly as she attempts to become more adept and experienced at decision-making she will want to try out the Guide. (See also the Appendix to Book Two, pages 237–245.)

A GUIDE FOR DEVELOPING
DECISION-MAKING ABILITY

In making a decision, some individuals will want to write out reactions to the statements in the Guide. Other persons will find it just as helpful to think through the statements as they relate to the decisions to be made. In general, the more difficult the decision the more helpful it will be to record your thinking. The more adept you become at decision-making the less recording will be needed. But however you proceed, your thinking in relation to each statement will help you clarify your thinking in the decision-making process.

1. I try to clarify what I wish to obtain from the decision to be made—my real goal.

2. I consider whether this goal reflects my values and standards. If not, where is the conflict?

3. I try to assess the relation of my goal to that of others.

4. I consider what personal, home, and community services and facilities are likely to be affected by the decisions I make.

5. I appraise whether the resources needed are available now or could be made available. Could they be made available by substituting one resource for another, using a combination of resources, or by saving or improving resources available—personal, home, community?

6. I assess how much, if any, personal or so-

cial pressure there is for or against the use of resources needed.

7. I choose what appear to be alternative ways of achieving my goal.

8. I consider the advantages and disadvantages of each alternative.

9. From among the various alternatives I choose the one or ones that I can support.

Consider the next two statements only if a group is involved in the decision-making:

I am willing to listen to the choice of others knowing they may be influenced by

  a. decisions previously made

  b. economic and other factors related to each possible decision

  c. feeling of risk in attempting anything different

  d. responsibilities and pressures from others that may be unrelated to personal feelings.

I accept wholeheartedly the fact that the most satisfactory method of settling conflicts is for different sides to reach a new and satisfying solution for all.

10. After a tentative decision has been reached I check probable reactions and make modifications as seem desirable.

11. After the final decision is made I plan, and put my plan into action. I remember that short-range plans need to be more specific than long-range ones. As each step of performance of a long-range plan comes up, specific planning will be needed.

12. I evaluate effectiveness of the decision as it is carried out. I try to face reality, knowing it may lead to greater achievement another time.

Now that you have made, carried out, and evaluated your decision, take time out to realize the satisfactions to be obtained from thoughtfully engaging in the decision-making process.

APPENDIX TO BOOK TWO

THE BUSINESS OF THE DEPARTMENT OF HOME ECONOMICS

MANAGING THE DEPARTMENT EFFECTIVELY

In its narrow sense, managing the department effectively usually includes such goals as: (1) putting the department in order for the opening and closing of the school year; (2) maintaining the facilities of the department through cleanliness, orderliness, and maintenance of equipment; and (3) caring for department business, which includes setting up the budget, keeping records and reports, attending to correspondence, taking inventory, and caring for records and instructional materials. All are important matters and a teacher is likely to find herself in difficulty if she neglects any one. On the other hand she is likely to feel rewarded if she handles them successfully. A more effectively managed department should be the result.

The following are suggestions for the three goals.

PUTTING THE DEPARTMENT IN ORDER FOR THE OPENING AND CLOSING OF THE SCHOOL YEAR

Few teachers will deny that opening and closing the department are important aspects of teaching home economics. At the beginning of the year the department needs to be ready for class use, and at the end of the year to be prepared for a period when regular classes will not be in session. It could be a tedious job for the teacher alone, but it is quite probable that student assistance can be considered as a major resource. However, in addition to the tasks that can be managed cooperatively by the teacher and the students, there are certain closing duties relating to inventories, budget reports, records, and the like which only the teacher can carry out. Since these responsibilities are of a business nature, they will be discussed in the section on department business.

SUGGESTED CLASS EXPERIENCES

Various class experiences can be planned around the tasks which need to be done. One such experience for a middle-adolescent group of students who are familiar with the department set-up could be the listing of management items and essential tasks for opening and closing the department. This list could serve as a yearly guide for different classes to consider what tasks they would like and are qualified to

237

do. An example of such a list is presented on page 239. Determining useful information needed for carrying out the tasks, setting up time schedules, and working out individual and group responsibilities could also become interesting class experiences for the opening and closing of the department.

EVALUATING RESULTS

Evaluation will need to be a continuous process from the time the tasks and experiences are undertaken to their completion. Here again, each participating group will need to decide how well the work is being carried out, where improvement is needed, and then to what extent the goal has been achieved. The final criteria for achievement could be these questions: Is the department actually ready for use? Is it adequately prepared for the period when it will not be in use? Is there satisfaction in what has been accomplished?

MAINTAINING THE FACILITIES OF THE DEPARTMENT

There are three important aspects of caring for the facilities of the department: cleanliness, orderliness, and maintenance of equipment. Every teacher is aware that a clean, orderly room makes the department more attractive, comfortable, and sanitary. In the long run, cleanliness and order also save money, time, and energy, especially when equipment is kept in good working condition.

The teacher and the students who cooperatively plan for the opening and closing of the department will be aware that many of the tasks will need to be continued throughout the year. Just what needs to be done, by whom,

when, and how can be discussed and decided on by the teacher and the participating groups each year. It is especially important to keep plans flexible from year to year and even throughout the year to meet new or changing situations. Some classes may need more information than others for carrying out the tasks related to keeping the department clean and orderly and in maintaining equipment. Experiences are likely to vary with different groups, depending somewhat on the approach taken toward achieving the goal.

PREVENTIVE HOUSEKEEPING

A particularly feasible approach to maintaining the facilities of the department is called "preventive housekeeping." The term speaks for itself. Examples of useful preventive measures follow (adapted, Illinois Teacher, 1962):

1. Know materials that resist soil and clean easily when choosing furnishings.

2. Displays behind glass will save many minutes of tedious dusting.

3. Using vacuum attachments for dusting is an efficient way of capturing the dust without scattering it.

4. End-of-class roundup will allow the next class to enter an orderly room.

5. A supply of paper towels should be readily available for immediate use in mopping up spills, drips, and splashes, keeping dirt and water spots from marring floors and furnishings.

6. Strips of felt glued on lamp and vase bases protect furniture and floor surfaces from scratches.

7. The installation of a ventilating fan can help in keeping grease and smoke off the walls.

ITEM	TASKS	
	OPENING THE DEPARTMENT	**CLOSING THE DEPARTMENT**
Storage spaces	Clean; organize for use	Clean; put into order
Equipment		
Ranges	Clean; prepare for use	Clean thoroughly
Refrigerator	Clean; cool for use	Defrost; wash inside and out; leave door open
Washer and dryer	Clean for use	Clean thoroughly; leave loading doors open
Sewing machines	Clean; test for stitching	Clean; oil; cover; list any needed repairs
Appliances	Clean; check operation	Clean; disconnect; store
Furnishings		
Upholstered furniture	Remove and store coverings; brush furniture	Clean surfaces; cover
Draperies and curtains	Unpack; press; hang	Clean; label; store
Linens	Unpack; press; distribute	Clean; label; store
Rugs	Unpack; vacuum	Clean; protect against moths if necessary; store
Shades or blinds	Clean; adjust for use	Adjust for summer lighting
Tables and other work surfaces	Clean	Clean
Kitchen service		
Utensils	Clean; distribute for use	Clean; inventory; store
Garbage containers	Clean; distribute for use	Clean by disinfecting; store
Food	Order; stock staples	Discard perishables; store staples carefully
Meal service		
Silverware	Unpack; clean; distribute	Clean; inventory; pack; store
Glassware, china, pottery	Unpack; clean; distribute to proper places	Inventory; pack; store
Instructional resources		
Books and other reference materials	Unpack; dust; arrange for use	Sort; file; store
Supplies for subject areas	Unpack; arrange for use	Sort; file; store
Visual aids	Arrange for use	Inventory; store carefully in dry place
Chalk board	Clean; arrange for use	Clean; store
Bulletin boards	Arrange for use	Clean; store
Fire hazards	Check for hazards; locate and learn to use extinguishers	Avoid leaving potential hazards
Household pests	Inspect for and campaign against	Take all necessary precautions

8. Having adequate supplies and equipment with some duplicates saves cleaning time and encourages teamwork.

9. Labeling and systematically arranging containers save searching time.

10. Knowledge of energy-and-motion studies as they apply to tasks frequently needing to be repeated is helpful.

11. A general storage box or tray for collecting odd items throughout the day will make short work of the end-of-day put-away chores.

12. Caring for equipment according to stated directions is essential for good maintenance.

13. Prompt attention to minor repairs and to the replacement of worn parts saves time and money in the long run.

14. Know how to make simple repairs on furniture and equipment but learn which repairs require professional skill.

EVIDENCES OF GOAL ACHIEVEMENT

As in the case of opening and closing the department, evaluation of maintenance should be a continuous process with periodic appraisals of the extent to which the goal is being attained. Although different groups will make these appraisals in various ways, there are certain evidences of how well task and goal achievement are progressing:

1. By indication that the department is ready for use as needed

2. By observation that there is a place for everything and everyone knows and uses the places

3. By checking equipment to see that it is in satisfactory condition and ready for use

4. By believing that resources are being used to the best advantage

5. By student self-appraisal that tasks leading to the goal are being learned

6. By student satisfaction in doing their tasks to the best of their ability

7. By observation that desirable housekeeping habits are being established and that managerial ability is developing

8. By believing that wise decisions are making achievement of the goal possible

TAKING CARE OF DEPARTMENT BUSINESS

Taking care of department business is an essential goal in managing the department effectively. Most teachers will agree that achieving this goal generally involves administering the finances of the department, keeping records and reports, attending to correspondence, taking inventories, and caring for instructional records and materials. Since a teacher's knowledge of business is often incidental rather than planned, it is important for her to acquire helpful information that will contribute toward the use of sound business procedures. The material here offers special information on business practices that are generally considered desirable.

CLARIFYING THE VALUE OF MONEY

One of the important resources in business management is money. The teacher's attitudes toward it will tend to influence her decisions concerning its use for the department. In order to clarify her values, the teacher will need to ask herself such questions as: (1) Do I think of money as a means to an end, or do I consider it an end in itself? (2) Does money give me a feeling of power, or does it represent a responsibility? (3) Do I think of money in terms of what other teachers have to operate their departments, or do I value it on the basis of what I can do with what I have?

The value of money as it is used to operate the department lies in what it can do for the teacher and for the students in achieving class goals. Money thus acquires value through the needs and wants it satisfies. However, the amount of money is not so important as the way the money is managed. Greater feelings of satisfaction can be derived not from having a certain amount of money but from knowing that wise decisions have been made in spending what one has.

SETTING UP THE BUDGET

At the present time most home-economics departments are financed by an allotment from the local school board, based on a yearly budget submitted by the head of the department. In determining the budget, several factors need to be taken into consideration:

1. The number of persons enrolled in home-economics courses and anticipated enrollment

2. Expendable equipment and supplies covering each area being taught

3. Current upkeep of the department—needs for maintenance, repair, and replacement

4. Expenditures of previous year or years

5. A three- to five-year plan for continued upkeep, development, and expansion of the department

In keeping with the spirit of democracy and with the use of human resources, budget-making tends to be more satisfactory when a number of people participate in the financial planning. School administrators, area and state supervisors, home-economics students, and persons serving on advisory committees may be helpful.

"PADDING" THE BUDGET

Every budget should be prepared on the basis of actual needs. Neither a large surplus nor a deficit is to be desired. A large unexpected balance is apt to give the impression that those planning the budget asked for an excess amount, whereas a deficit is apt to be construed as bad management. Making estimates in excess of actual needs with the hope that a cut in the budget will leave enough money with which the department can function adequately is a poor policy. A department which has the reputation of "padding" its budget loses social esteem. "Padding" makes it difficult for those who supply the funds to place a true evaluation on the home-economics program. It becomes impossible to distinguish between the expenditures that are superfluous and those that are necessary for the adequate growth and development of the students. The best budget is one in which the income and the expenditures balance at the end of the year.

EARNING AND SAVING MONEY
FOR THE DEPARTMENT

It is not to be expected in all cases that the home-economics program will be wholly financed by allotted funds. Some groups may want to earn money as part of the regular classwork. Special experiences may vary all the way from buying an additional lamp for the living center to equipping an outdoor play area for preschool children who are participating with the students as part of their classwork. In general, it may be advisable to select experiences for which there might be uncertainty about obtaining funds. This will indicate a willingness on the part of the teacher and the students to earn money for something that they believe is especially worthwhile.

The largest item of expenditures for the different areas is generally the supplies for food-preparation classes. Some of the cost can be reduced by freezing fruits and vegetables and making jellies and jams during the preserving season to be used by the classes during the year. Careful buying of other food products and needed small items also helps the budget. If the school policy permits, giving students an opportunity to gain experience along this line aids in the development of money management. Both the teacher and the students will need to keep up with consumer information because of the large and growing number of items available for selection.

KEEPING RECORDS AND REPORTS

In every home-economics department there are innumerable records and reports to be made, some for the school, others for the teacher's use. Since this is a time-consuming task for which the teacher herself is responsible, every effort should be made to do it as efficiently as possible. To expedite matters the teacher should know the school and department policy of keeping records and reports. She will then be able to set up a plan for doing what is required and in addition what she may feel is needed. As a rule, the records and reports a teacher may handle include the following.

1. Financial records. Good business practice requires that the teacher keep a record of expenditures in line with the budget that has been set up. In some schools special forms are provided. If not, any form is generally acceptable if it presents a clear picture of what is spent. The receipted bills should be clipped to the form, indicating the nature of the purchase, the amount, the date, and from where and by whom the purchase was made. In situations where small items are purchased and no receipts given, a petty-cash book should be provided in which items can be recorded at the time they are purchased. The total amount can later be indicated in the record of expenditures. Petty-cash accounts should never be carried in the memory. A teacher needs to be very careful to protect herself from any misunderstanding in the way she handles money for which she is responsible. Briefly there are four outstanding characteristics of a good financial report: (1) It is carefully and accurately prepared; (2) it is easy to interpret without too much detail; (3) it presents facts honestly, fairly, and clearly; (4) it follows, as far as possible, standard procedures.

2. Miscellaneous records and reports. These will vary in different situations but may include the following:

A class book for taking roll, for achievement scores, and for the final grade for the term or year

Individual student records

A record of the Future Homemakers of America program of work and information on any other cocurricular responsibilities and extracurricular activities

A record of evaluation devices for future reuse

Inventory records

An annual report summarizing and evaluating the year's program

ATTENDING TO CORRESPONDENCE

A particularly time-consuming but necessary task for the home-economics teacher is attending to the large amount and variety of reading material sent to the department. Regardless of its nature, all mail should receive attention, but it can be sorted according to material that is to be read carefully, studied, scanned, deferred, or discarded.

Prompt attention needs to be given to communications that require an answer, and the teacher should follow certain procedures which are considered essential in writing business letters:

1.   Type the letter, if possible, using a good grade of white stationery with an envelope to match. The stationery may include a printed heading identifying the department or the teacher.

2.   Direct the letter to a particular individual, if possible, using name and title if known.

3.   Date all correspondence, signing full name. Keep a carbon copy or a notation to whom and when the letter was written and the nature of its content.

TAKING INVENTORY

Many schools require an annual or semiannual inventory of equipment and supplies and provide forms for this purpose. When special procedures are not prescribed, the teacher will need to work out her own so that an accounting of the equipment and supplies on hand will be periodically known. Duplicate or triplicate copies of an inventory are advisable so that copies may be available on demand.

Since taking inventory is usually considered a tedious task, student assistance can be an important resource. This not only saves the teacher time and energy but gives the students an opportunity to learn how to arrange supplies and materials so that they may be easily located and accurately checked. Taking inventory also helps the students to realize the importance of accounting for every article or piece of equipment. If certain items supposed to be carried over from one inventory to the next are missing, a record of these articles needs to accompany each copy of the inventory.

A good inventory may be evaluated on the basis of its clarity in showing: (1) The name of each article; (2) the amount or quantity on hand at the time of the inventory; (3) where each article is located; (4) the date of the inventory.

CARING FOR RECORDS AND INSTRUCTIONAL MATERIALS

Another task essential in business management is caring for records and instructional materials, which are usually of an illustrative nature. It is believed that this can be best achieved by using adequate equipment, by having a good filing system, and by giving constant attention to the task.

1.   Using adequate equipment. A commercial filing cabinet or a set of drawers which can be sectioned off is customary equipment, but, if expenses need to be kept down, wooden or corrugated paper boxes can be satisfactorily used. The quantity and size of equipment will vary in accordance with the amount of instructional materials being used and the records being kept. Manila folders, large envelopes, or improvised folders can be used to hold some

of the flat materials, but whatever is used needs to stand upright for ease of access. The more bulky and larger materials may need special containers. In general, the expense, the durability, and the ease and frequency of using the filed contents are factors that will need to be considered in deciding what equipment will be used.

2. Having a good filing system. A good filing system is simple, clear, and convenient. Records and instructional materials should be easily located without having to search for them. Each teacher will need to work out her own system, but the contents of the file should be carefully labeled. The personal records of students and the teacher's reports pose no special problem since they can be filed alphabetically and kept in a special section of the file. Instructional materials are more difficult to file because they are likely to vary in size and shape. Some bulky materials, such as pamphlets, bulletins, charts, posters, and models will probably need to be filed or stored by themselves. Materials in upright folders can be filed under major headings for each area being taught and subheadings for the class goals in each area. Cross references can be made for materials which relate to more than one area. There will probably need to be a section for cocurricular data relating to the Future Homemakers of America, adult education, advisory groups, public relations, and the like. The students may also want to have a special section for some of their own activities.

3. Giving constant attention to the task. Efficient care of records and instructional materials requires constant attention to keep the files up-to-date and in order. Here again, student assistance can be an important resource, providing another opportunity for them to develop managerial ability. Arrangements can be made for them to do certain tasks in rotation

with the guidance of the teacher. Such tasks might include:

Clipping and filing helpful material

Discarding clippings that are out-of-date

Repairing, discarding, or replacing materials that are worn

Checking pamphlets and bulletins to see that a sufficient number of up-to-date copies are on hand—neither too few nor too many

Handling the circulation of books and other reference materials

Keeping their own file of activities up-to-date

The teacher will also need to keep the records for which she is personally responsible up-to-date. These include the class book, individual student data, and periodic reports required by the school administration. Although such tasks may be tedious and time-consuming, giving them consistent attention tends to minimize the overall effort needed to make these records worthwhile.

EVALUATING PROGRESS TOWARD THE GOAL

Much of the evaluation related to managing department business will be the task of the teacher. It will consist of a self-appraisal of her efforts and what she believes she is accomplishing. It is quite possible that the teacher may want to check her progress toward achievement of her goals by answering such questions as the following:

1. Do I have a salutary attitude toward money, using it and other resources to the best advantage?

2. Do I make sound decisions in planning and administering the department's funds?

3.   Do I keep financial and other records in accordance with sound business practices?

4.   Do I attend to department correspondence promptly and use customary business procedures?

5.   Do I take adequate inventories periodically?

6.   Do I take good care of records and instructional materials by having adequate equipment, by using a good filing system, and by giving constant attention to the task?

7.   Do I provide opportunities whenever possible for students to acquire managerial ability?

REFERENCES

Ack, M. Is education relevant? *Journal Home Economics,* November 1970, **62,** 647–651.

American Home Economics Association. *Home economics new directions. A statement of philosophy and objectives.* Washington, D.C.: Author, 1959.

Amidon, E. J., & Flanders, N. A. *The role of the teacher in the classroom: A manual for understanding and improving classroom behavior.* (Rev. ed.) Minneapolis: Association for Productive Teaching, 1967.

Baird, J. Verbal behavior of student teachers in home economics. *Journal Home Economics,* December 1970, **62,** 725–728.

Bloom, B. S., et al. *Taxonomy of educational objectives. Handbook 1 : Cognitive domain.* New York: Longmans, Green, 1959.

Bogniard, J. N., & Dalrymple, J. I. The use of simulation techniques. *Journal Home Economics,* December 1970, **62,** 729–732.

Chaos and learning. The free schools. *Time Magazine,* April 26, 1971, 81–82.

The case for permissipline. *Time Magazine,* June 21, 1971, 54–55.

Crews, J. W., et al. Micro-teaching and other uses of videotape in teacher training. *American Vocational Journal,* September 1969, 58–59.

Gardner, J. W. *Excellence. Can we be equal and excellent too?* New York: Harper Colophon Books, Harper and Row, 1962.

Gausman, C. H., & Vonnes, J. The single concept film—Tool for individualized instruction. *American Vocational Journal,* January 1969, 14, 16–17.

Gentile, J. R. The first generation of computer-assisted instructional systems: An evaluative review. *Audio-Visual Communication's Review,* Spring 1967, **15,** 23–54.

Hatcher H., & Andrews, M. E., *Adventuring in home living,* Book I. Boston: D. C. Heath, 1959.

Hawk, R. L. Individualized instruction in the school setting. *Educational Horizons,* Spring 1971, **49** (3), 73–80. Washington, D.C.: Pi Lambda Theta.

Holt, J. *The underachieving school.* New York: Pitman, 1969.

Illinois Teacher of Home Economics, February, 1962, V (6), 256–58.

Johnson, H., Clawson, B., & Sheffner, S. Using programmed instruction to teach a skill for transfer. *Journal Home Economics,* January 1969, **61,** 35–39.

Jorgenson, D. E. Analysis of verbal behavior of beginning home economics teachers as a basis for recommendations for inservice education. Unpublished doctoral dissertation, Oklahoma State University, 1968.

Kohlmann, E., & Smith, F. Assessing values related to home and family life. *Journal Home Economics,* November 1970, **62,** 656–660.

Kopstein, F. F. Why CAI must fail. *Educational Technology,* March 1970 (10), 51–53.

Kopstein, F. F., et al. CAL: Technological misconceptions. *Science,* 1970 (168), 1397–1398.

Krathwohl, D. R., et al. *Taxonomy of educational objectives. Handbook 2 : Affective domain.* New York: David McKay, 1964.

Mackenzie, L. Programmed learning for slow learners, *American Vocational Journal,* May 1969, 55–56; 80.

Mager, R. F. *Preparing objectives for programmed instruction.* Palo Alto: Fearon, 1962.

Mager, R. F., & Beach, K. M. *Developing vocational instruction.* Belmont, California: Fearon, 1967.

McClelland, W. A. Simulation, can it benefit vocational education? *American Vocational Journal,* September 1970, 23–25, 40.

McGrath, E. J., & Johnson, J. T. *The changing mission of home economics.* New York: Teachers College Press, Columbia University, 1968.

McGrath, E. J. The imperatives of change for home economics. *Journal Home Economics,* September 1968, **60,** 505–514.

National Education Association. *Educational leadership. Journal of the Association for Supervision and Curriculum Development* (Projects, Packages, Programs). Washington, D.C.: Author, 1971.

Reich, C. A. *The greening of America.* New York: Bantam Book, Random House, 1971.

Ridley, A. F. Inservice teacher education and the affective domain. *American Vocational Journal,* January 1971, 46–48.

Shear, T., & Ray, E. Home economics learning packages. *Journal Home Economics,* December 1969, **61,** 768–770.

Short, S. H., et al. Development and utilization of a self-instructional laboratory. *Journal Home Economics,* January 1969, **61,** 40–44.

Silberman, C. E. *Crisis in the classroom. The remaking of American education.* New York: Random House, 1970.

Simpson, E. J. The classification of educational objectives, psychomotor domain. *Illinois Teacher of Home Economics,* Winter 1966–67, **10,** 110–144. Urbana: University of Illinois.

Suppes, P. The uses of computers in education. *Scientific American,* September 1966, **215** (3), 207–20.

Torkelson, G. M. The Greeks had a word for it: Technologia. *Educational Horizons,* Spring 1971, **49** (3), 67. Washington, D.C.: Pi Lambda Theta.

Tyler, R. W. *Basic principles of curriculum and instruction.* Chicago: The University of Chicago Press, 1969.

Watson, P. G. CAL: From the educational technologist's point of view. *Educational Horizons,* Spring 1971, **49** (3), 81–87. Washington, D.C.: Pi Lambda Theta.

THREE

CURRICULUM
USE
AND
DEVELOPMENT

INTRODUCTION

One of the competencies associated with success in teaching home economics is the ability to plan and organize a curriculum that meets the needs of the people of the community where a teacher is employed. This aspect of curriculum development has long been an important part of any book on teaching home economics. Now, in addition, there are many more opportunities for home-economics teachers to work with others on developing curriculum materials. In fact, such cooperation will often be a definite responsibility of the teacher, even of beginners in the profession. Through the assumption of this responsibility, the teacher will have a better opportunity to keep abreast of what is happening in education and in the world.

At this point it may be worth taking a look at what appears to be developing in the curriculum aspect of education. Even though educational practices usually lag far behind educational theories, education is perhaps the most effective instrument available for helping people to adapt to place and time.

As long as society changed slowly from generation to generation, it was appropriate to use the same basic curriculum year after year. Then, with the industrial revolution, came the need to educate children for an entirely different kind of society, one in which educators attempted to produce the kind of adults the new society needed. According to Toffler in *Future Shock* (1970, "the solution was an educational system that, in its very structure, simulated this new world. This system did not emerge instantly. Yet the whole idea of assembling masses of students (raw material) to be processed by teachers (workers) in a centrally located school (factory) was a stroke of industrial genius. The whole administrative hierarchy of education, as it grew up, followed the model of industrial bureaucracy. The very organization of knowledge into permanent disciplines was grounded on industrial assumptions. Children marched from place to place and sat in assigned stations. Bells rang to announce changes of time.

"The inner life of the school thus became an anticipatory mirror, a perfect introduction to industrial society. The most criticized features of education today—the regimentation, lack of individualization, the rigid system of seating, grouping, grading, and marking, the authoritarian role of the teacher—are precisely those that made mass public education so effective an instrument of adaptation for its place and time [p. 355]."

Now there appears to be a new

technological revolution in which machines are freeing men from routine tasks to do more intellectual and creative ones. Instead of working as a machine does day after day people will need to cope with an increasing number of problems resulting from rapid, and more rapid change. Abilities, often not taught at all or certainly not well taught to most students will be needed, such as making effective decisions quickly under conditions of "overchoice," adapting to continual change, and attempting to penetrate the pattern of future events. As Toffler (1970) says, "the direction is super-industrialism. The starting point: the future [p. 359]." Super-industrial education must therefore make provision for life-long education on an in-out-in-out basis.

Home economists, like those in other fields of study, have long given lip service to education from nursery school to the grave, but not many have thought through realistically what this actually means. It would seem that we are now on a collision course with the idea of life-long education. Some people will go from one job to train for another job much of their working life. Others will do what many young people today are doing—stay out of school, especially college, for awhile to try to find out what life is all about. And there will be others who out of interest, or perhaps boredom because of a shortened working week, will be in and out of school periodically to learn recreational abilities. In this as in other areas, home economics has much to offer.

As was already mentioned earlier, almost all teachers who continue to teach for any length of time, and some beginning teachers, will be involved in cooperating with others in curriculum development. Such cooperation may be within the school, the county, the state. It may even cut across state lines. It may be based on developments of curriculum study centers or what is happening in truly experimental schools. However such developments come about, the teacher must be prepared to make effective contributions. Therefore the authors believe no consideration of curriculum development will be complete without answering the following questions: (1) How can I individualize the curriculum for my students and then plan most effectively for its use? (2) What can I learn about cooperating with others on curriculum development? (3) What is the teacher's responsibility following curriculum development?

Although there are many types of curricula and many different groups to be served, certain generalizations about curriculum use and development apply to all. What the teacher needs to do following curriculum development varies little from school to school although how she does it can be expected to vary greatly. The majority of the illustrations in this book are at the secondary level, because the majority of home-economics teachers work at this level. Nonetheless, the authors have used some illustrations for other levels of home economics and for specialized situations.

PART ONE

INDIVIDUALIZING CURRICULUM AND PLANNING ITS USE

Individualizing curriculum for students—individuals and groups—and planning effectively for its use is perhaps the most challenging aspect of the entire curriculum field. It involves fitting together what has been learned in college and what the teacher can learn in her school and community. Further, unlike the development of curriculum, which may have been through cooperative efforts, it is generally a teacher's own full responsibility, though there may be considerable discussion with others as questions arise.

No matter how effectively a teacher is able to individualize curriculum it is an ongoing responsibility. The students will vary with each group, the school and community is constantly changing, and the teacher will be developing in various respects. As the teacher gains experience what may have seemed difficult and time-consuming at first becomes far easier and an integral part of the teaching day. The more successful the teacher is in individualizing the curriculum the more interesting and exciting will teaching be. To become proficient the teacher will need to (1) become acquainted with the kind of curriculum materials which will be available for use, (2) learn ways of best using available resource materials, (3) understand some of the background of the various courses to be taught.

Some teachers will be working on an individual basis in the home or elsewhere. She will want to know the place of resource materials in this kind of situation.

ONE

WHAT IS AN EXAMPLE OF CURRICULUM MATERIAL AVAILABLE TO TEACHERS?

ILLUSTRATION OF RESOURCE MATERIALS

On the teacher's arrival at a new school, one kind of material most likely to be found in the home-economics department is a copy of a bulletin on curriculum material in home economics. Such material, sometimes known as resource material, may have been prepared by personnel from the state, the county, the city or elsewhere. There may be copies from several of these sources.

What is the teacher's reaction? After learning how important it is to study the needs, interests, and abilities of those to be taught as well as the contemporary life outside the school, the teacher's first reaction could be: "There wasn't any need to learn all those things I did. Here's what I'm supposed to teach. This will be easy." However, after some thought the teacher may think, "How wonderful it is to find such sources of help to supplement the things I've learned." Part One of this book will deal with planning to use wisely curriculum materials prepared by others.

Almost every group preparing resource materials for teaching home economics develops a somewhat different pattern, examples of which will be shown later in this book. There is no one right pattern to use in preparation of such materials or in planning their use. There

are, however, certain guides which are likely to result in satisfaction for the teacher who follows them. First, however, the reader will want to look at an illustration of the kind of curriculum material usually found in the home-economics department.

The illustration used is from a Resource Guide for Curriculum Development entitled *Preparing for Employment in Clothing and Home Furnishings Services* (Pennsylvania Department of Education, 1968). The Table of Contents is given first so the reader can obtain an overall picture of the bulletin. Then the section "Selected Factors in Our Job World," is shown as it appears in the publication. After the reader becomes familiar with this material a Guide to planning how to use it will follow in the next chapter.

Chapter I—Introduction

Chapter II—Program Organization

Chapter III—Program Design

Chapter IV—Curriculum Guide

Job Orientation of the Student: Employment Opportunities, Motivation, Guides for Job Success, Employment Services.

Clothing Skills and Understandings Organized for the Job World: Social Aspects of Clothing, The Body to be Fitted, Safety, Fabric, Clothing is an Art Form, Equipment and Garment Construction, Process of Fitting Individuals, Alterations.

Selected Factors of the Job World: Our Changing World, Contributions of Clothing and Home Furnishings Services, Person on the Job, Union and Non-Union Employment, Ways of Earning.

Appendix I—Forces in Motivating Students

Appendix II—Job Orientation

Employment Opportunities, Full Time and Part Time Employment, Variables in Job Situations, Guides to Job Success, Employment Services, Applications for Jobs, On the Job Cooperation, Helps Toward Success in Jobs.

Suggested Experience Material for Supportive Learnings

Appendix III—Job World Organization of Clothing Skills and Understandings

Social Aspects of Clothing, The Body to be Fitted, Fabric, Clothing is an Art Form, Equipment and Garment Construction, Process of Fitting Individuals, Alteration.

Appendix IV—Selected Factors of the Job World

Our Changing World, New Roles of Women, Contributions of Clothing and Home Furnishings Services, Union and Non-Union Employment, Ways of Earning, Selected Financial Aspects of Work.

Suggested Experience Material for Supportive Learnings

Appendix V—Dictionary of Occupational Titles

SELECTED FACTORS OF OUR JOB WORLD

OUR CHANGING WORLD

Key Concept: Employment opportunities in the clothing and furnishings area are constantly changing due to new technology.

Objective: Understand how: a. new machines and methods create new and different jobs; b. changes in society bring new opportunities and changing problems for women.

SUPPORTIVE LEARNINGS	LEARNING EXPERIENCES
Techological advances have changed the skill requirements needed for work in many areas.	Trace several occupations (such as secretary, garment sewer) from 1850 to the present, observing how technological changes have changed the work and the skills needed to do the work.
	Divide into four groups. Each group may present a list of innovations in a field which has come into use in the last 100 to 150 years. If time allows, the group could state what major

element the item gave to society. The fields are:

transportation and communication
household items and equipment
clothing and household textiles
foods

There is a need for persons who can modify factory made textiles and related items for individuals.

Collect and discuss illustrations of the statement, ready-to-wear dresses seldom fit all parts of most people.

Changes in our society have brought changes in the lives of women.

Have a panel discussion by mothers of students discussing how their own lives differ from those of their grandmother.

Changes in society have made it easier for women to work outside the home.

Discuss how the following and other items which have resulted from changing technology and changes in society have affected the lives of women.

Innovations in the home environment:
vacuum sweeper
phonograph
washing machine and dryer
television
telephone

Changes occurring in our society:
world wars
right to vote
education for all women
rapid world transportation
rapid world communication

The hours a woman may work outside the home are limited by law and dependent upon the hours she is free, what jobs are available, whether she needs the income, whether she likes working, etc.

Break the class into four groups. Give each an employment problem. Discuss the solution to the problem before the class. What would be the situation of the girl who would find this a good job opening? Note that employment may not be desirable in all situations.

The greater the number of working women, the more flexible the employer will need to become because women are the child bearers.

Use role-playing to illustrate various employer-employee situations. Have class discuss possible solutions because women are the child bearers.

Discuss how mothers of students have managed to work and if the employer has made any accommodations.

Key Concept: Women are protected through special provisions of labor laws.

Objective: Learn provisions of laws affecting employment with emphasis on those protecting women.

SUPPORTIVE LEARNINGS	LEARNING EXPERIENCES
Labor laws help to give women equal working rights and special protection.	Have a student committee make a bulletin board concerning types of laws which apply to working women.
There are special provisions for minors in Pennsylvania labor laws.	Have small group discussions concerning why particular labor laws would pertain to the selected situations.
	Present results to entire class.

Key Concept: Jobs in clothing and home furnishings are among those of real value to society.

Objective: Understand how employment in this area is important in meeting needs and wants of people.

SUPPORTIVE LEARNINGS	LEARNING EXPERIENCES
Persons with clothing and home furnishings skills are needed to adapt ready made items for other people.	Use role-playing situations to show the need for an alterationist to adapt ready made items for different individuals or situations.
Workers receive wages which help them to buy what they want and need.	Have class list the various uses of money based on their own home experiences, such as food, clothing, shelter, entertainment, etc. Discuss how money is secured in order to pay for the listed items.
Many things other than money can be obtained from having a job.	Have class members speak to friends, neighbors, etc., to see what things other than money they get from a job, such as fringe benefits, associating with others, helping others, feeling of satisfaction. Discuss results in class.

PERSON ON THE JOB

Key Concept: Ways to improve inter-personal relationships can be developed.

Objective: Develop a liking for and understanding of other people's needs and wants.

SUPPORTIVE LEARNINGS	LEARNING EXPERIENCES
When the workers and the employer try to understand each other, better work results.	Discuss the importance of "we-ness" in acceptable work relationships between: em-

The worker needs to have a good relationship with other workers and customers as well as his supervisor.

Being able to talk with all types of people help one to get along well on the job.

Honesty, dependability, and a liking for other people help one to get along well on the job.

ployee-employer, employee-employee, employee-customer.

Have buzz groups quickly list annoying mannerisms that they have noticed in an employee or customer. What suggestions could be offered to a person with such a mannerism?

Use role-playing skits to illustrate conflicts in work situations.

Discuss the importance of emphasizing the place of loyalty, responsibility, courtesy, tolerance, consideration in job situations.

Develop a checklist of qualities that are desirable in fostering good relationships on the job. Have each student rate himself on whether or not he would be a good employee.

UNION AND NON-UNION EMPLOYMENT

Key Concept: Prospective employees need to understand the function of labor unions and employment opportunities, both union and non-union.

Objective: Understand the difference between union and non-union employment.

SUPPORTIVE LEARNINGS	LEARNING EXPERIENCES
Unions are groups which represent the worker.	Have students give reports on topics such as: history, background, kinds of unions, membership, etc.
Almost every trade is represented by a union.	Ask students to take a survey of unions in the community which have members in clothing and home furnishings.
Jobs can be found in firms having unions and in firms not having unions.	Have students interview local union leaders who have members in clothing and home furnishings. Discuss advantages of joining unions.
	Have class members interview persons in clothing and home furnishings services that are not employed by union firms.
	Discuss results of interviews with all class members.
	Discuss differences of union and non-union employment through role-playing situations.

WAYS OF EARNING

Key Concept: Employment in large and small firms and self-employment have different advantages and disadvantages.

Objective: Understand pros and cons of self-employment and employment in both large and small firms.

SUPPORTIVE LEARNINGS	LEARNING EXPERIENCES
The organization of a large firm differs from that of a small firm and self-employment.	Ask resource persons from large and small firms and self-employed persons in the community to participate in a panel discussion which is centered around "differences between firms."
Small firms tend to be more concerned about its individual employees.	
Large firms are much less individual centered than are small firms	Use a chart to discuss differences between large and small firms.
A self-employed person is concerned mainly with himself and his job	Interview and report to class about self-employed persons in community to learn: how to become self-employed reasons for self-employment working conditions advantages and disadvantages of being self-employed
	Visit large and small firms related to clothing and furnishings, if available. Officer or supervisor may be asked questions if time permits.
	Read pamphlets supplied by various agencies regarding this area to have a little background before having speakers.
Financial aspects are important considerations when seeking jobs.	Have representatives from Social Security office, Unemployment Insurance office, and Workmen's Compensation office in town or county to speak to class.
Unemployment Insurance provides some income if one is unemployed	Have the school payroll clerk talk with the class about financial aspects of work in total and how deductions are made on paychecks.
Workmen's Compensation provides benefits for those who have accidents or job induced illnesses when working	
Social Security provides the old-aged, dis-	

abled, dependents or survivors of an employee with a partial income

| Fringe benefits can be considered as added income which help make the job more attractive. | Ask each student to obtain a list of fringe benefits that working members of their families receive and discuss differences in class. |

BIBLIOGRAPHY

** Allen, Donna. *Fringe Benefits: Wages or Social Obligation?* Distribution Center. New York. 1964.

** Baker, Elizabeth P. *Technology and Women's Work.* Columbia University Press. 1964.

 * Clarkadon, T. R. *Workers and Bosses are Human.* Public Affairs Pamphlet.

** Haber, William, Louis A. Ferman, and James R. Hudson. *The Impact of Technological Change.* Studies in Employment and Unemployment. Upjohn Institute for Employment Research. Kalamazoo. 1963.

** Kaplan, F. B. and M. Mead. *American Women: The Report of the President's Commission on the Status of Women.* Charles Scribner and Sons. New York. 1965.

** Women's Bureau. *1965 Handbook on Women Workers.* U.S. Department of Labor. U.S. Government Printing Office. Washington, D.C. 1966.

 * Worthy, James C. *What Employers Want.* Science Research Associates. Chicago. 1950.

 * Yoder, Dale. *You and Unions.* Science Research Associates. Chicago. 1951.

PAMPHLETS AND MAGAZINE ARTICLES

 * Ellis, Mary, *"Young Women and the World of Work," Teen Times.* September-October, 1964. p. 9.

** Uris, Auren. "Think Small," *Nation's Business.* May, 1965. pp. 94–98.

The following pamphlets are available from the Pennsylvania Department of Labor and Industry, Harrisburg, Pennsylvania 17120.

** *Regulations Affecting Employment of Minors*

** *Women's Labor Law* also **Abstract of Women's Labor Law*

 * *Abstract of Child Labor Law*

** *Industrial Homework Law*

** *Digest of the Pennsylvania Workmen's Compensation Act* with *Digest of Occupational Disease Act.*

Note: Send for this at the following address: State Workmen's Insurance Fund. P.O. Box 1066, Scranton, Pennsylvania 18501.

 * *Workmen's Compensation and Occupational Disease Information*

** *Highlights of the Fair Labor Standards Act as Amended—1966.* U.S. Department of Labor. Washington, D.C.

---

 * Recommended for students.
** Recommended for teachers.

TWO

HOW ARE CURRICULUM MATERIALS USED?

A GUIDE

In planning to use the kind of materials illustrated on the preceding pages, the answers to six questions should be helpful to the teacher:

1. In what ways can I best use available "resource materials?"

2. What immediate information should I secure from the administration?

3. How can I correlate above kinds of information with what has earlier been learned about teaching?

4. What organization for the course will best facilitate learning?

5. What kind of plans are best for day to day teaching?

6. What kind of planning is desirable for Future Homemakers of America?

USE AVAILABLE MATERIALS PRODUCTIVELY

Most curriculum materials have been prepared through the guidance of a supervisor: state, county, city, or other. For this reason such an individual should be in the best position to offer suggestions for using these resource materials.

There are many kinds of supervisors, just as there are many kinds of people. Nonetheless, the authors believe there is general agreement among members of this group that home-economics curriculum materials should serve as a guide to strengthen teaching in the classroom, the home, and the community. At the same time they should serve to promote better understanding of the home-economics program among those cooperating with it.

LOCAL NEEDS

Most resource materials are developed by a group of people with leaders who understand the process of curriculum development. Such development will be considered in Part Two of this book. At this time it should be sufficient to point out that a hard-working group of interested people with able state, county, city or other leaders should produce more useful ideas than one individual working alone. These ideas should be more comprehensive than those of an individual because they ordinarily represent a wider social group, a greater geographic group, a more varied economic background, and a greater range of ability. Unless a teacher is most unusual he or she is almost certain to gain new ideas from studying the resource materials available in the school.

Does the provision of such materials mean that a teacher is expected to use them exactly as they appear in the Guide? In nearly all instances, it is a supervisor's expectation that teachers will use the suggestions creatively to build a program around the needs of people in the local community. There is no intention that all schools or even classes within the same community will have the same program, because meaningful problems are likely to vary from one school to another and from one class to another. However, the supervisor will expect that where there is more than one home-economics teacher in a school, or in a community, these teachers will plan to avoid overlapping in sequence or gaps in the overall program. They will also need to share productive ideas.

Perhaps the greatest expectation of the supervisor is that the teacher will be guided by the suggestions in the resource materials to provide a balanced home-economics program meeting the needs of today and tomorrow. Life styles have changed and are continuing to change, so that home economics like most other school subjects, must also change to survive in today's world. This does not mean that some cooking and some sewing do not have a very real place in many home-economics departments; it does mean that a better balance must be achieved, to include along with these decision-making, nutrition problems, textiles, consumer services, housing and home furnishings, human relationships, development and care of children, and employment preparation. Most resource materials suggest time ranges for teaching the different areas: these may help the teacher in planning.

There are, moreover, some recently developed programs of home economics which are highly specialized, such as one-half or one-credit courses in food preparation, family-life education, or consumer problems. In some instances, these seem to meet needs better than some of the older kinds of programs. It is desirable to provide a range in such offerings, not just a total program, for instance, of work in foods. Even those responsible for employment programs are finding that their students need help with such problems as use of resources, personal appearance, and getting along with others.

PROMOTING UNDERSTANDING
OF THE PROGRAM

A home-economics trained leader in another country wrote, "Two days ago I received the home-economics planning books you sent. They have arrived as if sent from heaven. The entire project I had in mind has fallen through because those who thought they wanted to participate were not interested and maintained that home economics was taught in many places in our country. You and I know this is not so and the truth is they have no ideas as to what home economics is. I tried to explain, but in vain." Is this writer's experience unusual? In many communities in the United States it would be, because vast numbers of home-economics teachers have portrayed home economics at its best through their teaching. At the same time there are places in most of our states where home economics is not meeting today's needs for specific communities. It may be too far behind what people want and need or too advanced for life as they are forced to live it. It is in such places that the supervisor may find that curriculum materials are especially useful in working with the administrator, the teacher, and sometimes parents. And of course these same materials would be just as useful to anyone who wishes to present an up-to-date picture of home economics. The administration may wish to present such a picture to a particular teacher. Or a teacher may want to educate the administration or parents along such lines.

The curriculum materials presented on pages 255–261 are to be used for preparing people for employment. Programs of this kind are not very well known and the curriculum materials may be a useful resource in working with business leaders and others who have not had a part in the development of a program. It is easier for most people to understand a program that is described in objective terms rather than in generalities. In other words curriculum materials may serve as a bridge between those who understand a program and those who have considerably less understanding.

INFORMATION FROM THE ADMINISTRATION

The administration will have been responsible for a great deal of pre-planning before the teacher is ready to develop in detail the course to be taught. It is desirable for teachers to have participated in such planning and often they have, but not always, especially if they are new in the school system. Such a teacher will need the answers to certain questions at this time:

What kind of students will be in the course? What are their backgrounds? What are their needs?

What is the expected grade level? What is the expected duration of the class?

How many class periods are available each week and how long are class periods?

What space and facilities are available for the course? Are these to be shared with other classes?

What kind of a budget has been planned for the course?

Has an Advisory Board already been set-up for this course? If so what is the composition of the Board? How do I get in touch with members?

Later other questions may be answered by talking with administrators or by studying the material in Chapter 3 on preliminary planning.

CORRELATE NEW INFORMATION WITH EARLIER LEARNING

To be successful, a teacher must learn to correlate what she has already learned with new information, and apply them both in the way that is most appropriate to a particular situation. On the one hand, the teacher has considerable understanding of all the subject areas to be taught, of learners of different ages, of contemporary life outside the school, and of teaching-learning strategies and resources. On the other hand, there is a comprehensive amount of curriculum materials, new books, and professional magazines to be drawn on for suggestions, and there is specific information about such matters as actual students to be taught, class periods, and space and equipment available to be considered. In addition there are the beliefs, values, and standards, that is, the philosophy, which a teacher holds that are a basis for her choice making. Evaluating and correlating so much information and so many ideas is never an easy matter, but it is challenging to the person who gives it her best.

CHOICES RELATED TO THE CURRICULUM

Illustrations of the way three teachers were able to correlate some of what they had previously learned and the state curriculum materials are given here. An analysis of the procedures that were used will follow.

TEACHER NUMBER ONE

Let us assume that the teacher's philosophy includes a belief that people are happiest doing what they can learn to do well. She is scheduled to teach a new course in *Preparing for Employment in Clothing and Home Furnishings Services* (see pages 255–261). The range of ability in her group of students is greater than in most such groups. She decides that it is vital to discover a wider range of employment opportunities than an initial survey or the resource materials showed. She thinks that the survey covered too limited a geographical area in terms of where her students will be willing to live and work. She investigates and learns that there will be some jobs not previously considered for those students at both ends of the employment scale. Without this strong belief she would have accepted what on the surface appeared to be the only prospective jobs toward which her training should be directed.

This same teacher had done preliminary planning for such a course in her university work, so she now studied the goals she had considered then along with those suggested in the state resource materials. She found that in general the goals she had tentatively planned were at least as good for her students as those in the more comprehensive materials—perhaps because her home originally was in a community very much like the one in which she ex-

pected to teach. There were, however, important omissions in her goals, especially in the newer approach to the "Body to Be Fitted" and to the section on "Selected Factors in the Job World." She told herself she did not really have to do any more preplanning. Then she thought, "I believe in doing whatever I do to the best of my ability. I also try to think for myself and to work independently, making whatever changes are desirable." She decided to add to her goals, using the best ideas from both sources. She would also consider supportive learnings and learning experiences as she found better ideas. Her students would usually take part in the final decisions and they needed to have their thinking stimulated by the best tentative ideas she could develop.

TEACHER NUMBER TWO

Another teacher liked the state resource materials very much as a guide to her teaching, but she had some creative ideas that seemed better than some of those suggested. Her ideas would be more difficult to carry out. She believed that creativity was an important part of successful teaching, so she decided to explore the use of her own creative ideas whenever it seemed they might prove more effective. To carry out such ideas would require resources not presently available in the school. Was there any possibility the community could supply them if she and the students agreed on the ideas she was considering? Through talking with the Advisory Committee, she discovered there were many more resources available than she had thought possible, and these would be available to her and her students without financial cost.

She was grateful for the bibliography provided by the state resource material, because the one she had developed was inferior to it. She realized how important it was to have such materials available, not only for students, but her own use as well.

TEACHER NUMBER THREE

A third teacher found that the resource materials were useful in a general way, but her class on wage-earning was composed entirely of adults from the middle-economic level who wanted to learn to do home sewing for neighbors and others. It was a group who all had small children. These women hoped that the skills they could develop would enable them to supplement the family income and at the same time to meet interesting people. They had no interest in the job world outside their own homes, at least as they thought of the job world. The teacher learned some of the thinking of the group and then arranged for each member of the class to talk with someone who previously had or was presently having the kind of employment these women wanted.

Pooling the information gained from these visits and drawing ideas from the resource materials enabled the teacher and the class to plan a curriculum that was satisfactory to all concerned.

ANALYZING PROCEDURES USED

What steps did the three teachers follow when making choices related to a tentative curriculum? Certainly at some stage they had thought through at least part of the decision-making process presented in the form of an evaluation device (see pages 234–235). For example, each one already knew her goal and its relationship to other people. Each one realized a need for considering others in making any decision. In

some instances, parents and other lay persons had agreed to participate in planning the curriculum. At this point, then, what steps did each one follow in correlating new information and ideas with earlier learnings?

1.   They considered which of the things they had learned and believed seemed most useful in the present situation.

2.   They read carefully the new materials available, especially those parts that appeared to apply to their own situations.

3.   They began to choose from among the various alternatives and fit together those ideas which they could support. In doing so, they appraised whether needed resources were or could be available and whether there might be personal or social pressure against the use of needed resources.

4.   As they worked they made modifications in their thinking as seemed advisable. A few parents and other lay persons contributed some excellent ideas.

5.   They realized that their thinking should not be final because they would be listening to the choice of others in the final decision.

6.   They obtained satisfaction in knowing that this preliminary correlation of information and ideas would probably result in a better curriculum in the end.

CONSIDERING INTERRELATED PROBLEMS

Some problems, though not a part of the curriculum, may be related to it. These problems may offer suggestions which, if used, would improve the curriculum. Or there may be problems relating to parents, businessmen, or others. Correlating what the teacher knows, learns, and believes may be carried out by following in general the same process the three teachers followed. Examples of such problems follow.

1. Should I find time to help a community group that is working on the drug problem? It is causing so much heartache in so many families. If other work prevents my contributing to this cause, should I encourage a friend with more time at her disposal to help?

2. Should I actively support legislation aimed at helping the consumer or can others do all that is necessary?

3. Parties are apt to be hard on young people who are shy and lonely. Should I help some of these individuals feel more comfortable in social situations? Is it any of my business how they feel?

4. Someone told me that Susan, at fifteen, was trying to hold her family together since her mother died and her father is away from home quite a lot. Could we make some of her home problems class problems, thus vitalizing the class in home economics for her and other class members? Do I know enough about most of my students to be helpful?

5. Clare's father and mother came from one of the rapidly developing countries and believe that going to school and making the highest grades are all that matter, because these are essential to getting ahead. By working very hard Clare can make average grades but no more. Even though she is gifted in several other ways, Clare seems unhappy and is beginning to lose confidence in herself because of her parents' ambition for her to make high grades. The parents are unhappy also at what they consider lack of achievement in the one thing that matters to them. Should I try to help in this situation or should I adopt the attitude of the parents as far as Clare is concerned?

6. It is more fun and easier to teach home furnishings when I can use illustrations that look and are expensive, the kind of things I like best.

Then also, there are so many more of this kind of illustration. My students come mostly from homes with low average income and seem to be discouraged by the illustrations I enjoy so much. Should I satisfy their needs and their family's needs or my own desires? Can I do both?

ORGANIZE CURRICULUM TO FACILITATE LEARNING

After correlating in her thinking so much information and so many ideas about curriculum, there remains one thing for the teacher to do before planning day-to-day teaching. Some leaders think of this as the framework for planning the total program for the course. Others think of it in terms of a teaching unit, such as a unit on "Selected Factors of Our Job World." In either instance, it is an organization of how particular learnings are to be accomplished and evaluated with reference to specific purposes or goals. It is the adaptation of resource materials to students of a particular ability level, to grade, to course length, and to schedule. It is the teacher's picture of what will be taking place in a particular classroom for a specified period of time. It is not yet a completed picture, because ideas of students have not yet been incorporated. It does, however, enable the teacher to furnish the kind of leadership referred to in the *Dictionary of Education* (Good, 1959), which states that such a framework or unit is "An organization of various activities, experiences, and types of learning around a central problem, or purpose, developed cooperatively by a group of pupils under teacher leadership; involves planning, execution of plans, and evaluation of results [p. 587]."

The three teachers who had been making choices related to teaching a course on "Preparing for Employment in Clothing and Home Furnishings Services" knew they needed to write down their thinking while their ideas were still fairly clear. Teacher Number Two, who was least experienced, remembered that during student teaching she had obtained a copy of such a framework which proved helpful in writing her own unit plan. It was written for an entirely different area, but that did not matter. The framework which Teacher Number Two used for her own new course follows:

UNDERSTANDING AND
ENJOYING YOUNG CHILDREN

This material is prepared for senior-high-school students living in a town of 10,000 people. The students in the class will probably represent a considerable range in ability as well as different social and economic groups. The exact number of students is unknown but there will probably be 15 to 20 including both sexes. This year will be the second time the school has provided a Child Center for three- and four-year olds in relation to the classwork in child development.

The class meets 50 minutes a day five days a week for nine weeks. Tentative content for the class is broken down as follows (adapted from a unit developed for student teaching by Jane B. Harshbargar, then a senior in home-economics education at The Pennsylvania State University):

CONCEPTS	NUMBER OF PERIODS
Introduction and planning physical environment of Child Center	6
Planning daily schedules and procedures	2
Observational techniques and reporting	3
Experience at the Center	7
Post-experience discussion	7
Guided activities including stories, music, creative experience with painting and clay, dramatic play and puppetry	5
Learning more about young children	10
Evaluation and closing the Center	5
	45

The tentative schedule is as follows:

First week—Introduction and setting-up Child Center

Ninth week—Evaluation and final work related to the Child Center

Weeks between first and ninth:

Monday—Participation in one of three groups to obtain experience at the Center

Those who work with children

Those who observe

Those who plan and prepare curriculum materials and snacks

Students plan to work in each group during their seven experiences

Tuesday—Evaluation of previous day's experiences

Answering questions

Considering alternative ways of handling various situations that arise

Relating experiences to new learnings about children

Wednesday and Thursday—Learning more about young children through recognizing and understanding

Feelings of security

Emotional control

Motor coordination

Self-reliance and independence

Cooperation with others

Friday—Preparation for the following week's experience at the Center

Becoming acquainted with new schedule

Preparing materials needed

A description of the introductory experience as tentatively planned follows: The supervising teacher reports that the students are already enthusiastic about this part of the program. To stimulate even greater interest I plan on the first day of class to show two short educational films. One film is of the Child Center for last year. The other is of the Center from a neighboring school and was borrowed by my supervising teacher. I have also a number of slides to illustrate the physical environment of the Center, for that is where we need to concentrate our efforts at once. The supervising teacher and I together will teach this first week when the class is setting up the physical facilities of the Center. I will not know what is available in the school or community my first week on the job.

The daily schedule of the Child Center and procedures are described: The supervising teacher wanted to make the Monday schedule for the seven weeks one that would provide each student with some experience in all the activities of the Child Center. She was successful in doing this except for a very few who had conflicts. The class periods of the school for this part of the day are 9:00—9:50; 9:55—10:45; 10:50—11:40.

The schedule as planned for the Child Center is shown below:

9:00–9:15	Arrival, greeting parents and children, removal of wraps, and health inspection
9:15–9:45	Self-chosen activities indoors or outdoors, depending upon the weather and each child's interest at the time. However, some outside activities should be encouraged.
9:45–10:00	Toileting and wash-up time
10:00–10:20	Juice and quiet activities
10:20–11:15	Earlier activities may be continued and new ones introduced, such as story-telling, rhythm experiences, and the use of creative materials. Toward the end of the morning, quiet activities need to be encouraged
11:15–11:30	Clean up time, putting on wraps, and departure

Four objectives as developed for use at the Center are shown:*

Concept: Observational techniques

Objective: Be able to watch the way a child behaves without feeling a necessity for changing his behavior

Behavioral outcomes:

Can record exactly what is seen keeping it separate from any interpretation

Can record details accurately for given purposes without including trivia

Is very clear on all the factors of "being a good observer"

Generalization: The observation is a means by which certain aspects of a child's development can be recognized and evaluated.

KEY POINTS	LEARNING EXPERIENCES
There are four essentials which need to be followed to obtain a good observation. 1. Know what to look for before you begin to observe. 2. Record exactly what you see.	Utilize attractive bulletin board showing four essentials of a good observation. Class gives illustrations of each of the four points. Bring two young children to the class. Students record accurately for ten minutes the interaction among the children.
3. Eliminate trivia which does not pertain to your purpose for the observation. 4. Observe and then later interpret your observations; do not mix the two.	Class divides into four groups to study the observations made by individuals in the group. Members of the group offer each other suggestions for better observation reports.
Observations need to be made systematically; little is gained from one experience.	Class helps plan for the observations to be made at the Center. These will include detailed observation of only four children. See pages 274–277.
Observations show the real picture of the child only when well done and carefully evaluated.	Class learns that it will help evaluate all the observations made. Most of the last week for the Center has been reserved for evaluation.

* Concepts developed but not shown for lack of space include: (1) Physical facilities; (2) Techniques for guiding children at the Center; (3) Use of resource materials; (4) Recognizing and understanding (a) motor coordination, (b) self-reliance and independence, (c) cooperation with others.

Concept: Recognizing and understanding feelings of security

Objective: Be able to recognize when a child feels secure and understand what behavior indicates security

Behavioral outcomes:

Can verbalize what is meant by security and some of the causes of security and insecurity

Can explain what kind of behavior characterizes security in the young child

Is aware that the same situation can contribute to greater security in certain individuals depending on their past

Generalization: Understanding how a child is developing depends upon knowing about many aspects of his development.

KEY POINTS	LEARNING EXPERIENCES
Security in a child is his sense of adequacy or being able to cope with the problems he is expected to cope with. These problems are not always easy but the child does not fear for his status. He feels the need to grow rather than to hide. He has a sense of belonging.	Using circular response, each student states briefly what he thinks of as a feeling of security. Students then check references and write a definition of security. A small committee working with the teacher chooses the best definition to present to the class. The definition chosen may be a combination of ideas rather than a single student definition.

Possible explanation of why some children feel secure:
  Have parents who feel secure
  Have generally been "included" so feel they belong
  Have been given reasonable tasks they can accomplish with some feeling of success
  Have a readiness for group experience
  Feel accepted by individuals and the group
	The teacher and two mothers of small children who seem very secure hold a dialogue for the class in which they develop possible explanations of security in young children. The class supplements what it has learned from appropriate references.

Kinds of behavior characteristic of security in a child include:
  Joins group activity
  Talks to other children and adults
  Does not disturb other children at play
  Accepts other children who want to play with him
	At the Center class members each use a check list including the kind of behavior listed at the left. The check list also indicates the behavior characteristic of insecurity in a child. The lists checked by all students are to be kept for later analysis.

Does not demand constant attention
Willing to accept suggestions
Unafraid to try a new activity by himself
Speaks easily and can be understood
Has no nervous mannerisms

A child's past experiences influence him in many ways; one of these ways is in the extent to which he feels secure.

Analyze the possible effect certain situations may have on the extent of a child's security. Use sample situations such as:

Young child who is left by himself for some time during a bad storm, after he has been told his parents would be away for only a short time
Child who helps his parents with many activities and feels pride in doing his part

Why are children affected differently by the same experience?

Concept: Recognizing and understanding healthy emotional control

Objective: Understand what kind of behavior indicates healthy emotional control and be able to recognize such control in a three- to four-year old

Behavioral outcomes:

Knows the meaning of healthy emotional control

Can explain what kind of behavior indicates

healthy emotional control in the three- to four-year old child

Knows some of the causes of lack of emotional control in young children

Is aware that the same situation can cause different emotions in different individuals depending upon their past experiences

Generalization: Understanding how a child is developing depends upon knowing about many aspects of his development.

KEY POINTS	LEARNING EXPERIENCES
Healthy emotional control is the ability to adjust readily to a situation such as Parental separation for short periods	Class members read about healthy emotional control and then divide into small groups. Each group writes its own definition. The class helps choose the best definition and improves it if desirable.

Being with different people
Changes in the physical environment
Needing to cope with routines
in program

Kinds of behavior characteristic
of developing emotional control:
   When angry, may stamp feet or
   cry a little, or call object of his
   anger names
   Not easily discouraged; willing
   to make several trials to
   achieve something he wants
   to do
   Does not become upset when
   he cannot have his own way
   Able to relax during quiet
   activity period
   Has longer attention span than
   child lacking healthy emotional
   control

At the Center class members each use
a check list including the kind of behavior listed at the left. The check list
also indicates the behavior characteristic of poor emotional control in a
child. The lists checked by all students
are to be kept for later analysis.

Possible explanation of why some
children are developing healthy
emotional control:
   Are mature individuals for their
   ages
   Are seldom bored
   Can express themselves when
   called upon to do so
   Expectations of others for them
   are reasonable

A child's past experiences influence him in many ways; one of
these ways is in the extent to
which he is developing healthy
emotional control

Half of the class interview mothers of
three- to four-year olds who appear to
be developing healthy emotional control to discover
   (1)   what these mothers think contributes to developing emotional
   control
   (2)   what kind of past experiences
   they have provided to help their
   child develop such control

The rest of the class looks for answers
in appropriate references. One person
from each of the two groups summarizes what was learned. The teacher
adds comments only if needed.

Concept: Evaluation at the Child Center

Objectives: Be able to evaluate the effectiveness of facilities at the Child Center and its
contribution to learning

Behavioral outcomes:

   Can describe certain aspects of development
   or lack of it in a child

   Can show at least part of what the individual

student gained through her experience with children

Can point out the strengths and weak points in the facilities provided for the Child Center

Generalization: Effective evaluation in terms of comprehensive goals for an area clarifies how much has been achieved and the quality of achievement.

KEY POINTS	LEARNING EXPERIENCES

Evaluation should
  Be planned and carried out co-operatively with the students
  Be continuous and woven into the curriculum
  Use ingenious ideas at least part of the time
  Be in terms of the goals
  Be as accurate as possible and still in terms of the goals
  Be possible to administer and score
  Be enjoyable
 	
Students have to learn to evaluate in the same way they learn other things
	To discover possible changes in behavior of the four children:
	  Have check-list information from observations tabulated chronologically
	  Have class divide into four groups and each group analyze tabulated information for one child
	  Present what is learned to the class
	Teacher assisted by student answers questions such as, "Will a child who has just begun to show indications of desirable behavior continue to improve as time goes on?"
	
	To discover what each student has gained personally, teacher will suggest that each one write a paragraph on "What the Child Center Meant to Me." Teacher will have available samples written by other students. See example following this part of the framework. If good ideas for evaluation are presented by students these will be used instead of the teacher's suggestion.
	
	To evaluate the facilities of the Center, show class several ways this might be done. Encourage students to choose and adapt one of these or develop an idea of their own. Illustrations are not given because I need to work more on them before showing them to the class.

Paragraph by student: "What the Child Center Meant to Me."

The Child Center meant a great deal to me, because it gave me a greater understanding of myself. At first I didn't like the procedure used when one child hit another child. I was always spanked when I hit my brother. And I don't have to think very far back to remember when. No one ever tried to find out why I hit him. But I was sure I had a good reason. There were other children in the family, and my mother was busy. She probably didn't have time to help my brother and me settle our difficulties together in a friendly way. If we had learned to get along together when we were younger, we might be more friendly now. I can see how important it is to understand why children behave as they do, and to learn the best ways of guiding them.

OBSERVING A CHILD'S DEVELOPMENT THROUGH HIS BEHAVIOR

Name of child: Name of observer:

Date observed: Directions: Check (√) for each behavior observed.

Feelings of insecurity:

_____ Prefers to play alone
_____ Seldom talks to other children or adults
_____ Disrupts other children at play
_____ Attacks anyone who interferes with his play
_____ Constantly wants to be the center of attention
_____ Unwilling to accept suggestions
_____ Timid; will not try a new activity without adult help
_____ Stutters or stammers
_____ Sucks thumb or finger, or has other nervous mannerisms
_____ Seldom smiles or laughs
_____ Displays no enthusiasm about any of the activities

Feelings of security:

_____ Joins group activities
_____ Talks to other children and adults
_____ Does not bother other children at play
_____ Accepts other children who want to play with him
_____ Does not demand constant attention
_____ Willing to accept suggestions
_____ Unafraid to try a new activity by himself
_____ Speaks easily and naturally
_____ Has no nervous mannerisms

_____ Smiles or laughs frequently
_____ Claps hands when a new activity is suggested; hums or sings spontaneously

Poor emotional control:

_____ When angry, resorts to destructive behavior, such as throwing or breaking things, hitting or biting people, tearing his clothes

Developing emotional control:

_____ When angry, may stamp feet or cry a little, or call object of his anger names

_____ Becomes very much upset when he fails to achieve something he tries to do; gives up after one effort

_____ Cries, whines, or sulks when crossed

_____ Tense; unable to relax at quiet activity period or during other play

Poor motor performance:

_____ Awkward about maneuvering tricycle or wagon; bumps into objects or persons

_____ Cannot pour juice from pitcher into cup without spilling

_____ Holds paintbrush or crayons awkwardly

_____ Manages tools such as hammer and small saw awkwardly

_____ Cannot button or unbutton coat

Poorly developed self-reliance and independence:

_____ Has to be reminded when to go to the toilet and to wash hands

_____ Depends on someone to help him select activities

_____ Needs assistance in taking off and putting on wraps

_____ Leaves equipment and materials where he last played with them

Poorly established cooperation with others:

_____ Does not share without being urged

_____ Resents taking turns

_____ Not easily discouraged; willing to make several trials to achieve something he wants to do

_____ Does not become upset when he cannot have his own way

_____ Able to relax during quiet activity period; plays easily and naturally

Developing motor coordination:

_____ Able to ride around room on tricycle or wagon with ease, and to gauge distance

_____ Can pour juice into cup with little or no spilling

_____ Holds paintbrush or crayons as directed

_____ Shows ability to handle tools such as hammer and small saw

_____ Can button and unbutton coat easily

Increasing self-reliance and independence:

_____ Goes to the toilet and washes hands when necessary

_____ Plans his own activities

_____ Takes off and puts on own wraps

_____ Helps put away equipment and materials without being urged

Improving cooperation with others:

_____ Shares on his own accord

_____ Takes turns freely

———— Tries to take anything he wants from another child
———— Has not learned to compromise

———— Recognizes the property rights of others
———— Willing to compromise

Questions:

_____

Teacher Number One knew how to develop her own framework for the course but, at this point, decided to study publications of Future Homemakers of America (1970) and supplementary material on HERO-FHA (1971). She wanted to organize a HERO-FHA chapter, and believed that whatever framework she developed for the curriculum should include suggestions for HERO activities related to course goals for *Preparing for Employment in*

Clothing and Home Furnishings Services. The resource materials she used (see page 260) included the goal "Understand pros and cons of self-employment and employment in both large and small firms." One aspect of this goal related to financial considerations. The table below shows how Teacher Number One planned tentatively to correlate a HERO experience with this particular classwork, thus contributing to more interesting and vital teaching.

SUPPORTIVE LEARNINGS	LEARNING EXPERIENCES
Financial aspects are important considerations when seeking jobs. In addition to salary,	Have the payroll clerk talk with the class about financial aspects of work in total and how deductions are made on paychecks.
Unemployment Insurance provides some income if one is unemployed.	Have representatives from Social Security Office, Unemployment Insurance Office, and Workmen's Compensation Office in town or county speak to class.
Workmen's Compensation provides benefits for those who have accidents or job induced illness when working.	
Social Security provides the elderly, disabled, dependents or survivors of an employee with a partial income.	
Fringe benefits can be considered as added income which help make the job more attractive.	Suggest that each student talk with one or more working persons to obtain a list of fringe benefits each one receives.

Changes in a person's life style may change his financial condition.	For HERO–FHA: Bring in a psychologist, an unwed mother, or a doctor or some other capable person, to explain how teenage pregnancies affect job opportunities and income of girls. Discuss such things as: What can I do? Can I return to my job? What about unwed young fathers? What responsibilities are they to assume? How do income expenditures change when you become a teenage mother or father?

Teacher Number Three, who had had successful teaching experience for some years, developed a framework for her class much like those of Teachers Number One and Two. However, Teacher Number Three felt so secure in what she had planned that at certain spots in the framework it seemed unnecessary to write in part of the suggested experiences. If she failed to produce ideas quickly students might be stimulated to offer more suggestions.

Although there were some differences in the way in which each of the three teachers developed the framework for her wage-earning course all should have at least considered the following:

Introductory statements about such things as the number and ability level of the students, length and schedule of the course, and other appropriate information

Name for unit which will appeal to the class

Introduction to stimulate the students and give them an awareness of the breadth and depth of possible content for the unit

Concepts to help structure and organize appropriate content and to serve as a guide for other curriculum decisions

Objectives related to pupil's developmental needs which define what students will attempt to achieve

Generalizations and supportive learnings which students will be learning in achieving their objectives

Learning experiences to involve students in situations directed toward their goals

Evaluation of various kinds directed toward helping students understand the extent to which they have achieved each objective

Daily time plan to serve as a guide to the teacher in her use of time in the classroom

In concluding the discussion on organization of the curriculum to facilitate learning, it seems important to include what a highly experienced and successful teacher wrote about developing the framework for her own teaching, using the "Cooperative Approach." (The material was prepared in 1959 by Catherine W. Birth, Vocational Consultant for Luzerne County Schools in Pennsylvania.)

How do I plan my homemaking program? Well, it's a little difficult to explain. Maybe I don't write things down as much as I should either. Anyway, I know I just love to teach. Let's see whether I can explain my viewpoint.

You might say that I consider the

teaching of homemaking as a sort of guided tour through a variety of learning experiences, all of them interesting because they're based on the real problems of my students and their families. At the end of each group of related experiences, we arrive at our desired destination, and our arrival gives us a feeling of satisfaction and accomplishment.

Where do I fit into the picture? I seem to function as a guide, or a tour director. In the first place, I do some advance planning. Before I can plan a trip with my students, I have to have some possible destinations in mind. I like to look over maps, and maybe plan several different routes. I'm more apt not to miss anything if I list all the points of interest and the learnings which should take place as we travel along.

But after I've done some advance planning, I like to have my students plan with me. After all, they're going with me on the trip, and it's going to be pretty tough going if they aren't as enthusiastic about it as I am. How would you like to be the guide of a tour to Alaska when everybody in the group has his heart set on going to Hawaii? If we haven't mutually agreed on our destination, how do I know they'll stay on the bus till we get there? And how will they experience any satisfaction over their arrival at their destination if they didn't know where they were trying to go in the first place?

What happens if we can't agree on a destination? You mean that I want to go to the Metropolitan Museum of Art and they want to go to Coney Island? It shouldn't happen if I have done a good job of preplanning. You see, during that process I not only consider my own desires, but also those of my students. If we're miles apart, as we sometimes are,

maybe I should try to find a destination half way in between on which we can agree. And here's a confession I must make. Sometimes the students are more right about it than I am. If I had been truly familiar with their homes and backgrounds, their values and aspirations, I wouldn't have tried to take them to a museum to study period furniture. Maybe it is much more important to them to see something else in New York City. Maybe Coney Island isn't going to be the answer, or maybe it should be at least part of the answer.

Do I use the "Homemaking Education Resource Materials?" You bet I do. Who doesn't like to have a good road map with all the points of interest listed when they plan to make a trip? But the biggest thrill of all is when you discover something that the map makers missed, and you send in your discovery to be added to the next edition of the road map. That's a real achievement.

PLAN FOR DAY-TO-DAY TEACHING

The daily lesson plan has long been the subject of differences of opinion. On the one hand there are those, including Silberman (1970), who state that "the tyranny of the lesson plan in turn encourages an obsession with routine for the sake of routine. School is filled with countless examples of teachers and administrators confusing means with ends, thereby making it impossible to reach the end for which the means were devised [p. 125]." When teachers follow a lesson plan exactly, activities may begin before students have any interest in them and end while interest is still high. On the other hand all kinds of problems arise when students are encouraged to learn only what interests them, to learn only in their own way, and to stop learning whether or not they have achieved anything of consequence. Illustrations of this latter kind of situation may be found in books and magazines, on television programs, and in real life where, in such circumstances, the student says essentially, "Do I have to do what I want to do today?"

Do Silberman and others believe there is no need for a lesson plan? There are exceptions, of course, but in general what such people are really discussing is not the fact that there may be a lesson plan, but the way in which it is often used. In other words, there are times when it is wise to depart from the lesson plan, but there are other times when it would prove wholly unrewarding to do so. What to do in a particular situation is usually a teacher's decision. Making such a decision is not always easy for even the most experienced teacher. A beginner can use only his or her best judgment, knowing that each judgment can be a learning experience leading in time to more satisfying decisions.

What kind, then, of a lesson plan is needed to organize a teacher's thinking for the day in relation to the unit or area the class is working on? There is no pattern that is best for everyone. The amount of detail which is helpful to one teacher will be unnecessary for another. In fact, the amount of detail a teacher believes to be important for one situation may be entirely different in another situation. Many experienced teachers find it more helpful to project a daily class session in their minds than on paper. A student teacher, a beginning teacher, and some experienced teachers will find security in a well thought-out written lesson plan which guides teaching without destroying the creativeness of teacher or students.

The three teachers preparing to teach in an area entirely new to them thought it would be helpful to look at a sampling of different kinds of daily lesson plans. Several such plans are given here.

The following daily lesson plan was developed by a student teacher who was beginning to teach in an area in which she felt less secure than in other areas of home economics. (The material was originated in 1970 by Suellen Wayda, as a student at the Pennsylvania State University.)

Class: 12th-grade Home Economics; 15 students

Unit: Money Management

Day 1: Lesson on values, goals, and how they influence spending

Class Period: 43 minutes

Objectives: To better understand how values and goals influence spending.

Behavioral outcomes

Is able to verbalize what happiness means personally

Can analyze what determines the relative importance of various things (i.e. feelings)

Is able to make decisions about possible ways of spending a specified amount of money and then make a first choice, explaining reasons

Can suggest certain decisions that a newly married expectant couple would have to make with reference to spending (relates back to an earlier lesson taught by the supervising teacher)

Concepts: values; goals; decision-making

Generalizations:

1. Values and goals are interrelated forces that influence the decision-making process and thus spending.

2. Values are a guide in setting goals.

3. Each person needs and wants certain things that may be obtained by setting goals.

4. One must decide what to buy by considering what is important to him.

5. Sometimes things change in importance to the individual or the family.

Key Questions:

What are some things that are important to you?

What do you want from life?

How do values and goals change from infancy to youthful marriage and throughout the life cycle?

Who or what influence your values and goals?

How do values and goals affect your spending habits?

Sequence of Events: Most people do not have enough money for all the things they need and want. What should we know before we try to develop a spending plan that will contribute to greater happiness as we spend money to achieve goals?

1. Use a big drawing of Snoopy to motivate students to complete the phrase "Happiness is . . ." Have one student write everyone's responses on board.

2. Tie in how these things reflect what is important to them. Choose one response and explain that everyone has a different idea of what is important. Each person is different with different ideas. No two people agree on what is most or least important. (*Values*)

3. To further explain values and goals, show these things: Keys to a series of doors; have to unlock doors to reach what you want to achieve.

What Is Important

How To Reach the Goal

4. In order to reach the top of the stairs, you have to choose certain paths and decide to follow them. (Decision making) We have already seen that a young married and expectant couple had certain problems. What were some of them? How might they solve these problems? (Show how they have to make decisions)

5. Life cycle: (Different things are important at different stages in life cycle. One must make decisions to get what one wants at each level)

Infant
6–12
Teenager
After high school
Young married
Middle age
Old age

6. If I gave you $10, list five things you could buy that cost $10 (What is important to you); but you only have $10—choose *one* thing that is most important to you. Why did you make that particular choice?

Homework:

If you do not know how much you spend each month, list all the things you spend money on and then total.

Generalization: Knowing the amount of money available is essential in developing a spending plan.

The following daily lesson plan shows what an experienced teacher thought would be useful to her. She knew her subject matter well but often had difficulty achieving what she wanted in the available time. She needed to plan time carefully.

Area: Housing, home furnishings, and equipment

Grade 10

Goal: To plan the living area in my home to meet the needs and desires of my family

Subgoal: To learn how to make a living area convenient for family activities

Introduction: 5 minutes

Brief review of previous classwork on kinds of activities family members are likely to carry on in a living area and how furniture could be arranged for these activities.

Plans previously made for present lesson: To get as much firsthand knowledge as possible about different types of living areas—class to divide into 3 groups. Group 1 to visit private homes; Group 2 to visit stores with model rooms; Group 3 to visit places where model furnished homes are on display. All groups to use reference materials, such as pictures, books, and magazines. Each group to select a chairman to give a 3- to 5-minute report.

Each student to keep a list of main points as reports are being given

Reports: 15 minutes

Summary written on board of important points in reports: 10 minutes

Learnings expected to be similar to those listed in plan for advance work

Future plans: 15 minutes

Bring up subject of starting a file for the home-economics department on "Hints for Living Areas." Have class select a committee to handle contributions. Students to start file with information for setting up different activity centers and to bring in suggestions— pictures, written material, and the like—by the end of the week

Discuss briefly problems that families might have in sharing a living area. Before next meeting, students to consider problems of their families, or any family they know, and to think about how the difficulties can or are being met.

Class to present these problems at next meeting and to show satisfactory ways of handling them. Students will decide how the

problems and solutions are to be presented, possibly through role playing.

An experienced and effective teacher able to visualize her class as it probably would develop might need only to jot down reminders to herself such as:

1.   Remember that I need to use simpler terminology with this class than my other classes. I too often forget to do this.

2.   Cathy seems to go to sleep in class often even though she is very interested when awake. After class, talk with Joan who is Cathy's best friend to see if she or I can help Cathy with whatever is troubling her.

3.   Remember that John and Marilyn need to work at experiences in which each can feel success. They learn more slowly than most of the group.

4.   Try to challenge Larry. He is brighter than most students in this group and needs to achieve much more than at present.

In summary, the following major points apply to daily lesson planning.

1.   Visualize the class not only as a group, but as different individuals with different abilities and needs.

2.   Keep in mind the objectives, new learnings, experiences, and evaluation when developing the details involved in the daily plan. Details may include (a) participants, (b) equipment, (c) resources and materials to be used, (d) possible problems that may arise and how they can be handled, (e) how the learnings can be stressed and summarized most effectively, (f) how time can be distributed to the best advantage.

3.   Write the plan for the lesson in as much detail as is needed. This will vary with the same teacher in different situations and at different periods in her development as a teacher. A beginning teacher usually finds it helpful to have

a carefully developed plan. Her plan, of course, should be considered tentative and flexible, subject to modifications if ideas and conditions change.

4. There is no prescribed way for preparing a written lesson plan, since no two class situations are alike and no two persons teach the same way, even though they may be teaching the same subject.

5. A comprehensive lesson plan will generally include the characteristics of the daily lesson plan shown on pages 280–281.

6. In most instances, students do not enjoy a teacher who reads from her plans. Plans are only a guide, not a book to be read aloud. Sometimes a teacher who needs to refer to her plan during class may do so by commenting, "I'll just check to see if I thought of anything you didn't." Or, "That was a good idea. Maybe I thought of another one when thinking about today's lesson. Let me check a moment."

7. A lesson plan may be set up to cover a single day or it may be planned for a longer period of time. For example, when single class periods are used, work in meal preparation is often more successfully carried out if it is planned on a basis of several days. In any area where experiences are likely to extend over an even longer period of time, a running plan may be advisable.

PLAN FOR FHA MEETINGS

The question of planning for FHA meetings is often raised. The times of meetings of FHA or HERO-FHA organizations differ greatly from school to school. Some groups use regular class periods, other groups use activity periods of the school, some groups have evening meetings, and occasionally a group may meet during the noon hour. Groups may even use a variety of times for meeting, such as planning some meetings at noon, some in the evening, and an occasional one on Saturday afternoon.

Whatever plan is chosen, the overall goal is to integrate the Future Homemakers Program of Work with the home-economics curriculum as illustrated on pages 277–278.

One FHA group chose to concentrate their club work for three months on the National Program of Work related to "To Dare Is to Care" (pages 309–311). They decided to begin by having members of each class in home economics choose a different project to be presented to the total FHA membership, either in a special program or in several progress reports during a regular meeting. One group studying child development volunteered FHA help to some of the less fortunate children in the area. They also planned to do something special for children in a nearby children's home.

A class working in the clothing area at this time promised to present a "Holiday Around the World" program shortly before Christmas. This program would show the heritage of three countries in traditions and clothing. The countries chosen would be represented by FHA members with backgrounds in them.

An advanced class in foods promised to have a demonstration on the preparation of several foods from other countries. They believed they could obtain the cooperation of several women in town who had come to the United States from some other country.

An FHA member in a fourth class invited the group to her home for a Saturday afternoon meeting. Her parents had many furnishings and decorations from India. They also had films showing Indian life which the group could see if they chose.

At this point a small committee was appointed by the President to correlate the program, arrange the most appropriate time for meetings, and publicize those programs to which outside guests could be invited. Each group was responsible for the program it had volunteered to present. The teacher and FHA officers were available for conferences as needed.

THREE

WHAT PRELIMINARY PLANNING IS NEEDED FOR EFFECTIVE PROGRAMS?

PLANNING FOR A NEW PROGRAM

A school program, whether for a comprehensive secondary school or a vocational-technical school, does not just happen. It could be the result of requests by the teacher, business and industry, the State Department of Education, the local administration, or others who are interested. It is the administration, however, who is usually responsible for the development of a program at an early stage and continues to work with the program as it develops, or designates others to do so. The teacher may or may not participate in the pre-planning. If not, it is important that she know what has been accomplished and what remains to be done in initiating the program.

The wage-earning course in *Clothing and Home Furnishings Services* taught by each of the three teachers described earlier was a vocational-education course developed according to an educational plan. Content for such plan development will be discussed on the following pages.

FINANCING

Financing is often one of the first considerations in developing any new program. When the program desired is a vocational one, partial or in some instances total financing may be obtained through the state and federal government. The school district under the direction of the school administration is responsible for preparing an "educational plan" describing the program desired. This projected plan must meet both state and federal approval before funds for the new program are made available. For application forms and other help, the local district contacts the appropriate division in the State Department of Education, which in turn contacts the appropriate division in the U.S. Office of Education in Washington. It is important to remember that vocational education, whether carried on in a comprehensive high school or vocational and technical school, is basically a state and local program aided in part by the federal government. As federal funds increase, state and local funds usually increase proportionately.

ADVISORY COMMITTEES

An advisory committee may prove to be the most important factor in the success of a home-economics program. This is true whether or not the program is vocational. Some of the most successful teachers over the past forty or fifty years have organized and worked with such committees even though doing so was not required. At the present time an advisory committee is required for all wage-earning programs. The formation of such a committee is written into the Federal Vocational Education Act under which the program operates.

To a teacher who has not had an advisory committee a number of questions may occur. Who should be the members of such a group? Who takes the initiative for organizing and choosing members? How many members are needed? What can such a group do to promote a wage-earning program?

The number of members for such a committee varies. In a relatively small school district three to five members may be sufficient. More will probably prove desirable for larger school districts. There is no magic number. The real question is: What groups should be represented on a particular advisory committee? Representatives may be leaders from the lay public, business and industry, professional groups, school-board members, civic groups, church groups, the state employment service, labor unions, self-employed individuals, area redevelopment authority, and chambers of commerce.

Often the organization of an advisory committee is the first step in developing a new program. In this case the administration may take the initiative for such organization, the teacher may be asked to assume the responsibility, or it may be done cooperatively with the chairman of the group responsible. Whatever the teacher's responsibility is in the beginning, she is the one who will probably work most closely with the advisory committee over a period of time.

Once organized, what will the new committee do? One of the first important responsibilities may be to help conduct a survey in order

to document the need for training in the particular area under consideration. Such documentation may be an essential part of the educational plan developed by the administration. Projection of future needs in an area can be made with some confidence. A competent specialist, or at least an individual familiar with conducting surveys, will probably be in charge. Sometimes a steering committee of representatives from school administrators and teachers may assist in developing plans and procedures for the survey. The advisory committee often assists in gathering and reviewing data. It provides consultants on special problems and in general promotes the work of the survey.

In addition to assisting with the survey, this important committee may be active in fund raising if special funds are required. It may provide professional guidance in preparing a job description, in building the curriculum, and in disseminating information about the program. It may be especially useful in advising on facilities, in recruitment, and in helping arrange cooperative work experience and on-the-job training. Finally, it may be the most important asset the school has in placement of students, evaluation of the program, and follow-up.

DESCRIPTION OF COURSE AND PROGRAM OF STUDIES

Nearly every plan presented, whether it be to the school board, the state, or the federal government, includes at least some suggestions for the new program under consideration. These suggestions may include the results of the survey conducted to discover student and community needs. It may include objectives for the new course to be taught and, sometimes, a fairly complete description of such a course.

The steering committee, if there is one, and the advisory committee if it has been appointed, assist the teacher in development of whatever outline of the program is needed as part of the plan being developed. Often outlines can be quickly adapted from available resource materials, but there are some appropriate jobs for which resource materials may not be readily available. If the teacher is new or not present at this time, a leader in home economics from the State Department of Education may furnish needed help. In fact such an individual probably has conferred with the administration earlier than this in the development of the new program.

Students majoring in a career vocation in home economics need to be guided by a suggested program of studies, just as do college-bound students and business majors. Recommendations of appropriate courses to be taken in the 10th, 11th, and 12th grades need to be stated. Flexibility to meet individual needs and interests of pupils is desirable to the extent that the required courses meet basic needs for which the student is in training. Any program of studies should be adapted to local education situations.

FACILITIES AND EQUIPMENT

Needed facilities and equipment for a new program are a major consideration, and any plan generally asks for a listing of both large and small equipment needed and an estimation of its cost. Such planning depends on the objectives of the course, number of students to be served, and existing facilities in the school and community. Sometimes there may be available space in the school which can be renovated, or there may be appropriate community facilities which can be adapted and used

for the program. It may be necessary to provide a completely new facility.

Whatever the problem of space and equipment may be, the state supervisor of home economics and the school architect will be among those with most useful ideas. In much of the planning that is going on around the country, school leaders are thinking of schools of the future, and are attempting to incorporate newer ideas wherever practicable, even though the planning of teaching-learning spaces still needs to be dictated by the programs.

Perhaps the best summary the authors have found of the setting for any kind of home-economics program is in the chart on page 287, by Simpson and Barrow (1964, p. 78).

TEACHER FOR PROGRAM

Requirements for the teacher of wage-earning programs, such as the one described on pages 255–261, vary from state to state but in general the requirements are of three kinds:

Certificate to teach in the program area in the secondary school and often some teaching experience

Experience in the business world in the kind of work for which students are to be prepared

Personal qualifications desired by the administration. These may include such qualities as skill in the area of instruction, ability to work cooperatively with business, and high professional standards.

Many home-economics teachers qualify to teach wage-earning classes without being aware of it. They may have had previous experience during the summer, they may have held

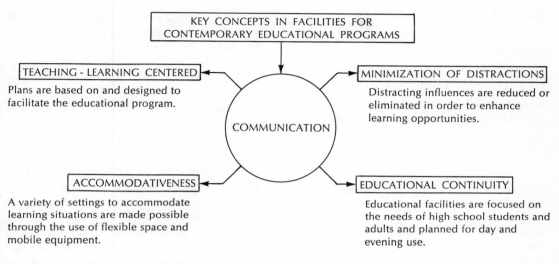

The Planning of Teaching Learning Facilities

jobs during college, or even had full-time experience in the business field. Sometimes an individual with experience and competency in a certain kind of work such as tailoring may be granted an interim teaching certificate. The important thing to remember is that professional skills, teaching ability, and satisfactory personal qualifications are all important needs in preparing students for employment. The three teachers who planned to teach "Clothing and Home Furnishings Services" (pages 265–266), had the qualifications which would probably need to be stated in any plan developed in order to obtain funds.

TRAINEE QUALIFICATIONS AND SELECTION

A description of trainees for a career vocation such as in "Clothing and Home Furnishings Services" was doubtless a part of the plan developed. According to the Federal Act supporting the program, the trainees for such a class would be chosen from any one of the following groups: high-school students, individuals who have completed or left high school, persons who have already entered the labor market and need training or retraining, and finally persons who have handicaps that prevent them from succeeding in the regular program. The estimated number of students in the course was also stated in the plan. The teacher, if available, and the guidance personnel in the school probably worked together in choosing high-school students for such a course. However, if the training was to be provided for the other groups listed, the advisory committee might well be in a position to render invaluable assistance.

Belonging to one of the above groups would not necessarily enable a student to join a particular career course. He or she would need other qualifications appropriate for the job training to be offered. In the case of clothing and textiles such qualifications might be:

Being fourteen years of age or over

Planning to complete the program and then be employed as a result of training

Having some skill and manual dexterity in sewing and clothing construction

Being perceptive of space relationships as required for garment construction and fit

Being in good physical and mental health

LENGTH OF COURSE AND SCHEDULING

Scheduling for the new course and its length are the responsibility of the administration. However, the state supervisor, the teacher, and the advisory committee may offer suggestions. If cooperative work experience or on-the-job training are planned as part of the course, those doing the scheduling need to take it into consideration. The time of day the course is offered and the length of time required outside the classroom are important to the teacher, students, and their parents.

The course may be set up so that the students attend school part-time and work part-time. Or outside experiences may be provided after school, on weekends and holidays, or in the summer. The more specialized the skill being developed the more additional clock hours will be required. The purpose in all instances, is to attain the objectives of the course.

COOPERATIVE WORK EXPERIENCE AND ON-THE-JOB TRAINING

In order to make a transition from the classroom to the responsibilities of a job, work experience of some kind is needed. For a course such as *Clothing and Home Furnishings Serv-*

ices the beginning work experience may be offered in a work-room set up for the purpose. The regular clothing laboratory would be desirable but may not be available for such use.

On-the-job training is supervised training in a situation of the kind in which the student later expects to be employed. The advisory committee can be especially useful in helping the teacher with contracts for the job training. It is a situation in which all those concerned need to work closely together. Self-evaluation by the student, employer evaluation, and teacher evaluation are all important facets of work experience, whether carried on in the school or in the community. Suggested forms of evaluation which will be needed may be found in available resource materials. Others may be secured from industry and business and some may be developed cooperatively by participants and the teacher.

JOB PLACEMENT AND FOLLOW-UP

The outcome of an employment program depends on the success of its students in securing jobs in the kind of work for which they are trained or in related work. Those best able to identify job openings and, in some instances, to recommend trainees to employers include the teacher of the course, the guidance counselor assisted by the advisory committee, and the Bureau of Employment. It is important to remember that a job needs to match the trainee's ability and skill if the trainee is to be productive and able to advance in employment.

All too often students are trained, graduated, and forgotten. As Voelkner (1971, p. 60) says,

If programs are to be evaluated, the products of the program must be periodically examined. There are innumerable factors about which data could be collected. Some variables which could be examined are:

The length of time a graduate takes to find a satisfactory job

Employment security, that is, once in a job, is the graduate subject to dismissals and/or lay-offs?

The length of time the graduate stays in his job

Earnings progression

Rate of advancement from entry level jobs, if any, to more responsible positions

Voelkner's list is not complete, as he himself stated, but it does indicate the need for follow-up and evaluation. The kind of self-evaluation experiences carried on during course work and on-the-job training are very important, but such evaluation as Voelkner speaks of may lead to learning how well students have developed skills which are salable in a free employment market. Such evaluation may lead to improvement of the overall program and to answers to other educational problems in vocational education. All of these are major goals of vocational education. At the present time, follow-up evaluation is part of the federal program of vocational education.

In conclusion, all the topics discussed under preliminary planning may become a part of the plan developed for the school board and the state and federal government. The content of such plans varies from time to time. However, all of the topics discussed will be used in developing the plan and/or carrying it out.

FOUR

HOW ARE RESOURCE MATERIALS USED IN INDIVIDUAL–BASIS TEACHING?

MATERIALS FOR INDIVIDUALS

Up to this point, the discussion on curriculum has been concerned chiefly with the class group. In certain situations, however, the teacher will be working on an individual basis in the home or elsewhere. Teaching on this basis is sometimes the only effective way in a particular situation. As new programs open up to home economists, such teaching will probably assume importance for more teachers than at present. For example, home economists are being employed to work with individuals in retirement homes and with older persons who may be able to continue living independently if they can be helped to simplify their housekeeping. Others are employed in homemaking rehabilitation and may work with the physically handicapped, the mentally retarded, the emotionally disturbed, and the economically and culturally deprived. Part of such work, to be effective, may have to be done on an individual basis.

To visualize this kind of teaching more clearly, it may help to know about a cooperative program developed in Alabama by the Division of Continuing Education in Home Economics at the University of Alabama and the Vocational Rehabilitation Service of the Alabama Department of Education (1971, 1972). In

Alabama, there are approximately 50,000 homemakers with disabilities. In addition, the Crippled Children's Service has identified 18,000 children in the state as crippled or otherwise handicapped. There are other homemakers with invisible difficulties such as, for example, deafness or heart disease.

Through a fourteen-show television series entitled "On Your Own" and produced for educational TV, it was possible to supply suggestions, ideas, and thoughts on activities of daily living for homemakers and others with visible and invisible disabilities. Even with these programs and training at the Rehabilitation Center, there was need for teaching some clients in the home situation. Such a pilot-program is now in operation in Alabama, and Vocational Rehabilitation Service officials anticipate that it will grow into a state-wide program. In the pilot program, a home economist works as a specialized counselor with a general caseload of disabilities, such as partial paralysis, amputation, and cardiac disease. The home-economics counselor makes home visits to rehabilitation clients who need help as homemakers on referral from other rehabilitation counselors.

The general objective of the program is to help both the homemaker and the family make more adequate adjustment to the homemaker's role within the limitation of his or her disability. This includes counseling with the clients and family members as well as teaching the clients. Recommendations for work simplification procedures and devices are usually made for various aspects of household tasks and personal daily living activities. Curriculum needs for such a specialized counselor will be different from those of a teacher confronted with a group of students. The counselor will probably know quite a lot about the objectives of the homemaker before the first visit, because generally hers are referral cases. In addition to counseling ability (which is an asset in any teaching) she will need either to know or be prepared to find out the answers to the following questions: What curriculum resources are available for helping the client with this special disability? How can I adapt appropriate information so it will be most useful to my client? How can I encourage as much participation as possible from the client and the family in using available helps? In some instances the client will be aware of progress as it is made, but in others the counselor may need to consider how best to help the client realize that progress toward goals is being made?

There is a rapidly growing amount of information available for helping homemaking rehabilitation clients. There are some generalizations which may apply to many clients such as:

The homemaker's role may have to become one of planning and taking part in family decisions without actually doing household jobs.

If the family accepts the disability and cooperates with a change in household routines and equipment plus added responsibilities, the whole family will benefit.

While the principles of work simplification apply to all homemakers, they are essential to the homemaker suffering from a disability.

People with handicaps may become not only self-supporting but can make valuable contributions to society.

Two persons with similar afflictions can perform vastly different tasks depending on each person's capability and spirit.

In addition to generalizations, there is general subject-matter material available concerning such things as simplifying tasks within the home, handy helpers for the disabled, clothing for children with handicaps, and sources of information and help for homemakers with handicaps. Then there is specialized and detailed information and equipment available for specific disabilities such as hand limitations, limited use of the lower extremities, and blindness. Finally, desirable responses of the non-disabled to various categories of handicapped persons is important.

The specialized counselor may have problems similar to those of other teachers in helping the family and individuals decide how best to achieve various learnings in terms of the objective. For example, the family may have learned a number of ways to help the homemaker with hand limitations. There are still decisions to be made on how to teach these techniques to avoid frustration on the part of the homemaker. Evaluation of accomplishment can be quite informal, such as complimentary comments by family members, but the disabled homemaker may need even more than others the encouragement which comes with accomplishment.

In conclusion, the teacher working on an individual basis needs to have readily available and well organized all the kinds of materials discussed. Instead of developing a curriculum for a class, she will be developing an ongoing one for each individual as she plans and works with her client. She, as well as the classroom teacher, will need to evaluate long-established and innovative learnings and correlate them in the way that is most appropriate for each situation.

SUGGESTED TEACHER EXPERIENCES

1.   The teacher may find it helpful to assemble and study several resource publications related to curriculum planning, including those set up for local teachers. Individual class members can exhibit and report on other kinds of materials that might be especially helpful to a beginning teacher and indicate why.

2.   Arrange to interview experienced home economics teachers regarded as particularly successful to find out how they go about planning a program. Questions such as the following may be asked:

(a) How do you use curriculum materials available to you from the state or locally?

(b) What kind of information from the administration do you find helpful in using resource materials for curriculum development?

(c) How do you manage to correlate so many ideas learned in college and at your school when thinking about the curriculum for a particular class?

(d) In what and how detailed a form do you develop the framework for your classes? Did you do this in a similar way as a beginning teacher? If not, what kind of framework did you use then? What kind of overall plan do you show your administrator? Is she pleased with this form? Has she ever suggested other ways that she believes might portray the program more clearly? If so, what were they?

(e) How much part, if any, do you have in the preliminary planning for new courses in your department? Would you like a greater part? If so, why? Have you ever spoken with the administration about this matter? If so, what did you learn?

3.   Select an area which you would like to teach or, preferably, will be teaching very soon. After choosing possible goals for this area, make two sets of plans: an overall plan for the area and one for a daily lesson or several lessons. These plans can be made in whatever form seems desirable and need not follow the material given in the text.

4.   With the class, develop an evaluation device for appraising the unit plan and the daily lesson plan. It is important in doing this to include planning for Future Homemakers of America.

5.   The class can examine the different plans worked out in Experience Number 3. Any procedures which vary from those described in the text can be discussed. All the plans can be appraised on the basis of the form of evaluation set up in the preceding experience.

6.   The class may want to put on a role-playing skit characterizing the teacher whose viewpoint on curriculum planning is given on pages 278–279. It might be interesting to evaluate the attitude of the person portrayed in relation to success in teaching.

7.   Hold a debate on the extent to which the home-economics teacher should participate in the preliminary planning needed for an effective program.

8.   With the class, compile as many examples as possible of teaching home economics on an individual basis. What are some of the advantages and disadvantages of such teaching?

PART TWO

COOPERATING WITH OTHERS ON CURRICULUM DEVELOPMENT

Anyone who understands the complexities of forecasting the future knows it is extremely difficult and that he cannot be absolutely sure of his forecast. Nevertheless, people today are living in a more rapidly changing environment than at any time in past history. The greater the lag between the rate of change and the response to this change, the greater will be the problems facing all of us. What can be said about society in general can be said also of education.

Few disagree that education needs to change in such a way that what is taught is worth knowing now and will be worth knowing in the future. How to select such knowledge is another matter, but one with which educators are vitally concerned, especially those responsible for the curriculum in our schools. The curriculum may denote the courses and class activities of the students, or it may refer to the total range of in-class and out-of-class activities sponsored by the school. In an even broader sense it may be thought of as the total life experiences of any learner for which the school assumes responsibility in direction and guidance. In this book, the broad interpretation of curriculum will be used. The home-economics program, or curriculum, will be regarded as a learners' experience which will improve personal, family, and community living. In general, these statements about the school curriculum apply also to any organization wishing to plan similarly for the organization's personnel.

A survey of current curriculum materials shows a variety of patterns, as well as general agreement that better materials are needed whether for private or public organizations. Although the examples available are not all structured alike, all are intended to serve as a guide to learning. Part Two of this book will show a sampling of available curriculum materials and emphasize the desirable characteristics of such materials, as well as discuss procedures for curriculum improvement.

FIVE

WHAT VARIATIONS ARE FOUND IN CURRICULUM MATERIALS?

A SAMPLING OF AVAILABLE MATERIALS

Resource materials, or curriculum materials, are probably most often available to teachers of home economics through their own state department of education. These materials are usually the result of cooperative efforts of the state supervisor of home economics, teacher educators from the colleges and universities, and teachers in the field. There are other sources also for curriculum materials such as the county, the city, the local school, and special groups. Such materials are constantly in process of development.

It seems advisable to present a sampling of recently-prepared curriculum materials. Some are available at this time as working papers for teachers to use and evaluate. In fact, the authors believe that all the materials except Example 5 (page 309), are still in the process of being evaluated. These actual illustrations from resource materials are included for the following special reasons:

1. To present materials comprehensive enough to give beginning teachers, and those without experience, a clearer picture than was heretofore available of the kind of help to be gained from such curricula.

2. To furnish a common base for the discus-

sion which follows, as well as to illustrate certain content developed throughout the remainder of the book.

3. To illustrate what may develop into trends for home-economics curriculum.

4. To stimulate readers to visualize still other kinds of curriculum materials which may be especially appropriate for the kind of society that appears to be developing.

The selection was arbitrary, and illustrations from other parts of the country probably would have served equally well as a substitute for, or to supplement, the examples used. The number which could be included was determined by the matter of space.

A word should be said about use of the illustrations. As you read you may want to keep these questions in mind: (1) What are the parts of the curriculum? (2) In what respect is one illustration different from another? Similar to the others? (3) Does one seem easier to use than another? If so, why?

Your first reading should be for the purpose of obtaining an overall picture of curriculum patterns resembling those you may be using or helping to develop. The discussion on characteristics of curriculum materials which follows the illustrations will highlight the different characteristics of such materials. As the book develops you will be able to fit the parts together again; in other words, you should use a Gestalt approach, or the whole-part-whole method of learning.

EXAMPLE 1

The illustration used for this example (Pennsylvania Dept. of Education, 1971d, pp. 53; 64–65) is a sampling from resource materials prepared for five levels from kindergarten through adulthood. The material deals with "Human Development and the Family including Child Development"; "Home Management, Family Resources, and Consumer Decisions"; "Foods and Nutrition"; "Textiles and Clothing"; "Housing and Home Furnishings."

Each subject-matter area is subdivided into major concepts. The concepts for Housing and Home Furnishings that follow are illustrative of the other areas as well:

Creation of home environment

Influence of surroundings on home environment

Influence of heritage on housing

Influence of values and resources

Expertise in the selection of housing and home furnishings

Beauty in housing and home furnishings

Creativity in housing and home furnishings

Wage-earning skills

The objectives for each major concept are progressive, as indicated for "Beauty in housing and home furnishings." The major generali-

LEVEL	OBJECTIVE
1. Kindergarten through Elementary	Know what makes a house pretty (May I help make the house pretty?)
2. Middle School or Junior High	Develop my sense of beauty
3. High School	Become familiar with good examples of the "beautiful" in art and home decoration
4. Post-secondary	Apply aesthetic knowledge to housing and home furnishings
5. Adult	Retain the best of the old and adapt the best of the new in housing and home furnishings

zation is the same throughout. Supportive learnings and pupil experiences including evaluation are progressive for each level from 1 through 5.

The illustration which follows is for levels 1 *and* 5, or kindergarten through elementary *and*

adulthood. The other three levels are omitted because of space considerations; they were developed in the same manner as those shown.

Concept: Beauty in housing and home furnishings.

Objective: Know what makes a house pretty. (May I help make the house pretty?)

Generalization: Each person has a potential sense of beauty that can be developed and expressed in the place he lives.

SUPPORTIVE LEARNINGS	SAMPLING OF PUPIL EXPERIENCES INCLUDING EVALUATION
There are many things that can make my house pretty.	"Show-and-tell something pretty from home that I like." Why do you like it?
Suggestion: Caution the children about taking things from nature without the permission of the owner.	
Colors found in nature are pretty.	"Show-and-tell something pretty from nature that I like." Why do you like it?
Colors are fun when I feel happy with them. I feel good when my house is pretty.	Show color combinations with construction paper. Have children choose color combinations they like best. How do they feel when they see the colors? Do they feel happy and warm, cool, cozy? Discuss with them parts of the house where these colors might be used.

Objective: Retain the best of the old and adapt the best of the new in housing and home furnishings.

Generalization: Each person has a potential sense of beauty that can be developed and expressed in the place he lives.

SUPPORTIVE LEARNINGS	SAMPLING OF PUPIL EXPERIENCES INCLUDING EVALUATION
New concepts of beauty and appreciations may be developed as new ideas are explored.	Have each person make a survey of his own living situation and determine possible changes which might take place such as: moving to a different place, redecorating present place. Discuss new concepts of beauty which would be involved.

Exciting trends in housing and furnishings are developing with the keynote being simplicity, flexibility, new materials, and old materials used in new ways.

To become acquainted with the new trends in housing and furnishings and apply them to own situations, class can:
a.   invite one or more resource persons to speak on new trends
b.   show samples or illustrations of new trends

Individuals can determine new ideas they personally like, that might fit into their own housing situations.

Objects which have meaning to the individual in terms of beauty are important to his everyday living.

Appreciation for older decorating ideas can be developed by:
a.   having antique dealer speak on value of antiques and methods of refinishing
b.   discussing use of antiques as accessories in relation to color, setting, and atmosphere. Individuals can show own personal antiques and tell the background of these
c.   having each person list decorative items, beautiful to him; select a new decorating item which would combine these attractively
d.   illustrating how new trends can blend with older ideas; this may be done by combinations of actual furnishings or magazine pictures.

Suggestion:

Problems expressed by individuals in the class will be a guide to selection of speakers. Ask class members for suggestions.

One room may contain furniture of different styles if done with care and understanding.

Concepts of beauty may be shared with others.

Suggestions for sharing possessions include gifts, museums, antique shows, schools.

Using his own personal situation, a person may be helped to decide which of his possessions to use and how to use them in a changing condition. This may be followed by a discussion of ways to share possessions with others who would really appreciate them.

In addition to the illustration shown, each subject-matter area provides a bibliography that includes student references, teacher references, magazines, films, filmstrips, bulletins, and reports. The material is published, loose leaf, in six sections that include the five subject-matter areas. The first section explains the terminology and curriculum structure used as the basis for developing the resource materials in each curriculum area.

EXAMPLE 2

This sampling taken from resource materials (Texas Tech University, Jan. 1971, pp. 33–39) was prepared for a one-semester course for both sexes at the eleventh- and twelfth-grade levels studying consumer education. The illustration that follows was from the first of four sections: "Allocation of Resources," "Consumer Buying," "Consumer Citizenship," and "The Consumer in the Economy." In addition to what is shown, the resource materials presented student references for books, pamphlets, and periodicals. Teacher references, visuals, and films were included also. The illustration is entitled, "Allocation of Resources—Budget or Spending Plan."

Behavioral Objectives: (1) comprehend the importance of setting up some type of spending plan (2) examine various types of budgets (3) select a personal budget plan that is suitable (4) apply the management process to setting up a budget.

Suggested learning experiences:

1. Write the first word that comes to your mind when the following terms are called out: bargain, rent, utilities, flexibility, planned spending, charge account, donations, insurance, savings, fixed income, emergencies, budget. Put a star by each word that has an unpleasant association for you. Compare your ideas with those of the other members of the class. With which words did you have an unpleasant association? Why?

2. Ask for a volunteer to put all the money he has with him on the desk, tell when he will secure more money, and identify the expenditures he has to make with this amount of money and tell how he will allocate this money. Discuss such questions as: Does your family budget? Do you budget? How does it work for your family? For you? How does your family reach long-term goals? Is your plan written? How often do you examine it for adjustments? Do you use the envelope system?

3. Conduct a survey to determine the various ways students in your school obtain money and the frequency with which they receive it. Ask such questions as: Do you earn your money; receive allowances, doles, or gifts; or receive money in a combination of these ways? Do you receive your money on a weekly, monthly, or irregular basis? What are the major items for which your money is spent?

4. Keep a record of all your income for the next two weeks, indicating sources from which it is received. Also keep a record of all expenditures. You will use this information later in this unit to analyze your spending habits.

5. View the Visual Master TM 10—Basic Budgeting—from *Coed* to introduce general principles of money management and budgeting as they apply to teen-agers. Discuss.

6. Read the play, *Mama's Bank Account*, by Kathryn McLean. When Papa brought home his week's earnings, what did Mama do? When all the money had been accounted for and put into the various piles, what did Mama do and say? Do you think she budgeted? Did she have short- and long-term goals? Was her budget successful in relation to her family's needs?

7. Read the "Thought of the Day" on the bulletin board. Discuss what this means in relation to budgeting. (Note to teacher: Be sure to put up a new quotation concerning budgeting each day while studying this concept and use it as a basis for discussion. See the Sears booklet, *A Department Store in the Classroom*, or ask your librarian to help you find quotations if others are not available.)

8. Take the $25.00 in play money given to you by your teacher and list ways in which you would spend it. Does your spending reflect your values and goals? Do not sign your name to the paper. Hand in your paper to the teacher, who will shuffle them and distribute them. Evaluate the anonymous paper you got for the values and goals reflected by the items purchased. Discuss.

9. Make a list of all the categories a family must consider when building a spending plan. Are there items that you had not considered before? Take a look at the various categories and see how these might change in relation to the family life cycle. Discuss. Which items are fixed expenses? Flexible expenses?

10. Look in textbooks and pamphlets to find a variety of forms and guides to be used in setting up a budget. Compare these forms. What are the items that need to be included in a budget? What are some guides that would work for you in setting up a budget?

11. Devise a form that you believe would meet your needs and goals. (Note to teacher: Students will use the form they devise later on in the unit.)

12. Listen to case studies to see the problems families face in planning their budgets. Situations can be obtained in local newspapers prior to the Good Fellow Fund Drive in Texas. Discuss.

13. Interview a case worker or someone who works with various families in your community. Find out what is being done to help families live within their income. Report your findings to the class.

14. View the film, *The Owl Who Gave a Hoot*, from the Office of Economic Opportunity to see how foolish everyone was who did not budget his money. Notice the names given to the various people in the film. Also listen carefully to the words of the song. Discuss such questions as: Why were the Pigeons unwise in what they purchased? Why were they named Pigeons? Who were the Owls? Why were they named Owls? How were the Owls "smart buyers"?

15. List a purchase from which you received so much satisfaction that you felt you had gotten more than your money's worth. What enhanced its value to you? Had you earned the money for it? Planned to buy it and wanted it for a long time?

16. Visit with homemakers or other students in the school to see how they satisfy their needs and wants and still live within their budgets. Are all family members involved in planning? Discuss your findings.

17. Read the booklet, *A Guide to Budgeting for Young Couples*, from U.S. Department of Agriculture or *Money and Your Marriage* by National Consumer Finance Association and write a short paper on "Two Can Live as Cheaply as One" or "Two Cannot Live as Cheaply as One." Justify your reasoning.

18. Use the information you have accumulated about your own spending habits and plan a budget that you might be able to live with. Work out your spending plan by applying the management principle to it. Use the form that you developed under item 11 of these experiences.

(Note: 17 other experiences not included for lack of space.)

Key points:

Plans may incorporate more than one decision.

Organization is the way in which individuals and families carry out activities.

The organization of different individuals and families differs in aim and effect.

The implementation of plans may involve reappraisal and adjustment of procedures to meet changing conditions.

Effective organization is related to optimal use of resources.

Anticipated outcomes and incentives energize organizational processes.

Management by individuals and families reflect differences in values, goals, and standards.

The perception of available resources may enhance or limit the management potential of individuals and families.

A financial plan is a necessary tool in managing money.

The four parts of a financial plan are related.

A successful plan is based on realistic facts and figures.

Good consumer habits help make a budget work.*

EXAMPLE 3

The following illustration, taken from one state's curriculum material (Tennessee State Board, 1970), shows specific objectives stated in the pattern of the Taxonomies—the cognitive and affective domains. The illustration was intended for use in junior and senior high schools. It covers only the psychological needs related to consumer education. The emphasis placed on consumer education by Part F of the Vocational Education Amendments of 1968

prompted the development of a wide variety of materials in consumer education.

In addition to what is given below, this particular resource material includes supporting generalizations, learning experiences and evaluation, and such resources as books, magazines, pictures, charts, and transparencies.

Major Concept: Psychological Needs

Long-Range Objective: Deeper understanding of how psychological needs affect national economy

Broad Generalization: There is a close relationship between psychological needs of the consumer and the national economy

Specific Objective:

Affective Domain—Receiving

An awareness that psychological needs influence consumer spending.

Such as: Belonging, achievement, freedom from fear affects the way money is spent.

Cognitive Domain—Knowledge

Recognizes psychological needs and how some of these can be satisfied through consumer.

Such as: Need for belonging, achievement, economic security, freedom from fear, love and affection, freedom from guilt and self-respect.

Belonging—buys certain products in order to belong to a group

Economic security—uses talent to earn money

Freedom from fear—saving for emergencies

Self-respect—plan long-range goals

Cognitive Domain—Comprehension

Comprehends that psychological needs are influencing factors which give priority to decisions made by consumer.

---

* The first eight statements were taken from *Concepts and Generalizations: Their Place in High School Home Economics Curriculum Development.* Washington, D.C.: American Home Economics Association, 1967. The other four statements were taken from *Your Family and Its Money* by Helen Thal and Melinda Holcombe. Boston: Houghton Mifflin Company, 1968.

Such as: Expensive car for status, overspending on children due to guilt feelings.

Cognitive Domain—Application

Relates family spending habits to psychological needs.

Such as: Spending more money on "things" —cars, boats, big houses, beach homes, trip to Europe, country club membership.

Cognitive Domain—Analysis

Recognizes the relationship between outcomes of positive and negative ways of satisfying psychological needs upon financial planning.

Such as: Overspending for status; gains through educational accomplishments; impulse buying versus planned spending; long-range goals versus immediate satisfactions; savings versus extended credit.

Cognitive Domain—Synthesis

Develops plan where psychological needs are recognized as a factor which influences the way in which families use resources to achieve goals.

Such as: Family makes temporary sacrifices to achieve advanced education or more training; all members pool resources to help achieve major goals to meet needs for achievement, security, and belonging.

Cognitive Domain—Evaluation

Appraises how decisions influenced by psychological needs relate to the economy of the national community.

Such as: Contributions to community agencies, heart fund, cancer drive; membership in community recreation facilities.

Affective Domain—Valuing

Seeks to influence consumer decisions of others in order that their psychological needs are met.

Such as: Responsibility to share information and assist others.

EXAMPLE 4

The illustration on "Family Influence and Responsibilities" that follows (Commonwealth of Virginia, 1971) was developed for tenth-grade students. It is a sampling from the life area known as "Individual Development in the Family." It is one of four areas around which the consumer and home-economics education programs in secondary schools are organized. The other three areas are: (1) "Management in the Family," (2) "Consumption of Goods and Services in the Family," (3) "Cultural Development in the Family."

Some educators recommend that all education be organized around major life problems or areas. The traditional subject matter in home economics is utilized in instruction as it makes a contribution to the development of concepts in the various family life areas. For example, food is a part of "Individual Development in the Family." What foods are right for the young child? Is the teenager's diet adequate? What foods are good for "snacks"? Why is the teenager the most poorly nourished member of the family, as is known to be true, and the mother the second most poorly nourished? The curriculum which follows illustrates how different areas of home economics may contribute to a life area. Three specific concepts are examined: "Importance of Living in Families," "Qualities of Family Membership," and "Responsibilities of Families." A suggested instructional procedure is included for each.

Unit Objective: Upon completion of this unit of instruction, the student will evidence a higher regard for his own family and will evidence qualities of good family membership.

SPECIFIC CONCEPTS AND CONTENT	SUBJECT MATTER

1. Importance of Living in Families
Emotional support
  Belonging
  Love
  Sense of trust
  Self worth and identity
  Release of feelings
Guides for behavior
  Values, goals, standards
  Spiritual beliefs
Traditions and customs
	Child Development
	Personal Development
	Family Relationships

2. Qualities of Family Membership
Individual worth and dignity
  Appreciation
  Consideration and kindness
Communication
Cooperation
Responsibility
Loyalty
	Child Development
	Personal Development
	Family Relationships

3. Responsibilities of Families Protection Economic support Affection and regulation of behavior Education and opportunities for development Environment for sociability Entertaining friends in the home Citizenship preparation	Personal Development Family Relationships Health and Safety Consumer Education Housing

1. Importance of Living in Families

Specific Objectives:

Appreciates the privileges of membership in a family group (Affective—Receiving).

Analyzes influences of family on individual development (Cognitive—Analysis).

Realizes that life in parental home provides a model for family life in future home (Affective—Responding).

Knows ways in which the family provides the first education a child receives (Cognitive—Knowledge).

Values being a member of a family (Affective—Valuing).

Generalizations:

The nature and quality of family life affect the development of individuals in the family.

Family influences in the first years of a child's

life have enduring effects on a child's aspirations and development.

Family membership is both a privilege and a responsibility.

An individual's development is affected by what he inherits, what he gains from the influences of his family, and the use he makes of these.

Each family member affects and is affected by his family.

Parental home life provides a model for future family life.

CONTENT	SUGGESTED EXPERIENCES (Learning—Evaluation)

1. *Importance of Living in Families*
Emotional support
  Belonging
  Love
  Sense of trust
  Self worth and identity
  Release of feelings
	Describe a family that you consider a close family. Try to determine why this family is close, as opposed to some other family.
	
	Several groups role play situations in which one of the emotional needs of young children is portrayed. Begin a listing—to be completed by the end of the unit—of what families and individuals do to provide emotional support for members.
	
	Students find out about, observe, and discuss how one can give emotional support or cause emotional damage as they help with feeding, dressing, bathing, and supervising the play of young children.

Guides for behavior
  Values, goals, standards
  Spiritual beliefs
	Students cite ways in which families influence values, goals, and standards. Instances can be cited from reading, TV shows and other impersonal sources. Relate these instances to the family they hope to have in the future.
	
	Analyze ways in which families influence the spiritual development of family members.

Traditions and customs	Prepare and present a skit illustrating the effect of different attitudes and habits of family members, such as picking up belongings, leaving the bathroom orderly, taking turns doing housework. Students list on chalkboard some customs and traditions of families. Analyze ways each

may contribute to important facets of family living.

Students talk with family members or others as a future basis for deciding on some customs they wish to continue.

---

2. *Qualities of Family Membership*

Specific Objectives:

Plans activities which further family solidarity (Cognitive—Synthesis).

Discovers ways to increase effectiveness as a family member (Cognitive—Analysis).

Generalizations:

Children contribute to satisfactions in family living and parents contribute to satisfactions of children.

Love, understanding and positive direction enable a child to develop a sense of personal worth.

CONTENT	SUGGESTED EXPERIENCES (Learning—Evaluation)
2. *Qualities of Family Membership* Individual worth and dignity Appreciation Consideration and kindness	Have students role play some ways of expressing appreciation to family members and feelings of satisfaction when appreciation is expressed.
	Students prepare and use a checklist on consideration and kindness in families. Check on practices.
	Have students, for a period of days, watch for acts of consideration and kindness at home, on television, in comics. Report in an interesting way to the class.
Communication	Describe how communication may be used to narrow the generation gap between children and parents. Discuss from children's and parent's points of view. Invite parents to participate in the class discussions.
	Students suggest key topics for communication considered important in families. Have students add to this list throughout the discussion. Use these ideas for communication in a skit for a Future Homemaker's program.

Cooperation

Plan a role-playing session, a "family discussion," for the purpose of solving family problems that require the cooperation of every member. The following problems may be discussed:

What should be the proper dating days and hours?
What amount should be included in the allowance?

Hold discussion on how younger and older members may cooperate in family activities, such as home care, hobbies, and entertainment.

Responsibility

Each student describes a responsible family member and explains why the individual is thought to be responsible.

Have students discuss the importance of assuming personal responsibility in the family. Students cite examples of experiences. Follow with selection of individual project in assuming a new home responsibility.

Loyalty

Have each student think through a way family loyalty may be demonstrated. In circle responses, have each student report.

Have a round table discussion on whether or not to be faithful to a family confidence. In what ways would you help younger children in your family to understand and practice loyalty?

---

3. Responsibilities of Families

Specific Objectives:

Understands responsibilities families have to members and members have to families (Cognitive—Comprehension).

Perceives significant ways in which family influences affect family members (Cognitive—Synthesis).

Generalizations:

The family has responsibility for guiding all aspects of development.

The family provides an environment for responsible individual development.

A combination of affection and control is conducive to development of emotional support.

CONTENT	SUGGESTED EXPERIENCES (Learning—Evaluation)
3. *Responsibilities of Families*	List the various ways in which a family provides protection for its members.
Protection	Discuss areas in which adults may give guidance in personal security for family members.
	Discuss role of family members in meeting emergencies and illnesses within the family.
Economic support	Use references to differentiate between real income and money income, taking account of such things as abilities in homemaking.
	Interview recently married couples to find out what advice they would give young couple concerning the financial obligations marriage involves.
Affection and regulation of behavior	Have students discuss affection to understand its meaning.
	Discuss characteristics of family living which may help children to learn desirable behavior.
	Students role play situations which show reasons back of parents' efforts to help you to maintain standards of behavior.
Education and opportunities for development	Present resource persons to work with class on the importance of an eagerness and innate urge to continue learning through experience and study throughout life.
	Have different students report on opportunities for continuing development, both in school and out of school.
Environment for sociability	Students carry out individual project over a period of time to (1) take time to engage in conversation with young child or adult visitor in the home and/or (2) make opportunity for own friends to be engaged in conversation with young family members and parents.
	Students (individually) keep a record of the topics discussed by family members when

	family is together. Carry out individual projects in increasing topics discussed.
Entertaining friends in the home	Consult references for help and discuss advantages of family's making a long-time plan for entertaining friends. (Include friends of all members of the family.)
	Carry out an individual project in simple entertaining for some family member, within a budget agreed upon by parents.
Citizenship preparation	Students demonstrate how concept of parents authority can be democratically exercised citing instances, real or fictitious.
	Students list facilities for children's recreation that community provides. Discuss means of support and the individual's responsibility for the care of such facilities.
	Design and use self-evaluation score sheets on citizenship in the home.

4. Unit Evaluation

Evaluation of progress toward reaching the unit objective: upon completion of this unit of instruction, the student will evidence a higher regard for his own family and will evidence qualities of good family membership.

SUGGESTED EVALUATION EXPERIENCES	EVIDENCES OF CHANGED BEHAVIOR
Prepare a balance, each side of which has a mobile suspended from it. On one mobile, use words showing what the family provides its members; on the other, show responsibilities of family members to the family.	The student: Realizes own potential contribution to the family. Accepts responsibility for making home for other family members. Helps foster the development of younger family members. Accepts increasing responsibility for behavior, with parental guidance.

EXAMPLE 5

This sampling was selected from the 1969–1973 *National Program of Work. Action Plan for the Future Homemakers of America* (1970, pp. 18–19). The entire program of work designed by FHA'ers is based on concerns expressed by youth.

The Table of Contents which follows shows two major objectives supported by seven projects. The project presented in full, "To Dare Is to Care," is intended to help students work toward eliminating prejudices and inequalities involving differences in culture, race, and creed. This curriculum material provides activity suggestions for awareness and involvement as well as resource suggestions for booklets, films, filmstrips, games, and plays.

As has already been illustrated in Part One of this book, FHA and HERO-FHA activities are intended to correlate with class work in home economics and in so doing to enrich the classroom program. This means that experiences are planned to relate to course objectives and learnings arrived at by the teacher and students. In some instances, teachers and students may choose projects which are developed as a continuing unit for club members rather than being correlated directly with a specific class unit. Illustrations of both ways of using material from this curriculum are given on pages 277–278; 283.

TABLE OF CONTENTS

OBJECTIVE: TO STRENGTHEN BONDS WITHIN THE FAMILY AND BETWEEN THE FAMILY AND COMMUNITY

Our Future as Homemakers
    To help prepare individuals for the responsibilities of homemaking.

Stable Home—Stable Life
    To stress the influence of the home on family members.

Make Time Work for You
    To emphasize the importance of using your time wisely.

Decisions That Count
    To encourage youth to formulate and work toward educational goals attributing to future success.

OBJECTIVE: TO HELP YOUTH COMPREHEND THE PROBLEMS OF SOCIETY AND CONTRIBUTE TO THEIR SOLUTIONS

To Dare Is To Care
    To work toward eliminating prejudices and inequalities involving differences in culture, race, and creed.

Our World—A Growing Heritage
    To arouse youth interest and participation in solving of world problems.

Preparedness—The Key to Opportunity
    To help youth develop initiative and resourcefulness in creating employment and preparing for work.

ACTIVITY SUGGESTIONS FOR AWARENESS AND INVOLVEMENT

Appreciation for Differences

Show the film, *The Religions of Man*, from NET Film Service, Indiana University. Talk about different religions in the world and discuss commonalities.

Make a survey of the different races and nationalities found in your town. Discuss their individual contributions to the community and what a pride in one's heritage can add to total community spirit.

Sponsor a progressive dinner party, dividing FHA members into groups—each representing a different country based on backgrounds of the individuals. At each home a dish native to that country would be served, and an informative presentation made.

Study both distinctions and similarities in races and cultures. Build a discussion around the strengths of each.

Read books about the history of different races and involve your family in your learning.

Create opportunities to become acquainted and establish a close friendship with a person or persons of a different race or nationality.

Establish a "personal plan" on how I can be open-minded when encountering and listening to different points of view from which I can learn.

"Save a Saturday for serious" and hold a symposium at school with a speaker and open-subject discussion to which teenagers and adults both are invited.

Pressures and Conscience

Ask ministers from various denominations in your community to speak at chapter meetings. Explore concerns and feelings about the dilemma of authority and conscience.

Discuss individual experiences of social pressure—conforming with crowd, cliques, dress, and organizations. Use as a resource the April/May 1969 Teen Times article on "Forming Convictions."

Sponsor an all-school assembly or a panel discussion on racial and cultural problems that could arise in your community as a result of hidden prejudice. What are these "hidden prejudices"? Select as a moderator a capable adult who knows the community.

Analyze prejudice projected by the media. Discuss how to discern bias and what youth might do to influence change.

Invite a social worker to give a talk on the unmet needs of persons right in your locale, how they experience prejudice, and its effects upon them.

Change of Heart, Opinion, Attitude

Explore in a chapter round-table-exchange the question: What is prejudice and what kinds of prejudices exist? Individuals may express types of prejudices they have experienced.

Sponsor a panel on human rights, using as a basis the "Human Rights and Fundamental Freedoms In Your Community" formulated by United Nations. Invite prominent community members of various backgrounds to serve on a panel.

Use the pamphlet, Prejudiced—How Do People Get That Way?, and develop a skit around the idea of the boy with green hair. Present the skit to grade-school youngsters.

Put on a "living play" for the total community or school to arouse their interest and concern about racial situations "at home" or nationwide.

Sponsor a youth/adult forum, discussing the question: If we dare to care, how can we be effective? Have representation from political groups, pressure groups, and the different classes of our society talk on present and future improvements needed in our society.

In a family night program of your own discuss and compare your prejudices with those of your parents. Explore how you might work together to strive to eliminate prejudices you feel.

Focusing on Positive Action

Have your Program of Work Planning Committee order the paperback book, *Human Rights and Fundamental Freedoms in Your Community,* and underscore from its many suggestions possible avenues of action for your chapter.

Conduct "sit-ins" to talk or just listen with the aged in rest homes.

Plan a chapter activity for the less fortunate children in your area.

Sign up chapter members for a project with a children's home to relate on a one-to-one basis with an individual child and do something special for them or with them.

Organize a FHA Caring Bureau. Distribute "FHA Help Needed" cards to aged in the community to put in their windows when they need errands or service.

Volunteer FHA help to a foreign or new family in your community to help them begin to feel a part of the school or community.

Invite a qualified person, youth or adult, to a chapter meeting to talk on the subject, "Morals Do Matter."

Start a clothing bank or volunteer to staff one in your community for the experience of relating to and understanding better the problems and needs of low income people.

SIX

WHAT QUALITIES ARE IMPORTANT IN CURRICULUM MATERIALS?

DESIRABLE CHARACTERISTICS OF RESOURCE MATERIALS

Concern about curriculum development increases when there is need to update the existing program of home economics. In 1968 Congress passed Amendments to the Vocational Education Act of 1963. Senator Yarborough from Texas, one of the sponsors of the 1968 Vocational Act, graphically explained the new emphasis for consumer education and home economics when he spoke in the Senate thus (Congressional Record, 1968) ". . . we are talking about learning how to run a home, balance a budget, shop wisely, establish a good credit rating, and avoid being bilked by the sharks that we all know are out on the open market to scuttle the unsuspecting uneducated housewife."

Home economists are presently concerned with developing programs which carry out the purposes of the Vocational Act of 1968 and meet the following requirements:

Encourage greater consideration to social and cultural conditions and needs, especially in economically depressed areas;

Encourage preparation for professional leadership in home economics and consumer education;

Meet the needs of youth and adults who have

entered or are preparing to enter the work of the home;

Prepare such youth and adults for the role of homemakers or to contribute to their employability in the dual role of homemaker and wage earner; and

Include consumer education as an integral part thereof.

Perhaps chiefly because of the 1968 Amendment, there have been a number of publications the last few years devoted wholly or in large part to the consumer aspect of Consumer and Homemaking Education. A sampling from several of such publications was shown in the examples on pages 296–311 of curriculum materials prepared by states or the Future Homemakers of America.

But whatever is stressed in curriculum development at a given time, the major concern of leaders in home economics always is to produce materials which, used as a resource by teachers, will result in programs that better meet the needs of all concerned. Curriculum resource materials which fulfill this major purpose will in general (1) provide up-to-date and stimulating content, (2) include all the parts of curriculum material needed by teachers, (3) be structured for ease of use, and (4) show a balanced program. Each of these four will be considered in turn.

UP-TO-DATE AND STIMULATING CONTENT

There has always been a need to produce up-to-date and stimulating curriculum material. But today it is important in addition to provide advance information about what lies ahead. And according to Toffler (1970), "Even more important than any specific bits of advance information, is the habit of anticipation. This conditioned ability to look ahead plays a key role in adaptation. Indeed, one of the hidden clues to successful coping may well lie in the individual's sense of the future [p. 371]."

Illustrations of experiences which force students to look toward the future are:

Conduct a series of discussions and debates by youth on the roles they see they will play as young adults in the future success of our world.

Attend Career Days or College Nights and ask questions about the future in fields toward which you feel attracted.

Have three students volunteer to imagine that each has had a dream about the kind of food preparation which will be carried on in most homes twenty years from now. Students chosen as well as other class members read on life in the future. Each student pantomimes his own dream about such food production. Follow this by a circular response session in which other class members state a reaction to the three pictures presented.

Through the following questions, students summarize ideas on housing trends:

What housing trends do you see best for your community?

What housing trends would be impractical? Are planned developments feasible in your areas? What are the advantages? Disadvantages?

Through their new curriculum material (Arizona Department of Education, 1972) one state has attempted to provide up-to-date and stimulating material on housing and home furnishings by capitalizing on the stimulus given to contemporary housing by Frank Lloyd Wright and continued by other architects in the state. Such materials could encourage young people to look toward the future with reference to housing. Illustrations of such experiences are:

1. Students are shown pictures of prehistoric housing in Arizona such as cliff dwellings, Casa Grande Ruins, tepees, caves, and protected shelter. Students discuss how nature, available natural materials, human resources, and the technology of materials influenced the homes these people had. Are the same influences observable in today's housing? In tomorrow's housing? Explain using illustrations you have read about or have seen.

2. Students view pictures of various ways (1) man has worked with nature in providing housing, and (2) man has worked against nature.

Examples of working with nature:

New York City built on granite rock
Towns founded near water
River boats on delta
Cliff dwellings
Adobe buildings in desert
Wood homes near forest
Stone homes in rocky areas

Examples against nature:

Buildings too close to shorelines
Destruction of scenic beauty (e.q., Camelback Mountain)

Buildings on California hillsides with woodland and ground covers destroyed
Subdivisions on farmland
Homes close to rivers that flood
Homes in river beds
Homes filled with undesirable odors from being placed next to feed lots and stockyards
Homes filled with noise from being near freeways or in an automated society

3. Students visit Paoli Soleri's desert site where he and his students have experimented with many architectural ideas. There students would be able to observe a model of Arcosanti, his plan for an arcology.

This same state is also encouraging students to think of people around the world in such experiences as:

1. Students are shown pictures of varied types of housing such as straw huts in African village; stilt houses; igloos; sod houses; skyscraper apartment buildings; and castles in Europe. They then answer the following questions:

What facts about nature were considered?

What materials could be used and why?

What economic and technological factors needed to be considered?

What human factors do you think were considered?

2. In nearly all countries around the world individuals may be found living in 35 square feet or less. Students experiment with living in a space of no more than 35 square feet. Such spaces may be sectioned off with masking tape and after students spend time in their allotted room reactions may be obtained.

COMPREHENSIVE CONTENTS

Although the patterns for all curriculum material developed by public and private groups vary, they all contain about the same parts unless there is some special reason for not including certain ones. Future Homemakers of America, for instance, develop most of their material to correlate with that of other groups and for this reason can afford to omit some parts that most groups cannot wisely omit.

The five examples of curriculum shown on pages 296–311 have illustrated in some way the different parts, but in limited detail. At this point the writers will consider each part further.

SCOPE AND SEQUENCE

Clearly defined and comprehensive scope is essential to development of curriculum-resource material, whether for the program of one teacher or for a state-wide program. The material below, from an Oklahoma curriculum guide (1969, pp. 13–15), shows suggested scope and sequence for teaching consumer education at three levels. Planning such scope and sequence is necessary before any real progress can be made in developing curriculum materials.

BEGINNING LEVEL—EARNING AND MANAGING

1. Sources of Family Income
   a. Earnings
   b. Investments
   c. Public assistance
   d. Miscellaneous

2. Factors Influencing Distribution of Family Income
   a. Attitudes
   b. Values, goals
   c. Needs
   d. Alternatives in the marketplace
   e. Impulsive buying
   f. Stage in family life

g. Claim on future earnings
h. Emergencies

3. Sources of Personal Income
   a. Earnings
   b. Allowance
   c. Dole
   d. Gifts

4. Factors Influencing Use of Personal Income .
   a. External influences
   b. Values
   c. Goals
   d. Knowledge

5. Managing Personal Income
   a. Establishing priorities
   b. Practicing self discipline
   c. Buying practices
   d. Record keeping

6. Maximizing Value of Money Spent on Care and Maintenance
   a. Care of clothing
   b. Care of resources

INTERMEDIATE LEVEL—FUNCTIONS AND USES OF MONEY IN OUR ECONOMY

1. Money in Our Society
   a. Money and the price level
   b. Money as a measure of relative values
   c. Money as a medium of exchange
   d. Money as a saving of wealth
   e. Money as a standard of debts
   f. The circular flow of money in the economy

2. Banking Services
   a. Checking accounts
   b. Savings accounts
   c. Loans
   d. Safe deposits
   e. Miscellaneous

3. Credit
   a. Evaluation of credit
   b. Savings accounts

c. Interest rates
d. Credit ratings
e. Guidelines for using credit
f. Influence of credit on national economy

4. Buying Practices
   a. Factors which influence buying decisions
   b. Planning and making clothing decisions
   c. Planning and selecting gift items
   d. Planning and selecting entertainment equipment
   e. Utilizing consumer information
   f. Balancing wants with resources

ADVANCED LEVEL—
ACHIEVING FINANCIAL SECURITY

1. Planning
   a. Organizing
   b. Establish priorities
   c. Implement plans
   d. Record keeping

2. Buying
   a. Food
   b. Clothing
   c. Shelter
   d. Transportation

3. Borrowing
   a. Conditions for obtaining a loan
   b. Lending agencies
   c. Types of credit
   d. Shopping for credit
   e. Responsibilities and problems

4. Saving
   a. Establishing the habit of saving
   b. Types of savings
   c. Selecting a savings plan

5. Investing
   a. Types of investments
   b. Investment principles and procedures

6. Protecting
   a. Types of insurance protection

b. Shopping for insurance protection

c. Family protection through estate planning

7. Sharing

a. Opportunities for sharing

b. Philosophy of sharing

8. Earning More

a. Adjusting attitudes to the changing world of work

b. Continuing education and training

c. Human relationships

9. Utilizing

a. Consumer information

b. Consumer services

c. Continuing educational opportunities

At this point it should be pointed out that those responsible for curriculum development need to see that the scope and sequence planned can fit, in some way, the existing program or that the program can be changed to fit the scope and sequence. The chart on page 317 shows a variety of courses into which the content of the scope and sequence for consumer education would fit in this particular state. It does this by providing a guide and recommendations. At the same time allowance has been made for flexibility, which is important. One of the generalizations relating to curriculum development is: development of sequence is more satisfactory when it allows flexibility in relation to time allotment, areas of work, maturity level, and individual and community differences. For example, a particular class in an underprivileged community may need to spend more time and work on some concepts than another group their age if teaching is to be meaningful.

The foregoing discussion is applicable not only to extensive curriculum development such as that carried on by states, but to teachers planning units or their total programs. Scope and sequence is related to a central idea, which is organized about some aspect of home

economics, and the parts of which are arranged in sequential order (pages 314–316). Such arrangement makes it easier to develop objectives which do not overlap or show omissions. At the same time such scope and sequence arranged for different courses will give the administration a brief but overall picture of tentative planning for classes.

OBJECTIVES

Objectives were considered in some depth in Book 2, where it was learned that there are many different ways of stating what a person is trying to achieve. There are two problems related to objectives which are likely to occur when working on curriculum materials. These problems are (1) stating objectives in sequential form, for example, from early childhood through adult life, and (2) being consistent in the form used within the same grouping unless there is a good reason for not doing so.

Example 1 on page 296 illustrates objectives developed for the same major concept in the following sequence: kindergarten through elementary, middle school or junior high school, high school, post secondary, and adult. In studying the objectives it seems clear that each level is somewhat more advanced than the preceding one, but this does not mean that individuals and groups need to study at the levels indicated. Certain individuals need to work either behind or ahead of what might appear to be the appropriate level for them. This may be the result of the kind of education experienced earlier, interest in the subject up to now, ability, home and/or community background, or a combination of these and other factors.

Further, the fact that an individual or group needs to work at a certain level with reference to the objectives on page 296 does not mean the same level will be appropriate for that individual or group when working with other

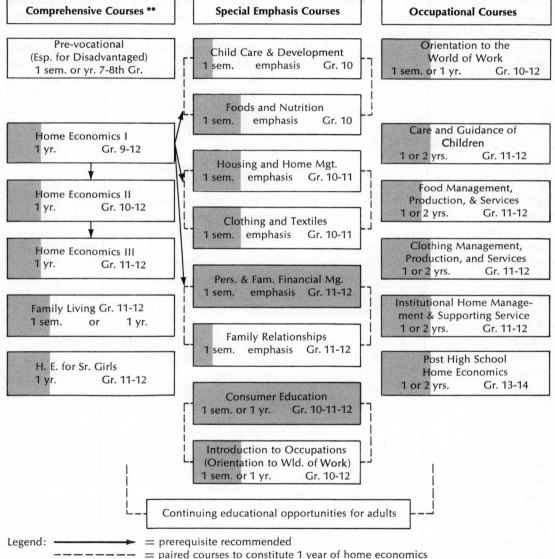

Comprehensive Courses **	Special Emphasis Courses	Occupational Courses

Comprehensive Courses: Pre-vocational (Esp. for Disadvantaged) 1 sem. or yr. 7-8th Gr.; Home Economics I 1 yr. Gr. 9-12; Home Economics II 1 yr. Gr. 10-12; Home Economics III 1 yr. Gr. 11-12; Family Living Gr. 11-12 1 sem. or 1 yr.; H. E. for Sr. Girls 1 yr. Gr. 11-12

Special Emphasis Courses: Child Care & Development 1 sem. emphasis Gr. 10; Foods and Nutrition 1 sem. emphasis Gr. 10; Housing and Home Mgt. 1 sem. emphasis Gr. 10-11; Clothing and Textiles 1 sem. emphasis Gr. 10-11; Pers. & Fam. Financial Mg. 1 sem. emphasis Gr. 11-12; Family Relationships 1 sem. emphasis Gr. 11-12; Consumer Education 1 sem. or 1 yr. Gr. 10-11-12; Introduction to Occupations (Orientation to Wld. of Work) 1 sem. or 1 yr. Gr. 10-12

Occupational Courses: Orientation to the World of Work 1 sem. or 1 yr. Gr. 10-12; Care and Guidance of Children 1 or 2 yrs. Gr. 11-12; Food Management, Production, & Services 1 or 2 yrs. Gr. 11-12; Clothing Management, Production, and Services 1 or 2 yrs. Gr. 11-12; Institutional Home Management & Supporting Service 1 or 2 yrs. Gr. 11-12; Post High School Home Economics 1 or 2 yrs. Gr. 13-14

Continuing educational opportunities for adults

Legend: ——————▶ = prerequisite recommended
– – – – – – – = paired courses to constitute 1 year of home economics

Shading denotes recommended proportion of time for study of consumer problems.
**Comprehensive courses include offerings in all home economics subject matter areas, i.e. child development, family relationships, consumer education, home management, housing, clothing and textiles, and food and nutrition.

Opportunities in Vocational Home Economics
Consumer and Homemaking Education - Cooperative Education
Consumer Education Emphasis

objectives relating to the major concept, for example: creation of home environment. The effective teacher helps students choose objectives meaningful to them rather than objectives which are supposedly at their age and grade level.

The illustration on pages 301–302 shows a way of classifying objectives in levels or steps different from age and grade level. Example 3 uses the classification of the Taxonomies but shows a sampling of statements which for the purpose did not need to be stated in a progression. When speaking of sequential form with relation to objectives, persons usually mean progression of age and grade level.

The samplings of curriculum shown in Examples 1 through 5 appear to be consistent. It may be interesting to note that Example 1 states objectives in a consistent way for kindergarten through elementary school, and places in parentheses under each a question which to the young child probably would be more meaningful than the first form. This was done consistently throughout the curriculum materials developed for the five subject matter areas.

CONCEPTS AND GENERALIZATIONS

Looking again at Example 1, pages 296–298, and pages 314–316, it may be seen that both curriculum groups worked essentially the same way except for one thing. Both groups developed sub-concepts along with major ones although the sub-concepts are not shown in Example 1. The difference was in the progression of concepts shown on pages 314–316. Those who developed Example 1 consciously omitted any reference to grade levels in presenting the resource materials. Although it seemed necessary to think of five levels from kindergarten through elementary to adult, levels were not indicated in the resource materials as shown on pages

296–298. The reason was that, regardless of what they have been taught, teachers frequently seem to believe they must teach at the level indicated regardless of the background of their students. At the present time, and even more so in the future, the interests of education may be best served by forgetting grade levels and concentrating on the most appropriate concepts and objectives.

In looking for concepts in Examples 2, 3, and 4, it should be remembered that (as was pointed out in Book 2) some educators use the words *concepts* and *generalizations* interchangeably. Further, all illustrations are a sampling which may include only part of the curriculum itself. As an illustration, Example 3 was included primarily to show objectives developed according to the Taxonomies.

The pattern for generalizations varies greatly in the four samplings (Examples 1–4, pages 296–308), which include:

Generalizations with supportive learnings

Key points which include generalizations

Generalizations and content; the latter appears to be concepts as differentiated from generalizations

So far as is known one way is not better than another. Teachers do, however, need help with generalizations, which are an important part of the curriculum.

LEARNING EXPERIENCES *

The three most common criticisms heard when considering learning experiences are: (1) too high a proportion of the experiences use only

_____

* Many of the experiences are from curriculum publications of the Pennsylvania Dept. of Education. (See list of references at end of Book 3.)

the discussion method, (2) too many experiences are not explained in enough detail to be useful, and (3) the amount of space devoted to experiences in contrast to learnings is out of proportion.

Although the first criticism is not true of the curriculum samplings shown in this book it is often true of curriculum materials. Some resource materials propose the discussion method for most experiences. The discussion method is useful and may be employed alone or in combination with other methods. However, when it is recalled that in Book 2 something like fifty different kinds of teaching-learning resources are suggested, such extensive use of the discussion method seems unwarranted and out of proportion.

The statement of discussion questions is important also. The following two illustrations show a marked difference. The second would probably be more clear to more people than the first example.

1.   Discuss similarities and differences of costumes from other countries.

2.   Mrs. Smith has young children, and due to the illness of a member of the family, is unable to get to the grocery store. It is Tuesday, and there are no special bargains at the store on this day. The list she gave Mr. Smith to use is as follows:

cheese	orange juice
pears	margarine
potatoes	peaches
canned tomato juice	tomatoes
eggs	

When Mr. Smith returned home, he unpacked his purchases. They included:

sliced cheese in a package
fancy pears
a small box of frozen peeled potatoes
one No. 2 can of tomato juice
one dozen extra large eggs—Grade A
carton of frozen orange juice, six 8-ounce cans
whipped margarine
frozen peaches
canned whole peeled tomatoes

What additional information would have helped Mr. Smith in purchasing the food items on the list? How did his choice affect cost?

Experiences other than those using primarily the discussion technique need to be explained in more detail than is often done. The following two experiences are examples of those which should be clear either to use as stated or to adapt.

1.   Set up a "play store." Distribute "play" currency to each child. Allow each to "buy" items from the store such as milk, juice, art paper, pencils. Use this experience to point out that we use money to buy things we want and that once we spend it, it is no longer ours.

2.   Write skits and present them to the class. Be sure skits show some ways individual goals as well as family goals influence management of daily life. Some skits may also point out that differences in management among families is due to their values, goals, and standards. Skit ideas may be:

Mother of a daughter holds goals of neat room, well-pressed clothes, well-groomed face and hair. The teenage daughter does not hold these goals.

The Carters have spending leisure time with their children as a family goal; therefore, their house is less immaculate than the Campbells, who insist on everything being clean and in order at all times.

It is difficult, if not impossible, to know what to say about the relationship of space allotted to experiences as contrasted with learnings. Perhaps the important thing to remember is that, in general, resource materials should not indicate that "much is done but little is learned." Rather the completed materials should show that "much was done in learning a great deal."

If generalizations are presented without supportive learnings or other content, and experiences are written in enough detail to be useful, a pattern like that in Example 2 (pages 299–301) may prove useful. It is important at the same time to relate specific learnings and experiences to each other.

EVALUATION

As was indicated in Book 2, evaluation should be continuous and interwoven with the curriculum so as to appear inseparable from it. In other words, evaluation may be used at any stage of the learning process from the original setting of goals to the conclusion of a unit or area of work. Many teachers find that evaluation seems more difficult than other aspects of education. Further, some believe they do not receive enough help with it. A common criticism of curriculum resource materials is that too few illustrations of evaluation are included. It seems probable that resource materials will never include the amount of help some teachers would like; it is too space consuming and good examples are often not available.

All of this may sound discouraging to the teacher but there is one helpful development. Well-written learning experiences may be easily and quickly developed to include evaluative experiences or even term-end evaluation if the teacher and students have learned to write different types of questions and check lists.

Examples from resource materials of experiences easily adapted to include evaluation follow (Examples 1, 5, 6—Pennsylvania Dept. of Education; Example 3—Future Homemakers of America, 1970):

EXAMPLE 1

Objective: Recognize that values and goals are important to individuals and families in making decisions

One learning: Individual and family goals need to be in harmony in making decisions to assure goal attainment

Pupil experience: Use open-end situations to relate how goals need to be in harmony with values. An example might be as follows: A value that may rank high in order of importance to a couple is that of education. They will work hard toward the goal of a college education for their son, saving money, often depriving themselves in order that this goal may be accomplished. In what ways must the son's values be in harmony with his parents' values to accomplish this family goal?

Possible evaluation: A question that should show each class member whether he or she understood the learning might be:

Explain how one of your values is in harmony, or lacks harmony, with a family goal.

State one value which ranks high for your family.

Give an example of how this value has affected one of their goals.

What is your value in relation to their value?

As matters stand now, will the family probably achieve its goal? If yes, explain why. If not, explain why not.

EXAMPLE 2

Objective: Know resources available to the individual and family and how to use them

One learning: Resources require management if the family is to attain its goals

Pupil experience: Divide class into groups to write and present skits showing examples of how individuals use resources

Possible evaluation: After or during the skits students might evaluate their understanding using the format below.

After students have finished the evaluation, they may wish to summarize how effectively different groups used some of their resources.

SKIT NUMBER	RESOURCES USED IN SKIT	RESOURCES USED		
		EFFECTIVELY	INEFFECTIVELY	NOT CLEAR
1.				
2.				
3.				

EXAMPLE 3

Objective: Understand how the preservation of foods can control the natural maturing processes and effect chemical and physical changes

One learning: Foods may be preserved in a variety of ways to prevent spoilage

Pupil experience: Arrange a field trip to a food processing plant. Structure questions for student observation such as:

What types of foods are being processed?

What methods of preservation are being used?

What sanitary practices are in effect?

How is the equipment being handled?

Possible evaluation: The student and teacher could decide to use whichever of the suggested questions seemed appropriate and add others as seemed desirable. The questions could be adapted either to the questions as shown or to a check list.

EXAMPLE 4

Objective: Recognize that clothes help people express themselves

One learning: People tend to judge an individual by his dress

Pupil experience: The class had carried on a round table discussion on the subject, "People form opinions of us by what we wear." The experience which followed this was:

Have students develop a clothing rating sheet for their wardrobe.

Sample statements may be:

1. My skirts are:
   Flouncy
   Make me look bouncy
   Show every ounce of me

2. My dresses are:
   A sight
   Just right
   Skin tight

3. My hems are:
   Crazy lengths
   Wavy lengths
   "Suits me" lengths

Comment: With this much help provided pupils could easily complete a form they would enjoy using. This would give them a list of problems and could be followed by the filmstrip "Five Magic Mirrors." Points relating to the pupils' problems could then be discussed.

EXAMPLE 5

Objective: Learn how to use values in obtaining and maintaining a home.

One learning: A knowledge of what to look for in housing may help in determining realistic values.

Pupil experience: Make a check list of items to consider when planning housing, such as, neighborhood, exterior and interior design, construction, comfort, convenience, privacy. Visit several houses representing different levels of expenditure, and rate using the check list.

Comment: If the group has difficulty with points to consider in the check list it may want to brainstorm for ideas. A check list is relatively easy to set up if the content is clear.

EXAMPLE 6

Objective: Understand how to go about getting a job and seeing it in relation to training

One learning: Through an interview the employer and employee can learn about each other.

Pupil experience: Use role-playing situations to illustrate interview and application procedures. Divide the class into groups to act out the four role playing situations.

Employer Number 1. Large department store in which a young woman reports to the personnel department's office. The personnel director will interview her first. She is an abrupt but courteous person, offering her hand for a handshake. In the beginning of the interview she asks such questions as "Why would you like to work here?" and "Do you think you could handle the job?"

After this initial interview, the interviewee is taken to the alteration department where she meets the supervisor, who in turn interviews her again. The supervisor is very skilled and asks the interviewee some technical questions about the machines, but does so in a friendly way. She also inquires into the dressmaking education of the girl trying to discover what she is familiar with and how extensive her training was.

(Employers 2, 3, and 4 not shown here.)

Possible evaluation: Students could make a list of strengths and of weaknesses in each interview observed. Or if the group chose, it might formulate questions to be answered about each interview.

1. Did the student show an active interest in getting and doing well on the job? Explain.

2. Did she maintain easy courtesy and good manners by (a) being a good listener, (b) being responsive, (c) showing appreciation of the interviewer's time, (d) being ready to shake hands or carry out other courtesies?

3. Did she respond well to technical questions about the employment considered? Explain giving an example.

4. When asked, was she able to give a clear resumé of the kind and amount of preparation she had and the amount of dressmaking education as well? What suggestions do you have for making a better presentation?

Evaluation may be presented to teachers in a variety of ways other than suggesting the ideas for it through well-written experiences. Some curriculum guides use several kinds within a single publication. Examples from curriculum guides follow (Example 1—Oklahoma, 1969; Examples 2, 3, 4, 5—Pennsylvania Dept. of Education).

EXAMPLE 1

Evaluation is shown at regular intervals throughout the curriculum guide.

CONCEPTS AND BEHAVIORAL OBJECTIVES	LEARNING EXPERIENCES AND EVALUATION PROCEDURES
VI. *Maximizing value of money spent through care and maintenance* Identifies a relationship between the type of care given to property and its long-range usefulness	Discuss: "What are some reminders issued around the home which have as an objective the extension of usefulness of an item purchased or the maximum utilization of property?" Discuss: "How can negligence shorten the life or value of property?" (Cite money examples.)
A. Care of clothing: Identifies practices which help to prolong the life of clothing	Fill out anonymous questionnaire on "How Do I Care for My Clothing?" Discuss results of questionnaire. Present a skit showing a teenager who carelessly manages personal clothing. Discuss: "What are some consequences of carelessly managing one's clothing?" See a filmstrip on caring for clothing. Develop a bulletin board on caring for clothing. Caption example: "What Does Clothing Reveal About the Personality?" Discuss: "What characterizes clothing that 'looks like new'?" Divide class into groups to prepare illustrated demonstrations or lectures on how to keep that "new look" in clothing. *Evaluation:* List five suggestions for maximizing the value of money spent for clothing. *Evaluation:* Write a brief paragraph to explain the relationship of caring for clothing and maximizing the utilization of clothing resources.

B.   Care of resources:

Recognizes a relationship between waste and care or maintenance

Refer to list of reminders for saving money around the home. Organize list in categories. (Example: time, furnishings, supplies, food, etc.)

Discuss: "What are some of the most frequently wasted items in the household?" "What are some of the most abused items around the house?" "What items around the household are least used?"

Compare utility bills of one season with those of another. "What accounts for the differences?"

Discuss: "If $1.00 per month could be saved on household utility bills, would this be a worthwhile savings?"

Interview parents to find out the ages of some of your household furnishings. "Is there a positive relationship between age and care?"

Discuss: "What are some general care and maintenance suggestions that apply to many types of resources?"

Work hypothetical problems which show how care and maintenance prolong the life of merchandise purchased, thereby saving money or allowing the use of money for other items.

See a filmstrip on caring for household furnishings.

Evaluation: Summarize some principles of caring for property in order to get the most value from the investment.

EXAMPLE 2

Evaluation is shown, but irregularly, as a pupil experience in the column entitled "Sampling of Pupil Experiences Including Evaluation." Objective: Learn to make decisions and accept the consequences.

One learning: Evaluation of the decision can aid in making other decisions.

Evaluative experience: Use the sample questionnaire and the case studies below in showing how to evaluate a decision.

SAMPLE QUESTIONNAIRE	CASE HISTORY EXAMPLES
1. What was the goal of each girl?	*Case History 1:* A week before Christmas, Sally had stepped in at the exclusive Corner House to price the cornflower-blue cardigan in the window. It was her size and just matched her favorite skirt. She hadn't seen another like it, but $25 was more than she could afford to pay. Soon after Christmas, Sally saw a sign in the shop's window: "Sale —All Merchandise Reduced." She quickly headed for the sweater counter, and there was the blue cardigan! She looked at the price tag: $25 was crossed out and $15 was written in its place. Sally examined the sweater carefully. The label read 100% cashmere, and she recognized the manufacturer's name. She tried on the cardigan. A perfect fit!
2. Which girl do you think made the best decision and reached her goal more satisfactorily?	
3. List the points in the case that would back up the answer above.	
4. What alternatives did each girl have in her decision?	
5. What seemed the most influential factor in bringing the decision to a close?	
6. What knowledge was necessary in making the choice?	*Case History 2:* Jean, too, had longed for a cashmere cardigan. She saw a sign in the Empire Store window: "Never Again! $30 Value! Cashmere cardigans! Now—Only $10! Jean had never been in the store before. In a moment she was frantically digging in a bin. The color choice in her size was limited, so Jean wasn't able to get the go-with-everything blue she wanted, but the price was far lower than she'd seen for a cashmere sweater, and she figured that somehow she could find a use for gray. Jean didn't have a chance to try the sweater on, nor did it have any labels to check other than a size tag. Jean bought the sweater.
7. How risky was the choice?	

Examples 3, 4, and 5 show evaluation devices referred to in the experiences but shown elsewhere in the resource materials.

EXAMPLE 3

Objective: Develop a basis on which choices in housing are made.

One learning: There are advantages and disadvantages in any choice of housing.

Experience: Refer to the table on page 326, which illustrates the situation of an engaged couple. If this is not a realistic situation for you, adapt the problem and evaluation to one that is real either for you or someone you know well. The class may choose to work in small groups based on common problems.

Self-Evaluation Device

Problem: An engaged couple are making a decision as to where they will live after their June wedding. They must first decide if they will live: (A)Away from their parents, or (W)With their parents.

Directions: Certain considerations must be weighed in making this decision. To the right of each consideration listed below, circle (A) if the consideration would be more true in living *away* from their parents. Circle (W) if the consideration would be more true when living with their parents after marriage.

CONSIDERATION	WITH PARENTS	AWAY FROM PARENTS
1. More privacy	W	A
2. More economical	W	A
3. More responsibilities	W	A
4. More sharing of chores	W	A
5. More freedom of activities	W	A
6. More personalized entertaining	W	A
7. More role conflicts and disagreements	W	A
8. More satisfaction in keeping house	W	A

(Note: This key could vary if good reasoning is used in answers.)
Write one reason for each of your decisions in sentence form.

EXAMPLE 4

Objective: Understand the factors involved in the distribution and consumption of food.
One learning: Consumers may use information on labels in determining their choices.

Experience: Students bring in labels from food items. Categorize label information which would be useful in making selections. Show films "Behind the Label" and "Learning from Labels." Use "Find Your Label IQ" as an evaluation.

FIND YOUR LABEL I.Q.	TRUE (T)	FALSE (F)
The label is defined as the written, printed, or graphic material found on a food item.	_____	_____
It is legal for a food label to illustrate the contents of the package to make it appear better than it really is.	_____	_____
A food standard is a precise description of a food item established by the Food and Drug Administration.	_____	_____
Foods with standards do not need a list of ingredients on the label.	_____	_____

Bread must always show a list of ingredients on the label. _____ _____

The list of ingredients on the label of a non-standard food must be in order, with the ingredient in greatest amount listed first and so on. _____ _____

In addition to the name of the product and the name and address of the manufacturer, packer, or shipper, the label must tell the style or variety of a product when such information applies. _____ _____

The net weight of a package includes the weight of the contents as well as the container itself. _____ _____

On the label, "Fruit Juice" means the same as "Fruit Drink." _____ _____

The label on cans must include information on the approximate number of cupfuls and average servings contained. _____ _____

EXAMPLE 5

Objective: Be able to implement and evaluate a plan.

Major learning: The processes of plan imple-mentation involve decision-making and are usually integrated processes.

Pupil experience: Use the Planning Check List to evaluate your plan made earlier.

EVALUATION OF PLANS	YES	NO
Planning:		
1. Did my plan work smoothly with little control necessary?		
2. Did it work because the control was good?	_____	_____
3. Should my plan have been more detailed?	_____	_____
4. Did unforeseen conditions affect my plan?	_____	_____
Controlling:		
5. Did I keep my goal in mind as I carried out my plan?	_____	_____
6. Did I keep check on the resources being used, such as time, money, energy, etc.?	_____	_____
7. Did I remember to use effective work techniques?	_____	_____

8.   Did I note how my activities fitted in with my family or group?

_____   _____

Evaluating:

9.   Did I consciously look back to see how well I managed?

_____   _____

10.   Were my goals attainable?

_____   _____

11.   Did I honestly face the strengths and weaknesses in my management?

_____   _____

12.   Would some other alternative be better than the one I chose?

_____   _____

13.   Can some of my weaker points be improved the next time I have a similar managerial problem?

_____   _____

Note: The best answer is not necessarily "yes" to all questions. You may wish to revise some questions and add others.

In conclusion, all of the ways of presenting evaluation in curriculum guides or in unit plans will be useful in certain situations. The most important thing to remember is that teachers need a great deal of help in evaluation.

OTHER RESOURCES

Curriculum content varies greatly; however, two generalizations should be true of all curriculum content: (1) Instructional material that is up-to-date, easily obtainable, and geared to student ability level is incorporated for each area. Teacher helps may also be included; (2) supplementary material that meets current need is presented in forms that are useful, understandable, and inclusive.

Instructional materials are mentioned in some of the illustrations on pages 296–311, but all the curriculum material from which the illustrations were taken include resources for students to refer to such as books, pamphlets, leaflets, periodicals, charts, pictures, films, film strips, games, plays, socio-dramas, and recordings. References for teachers were also included some of the time.

Neither suggestions for, nor illustrations of, supplementary material are given in the sampling of curriculum materials presented. Nonetheless, such materials are especially needed when developing resource materials for new groups and new situations. One state which developed resource materials on *Consumer Education for Families with Limited Incomes* (Texas Tech University, 1971) wisely presented background information on such topics as: "What is poverty? Who are the poor? Characteristics of the poor. Limitations of the poor. Needed adaptations for this group to program planning and procedural considerations. Teaching methods and evaluative techniques for use with disadvantaged adults." It may be readily seen that such materials, well prepared, will help teachers immeasurably.

A section of the material mentioned above (pp. 9–11) is included at this point.

CHARACTERISTICS WHICH AFFECT LEARNING

People with limited incomes have the same need for expression, attention, and recognition as other people. Self-confidence and self-respect are powerful motivating forces, and every opportunity should be taken to help class members feel accepted, wanted, and worthwhile.

A number of factors affect not only the ability of the disadvantaged to learn, but also the likelihood of their participating in educational groups. The educationally deficient individual lacks the skills necessary for enjoying a formal learning situation. He may lack both the social skills for group participation and the initiative or motivation to join a group without considerable encouragement. In addition, he may fear outsiders or people he does not know. If he has previously experienced failure in school activities, he may be insecure, lack self-confidence, and fear failing again. His level of aspiration may be low because he does not know what he may reasonably expect to attain.

Adults in limited income groups are characterized by a number of factors which affect learning. Awareness of these factors is an important aid for the teacher of disadvantaged adults in planning programs which will provide opportunities for class members to receive the fullest benefit from the class.

Characteristics which encourage adult learning include:

1.   Recognition of immediate problems. Adults should be encouraged to express their immediate problems, so these can be used as the basis for beginning lessons.

2.   Meeting basic needs. Because limited income adults, like other people, are striving to meet their needs, classes should be planned which deal with meeting these needs.

3.   Influence of admired person. If the teacher can gain the confidence and admiration of the learners, their desire to learn is increased. This also places her in a position to help meet their basic needs for recognition and approval.

4.   Interest in relevant learning. The disadvantaged learner must see a relationship between what is being taught and his own situation. If this relationship is established early in the course and frequently reinforced, interest is more easily held.

5.   Learning by doing. Disadvantaged adults learn most easily when they are personally involved in the experience through guided practice.

Characteristics which are barriers to learning include:

1.   Fear of failure. Many disadvantaged adults have experienced repeated failures in school. A new learning situation may carry threat of further damage to an already battered self-concept, so they may avoid new learning situations. If a teacher can give students opportunities to succeed, she will do much to increase their likelihood of learning.

2.   An acquired dislike of school. There is some evidence that school has a negative connotation in many disadvantaged homes. Therefore, it may be important for the teacher of adults with limited incomes to avoid associating her classes with school or education.

3.   Feeling of being too old to learn. A disadvantaged adult, like many other adults, may have the attitude that he is too old to learn. The teacher may need to emphasize small achievements at first so this false belief is corrected and new learning can take place.

4.   Lack of language skills. Because of their poor language development and their inability to speak standard English, learning experiences must be geared to the disadvantaged adults' level of language and a limited amount of time devoted to lecture and discussion. Many additional experiences other than verbal ones should be provided. The language problems of disadvantaged adults have several implications for the teacher. Most important, she must be a

good listener. Because students may use words incorrectly or inappropriately, she must be able to interpret what they are trying to say. By always listening carefully and by asking appropriate questions and probing to get at the meaning of their answers, the teacher will soon realize that her students have many important contributions to make to lessons. It is also important for the teacher to be supportive in helping the students say what they mean and to be careful not to alienate them by embarrassing or correcting them.

5. Need for immediate gratification. Because of their many past failures, disadvantaged learners tend to give up on tasks which provide no immediate sense of accomplishment. Encouragement and praise are necessary to promote completion of these tasks. In addition, practical rewards should be given as often as possible.

6. Short attention span. The short attention span of disadvantaged learners demands that learning tasks be short and varied. Listening for long periods of time may be particularly difficult for disadvantaged learners. Therefore, instruction should emphasize seeing and doing rather than a verbal approach.

7. Slowness to learn. Disadvantaged learners are slow in their performance of intellectual tasks. Slowness should not, however, be equated with dullness; it simply means that adequate time must be allowed for completion of each task.

8. Lack of time. Homemakers with large families and low incomes may have difficulty finding time to participate in classes. Husbands who work long hours at physically tiring jobs may be exhausted and may not be interested in attending classes at night.

9. Interfering past experiences. Cultural patterns which affect values and attitudes are likely to be different for the group than they are for the teacher. It may, therefore, be dif-

ficult for a "middle class" teacher to effectively communicate with a person or group of people holding different social values because her standards in many aspects of living, including sanitation, adequacy of diet, and home furnishings, are likely to be very different from those held within the lower socio-economic family. A teacher who is consciously aware of these factors and takes them into consideration when planning the lessons is more likely to be successful than one who does not.

10. Reading difficulty. Because the average educational level of the disadvantaged adult is between the fourth and sixth grade, reading ability is usually low. In addition, reading may be associated with failure in school, with the result that the adult may have done little reading since dropping out of school. Difficulties in reading must be taken into account in preparing handouts, visuals, and other materials.

In addition to the characteristics discussed above, other factors must be considered by the teacher when planning classes for a group of adults with limited incomes. It is often difficult for them to get to the meeting place. The reason for this may be that they have no place to leave the children, or they may not have transportation outside their neighborhood. It may be necessary for the teacher to help solve such problems or to plan the meeting place accordingly. Another reason for such adults hesitating to attend meetings is the feeling that their clothing is not suitable. Attendance of any one individual is likely to be inconsistent and absences are to be expected. Group size may vary from only a few to a large number depending on such extraneous factors as weather, community and church activities, or a death or marriage in the neighborhood.

The preceding illustration is of only one kind of supplementary material used in curriculum guides. Such materials may include anything which is believed to be useful and not easily available to teachers.

STRUCTURE FOR EASY USE

With reference to format, the important requirements are that the finished study be easy for teachers to use, have eye appeal, have an index system, be free from mechanical error, and be arranged so that it may be added to or deleted from with ease. There are many patterns for curriculum materials that meet these requirements. There are undoubtedly ideas for patterns that have not been tried but that would meet these same requirements. In making a choice it is important to keep an open mind and experiment with various patterns before choosing the one which appears to be most appropriate for those who will be using the resource materials produced.

BALANCED PROGRAM

The problem of maintaining balance in the home-economics curriculum is a constant challenge, partly because foods and nutrition and clothing and textiles have been prominent in home economics for many years. As a result, teachers have frequently had more college courses in these areas than in other areas where accomplishment has not been comparable until more recent years. The provision in many programs of specialized courses such as foods and clothing may be desirable, but in many situations there needs to be a balance in the overall program of home economics available to students.

A balance in curriculum material within and among all areas should encourage teachers to develop more balanced programs in their schools, not necessarily in any one course. Providing stimulating resource materials for all areas should also lead to better balance in the program. Does the program provide stimulating materials for career education in home economics? Does it provide such materials for the different age and economic groups who are interested? These are questions about balance in the total home-economics program.

SEVEN

WHAT ARE EFFECTIVE PROCEDURES FOR CURRICULUM IMPROVEMENT?

BASIC PROCEDURES

The reader at this point should have a fairly clear picture of the kind of resource materials useful to teachers. It is necessary now to say something about procedures for curriculum improvement, even though such improvement in most instances is an ongoing goal of educational leaders rather than teachers. It is true that the average teacher will not be guiding curriculum development, but he or she will be cooperating in ways already discussed in this book. To cooperate intelligently the teacher needs to know some of the basic procedures which will result in the development of curriculum material satisfying to all.

RECOGNIZE A READINESS OR NEED

Recognition of a readiness or need to embark on curriculum development in home economics may start when teachers within a group begin to complain that the resource materials they are expected to use are becoming outdated. Such individuals may first become vocal with fellow teachers and then with leaders. The local school administration may recognize that the home-economics program is not

taking into consideration relevant changes in society. Parents and other citizens may talk to each other and to the administration about the need for more real-life education in all areas including home economics. State leaders often realize before others do that more up-to-date materials are needed. As many persons become vocal on the subject, opinion about the necessity of updating the present curriculum will crystallize.

UNDERSTAND NEEDS AND RESOURCES

Curriculum revision involves decisions at all points in the process, but once it is recognized that such revision is necessary early decisions are of two kinds: What kind of curriculum improvement must be given priority? Do we have or can we secure the resources needed to provide this improvement?

Preparation of effective resource materials is usually time consuming and requires a great deal of effort on the part of many people. Lack of resources, both financial and otherwise, may indicate the need for working on some particular part of the overall program such as career education or education for the consumer. Whatever is decided, the decision is usually that of leaders influenced by expressed needs of interested persons.

CHOOSE SKILLED, EXPERIENCED LEADERS

Skilled and experienced leaders involving all those concerned in planning and carrying out curriculum improvement produce the most satisfying results. In some ways it would be much easier for a few persons to plan and write resource materials than to include many people. However, the more participation there is throughout the entire process the more likely are the materials to have maximum value and use. It is true that after the many ideas have been incorporated and the resulting material is in clear, but rather rough form, one or several persons must edit it for omissions, overlapping, consistency of form, and typographical errors.

Who should be the participants? Certainly there should be one or more persons with previous successful experience in curriculum development if possible. There should be also a wide sampling of teachers both experienced and inexperienced. Many groups like to include "listening participants" who are available both to give their own ideas and to react to the ideas of others. Such persons may include administrators, teachers from fields other than home economics, students, parents, and any other interested persons.

SECURE GROUP CONCURRENCE ON
SOUND EDUCATIONAL POLICY

It is true that development of curriculum is more satisfying when based on flexibility in

original conception and on an exploratory attitude toward development. Nevertheless, even though there are many ideas which need to be considered and explored, resulting decisions should be based on sound educational philosophy acceptable to the group.

Little or no progress can be expected so long as there are wide differences among the group on basic philosophy. Do members of the group believe in the democratic process? Do they believe that the democratic process includes responsibility along with freedom? Do they accept the fact that there must be a certain amount of "give and take" in group work? Do they believe that all levels of ability and economic background should be considered in the materials being developed? Do they believe in Career Education? There are many questions which may arise that will need to be answered in terms of the group's philosophy rather than in terms of a variety of individual and conflicting philosophies.

It should be stated that in addition to securing group concurrence on sound educational philosophy, consideration needs to be given to the philosophy of other related groups such as the school, the American Home Economics Association, the American Vocational Association, and the Future Homemakers of America. Philosophy for planning a specific curriculum needs to be in harmony with the philosophy of other related and cooperating groups.

CONSIDER RELEVANT CHANGES IN SOCIETY

Before considering details of the curriculum, any curriculum group needs to take into consideration relevant changes in society and the possible effect of such changes on the curriculum itself. The trend of change is important to consider for otherwise the new curriculum materials may be out of date before they are ready for use. On the other hand it is important to remember that not everyone in our society keeps up with rapid change nor has any desire to do so. Sections of the country may vary markedly in the amount of change they are willing to accept; individuals and groups within one area may also vary. These variations add to the complexity of curriculum development.

There are questions which the group may need to consider in view of current and expected changes. Such questions might be:

To what extent can we wisely make home-economics classes more mobile; that is, take the student out of the classroom to participate in significant community activity?

Should there be more emphasis on decision-making and less on skills? If so, what skills? How should general home-economics classes and those in career education vary on the matter of skills?

What are some implications of changes in the market place for teaching nutrition?

What does the trend toward a shorter work week suggest about recreation as an aspect of home economics to be considered?

As values change, what will be the effect on the generation gap? How can both students and parents be helped?

The questions that might be considered are almost without end. Questions should continue at intervals as the group works ahead on curriculum development.

Part One of this book attempted to show teachers how to correlate what they learned in college with what other groups, such as city, county, or state, provide to help them on the job. It tried to show also how to individualize the curriculum for students and then plan most

effectively for its use. Part Two considers the desirable characteristics of curriculum materials whether these be for a state-wide curriculum guide or for detailed unit plans for the administration. It summarizes briefly procedures for curriculum improvement. Part Three will continue with the teacher's responsibility following the actual preparation of new curriculum materials.

SUGGESTED TEACHER EXPERIENCES

1. Three members of the class role play, as Act 1, a situation in which they discuss and demonstrate the extent to which Part Two of Book 3 should be useful to each at the present time. The characters might be a student teacher, a beginning teacher, and an experienced teacher. Act 2 portrays the same characters a year later, after each has had new experiences related to curriculum. The cast for role playing may find it helpful to do some interviewing or questioning of others before planning the two Acts.

2. The sampling of curriculum materials presented on pages 296–311 as well as curriculum guides to which the class may have access should raise questions such as: What are advantages and disadvantages in developing curriculum materials (a) for all levels from early childhood through adulthood, (b) with the statement of objectives based on the Taxonomies, and (c) with the organization based on major life problems rather than on subject matter areas? In considering the question, use of the colloquy is suggested. One group of several individuals acts as resource persons whereas the second group, about the same size, raises questions, either their own or those obtained from the audience.

3.   Different groups within the class may each choose one aspect of the curriculum and develop a simple form for evaluating this aspect. The form may be presented to the total group for suggestions after which it should be used for evaluating whatever aspect it was developed for. The conclusions of each group may be presented to the class.

4.   Individuals or small groups may each choose the curriculum pattern they prefer of all those they have been able to study carefully. Then the individual or group should attempt to improve the pattern chosen to make it even more pleasing. What problems arose in trying to create a new and better pattern?

5.   Compare different areas within the same resource materials. Is the material equally stimulating for all areas? Explain. Does this resource material show a balance (a) among different aspects within the same areas as, for example foods, (b) a balance among the different areas? In what ways would you try to improve the balance?

6.   In how many different ways could a teacher facilitate curriculum improvement in her city, county, or even the state? What difference, if any, do you see between the contributions of an experienced teacher and an inexperienced one, assuming that both are able teachers?

PART THREE

THE TEACHER'S RESPONSIBILITY FOLLOWING CURRICULUM DEVELOPMENT

New curriculum materials in the hands of teachers usually meet a need that was expressed earlier. Such materials are like most new things in that they usually suggest other needs. For example, if one buys a new dress, certain new accessories may be needed. In the case of new curriculum material, its content may suggest a number of questions related to it:

This new material should bring me up-to-date if I use it well. How can I keep informed on subjects and events of concern to the home-economics program?

Is it possible to adapt the existing school environment to the new curriculum and trends portrayed? If so, how?

Real-life student experiences are emphasized in the new guide. What available means can I use to do a better job in providing such experiences?

What kind of program evaluation should be planned? What is my responsibility in such evaluation?

What ways of interpreting and promoting home economics promise to be effective?

In looking again at the questions, a reader may say, "But these suggest old needs too." That reader is undoubtedly correct. However, up-to-date curriculum materials often stimulate teachers to greater achievement. The period after new curriculum materials have been developed may be an especially good time to make new resolutions and keep those made earlier. The responsibility of teachers in each of the above areas will be considered in the following pages.

EIGHT

SPECIAL TEACHER NEEDS RELATED TO NEW CURRICULUM

PROGRAM FOR KEEPING UP-TO-DATE

Being up-to-date is not simply a matter of getting up-to-date but of keeping up-to-date. Although new curriculum materials may help a teacher feel more up-to-date in teaching, the faster pace of change demands that the tempo for continuous learning be accelerated. Not only must the rate of speed be accelerated but the kind of continuous learning must be far more inclusive than in the past. Some of the new learnings may be provided by the schools or other organizations employing home-economics educators. Many will need to be the result of an individual's own endeavors for educational and personal growth.

SCHOOL-DIRECTED EDUCATION

Most schools, today as in the past, provide a variety of ways to help teachers keep up-to-date. The more usual of these are faculty meetings, study groups, committees, workshops, and demonstration centers. New problems to be handled through cooperative efforts have arisen. For example, there are new schools which are all open space for team teaching. Though the teachers may have spent a summer working together on a new curriculum to fit the building, some have a very difficult time adjusting to the open space and less formal type of teaching. Another problem that many schools are having for the first time relates to the background of the students. Instead of a school population of students mostly from affluent homes the population now includes at least as many culturally deprived students. Yet another problem may exist where certain schools have spent quite a lot of money for some of the newer teaching equipment and materials. Now these schools find that many of the teachers do not know or want to know how to use these materials. Parents are complaining about taxes and cite the equipment and materials as one factor in increased school taxes. There are also problems related to year-round education, compensatory education for inner-city children, school programs run by business, educational research labs and centers sponsored by the Office of Education, a National Institute of Education, and many more.

The illustrations of some of today's and tomorrow's problems show the need for dedicated teachers. It is true that new and unusual ways of helping teachers may be needed and will undoubtedly be developed, but perhaps even more important is the necessity for teachers to cooperate in terms of today's certainties and to keep an open mind to tomorrow's developments. The job of any truly professional person involves life-long learning.

INDIVIDUAL ENDEAVORS FOR GROWTH

It is useful to know what the school may do to help you as a teacher keep up-to-date. The school's primary concern in most instances, however, will be with the kind of problems suggested above which cut across departmental lines. Individual endeavors for growth are likely to relate to personal problems and professional needs.

PERSONAL PROBLEMS

A teacher's personality is very important in terms of personal happiness, professional success, and even in the kind of personal problems experienced. The term *personality,* simply stated, stands for what a person really is. It includes such things as physical and mental characteristics and character traits, and it also involves the impression an individual makes on others through his or her personal appearance, behavior, and attitudes. All of these aspects of personality vary in kind and degree in different people. This is as it should be, for it would be inadvisable and futile to attempt to make all teachers just alike. Nevertheless, to be a successful teacher a person not only needs to *know* but to *accept* and *be* himself or herself.

Possibly no one factor can contribute more to knowing oneself than frequent self-appraisal. It is only by assessing strengths and weaknesses that a teacher can overcome deficiencies. Personal evaluation includes some recognition of the opinion of others as well as an individual's own evaluation of self. A teacher can begin self-analysis by trying to answer such questions as these, giving evidence to support the answers.

Do I show interest in my students as individuals?

Am I cooperative and helpful?

Do I give praise and recognize achievement?

Am I honest and impartial, holding no grudges?

Do I have a sense of humor?

Do I have a good disposition, showing courtesy, tactfulness, and sympathy?

Do I control my emotions as well as I should?

In most cases the answers should not be a simple "yes" or "no." An answer might be something like one below though more detailed:

Do I give praise and recognize achievement? Not as much as I should.

> The class did very well with a role-playing skit, but I was in a hurry to discuss future work and did not praise their performance.

> I failed to tell Joan how pleased I was about the improvement she had made in her personal appearance.

> I forgot to tell the class that Mr. Dean was pleased with their display in the school showcase.

Whenever there is any real difficulty in determining answers a friend should be able to help. He or she is likely to know both your strengths and your weaknesses.

Ultimately you will want to combine the different answers to answer more comprehensive questions such as:

Do I like myself? If not, how would I want to

be different? What should I do to become the kind of person I would like to be?

Am I the kind of person that students, parents, and co-workers respect? If not, why not? What can I do to earn the respect that I so much desire?

Am I a leader in today's world? If not, what should I be doing to assume more of a leadership role?

As an individual and a teacher, such analysis and self-improvement should help you to feel more secure. The feeling of security is the sense of adequacy or being able to cope with the problems you are expected to cope with. These problems will not always be easy: if they were they would not be a challenge that helps you grow. Other people are meeting such challenges every day; your success in meeting them will give you a sense of belonging which is important to each individual. Feeling secure, furthermore, will help you to be yourself. Friends and others may assist you, but success or failure is your own responsibility.

Although a teacher can modify and improve many personality traits, each person has certain limitations which she must accept. For example, basic physical appearance, physical handicaps, and mental ability may need to be accepted. Other people generally are less aware of any deficiencies you may have than you are, and it may help to remember that if such deficiencies were too marked you would not have been accepted as a teacher. It is of course important to fulfill your potential, whether physical, mental, or both. This can best be done by adjusting your activities to your personal potentialities, and by taking time to relax mentally and physically through play, rest, and intellectual pursuits. You can compensate for limitations by emphasizing strengths. The literature offers many illustrations from fiction or real life of those who successfully compen-

sated for different kinds of limitations. Finally, an effective teacher will exert some leadership in his or her community. There are many facets of leadership and the one most appropriate will vary with the individual.

PROFESSIONAL NEEDS

Although school-directed education may afford some opportunity of keeping up-to-date, or at least considering matters which relate to most or all departments in the school, it is less likely to consider other matters of concern to a home-economics teacher. These matters may relate to home economics, general education, and vocational education.

What, of all that is being learned in each of the subject matter areas of home economics, should be a part of the curriculum? What is outdated because of new learnings? Some areas such as consumer education or nutrition may be developing more rapidly than other areas, but changes are not confined to them. New learnings may be offered on such matters as ways to reach ghetto children or the physically handicapped. Educators certainly will hope to make available what is being learned about new teaching-learning equipment and other new resources. There will be research and reports on desirable features for new educational facilities. The list could be added to indefinitely, but the point to remember is that today we cannot even visualize what may come tomorrow. Keeping up with today's developments will put us in a better position for tomorrow. In vocational education there will be much to keep abreast of. What is the relation of vocational education to career education? What are some of the clusters-of-work categories being considered in career education? What are the meanings of new terms such as school-based model, home and community model, career mobility through personalized occupational education, incorporated student-run study-job project? All of this may sound overwhelming but there are important sources of help. Many teachers prefer to concentrate their efforts and available time on endeavors that will bring results through their own initiative.

An individual reading program is one effective way of keeping up-to-date. Some teachers may plan to read many short articles and summaries, whereas others who read easily and rapidly may plan a different kind of program. Some may need to concentrate their reading in fewer areas than others. Any or all of the following types of materials are available to choose from: current periodic publications; local newspapers; current journals and bulletins related to home economics, such as the *Journal of Home Economics* and government publications; and publications related to education, both general and vocational.

College courses, both on the campus and at centers around the state, are available to teachers. Some may be offered as summer school classes or workshops. If careful choices are made with regard to a teacher's professional goals there is probably no better way of keeping up-to-date. Furthermore, some boards of education adjust salary schedules to make graduate work possible and profitable, and often raise salaries when an advanced degree is obtained.

Membership in professional organizations can also contribute to teacher growth. These organizations generally fall into three groups: (1) state and national education associations, (2) organizations centering on a special field of education, and (3) organizations primarily for the improvement of teacher's working conditions, salaries, tenure, and the like. Providing reading materials and holding meetings to keep teachers up-to-date on developments are

two activities of all these organizations which may be especially helpful to teachers. Membership is generally voluntary, although some schools require all their teachers to join the State Teacher's Association and to attend its meetings. The American Home Economics Association, the American Vocational Association, and the National Education Association are organizations which home-economics teachers will want to know about in considering what memberships will best help to further their professional goals.

The educational value of travel has long been recognized by teachers. Individual visits to observe special teaching procedures, to see how certain equipment is being used, or to learn about any phase of a program should help teachers grow professionally. Travel in general, either in the United States or to other countries, will enlarge the vision of teachers and at the same time make the outside world more real to them and in turn to their students.

ADAPTING FACILITIES TO MEET NEW NEEDS

Few teachers have the perfect setting for teaching. But many, without much financial outlay, have been able to modify the setting so as to make it more functional and pleasing to them and to their students.

New curriculum materials frequently suggest experiences that sound interesting but not possible with the present facilities. What, if anything, can a teacher do in such a situation? For example, a home-economics department may not provide settings for presentations and demonstrations to small groups. Is there any way to adjust space to meet this need? Perhaps some experimentation is needed. The solution will vary with the situation. Again, the department has no space in which to have large groups together for films or discussion. Is there another place sometimes available in the school or nearby? Some of the new teaching resources indicate a need for independent study space. What adjustments are needed to provide such space? The new curriculum guide may recommend a better balance among all areas of home economics. If the department space is presently occupied by cooking and sewing equipment, how can the space also be adapted to teach home furnishings, to provide observation of and experiences with caring for small children, and to include certain aspects of foods, clothing, and other subject matter content of home economics not currently being taught?

A partial answer to all of these questions, of course, is to try to make what is available more functional by making it more adaptable, mobile, and malleable. This is less difficult when storage space is available nearby for storing furnishings and equipment not in use. Such equipment might include sewing machines, furniture and equipment for use with small children, and free-standing wall space on wheels for home furnishings. However, even if there is less storage space available than is desired, furnishings that are easily moved are useful. The goal is to have arrangements that do not get in the way of the program. In other words, space arrangements should not dictate the program.

There is need for beauty within and without the building. According to some researchers (Schneider, 1971), "the need for creating beauty in our school buildings is becoming less of a wish and more of a fact. Society is recognizing that ugliness, whether in our lives or in our surroundings, is not a matter for complacency; that beauty is as necessary for man's well being as is his physical comfort and mere shelter [p. 93]." And of course a reasonable de-

gree of cleanliness and orderliness is basic to beauty.

There are other important aspects in the teaching-learning environment such as temperature, humidity, ventilation, air filtration, sound conditioning, and lighting. Sometimes, the teacher can make simple adjustments that serve to improve the thermal, visual, and sound conditioning. Sometimes he or she can minimize or eliminate distractions. All of these aspects of the teaching-learning setting are important whether or not there is a new curriculum. Nevertheless, the study of new ideas for individual and class experiences found in curriculum guides should inspire the teacher to look more closely at the present facilities and to make possible improvements drawing on her knowledge, ingenuity, and originality.

SUGGESTIONS FOR REAL-LIFE STUDENT EXPERIENCES

Effective teachers avail themselves of many opportunities for real-life student experiences. Such teachers are aware that intellectual and social skills, leadership qualities, and other achievements may be developed through activities for which teachers frequently have some responsibility. Such activities may relate to:

Student organizations such as FHA and HERO-FHA

The food service program

Other related school programs including elementary-school programs, adult classes, and special programs such as those for teaching the handicapped or working with the elderly

Business, service organizations, and related groups

STUDENT ORGANIZATIONS

The organization, Future Homemakers of America, has been mentioned at many points in these materials. General information about both FHA and HERO-FHA has been included. The national program has been considered and illustrations of how the program can be integrated and correlated with unit and daily lesson plans have been given. Ideas for social and educational group meetings outside of school have also been discussed in relation to the national program.

In conclusion, the writers would like to stress anew the importance of this organization to teachers not now participating in the state and national organization. Over half a million boys and girls belong, through high school classes. It is an exciting and expanding program in which young people are encouraged to branch out in a variety of directions for self-growth and to evaluate the results. They may wish to tutor children, strive for better communications with parents or siblings, become more effective consumers, or work to overcome prejudices. Groups may have meetings with parents or they may tie in with school action to help control use of drugs or to work to overcome social pressures. FHA'ers may assist older citizens, work with Head Start and in Day Care Centers, assist with the handicapped and mentally retarded, and become involved in social issues such as pollution, poverty, and human relationships. Finally, all FHA'ers, but especially HERO-FHA'ers, may want to concentrate on job and career opportunities. There are many possibilities to consider, such as the role of working men and women in society; the availability of jobs; the know-how of specific jobs; the relationships and involvement in the working world; and home-economics programs in college, post secondary Vocational-Technical schools and junior and community colleges.

Of all the possible resources teachers and students may choose for providing real-life stu-

dent experiences, probably none has the potential of FHA and HERO-FHA organization because of its scope. The initiative remains with the teacher and students. Personnel at national headquarters of the organization and state leaders are ready to provide help when requested.

FOOD-SERVICE PROGRAM

Where a food-service program is in operation in the school, the home-economics teacher is often expected to cooperate in making the program more educational. Such cooperation works two ways because the food-service program furnishes the teacher with a ready-made means of providing students with real-life experiences. Such experiences may be improving the eating habits of students in the school or work experience for home-economics students interested in employment in food services.

The problem of developing good eating habits can be met only by a broad program of nutrition education reaching beyond the school into the home. The National School Lunch Program has helped in many instances, but there are students who, instead of a complete lunch, will eat only things like desserts. There are others who go elsewhere for lunch and buy a hot dog or candy bar, and a soft drink. Still others bring from home something far from adequate. The situation is challenging for the home-economics teacher and students, but especially for those students who look toward teaching as a vocation.

Promising procedures for improving whatever food-service program exists may be developed by a committee of interested students, faculty, school-lunch personnel, and parents. Such a committee may include representatives not only of home economics but of physical education, science, and whatever departments are especially interested. As the committee develops suggestions related to improving the food-service program, it should coordinate efforts of sub-committees in carrying out the suggestions. There is probably no department in the school unable to think of ways to cooperate on such a school-wide program, which should reach even beyond the school into the homes.

It is important to remember that the development of good eating habits is a long, slow process for many students, including those in home-economics classes. In fact, a program such as the one discussed will probably need to be a continuing one in most schools. It will tax the ingenuity of participants to provide meaningful and novel experiences. At the same time participants from home economics and other fields of study will learn the meaning of real-life student experiences. What could be better initiation for prospective teachers? And, if the goal of improving the eating habits of even some of the students is achieved, all the effort put forth will be worthwhile.

Vocational food-service training programs are designed to prepare students for entry level food-service jobs such as kitchen helper, cooks' helper, counter server, tray girl, and food stockroom clerk in a variety of food-service operations—in nursing homes, hospitals, school cafeterias, and restaurants. There is a rapidly expanding need for such training and high-school and technical programs are able to train students who can become effective Food Service Workers. However, on-the-job training in a variety of work experiences is fundamental in any training procedure. The food-service program in the school is one of many resource facilities which can make a contribution to the food-service aspect of career education.

Experiences will vary from one situation to another but could include any or all of the following: participation in menu planning, food preparation, serving food, and developing satisfying relations with school food-service personnel. Related problems might involve making market lists, purchasing supplies, keeping records, and supervising the dining room. The work should be rotated to provide actual work experience in a number of different aspects of food service.

OTHER RELATED SCHOOL PROGRAMS

There are some teachers who realize the truth of what Aristotle said years ago—that the exclusive sign of a thorough knowledge is the power of teaching. Such teachers capitalize on this truth, using whatever opportunities are available to give students the chance to learn through teaching others. For example, past studies of nutrition may mean little to a senior student until he is asked to work with an elementary-school teacher and two other home-economics students on a short series of lessons, "Learning to eat what is good for me." Or perhaps a student has developed a certain skill in some aspect of clothing which members of an adult class need to develop. Giving a demonstration to this group might serve to increase the high-school student's confidence in herself, something she may badly need. Perhaps an adult homemaker telephones the home-economics teacher for some special information which a student could just as well give the homemaker. The student is likely to gain confidence from supplying the answers.

There are other kinds of cooperation that individuals or classes may offer. There may be a home for orphaned children where a Christmas program would be welcome. There may be a disadvantaged family which needs the kind of help and encouragement young people could give. Perhaps there is a physically handicapped homemaker who needs the assistance the teacher and several students could give. On the other hand, students may prefer to cooperate on an all-school project like one initiated in California. As a summer project in horticulture, students there built a "Fragrance Garden" of herbs for blind people to feel and smell. The students and their guests enjoyed the garden so much that the students built a brick greenhouse to keep the garden stocked. The literature classes enjoyed seeing aromatic plants mentioned by Shakespeare. Both boys and girls in food classes learned to use the herbs. The biology and science classes learned about medicinal plants. The school principal believed that the garden served a number of educational functions.

There is no end to the real-life learning situations available to students in home-economics classes. Programs with elementary-school children, adult classes, and special programs such as those for teaching the handicapped or working with the elderly may be used. The situations suggested and others may be carried on through regular class work, through FHA and HERO-FHA, and perhaps as home experiences. Teachers who have learned to work cooperatively with students are not worried about what some other teachers are certain to call "extra work." They know that engaging in such activities may mean a different kind of work but not necessarily more work. They know also that the personal satisfaction to themselves and to their students is very great. As scheduling becomes more flexible in more schools, experiences such as those suggested will be easier to manage. Nevertheless many of the most effective teachers of today have found ways to provide such experiences.

BUSINESS AND SERVICE ORGANIZATIONS

The business community offers many opportunties for real-life learning situations. Successful employment courses cannot be carried on without the cooperation of businesses, but students in other courses may also find an outlet for their interests and at the same time make a worthwhile contribution to the business community. Programs may be expected to vary from place to place and even in the same place at different times. Probably the most successful programs have involved four-way planning carried on by one or more representatives of business, students, teachers, and parents. If representatives of the business community are convinced that students are serious in using the real-life situations which they can provide, there should be little difficulty in obtaining cooperation. In a grocery store on Saturday morning, a few students might like to demonstrate ways of using a particular food. Several students might help plan and arrange furnishings for a teen-age room in a demonstration center at a furniture store. Those especially skillful in making garments might volunteer to exhibit a few articles at a dry goods department store where they purchased the material. The articles exhibited could show the cost in dollars of making each garment. Other students might suggest telling stories to young children at the community library at a regular time for a specified period. At the Christmas season, the toy department of a local store might be delighted to have a couple of students demonstrate the use of certain educational toys. Once students have shown what they can contribute while learning, new sources for cooperation will undoubtedly become available.

PLANNING FOR PROGRAM EVALUATION

Evaluation up to now has been considered chiefly from the standpoint of evaluation in the classroom. Major emphasis has been on self-evaluation by students with the guidance of teachers. Self-evaluation by teachers has also been considered to some extent. Such evaluation is of the utmost importance if improvements are to be made intelligently rather than haphazardly. In fact, evaluation is important in almost every facet of an individual's life. The list of those who feel a need to evaluate is long and impressive. In addition to individuals nearly all groups, social or professional, at one time or another want to know what has been accomplished. There are national and state evaluation programs which attempt to discover the quality of education in general or achievement in specified subjects. For example, the Vocational Education Act of 1963, revised in 1968, requires evaluation of vocational-technical education at least every five years. Nearly all schools are evaluated at specified times by the State Department of Education, Middle States Association of Colleges and Secondary Schools, the school administration of a particular school district, or some other team of experts and specialists. Finally, teachers often wish to evaluate the overall program of home economics for which they are responsible. This desire may be especially strong after a new curriculum has been introduced and tried out in the school.

Comparing a nationwide evaluation program with an evaluation of home economics in one school may appear incongruous. It is true that in the one instance the home-economics teacher generally is only one of many participants, whereas in the other she is in charge of the evaluation. Nevertheless, the basic principles of evaluation for any program are the same as those applied in the classroom situation. However, far more extensive organization and planning is required at national, state, or even school levels than for one class. At this point it may prove most helpful to answer questions often asked by teachers about program evaluation:

Is it probable that I, as a classroom teacher in home economics, will have responsibility for program evaluation other than perhaps evaluation of my own program? If so, what kind of responsibility am I likely to have?

At the present time there is an awareness that growth as a teacher needs to include the development of ability to serve as an evaluator of a school program. Becoming qualified in this capacity takes time and experience, and for this reason a beginning teacher in home economics may not be expected to participate in such an appraisal. Nevertheless, it is important to realize that learning to appraise one's own program is only a part of the total picture of evaluation. In many schools the content of a comprehensive home-economics program cuts across other subject fields such as art, health, and science, which also have goals related to personal and family living. Coordinated evaluation with teachers in these fields could lead to improved procedures for achieving common objectives. Furthermore, there is a growing trend in education to help learners see relationships among many subject fields. Thus every teacher should be prepared to contribute to evaluation far beyond her own particular program.

Your school at some time may be evaluated as part of a state or national program. If so, you may be asked to prepare material or to answer questions. During an evaluation by a Middle States Association of Colleges and Secondary Schools you will be asked to help with a self-study developed by the school staff. A questionnaire supplied by the Middle States Association will serve as a basis for the study and your own preparation for it. Procedures of other groups in charge of similar studies may be expected to vary somewhat but the desired outcome of learning more about how effective a program is will generally not vary.

The curriculum for home economics in my state appears to be quite different as the result of a recent curriculum revision aimed at bringing the curriculum in line with today's world. Some teachers are frankly critical of the new materials. How can this new material be evaluated?

There are many ways in which a new curriculum can be evaluated. It is important to consider the specific purposes of the proposed evaluation before considering evaluation techniques. Any of the following to which a "yes" answer is given should suggest a purpose or objective.

Should evaluation aim at discovering in general how well the new material has been received by students? parents? others?

Should the evaluation provide suggestions for improvement in the first reprinting?

Should it serve to publicize home economics?

Should the plans include long-term as well as short-term evaluation?

Will there be adequate resources and facilities available for analyzing the results?

Will there be a time limitation?

Will the results be used in important ways?

In addition to determining purposes it is desirable to answer several questions about who will be involved in the evaluation. Such questions are:

Who will develop the evaluation?

Who will contribute answers?

Who will collect the data?

Who will analyze the data?

At this point those responsible for the evaluation may wish to look at as many illustrations of similar evaluation as possible. Sometimes illustrations are found in resource materials themselves. Ideas may be gained also from others who have worked in such programs. Sometimes books on curriculum development may offer helpful suggestions. Often the ideas must originate entirely from the group presently concerned with evaluation of the curriculum. The answers previously given about purposes and persons should help. For instance, if school administrators are expected to contribute answers, which of the usual techniques of evaluation seem most appropriate? If the evaluation is to be long-term as well as short-term, what if any modifications need to be considered in the overall plan?

An example follows of evaluation of a thirty-two-page handbook for teachers entitled "Clothing Construction for Beginners," with emphasis on saving time in construction, and introducing students to newer aspects of clothing. The handbook was developed in 1964 by three graduate students majoring in clothing and taking a course in evaluation. They believed that teachers who used the handbook could offer valuable suggestions on how effective the project was and at the same time give suggestions for improvement. The illustration was included at the back of the handbook with the idea that teachers would send their responses to the writers.

EVALUATION OF HANDBOOK

Has the handbook been helpful? You can answer this question best in terms of your own objectives. At the same time the writers will appreciate your answering the question in terms of their goals which were to teach clothing in less time than previously and to introduce students to the socio-psychological aspects of clothing. Your answers to the following questions will be appreciated.

How much time do you usually spend on teaching clothing to beginners?

Were you able to save time using this handbook? If so, how much?

What teaching and evaluation techniques saved the most time?

How did you use the questions pertaining to

the socio-psychological aspects of clothing? How valuable do you feel they were? What questions would you add? Omit?

Did you achieve better results from using the ideas in this handbook? Explain.

What teaching techniques and evaluation methods were the most effective?

In what ways do you feel that this or parts of this handbook could be improved?

Objectives
Generalizations
Teaching techniques
Evaluation devices

It is recognized that the illustration shows very simple evaluation compared to evaluating the curriculum for a state-wide or city-wide program or even the total program of any one teacher. However, it illustrates one possible way of evaluating a new curriculum for teaching clothing to beginners. The example illustrates some of the points made about program evaluation.

Additional questions often asked by teachers about program evaluation are included below:

Sometimes I think my own home-economics program is excellent but other times I wonder if it really is meeting the needs of students and how satisfied parents really are with it. How should I proceed in evaluating my program?

Evaluating your own program follows the same educational process as any other kind of evaluation.

Step 1: Write the objectives or goals for your program. This will include those related to the school, home, and community. It is rarely feasible to evaluate in terms of all the objectives, but it may be as important to know which ones are not being evaluated as those that are. In the end such knowledge will make any interpretation of results more meaningful. For example, if nothing was learned about the teacher's relationship to other teachers in the school, the final result would be more meaningful if this was stated. To put it positively, some teachers would prefer to indicate the objectives which are covered.

Step 2: Clarify what needs to be learned with respect to each objective. For example, if student-teacher relationships are to be examined, it should be noted that many authorities believe that student respect is an important facet of desirable relationships. The evaluation to be developed should show whether or not the teacher has the respect of students.

Step 3: Consider what kind of evaluative experiences will provide the information needed with respect to the various objectives. Among the possible techniques are observation, demonstration, interview, written questionnaire, check list, and tests of various kinds. It may be necessary to experiment with more than one kind to decide the best way of evaluating a particular objective.

Step 4: Develop the evaluation instruments needed. For each of the techniques there is a wide variety of possible forms among which the teacher may choose. Ideas may be secured from available instruments or it may be possible for the evaluator to develop entirely new ideas.

After the evaluation has been developed, plans may be put into effect for collecting the data, analyzing it, and using the results.

I do not feel as up-to-date as many teachers feel about evaluation and I am almost certain the administration in my school would agree. How should I plan to get up-to-date and then stay there?

It is not easy to produce effective evaluation, but many teachers who become proficient in this area of education say that the more they evaluate the easier evaluation becomes. Their advice to other teachers is to understand the process of evaluation, learn the well-known types and forms, look at available examples developed by others, and then begin by adapting evaluation done by others, developing original ideas, or both.

Teachers seek different kinds of help in an effort to improve their ability in evaluation. Such help includes:

Reading widely but discriminatingly about evaluation

Taking a graduate course or two in evaluation

Attending a special meeting or short workshop which plans to concentrate on evaluation at the request of teachers

Looking for special helps on evaluation at professional meetings

Working on an exchange basis with one or two other home-economics teachers interested in trying out ideas for evaluation

After teachers feel some satisfaction with their progress in developing evaluation, they may want to consider further suggestions for improvement. Trying out evaluation that has been developed and analyzing it for effectiveness is an integral part of the total process and should not be neglected. Further, being up-to-date in evaluation generally offers so much satisfaction that most teachers plan to keep this way. Although the basic process will probably not change, developments in the field should result in new types and forms of evaluation as well as new ways of analysis.

PROMOTING HOME ECONOMICS

With or without new curriculum materials, every home-economics teacher needs to develop a well-planned program of publicity to interpret and promote home economics. However, new curriculum materials afford an especially good opportunity for the alert teacher to let the public know of efforts to keep home economics up-to-date and meaningful to students. In American education there has always been a close relationship between educators and the public they serve. Since schools exist for the welfare of the people and are dependent upon them for support, financial and otherwise, it is essential that the public be kept informed of the objectives, needs, and existing conditions in the schools. This constant need for interpreting educational values is vitally important, for schools can be improved and developed only to the extent to which the general public understands these values. All too often there is a lack of knowledge and sometimes a misunderstanding of what the school is trying to do for young people. In fact, the public's concept of home economics is frequently not the same as the concept held by persons in the profession. The same is often true of others on the teaching staff and of the student body as well as the general public. It is therefore necessary for the teacher not only to interpret home-economics education more effectively as a means of changing misconceptions, but to present an up-to-date picture of the program as a means of strengthening home economics in general.

There are various ways of publicizing home economics and each teacher will need to determine which ones will best meet her particular situation. Many of the activities which will contribute toward an effective program can be planned and carried out cooperatively with the students in connection with their regular classwork. In fact, as the teacher plans for the yearly class program, it is a good idea to keep a folder for publicity ideas, adding to it from time to time as class goals and experiences are determined. From this folder the teacher and students can select the best possibilities for publicity. There are certain avenues of approach which are open to most teachers.

NEWSPAPERS

Local newspapers are important outlets for informing people about home economics through news stories and feature articles. Handling this channel of publicity requires a knowledge of newspaper procedures coupled with discretion and judgment on the part of the teacher. A person who is inexperienced in dealing with newspapers therefore needs to learn what editors to contact, what news really is, and how news stories and features are written and submitted.

CONTACTING THE APPROPRIATE EDITOR

Knowing which editor to contact is the first step in establishing relations with a newspaper. On a weekly publication "the editor" usually handles all types of news. On metropolitan papers there are generally different editors for various areas of news. These include the city editor, who has over-all responsibility for local news, and other editors who handle news of sports, amusements, business, churches, society, women's interests, and so on. In some localities the women's editor may handle news of home economics, whereas in other places

the food, family, or homemaking editor may be responsible for this news. Once the teacher knows what editor to contact, the type of material in which the editor is most interested can be discussed.

It is quite possible that the teacher will encounter an editor who appears to have reservations about the news value of home economics. One reason for this attitude may be that the editor knows very little about the profession except vague details. As a taxpayer he may feel that he should resent the expenditure of tax funds for such courses. A vital phase of any publicity program is discovering these negative attitudes, learning why they exist, and then doing something constructive to correct them. There is no particular point in arguing with a prejudiced editor. Home economics needs no defense, but it may need explaining in order to correct mistaken ideas about it. This can be done by preparing articles highlighting the broad and varied aspects and activities of home economics and pinpointing these activities to the local program. Students may help with writing, pictures, or in other ways.

NEWS STORIES AND FEATURE ARTICLES

All editors are interested in news and from their point of view, news is a timely and accurate report of what has happened, what is happening, and what is going to happen. It must also be of potential interest to at least a segment of the newspaper's readers. News may be of two kinds—news stories and feature articles.

In a news story, timeliness is of essential importance. The news may be an announcement of a talk by a visiting home economist, the organization of an adult education class, or a new development in nutrition or textiles.

Names can also make news if the names are sufficiently notable or are associated with unusual or striking facts.

In a feature article, the time element is of less importance than in a news story. Instead such qualities as human interest, personalities, and ideas are emphasized. For example, a story about a home-economics student receiving a scholarship would be a news story. An account about a student who attends school during the day and manages a baby-sitting agency in after-school hours would be a feature article. A feature on new ideas for outdoor cooking would be a possibility for early spring or fall. A Child Center for young children might provide an opportunity for good pictures and an interesting article, since it would have special appeal for parents in the community. Students having job experience in relation to a career-education class might have a story that would interest people in the community, especially if accompanied by good pictures.

In connection with news stories and feature articles, the following suggestions based on newspaper protocol might be helpful:

1. Notify an editor in advance about a coming news event. If it is sufficiently important, the paper may send its own reporter and photographer. Such an assignment needs to be scheduled ahead of time.

2. Provide the press with essential materials for an important meeting, speech, or special program. In addition to copy already prepared by the teacher, the press needs to have texts of important speeches and brief biographical sketches of the chief individuals participating in the program.

3. Send a copy to the editor correctly typed. The material that is sent in should be typewritten, double-spaced on plain white paper 8½-by-11 inches without a letterhead. Use only one side of the paper, and ample margins at left and right. Always give the newspaper the top copy, never the carbon, since the latter is frequently blurred or difficult to read. Include in the upper left corner the name, address, and telephone number of the person who should be called for additional information.

4. If photographs are to be used, be sure they accompany the copy. Glossy 8-by-10 prints are generally satisfactory. The content of the pictures needs to be well composed showing persons engaged in some activity. A choice of pictures should be submitted if possible.

5. Get copy in well before the deadline. The deadline is the last minute at which copy can be received with any chance of its being printed in the edition of the paper in which the material is scheduled to appear.

Newspaper writing requires an approach somewhat different from that of ordinary writing. For this reason, in preparing articles for publication, the following suggestions based on newspaper policies may be helpful to the teacher:

Remember that the material is for nonprofessional people. It should be simple, direct, and as unacademic as possible. Information which contains names and personal experiences has more general appeal than statistics and data with unfamiliar terminology.

Create interest in the first sentence. Many people do not bother to read an article unless the first sentence interests them.

Double-check the final draft for accuracy of content. Students who plan to submit articles should check with the home-economics teacher to be certain that all information is factually correct. All articles may need to be cleared with the principal or with the school publication chairman.

RADIO AND TV

Another excellent means of publicizing home economics is through radio and television. If these facilities are locally available, every effort should be made to use them. Most stations will announce current meetings and events, and in such cases the person responsible for local-news reporting will need to be contacted. It is quite possible that arrangements can be made with the program director for various presentations. But the teacher and students should decide beforehand what programs they are best able to present, for whatever goes over the air should be of superior quality. Several students experienced in giving talks might tell about various aspects of the home-economics program. Or the teacher and a few students may speak on some special phase of home economics such as the wage-earning program. A panel of students could discuss a current controversial problem. Demonstrations of certain home-making skills may also be feasible for television publicity. Although student participation in all these activities would be limited, the class as a whole can help in planning and carrying out the details involved in this type of publicity.

EXHIBITS AND DEMONSTRATIONS

Exhibits and demonstrations have long been a popular avenue through which people can learn about the home-economics program. A well-arranged, colorful exhibit that catches the attention and holds it long enough to tell a story is not only informative but can move a person to action. "I'll go home and try that." "Guess I better check the baby's toys for safety." "I'll talk to Joan about taking home economics"—these are reactions that might result from viewing a good exhibit.

Like other forms of publicity, exhibits can be cooperatively planned by the teacher and students to tie in with class goals and experiences. Since setting up an exhibit is considered a valuable technique for effective learning, the subject was discussed in Book 2 on pages 162–163. This material gives the important points to consider in planning and setting up small exhibits, and should be carefully studied by the teacher as the publicity program is being planned.

A number of small exhibits may be as effective as a large one at the beginning or toward the end of the school year. Small exhibits may be set up in the home economics department, at other points in the school, in downtown stores, and wherever needed for special occasions such as evening meetings for parents. Such exhibits usually focus on one aspect of the field, though it is not essential that they do so. The advantage of an occasional large exhibit is that it is usually possible to present a picture of the overall home-economics program. Too often, in the past, teachers have emphasized foods or clothing exhibits and then have wondered why parents did not have a broad view of home economics.

A sampling of suggestions for use in exhibits shows only a few of those which might be used for publicity purposes:

A job spectrum for whatever wage-earning courses are, or could be, offered in the school. Spectrum shows the variety of jobs for present and projected employment opportunities.

Illustrations or displays relating to the different areas of a home-economics program placed in shadow-box frames. The caption might be "Portrait of Home Economics."

A corner of a room arranged as a child's play room. Furniture used should be simple and scaled to a child's size. Pictures need to be carefully selected and hung low.

A collection of toys and books suitable for pre-school children at different age levels. Some of the toys can be of the homemade type, but all should stress safety features.

A display of self-help clothes for young children.

A school wardrobe for teen-age boys and girls. Some of the articles constructed in class can be used.

Clothing labels indicating what to look for when purchasing certain garments.

Pictures of good and poor standing, walking, and sitting posture, showing how posture affects personal appearance.

A good school lunch contrasted with a poor lunch.

Ideas for one-dish meals.

Suggestions for maintaining good eyesight through adequate lighting.

Window arrangements showing draperies, curtains, and shades for windows of different sizes and shape.

Samples of wallpaper, stressing patterns suitable for large and small rooms.

Work areas in a kitchen, showing suitable heights, advantageous placement of large and small utensils, and storage facilities.

Furniture arrangements in a bedroom shared by two young members of the family, showing how each person can be assured of a certain amount of privacy and individuality.

Illustrations of three different life-styles.

BANQUETS AND LUNCHEONS

The preparation and serving of a banquet or luncheon to a civic group is sometimes considered a feasible way of directing the attention of the general public to the home-economics program. Carefully planned and well-served meals reflect great credit on a home-economics department and can provide valuable experiences for the students. However, successfully planning and executing all the details of a banquet or luncheon not only require experience and superior leadership, but involve a considerable amount of time and energy. Such a heavy burden of responsibility is placed upon the teacher that, unless this type of publicity is really needed, too many banquets and luncheons are not advisable except, perhaps, for wage-earning students in the area of foods.

It is still possible, however, to utilize banquets and luncheons in another way to publicize the home-economics program. A clever skit about family relationships, an interesting demonstration on meal planning and preparation including outdoor cookery for men, and colored slides or movies of wage-earning students on the job can sometimes be presented as part of a banquet or luncheon program.

PUBLIC RELATIONS WITH FACULTY AND STUDENTS

All too often some of the faculty members and many students in the school do not have a clear picture of what the present home-economics program includes. It is therefore essential to find ways of focusing the attention of these people upon the various aspects of home economics so that they may acquire a better understanding. There are many avenues of approach, some of which can be planned and carried out cooperatively with the students.

Home-economics students can present an assembly program dealing with some less-often-publicized aspect of home economics in place of the traditional fashion show. Frequent small exhibits in the school display case or elsewhere in the school can call attention to some of the current class work. The class work can be coordinated with such activities as redecorating the teachers' lounge or entertaining children during open-house programs. The home-economics department can also offer to cooperate in joint projects with other departments. Mention has already been made of news stories and feature articles for the local paper and many of the same procedures can be followed for the school newspaper. In the early fall when committees are being set up, the teacher can volunteer to work with an academic group rather than wait for an assignment to the refreshment committee. The best publicity, however, can be given by interested and enthusiastic students who have studied or presently are enrolled in home-economics classes.

VOCATIONAL INFORMATION

Every publicity program should provide information concerning the various kinds of work available to students with appropriate training in the field. Technical education during high-school years or later and college education may both lead to some aspect of work in home economics. This information is important to students trying to decide what to take in high school, to students considering college, and to people who guide students in making vocational decisions.

Printed material can be placed on the reference shelves in the home-economics department, in the school library, in the offices of the principal and school counselor. Arrangements can be made to distribute material to parents who may be interested. A clever exhibit and interesting talks by former students who have

positions in various lines of work are other possibilities.

ADVISORY COMMITTEES

The interpretation and promotion of home-economics education can also be facilitated through use of an advisory committee. Such a committee has already been discussed; one is required in federally supported programs for gainful employment. Many effective teachers in other home-economics programs have had the support and assistance of such committees for many years. Members are somewhat different in background than those contributing to wage-earning programs. A committee of five to seven men and women representing diversified interests is a good size. The following qualifications for a lay person are generally regarded as desirable:

Knowledge of the community

Respect of the community

Sensitivity and sympathy with educational values

Willingness to give time, enthusiasm, and best judgment to the work of the committee

Understanding of the importance of working cooperatively

Such persons are especially helpful in interpreting to others the contributions the program makes for better home and family living. They may assist in making and carrying out program plans and in securing community cooperation for the department. If the teacher is able to work cooperatively, the total program should be greatly strengthened. There will be many kinds of student experiences possible through working with an advisory committee.

SUGGESTED TEACHER EXPERIENCES

1. Working in two or more groups, it should be interesting for the class to assume that members of the groups are composed of teachers of different ages and backgrounds. Some teachers from each group have helped in developing new curriculum materials for home economics. Now that the new materials are available and class members are fairly well acquainted with them, the groups should consider a particular community known to all and attempt independently to answer within their own groups such questions as:

What special problems are raised by the new curriculum? The class may think of some of the same problems discussed in this book, but in addition there may be other problems of interest to them.

What suggestions should be helpful in trying to meet these problems?

What resources would probably be of particular help with the problems?

Finally the groups should exchange ideas on special problems related to new curriculum materials and ask a committee composed of one student from each group to summarize the most important ideas presented.

2. Individually or in small groups, arrange to interview at least one experienced teacher to obtain his or her personal reactions to inservice education. Questions such as the following can be asked:

What forms of professional development or other inservice education have you engaged in since the completion of your undergraduate work?

Are you now engaged in any form of inservice education other than the cooperative enterprises in which you are expected to take part? If so, what?

What form or forms of inservice education contributed most to your teaching career? Why?

What are your future plans for inservice education?

Then under the headings (1) *Cooperative Enterprise* and (2) *Individual Endeavors* each class member may wish to jot down ideas for herself.

3. Working in small groups, select a home-economics department known to the class. Each group decides on the goals toward which it will work in order to make minor, inexpensive improvements. For example, one goal might be to provide more satisfactory seating arrangements for class discussion. Another might be to develop some plan whereby the facilities could be adapted to more realistic teaching of child development. An evaluation of the plans can be made by the entire class. The best ideas, in some instances, may be given to the teacher of the department for which the plans were made.

4. Collect examples of illustrations of interesting and adequate storage facilities for a home-economics department. Have a committee screen the offerings and present those that appear to have the best potential value. Examples may be supplemented by verbal descriptions of such storage facilities.

5. The class may find it stimulating and worthwhile to take a look into the future and offer ideas on how space and equipment for home-economics departments might be made more mobile, adaptable, and malleable, thus more functional.

6. Members of the class who are unfamiliar with the school food-service program can arrange to visit schools where such a program is in operation. Plans can include talks with a home-economics teacher to obtain the following information:

How much time, if any, is devoted to the program?

To what extent does the program tie in with class goals and experiences?

How could operational procedures be improved?

Reports of the visits can be given to the class. Those who are already familiar with the school food-service program can compare their experiences with what the visiting members learned.

7. Collect the most interesting ideas you can of real-life student experiences and after presenting these to the class discuss their effectiveness insofar as you are able to do so.

8. A series of talks by teachers of home economics who have participated in different types of evaluation experiences leading to program improvement could be helpful and stimulating. Speakers can include:

A teacher who has served on several staff committees

A teacher who has been a consultant outside her own school

A teacher who has served as a member of a team of experts and specialists

Before the talks, the class can divide into three groups—each to be prepared to summarize briefly one of the talks. Questions relating to each teacher's experience may follow the talks. After the summaries are given, the class should attempt to evaluate the different types of appraisal used for facilitating program improvement.

9. Hold a panel discussion of effective ways of interpreting home economics to the general public. Panel members may be experienced teachers and selected students with a member of the class acting as moderator. Time can be allowed for questions by the class.

10. Collect and bring in news stories and feature articles which newspapers and other publications have printed in relation to home economics. Read these materials carefully and analyze them from a publicity viewpoint on the basis of:

How well the articles were written
Improvements, if any, which might have strengthened the articles

11. Several members of the class can volunteer to tell the others how they secured vocational information about home economics. Was the information publicized through the efforts of the high-school home-economics teacher, and if so was it sufficiently adequate and stimulating? Or was it secured by the interested persons themselves, and if so how was it obtained? Suggestions can be offered for publicizing vocational information effectively.

REFERENCES

American Home Economics Association. *Home economics teacher education—The state of the art.* Washington, D.C.: Author, 1970.

American Home Economics Association. *Consumer and homemaking education—Opportunity and challenge.* Washington, D.C.: Author, 1971.

Arizona Department of Education, Division of Vocational Education, Home Economics Section, *Environmental housing and life styles.* Phoenix: Author, 1972.

Congressional Record of Senate S11770. October 1, 1968. Washington, D.C.

Commonwealth of Virginia, Division of Vocational Education, Home Economics Education. *Discussion draft. Individual development in the family,* pp. 29–41. Richmond: Author, 1971.

Council of Educational Facility Planners. *Guide for planning educational facilities,* p. 114. Columbus, Ohio: Author, 1969.

Educational Testing Service. *Proceedings of the 1970 invitational conference on testing problems. The promise and perils of educational information systems.* Princeton, N.J.: Author, 1970.

Future Homemakers of America. *1969–1973 national program of work. Action plan for the Future Homemakers of America,* pp. 18, 19, 91–92. Washington, D.C.: Author, 1970.

Future Homemakers of America. *Unfolding the action of HERO-FHA. A supplement to the 1969–73 program of work,* p. 8. Washington, D.C.: Author, 1971.

Good, C. V., Editor. *Dictionary of Education.* New York: McGraw-Hill, 1959.

Hatcher, H. M., & Andrews, M. E. *Adventuring in home living.* Book 2, pp. 463–464, 473. Boston: D. C. Heath, 1959.

Mager, R. F., & Beach, K. M. *Developing vocational instruction,* pp. 29–30. Belmont, California: Fearon, 1967.

Oklahoma State Board of Vocational and Technical Education, Division of Home Economics Education. *Consumer education. The management of personal and family financial resources. Curriculum guide,* pp. 13–15; 46–47. Stillwater, Oklahoma: Author, 1969.

Pennsylvania Department of Education, Bureau of Vocational, Technical and Continuing Education. *Preparing for employment in clothing and home furnishings services—A resource guide for curriculum development,* pp. 8–9, 29–33, 41. Harrisburg: Author, 1968.

Pennsylvania Department of Education, Bureau of Vocational, Technical and Continuing Education. *Resource materials for home economics education in Pennsylvania schools. Home management and family resources,* Book 3, pp. 20, 22–23, 28, 48–49, 65. Harrisburg: Author, 1971. (a)

Pennsylvania Department of Education, Bureau of Vocational, Technical and Continuing Education. *Resource materials for home economics education in Pennsylvania schools. Foods and Nutrition,* Book 4, pp. 30–31, 33, 45. Harrisburg: Author, 1971. (b)

Pennsylvania Department of Education, Bureau of Vocational, Technical and Continuing Education. *Resource materials for home economics education in Pennsylvania schools. Textiles and clothing,* Book 5, p. 21. Harrisburg: Author, 1971. (c)

Pennsylvania Department of Education, Bureau of Vocational, Technical and Continuing Education. *Resource materials for home economics education in Pennsylvania schools. Housing and home furnishings,* Book 6, pp. 5, 21, 40, 53, 64–65. Harrisburg: Author, 1971. (d)

Schneider, R. C. Instructional technology and the teaching-learning environment. *Educational horizons, Spring 1971,* **49** (3), 88–95.

Silberman, C. E. *Crisis in the classroom.* New York: Random House, 1970.

Simpson, E. J., & Barrow, J. M. The setting for the home economics program at the secondary level—A new look. *Illinois Teacher of Home Economics,* **8** (1964–65), 74–78.

Tennessee State Board for Vocational Education. *A curriculum guide for teaching consumer education,* pp. SCE34–SCE40. Nash-ville: Author in cooperation with Division of Vocational-Technical Education and University of Tennessee, Home Economics Education Department, June 1970.

Texas Tech University, Home Economics Instructional Materials Center. *Consumer education part one,* pp. 33–39. Lubbock, Texas: Author in cooperation with Texas Education Agency, Department of Vocational and Adult Education, Division of Homemaking Education, January 1971.

Texas Tech University, Home Economics Instructional Materials Center. *Consumer education for families with limited incomes,* pp. 9–11. Lubbock, Texas: Author in cooperation with Texas Education Agency, Department of Vocational and Adult Education, Division of Homemaking Education, February 1971.

Toffler, A. *Future shock,* New York: Random House, 1970.

University of Alabama, Division of Continuing Education in Home Economics, and the Vocational Rehabilitation Service of Alabama, Department of Education. *On your own* (Series of newsletters), 1971–72.

The Vocational Act of 1963—Public Law 88–210 and Title 1—Amendments to the Vocational Education Act of 1963.

Voelkner, A. R. What every teacher should know about evaluation. *American Vocational Journal.* September 1971, 59–61.

Whitmarsh, Ruth. An annotated bibliography on employment education in home economics. *Illinois Teacher of Home Economics,* **8** (1), 33–55.

HOME ECONOMICS AS PART OF VOCATIONAL EDUCATION

Vocational home economics is one member of a large family of programs which have been brought together under the title of "vocational education." Such programs are designed to provide the occupational education and the training needed by individuals to fulfill their roles in today's society. Traditionally the focus of vocational home-economics programs has been on preparing women for the occupation of homemaking. This has been an important vocation which had as its goal maintaining and improving the quality of life. Providing the basic needs of the family for food, clothing, and shelter has been recognized in the past as a bona fide role for women.

Early in our history the home was the center of production for many of the goods and services necessary to satisfy the basic needs of the American family. School programs were developed in keeping with this philosophy to provide instruction in needlework and housewifery.

As the American family shifted from being primarily a producing unit to a consuming unit, and as women became interested in the world beyond the home and joined the labor force, home economics reflected these changes in the nature of its program offerings. Not only is vocational home economics essential to the economic well being of our nation, but it also plays a major role in helping people adapt to societal changes which affect individuals and families. It is being challenged to redirect and expand its offerings to focus upon the dual role and the employability of people. This concept is not limited to women but has been expanded to include all people of all ages in all communities.

VOCATIONAL LEGISLATION AND FEDERAL AID FOR HOME ECONOMICS

The federal funds provided for in the numerous vocational acts have tended to change secondary-school curriculums in vocational education and have contributed to the development of home economics. As early as 1917, the Congress of the United States passed a vocational education act known as the Smith-Hughes Act which provided funds for home economics. These funds were designed to promote the organization and development of programs, and most of them were granted with the provision that they be matched by state or local monies or both.

Since 1917, additional funds have been made

available for vocational home-economics programs through numerous supplementary and related acts. Until the Vocational Act of 1963, these funds were provided for vocational homemaking education programs designed to train persons for the occupation of homemaking. The emphasis was on such areas as foods and nutrition, clothing and textiles, housing and home planning, home management, child care, and family relationships.

A brief résumé of the Smith-Hughes Act and subsequent laws providing additional funds for home economics follows.

THE SMITH-HUGHES ACT

The Smith-Hughes Act provided a continuing appropriation for vocational education in agriculture, trades and industry, and in homemaking. This original vocational act not only initiated and stimulated recognition of vocational education at the secondary level but also provided for teacher training in each of the fields mentioned. The states under the provision of the law were permitted to use 20 percent of the total funds allocated for salaries of teachers of trades and industry for the purpose of paying salaries of home economics teachers. Federal financial support was provided also for state administration of vocational education. The Smith-Hughes Act of 1917 created a federal-state-local partnership whereby schools became the vehicle for preparing students for employment. It set standards regarding age, kind of student to be enrolled, space and equipment to be used, the form and content of the curriculum, the grade levels at which the program might be offered, the length of the school year, and the qualifications of instructors and administrators. Although this Act was

amended twice by Congress and three times by executive order with the consent of Congress, none of the amendments or revisions changed the fundamental purpose of the Act.

VOCATIONAL EDUCATION ACTS OF THE THIRTIES AND FORTIES

THE GEORGE-REED ACT

The George-Reed Act of 1929 authorized an annual appropriation for vocational agricultural education and vocational home economics for a period of five years. The monies were divided equally between agricultural education and vocational home-economics education and were additional to the funds provided in the Smith-Hughes Act.

The organization and administration of the programs under this Act were similar to the provisions of the Smith-Hughes Act. One basic difference was that allocation of funds to the states for home economics was based on rural population rather than urban. This Act was an authorization of funds, while the Smith-Hughes Act provided for an appropriation. Some changes were made in the organization and administration of home economics so that it might be similar to that provided for agricultural education.

THE GEORGE-ELLZEY ACT

In 1934 the George-Ellzey Act replaced the George-Reed Act, which had expired. The funds allocated in this Act were to be divided equally among agricultural education, vocational home-economics education, and trade and industrial education. The funds for agricultural education and vocational home-economics education were allocated on the same basis as the George-Reed Act; the funds for trade and industrial education were allocated on the basis of urban population. For the most part the Act was administered in the same way as the Smith-Hughes and George-Reed Acts.

THE GEORGE-DEEN ACT

When the George-Ellzey Act expired Congress recognized a need to provide additional funds over and above those provided by the Smith-Hughes Act. On July 1, 1937, the George-Deen Act became effective. This Act not only authorized a sum of money to be divided equally among agricultural education, vocational home economics, and trade and industrial education but also provided a sum for distributive education. The authorizations for home economics in this Act were subject to the same conditions and limitations as those of the previous Acts.

THE GEORGE-BARDEN ACT

In 1946, the George-Deen Act was amended and supplanted by the George-Barden Act. Under this law increased appropriations were provided for the same four field services including agriculture, home economics, trade and industrial, and distributive education. The George-Barden Act provided for greater flexibility in the use of these funds. The funds provided in this Act would be used for the salary and expenses of state directors of vocational education and vocational counselors, for training and work experience programs for out-of-school youth, and for purchase of rental equipment and supplies for vocational programs.

THE VOCATIONAL AMENDMENTS OF 1963

The Vocational Act of 1963 made its mark on home economics education. With its overall commitment to the family, home economics retained under this Act the right to develop the competencies needed for the occupation of homemaking. A challenge was given to develop a new thrust in occupational education by initiating wage-earning programs using the knowledge and skills of home economics.

The new types of programs and new program emphasis were made possible under the following provisions in the Act:

1. Maintain, extend and improve vocational education

2. Develop new vocational education programs

3. Provide for part-time employment of students while participating in vocational education programs

4. Expand training opportunities for all ages in all communities.

The 1963 Act guaranteed equal access to education and training of a high quality for all, but particularly for the least able and disadvantaged. At least 10 percent of the funds allocated to the States for home economics was to be used to train individuals for gainful employment. Research and development were assigned an important place in the 1963 Act, with 10 percent of the total appropriations for each year reserved to make grants to educational agencies such as colleges, state boards, or other public nonprofit agencies.

Neither the Smith-Hughes nor the George-Barden Acts were eliminated, but the State Board upon approval of the United States Commissioner of Education could transfer funds from one category to another according to need. The Act also provided for an Advisory Committee on vocational education to study the nation's needs and to make recommendations to Congress. The investigation of the Advisory Committee opened the door to new vocational legislation which culminated in the Vocational Amendments of 1968. This Act also made permanent the authorization of Practical Nurses Training.

VOCATIONAL EDUCATION
AMENDMENTS OF 1968

The 1968 legislation consolidates and supplants both the Smith-Hughes and the George-Barden Acts. It implements the provisions of the Vocational Education Act of 1963 as amended, which provides for federal grants to states (1) to assist them to maintain, extend, and improve existing programs of vocational education, and (2) to develop new programs of vocational education for persons of all ages in all communities of the state. It applies to those in high schools, those who have completed or discontinued their formal education and are preparing to enter the labor market, those who have already entered the labor market but need to upgrade their skills or learn new ones, those with special educational handicaps, and those in post-secondary schools.

The basic purpose of the Act is to provide instruction related to the occupation or occupations for which the students are in training; that is, instruction which is designed upon its completion to fit individuals for employment in an occupation or a cluster of closely related occupations within an occupational field. This instruction shall be suited to the needs of those involved in or preparing to engage in such occupations. The instruction shall include classroom, related academic and technical in-

struction, as well as field, shop, laboratory, cooperative work, apprenticeship, or other occupational experience.

Home-economics programs may benefit from sharing in the resources made available under Parts B, C, D, E, G, and H of the Act. In order to qualify for such funds the instruction in home economics shall be designed to place the individual in employment in an occupation using the knowledge and skills of home economics.

Part F is of major importance since it authorizes special funding for consumer and home-making education. The funds are allocated to the states on a matching basis. At least a third of these funds are to be used for programs in depressed regions or in areas of high unemployment. The following are the criteria for the use of such funds:

1. Encourage home economics to give greater consideration to social and cultural conditions and needs especially in economically depressed areas.

2. Encourage preparation for professional leadership in home economics and consumer education

3. Be designed to prepare youths and adults for the role of homemaker or to contribute to the employability of such youth and adults in the dual role of homemaker and wage earner

4. Include consumer education programs

5. Be designed for persons who are entering or preparing to enter the work of the home

Funds may also be used to provide ancillary services and activities and other means of assuring quality in all homemaking education programs such as teacher training and supervision, development research, program evaluation, experimental programs, development of instructional materials, provision of equipment, and state administration and leadership.

REFERENCES

Baldwin, K. *The AHEA saga*. Washington, D.C.: American Home Economics Association, 1949.

Hurt, M. L. Vocational home economics present and future. *Journal Home Economics*, May 1972, **64** (5), 26–32.

Law, G. F. (Ed.) *Contemporary concepts in vocational education*. Washington, D.C.: American Vocational Association, 1971.

National Association of Secondary-School Principals. Vocational education: time for decision. *The Bulletin*, May 1965.

National Working Conference on Vocational Home Economics Education. *Papers on vocational home economics education, consumer and homemaking education, occupational home economics*. Washington, D.C.:

U.S. Dept. of Health, Education, and Welfare, Division of Vocational and Technical Education Program Services, April 28–30, 1971.

Stout, B. L. Federal legislation affecting home economics education. Unpublished study, University of West Virginia, March 1971.

U.S. Congress Committee of Conference. *Vocational amendments of 1968*. 90th Congress, 2nd Session, Report No. 1938. Washington, D.C.: Government Printing Office, 1968.

U.S. Department of Health, Education, and Welfare. Office of Education. *Federal Register*, Jan. 1970, **35** (4), Part 2.

Venn, G. *Man, education and work: postsecondary vocational and technical education*. Washington, D.C.: American Council on Education, 1964.

INDEX

list classes p.317